MADONNA

By the same author

Call Her Miss Ross

Michael Jackson: The Magic and the Madness

Sinatra: Behind the Legend

Jackie, Ethel, Joan—Women of Camelot

An Intimate Biography

J. RANDY TARABORRELLI

Simon & Schuster

New York   London   Toronto   Sydney   Singapore

SIMON & SCHUSTER
Rockefeller Center
1230 Avenue of the Americas
New York, New York 10020

This book was originally published in Great Britain in 2001
by Sidgwick & Jackson, an imprint of Macmillan Publishers Ltd.

Simon & Schuster and colophon are registered trademarks of Simon & Schuster Inc.

For information regarding special discounts for bulk purchases,
please contact Simon & Schuster Special Sales:
1-800-456-6798 or business@simonandschuster.com

Picture research by Natalie Goldstein, NYC
Insert design by Jeanette Olender
Manufactured in the United States of America

1   3   5   7   9   10   8   6   4   2

Library of Congress Cataloging-in-Publication Data is available.

ISBN 0-7432-2709-3

For my father, Rocco

Contents

✝

Author's Note

✝

When I first met her at a press conference in the spring of 1983, Madonna Louise Veronica Ciccone—twenty-five at the time—struck me as brash, cocky, petulant and self-indulgent. Never one to put on an act for a journalist, she was just what she was—and without hesitation. "Look, I never had money," she told me of her early, struggling days in New York. "Each month it was a scramble to pay the rent and get some food in the apartment. I literally had to eat out of garbage cans in those days. Now that I have a record out and it looks like it'll be a success, hell yeah, I feel like I deserve it," she concluded. She fixed her hazel eyes on me. "People don't know how good I am yet," she said, holding me with her gaze. "But they will soon. In a couple of years everyone will know. Actually," she concluded, "I plan on being one of this century's biggest stars."

"And with no last name?" I asked, uncertain that "Madonna" was even an authentic appellation. (Surely, it couldn't have been.)

"It's Madonna," she snapped. "Just like Cher. Remember it."

It was difficult to argue with her, mostly because she wouldn't hear of it. Poor thing, I thought. Let her have her illusions. No reigning beauty she, and—judging from her first record—equipped with only a fair voice, yet she thinks she's going to become a dominant influence in pop music, a big star. Well, we'll see . . .

Of course, it didn't take long for Madonna's prediction to come true.

Everything she is today has been hard earned. With nothing ever handed to her on the proverbial silver platter, her life and career have been built on single-mindedness of intention, the most exhausting work (in recording studios, on movie and video sound stages, and on concert tours), dogged determination and, often, unmerciful and extreme sacrifice. Today, Madonna is arguably one of the most memorable, celebrated and highest-paid women of the twentieth century . . . and to think that I doubted her resolve.

I first began the challenge of writing this book in 1990, but decided to put it away for a few years. I thought then that Madonna should have an opportunity to do more living before I, as her biographer, would be able to do her story justice. Though she was already one of the most famous people on the planet, it takes more than just the accurate documentation of a person's celebrity to make for a good character study. Most subjects need time for evolution and personal growth before their stories are ripe enough to commit to paper. At the time, Madonna was in an ambitious, self-involved phase during which nothing mattered more to her than her career.

When I picked up work on this book again in 1994, I felt the same way about her. She had prioritized her life—career first, above all else—and would do almost anything to get to a certain point of creative freedom and financial security. I anticipated that when she was finally satisfied with her career, she would begin to work on her *life*. Happily, just such a personal evolution began to occur in 1996 when she had Lourdes, her first child.

Now, in the year 2001, Madonna has greater concerns than just the next big public relations spectacle in her career—especially since giving birth to another child last year, a brother for Lourdes, named Rocco. She has grown, changed and transformed herself (again) and, this time, in a way that not only inspired me to want to write about her, but admire her as well. Yes, she is still driven, still ambitious and still self-involved—that really hasn't changed. She's still Madonna, after all, an artist of calculation known for inventing and reinventing her image, usually for the purpose of publicity. However, as I now see it, in recent years she's also been shedding certain layers, slowly revealing who she really is as a person, as a woman.

Affluent, powerful and famous people like Madonna are, generally, different from most other people—at once more and less human, they're walking paradoxes, thoughtful and inconsiderate, generous and parsimonious, disciplined and uncontrolled, self-denigrating and self-important. While it may not always be easy to find the real Madonna amidst the hocus-pocus of public relations she manufactures to hide her true self, she's there just the same. In pursuit of her, one only has to be perceptive enough to look beyond the thick smoke, away from the confusing mirrors. There hides the real woman. As I found in the years of researching and then finally writing *Madonna: An Intimate Biography,* finding her is worth the effort.

J. RANDY TARABORRELLI

Los Angeles, January 2001

The Actress and the President

Perhaps the last place Madonna's fans would ever have expected to find her was crouched on the floor of an automobile racing down a bustling Buenos Aires street. Her destination: the home of the president of Argentina, Carlos Menem. It was Wednesday, February 7, 1996—just another day in the extraordinary life of Madonna Louise Veronica Ciccone.

While huddling on the floor of a black Spanish-made automobile, Madonna was being smuggled to meet the president. Her own rented Mercedes-Benz—surrounded by police on motorcycles—had successfully been used as a decoy moments earlier, confusing the ever-stalking paparazzi who had followed it in hopes of capturing on film whatever they believed Madonna was going to be doing that day, probably shopping. If only they had known the true nature of her plans; *that* would have been a real story.

From the day she arrived in Buenos Aires, Madonna had not been pleased with what she found there: an orchestrated political campaign in opposition to her movie *Evita*. Much to her dismay, it seemed that everywhere she looked she saw graffiti sprayed on walls with sentiments such as: "Chau good-bye Madonna," and "Evita Lives! Get Out, Madonna!" Many of those living in Argentina believed that Madonna would desecrate the memory of their beloved Santa Evita. They feared that Evita, as painted by the flagrant Madonna, would be an insult to her memory—and for no good reason other than the fact that Madonna would be the one essaying the role. Perhaps making matters worse for everyone on the *Evita* project was the fact that director Alan Parker's cast and crew were comprised mostly of British workers; the 1982 war between Argentina and Britain over the Falkland Islands remained a sticking point for many Argentinians.

Though a replica of the balcony at Casa Rosada, the presidential residence in Argentina, was re-created for the movie at great expense in London, Madonna had longed to film the climax of the movie (when Evita sings "Don't Cry for Me Argentina") at the actual location. Standing on the exact site at which Evita gave some of her most dramatic appearances would, no doubt, fill Madonna with genuine emotion, thereby enhancing her performance immeasurably. Originally, Menem had granted the film company permission to film at public buildings such as the Casa Rosada. However, because of the public outcry and controversy, he abruptly changed his mind. He now decreed that locations originally scheduled to be used as sites for filming were off-limits.

President Menem, Madonna noted, "was setting the tone for everything" that was, in her view, ruining her movie. "He made statements indicating that he agreed the film was an outrage," she said angrily. ("I don't see Madonna in the role," he had observed to *Time* magazine. "And I don't think Argentina's people, who see Evita as a true martyr, will tolerate it.")

It seemed clear that no producer, director or studio executive would be able to change the president's mind. This was a task that would have to be left to the lady herself, the movie's star. It was another one of those times in Madonna's career when a "handler" would not be able to do her bidding, when she would have to do something herself in order for it to be done to her satisfaction.

Madonna had met Constancio Vigil, a close friend of Menem's, who attempted to arrange a meeting between the star and the president. Menem, however, said that he wasn't interested in meeting Madonna; he refused to see her. Chagrined by his snub, she would not take no for an answer.

After much negotiating, the president relented and agreed to talk with Madonna, but only under the condition that the public not be made aware of the meeting—hence the clandestine manner of her journey on the floor of an automobile. "He didn't want people to think he was speaking with the enemy," explained one government official. When this stipulation was reported to Madonna, she was disappointed by it but also understood that it was the only way she would be able to meet the president. She would simply have to refrain from doing what she, a master public relations strategist, probably wanted to do: set up a press conference to announce that she and the president were about to engage in a face-to-face meeting.

Before she would sit down with Menem, it was only natural for Madonna to want to do a certain amount of research. A voracious reader, she asked for material about Menem which she would review prior to the meeting so that she could better understand his life and political career. As she put it to one of her associates, "I want to know who he is. He certainly knows who I am."

Through her research, Madonna would learn that sixty-six-year-old Carlos Saul Menem was the first Peronist ever elected to national office in Argentina. He was elected governor of La Rioja in 1973, the year Juan Domingo Perón engineered his political comeback. Jailed in 1976 when his wife, Isabel, was forced from power, he was released in 1981. He was reelected governor in 1983 and again in 1987.

From his early career as provincial governor, Menem rose to the presidency by preaching Peronist politics, the nationalistic style of government formulated by Juan and Eva Perón, which sought to reconcile the interests of industry, business, labor and the poor. Menem's personal charisma and dramatic oratorial style had won him the presidential election in 1989. That election also represented the first transfer of power from one constitutionally elected party to another since 1928. A Roman Catholic convert, Menem is divorced with two children, a son and a daughter. "Divorced, huh?" Madonna remarked. "Finally, something we have in common. We're both sinners . . . divorced Catholics."

When it was clear that they had evaded the press, Madonna and Constancio Vigil were driven to an airport and then flown by helicopter to an offshore island in the middle of the delta in El Tigre. They swooped low, flying directly over what was clearly a large estate in the direction of a nearby small airport. Madonna watched as rolling, green hills flattened out, making way for a concrete landing strip. The helicopter dropped gently.

As soon as Madonna and her friend disembarked, a dignified, elderly, casually dressed black man appeared before them. He bowed deeply. They were then escorted to a nearby Land Rover and driven to opulent grounds owned by a business associate of Menem's. There, surrounded by pink flamingos, as if in some magical fairy tale, Madonna would find the president of Argentina waiting for her. It was six P.M.

According to some of his aides, President Carlos Menem had been determined not to be impressed by Madonna. However, like many men before him who had tried to resist Madonna, Menem's cool reserve melted away almost immediately upon meeting her. According to a photograph of her taken that day, she was dressed in a thirties-style ensemble perfectly appropriate for the moment: a black crocheted cotton cardigan and a knee-length silk dress splashed with red, black and white. With black-and-white leather t-strap pumps on her feet, a sequined tulle clutch bag in one hand and what appeared to observers to be ruby antique French earrings, she looked as if she had just stepped out of a 1930s film. Because her hair was pulled into a chignon and covered by a thirties-style black horsehair hat with a gray lace overlay, it was difficult to tell if she was blonde or brunette.

As Madonna stood serenely before Menem, perhaps trying to maintain her composure (she would later admit she was nervous), the president began to compliment her profusely. First, he told her that he was amazed at how much she resembled Eva Perón, whom he had met as a young man. Madonna was flattered. She never expected such a compliment from the president of Argentina and, as she would later say, she couldn't help but feel "ten feet tall."

It was going well. They walked through a large courtyard. In the middle of a paved quadrant stood a huge carved fountain on which life-sized, bronze sea horses pranced among stone mermaids, octopuses and jellyfish. As they walked by it, Madonna couldn't resist dangling her fingers in the cool water. "I need one of these in my backyard," she joked.

As soon as they were seated in the center of a lovely brick patio, maids and butlers swarmed about, offering wine and cheese. Then, an attractive and formal-looking female interpreter walked over and introduced herself to Madonna. She indicated that she would be assisting in the event of any awkward communication between the actress and the president. While the interpreter spoke, Madonna noticed the president's eyes going "over every inch of me," as she would later recall, "looking right through me." She found him to be "a very seductive man."

Once relaxed in her wicker chair, Madonna quickly took stock of Menem, just as he had of her. She noted his tan, his small feet, the fact that he dyed his hair black. She also noted that he could not take his eyes off her.

As ravenous mosquitoes descended upon them, Madonna and the president—followed by his aides—retreated into a parlor furnished with expensive antiques; Madonna was unsure about their age and would later say she thought it "uncouth" to inquire. In the parlor, the owner of the estate in which the meeting was taking place suddenly appeared with a bottle of chilled champagne in one hand and a small tray of caviar and crackers in the other. After sampling the caviar, Madonna slipped a cassette tape into a player she had brought with her. The song on the tape was "You Must Love Me," a new ballad from the *Evita* cast album, which Madonna, as Evita, sings when she learns that she is near death. It's an emotionally involving performance, perhaps her best of recent years, and one of which she was most proud.

Fixing him with a stare to gauge his reaction, Madonna watched Menem rock back and forth, his eyes closed, as her voice filled the room. He then leaned back in his chair and put his hands behind his head as he continued to listen intently. When the song was over, he had tears in his eyes. As Madonna had hoped, the president had been moved. With the moment just right, Madonna then began what she would later refer to as her "spiel."

"I so want to make this movie," she told him, her tone passionate. Small television cameras, mounted on the walls and swiveling soundlessly, recorded her plea. The interpreter translated as Madonna continued: "I promise you that it will be fair. I want to be respectful to Eva's memory. You must understand that my intention is good." She seemed filled with emotion. "It's all about intention, you know?" she continued. "And mine is a good one, I promise you."

"Somehow, I think I believe you," Menem said as he inched closer to his guest. He reached out and patted her hand, seeming happy to be in the company of an attractive and intelligent woman. Madonna smiled warmly, just a little seductively . . . but not *too* seductively. When she leaned forward, he did the same. While this flirtatious moment was an interesting turn of events, it was not unexpected.

According to one eyewitness—the two were never left alone but were always in the company of Menem's aides—Madonna met

Menem's gaze with her own. "You know, you're a very handsome man," she told him. He didn't need an interpretation to understand the compliment.

"I caught Menem looking at my bra strap, which was showing ever so slightly," she would later recall. "He continued doing this through-out the evening with his piercing eyes. When I caught him staring, his eyes stayed with mine."

Over dinner, Madonna and the president talked about their lives and careers and, as Madonna later recalled, "our passions." They spoke of music, politics, mysticism and reincarnation. It must have been difficult for Madonna to come to terms with her circumstances, with how far she had come from her struggling days as a Detroit singer with a New York band called the Breakfast Club. Perhaps it would have been difficult for some observers to reconcile this woman who seemed to possess such a flare for diplomacy with the one who, when she finally did become famous, was often viewed as a tem-peramental and sex-starved pop star. Now, she was the perfect combi-nation of sexuality and brains. But, of course, she had always been just that.

"One always has to have faith in things that cannot be explained," the president told her as they discussed Catholicism. "Like God. And the fact that miracles can happen."

Madonna seized the moment. "Yes," she agreed. "And that's why I believe that you will change your mind and allow us to film on the bal-cony of the Casa Rosada."

He smiled warmly. "Anything is possible," he said, nodding. "Any-thing is possible."

Five hours passed. It was eleven o'clock. The president took Madonna's face in his hands and kissed her on both cheeks. "I wish you great luck with your film," he told her, speaking in English.

"But will you help me?" she asked.

"As I said," he answered, smiling, "anything is possible." With old-world courtesy, he helped her to her feet. Then he stood at the front door and waved good-bye as Madonna and Constancio were driven away.

Once at the airport, Constancio guided Madonna by the arm across the tarmac to a red-and-white helicopter whose rotor was already be-ginning to turn. Soon, they were heading back to the city.

Madonna later said she felt swollen with pride over her accomplishment. "We flew away," she later said, "and I was floating inside the cabin the whole way home. He had worked his magic on me. I only hoped I did the same."

Less than two weeks later, the Ministry of Culture contacted the film's production company. A second meeting—this time formal and public—was organized and attended by President Menem, Madonna, Alan Parker and two other stars of the movie, Jonathan Pryce (the Tony award–winning actor from the musical *Miss Saigon* who had now been hired to portray Juan Perón) and Antonio Banderas (Ché, the film's narrator). At that meeting, Menem gave his blessing to *Evita* by making available to the film all government buildings previously off limits—including Madonna's cherished Casa Rosada.

⁜

Restless Child

Just who is this person so capable of charming the president of a country into doing something he had no intention of doing, and doing it her way? What is it about this woman—an entertainer who isn't uncommonly beautiful and, while talented, perhaps not phenomenally so—that has kept her on the top rung of the show business ladder as the very symbol of success and glamour for the last fifteen years? Always comfortable and confident within her limitations, in her 1991 documentary film *Truth or Dare* she noted, "I know I'm not the best singer or dancer in the world. I know that. But I'm not interested in that, either. I'm interested in pushing buttons."

In the ensuing years since her original success in 1983, many journalists have gone back and explored her past, looking for keys to the mystery of Madonna. However, in her ordinary beginnings there was little to suggest what lay ahead for Madonna Louise Veronica Ciccone.

"I get nostalgic for a time in my life before I was an empire," Madonna said in September 2000 during an on-line chat with customers of the Internet provider AOL. Like many people who become famous, before she was "an empire" Madonna just wanted to be a star. A driving, burning ambition to be famous seemed to be born within her, just a part of who she was at the core. When, in fact, she did realize her dream, one of her most celebrated remarks would be "I have the same goal I've had since I was a little girl. I want to rule the world."

Though half French Canadian, Madonna seems to most identify with the other half, her Italian heritage. *"Io sono fiera di essere Italiana"* ("I'm proud to be an Italian") she told an audience of 65,000 fans at the Turin football stadium when she performed in Italy in the summer of 1987. Her Italian roots date back to the 1800s in the Abruzzi province of Pacentro. Her paternal great-grandfather, Nicola Pietro Ciccone, was born in Pacentro in 1867. At the age of twenty-six, he married Anna Maria Mancini, also from Pacentro. In 1901, they had a son, Gaetano, Madonna's grandfather. Eighteen years later, Gaetano married a woman named Michelina (there seems to be no record of her surname), also from the local village. Shortly thereafter, the couple immigrated to the United States, settling in the Aliquippa suburb of Pittsburgh. Unable to speak English, they forged their way in their new country, Gaetano working in the steel mills of Pittsburgh. They had their first child, Mario, in 1930 and then, four years later, their second son, Silvio—nicknamed Tony—Madonna's father. Four more children, all boys, would be born over the course of the next six years.

Of all the boys, Silvio was the most aggressive, the most intelligent and the most determined to carve his own niche in life; he was the only child to graduate from college with a degree. After graduation, Silvio met and fell in love with a beautiful French Canadian woman from Bay City, Michigan, with the unusual name of Madonna Fortin. Though engaged to another man at the time, Madonna was attracted to Silvio's strong charisma and dark good looks and soon she accepted his proposal of marriage. They married in 1955 at Bay City's Visitation Church. After settling in a small brick home at 443 Thors Street in Pontiac, Michigan—twenty-five miles northwest of Detroit—Tony took a job as an engineer at Chrysler Automotive Corporation.

Madonna Fortin Ciccone gave birth to the couple's first child, Anthony, on May 4, 1956. Another son, Martin, was born a year later, on August 9. While visiting her mother, Elsie Fortin, in Bay City, the again-expectant Madonna Fortin Ciccone gave birth, on August 16, 1958, to her first daughter, Madonna Louise (nicknamed "Nonnie" by her parents) at Bay City Mercy Hospital. She would give birth to three more children over the next three years, Paula, Christopher and Melanie.

"I grew up in a really big family and in an environment where you had to get over it to be heard," Madonna once recalled. "I was like the she-devil. It was like living in a zoo. You had to share everything. I slept in a bed for years—not even a double bed—with two sisters." She also recalled, "I would even hurt myself, like burn my fingers deliberately, to get attention."

"She was spoiled from the very beginning," recalls her brother Christopher. "She was the oldest girl, and was the one considered our parents' favorite. That, combined with the fact that she was really aggressive and wanted her way, and got it, made her a spoiled kid. But she was good-hearted. She liked to take care of the bunch. She was also very bossy," he says. *"Very bossy."*

While growing up, the young Madonna had always been a faithful fan of classic Hollywood and of its stars. At an early age, she somehow came to realize that many of the world's greatest stars suffered through volatile early lives rife with mystery and drama. A melodramatic child, she seemed to understand the importance of legend. Years later, Madonna seemed to want to give the impression in interviews that she came from a lower-income family—perhaps hoping to capitalize on the "good copy" value of the so-called classic rags-to-riches story. While this was apparently the kind of history she wished to claim for herself—one in which she had to overcome great childhood traumas and obstacles before she could ever think of attaining success—it wasn't true.

In truth, her father Silvio was never out of work. He did well, even with the responsibility of so many children and the financial burden inherent in such a large family. Madonna always lived a healthy, middle-class existence.

"Ours was a strict, old-fashioned family," she has said. "When I was tiny, my grandmother used to beg me to go to church with her, to love Jesus and be a good girl. I grew up with two images of women: the virgin and the whore."

As a young girl, Madonna was particularly close to her mother. The two Madonnas shared an intense and special affection, and throughout her career daughter would always speak of mother with great tenderness. "She was beautiful," Madonna once recalled, "and very loving and devoted to her children. Very children-oriented." Her earliest childhood memories, she has said, are happy ones because they revolved around her mother, whom she has also called "forgiving and angelic."

"When I was four and younger, I remember not being able to sleep at night," Madonna remembers. "I would walk to my parents' bedroom and push the door open. They were both asleep in bed and I think I must have done this a lot, gone in there, because they both sat up in bed and said, 'Oh no, not again!' And I said, 'Can I get into bed with you?' My father was against me getting into bed with them. Yet, I remember getting into bed and rubbing against my mother's really beautiful, red, silky nightgown . . . and going to sleep—just like that. I always went to sleep right away when I was with them. I felt really lonely and forlorn, even though my brothers and sisters were in my room with me. So, I wanted to sleep with my parents. To me, that was heaven, to sleep in between my parents."

Madonna's older brother Martin remembers her as a restless, rambunctious child. Though there was the usual sibling rivalry between them, little Nonnie never let her older brother intimidate her. If he spread Vaseline in her hair while she slept, or hung her on the clothesline by her underwear, she'd soon retaliate by snitching on him the next time he sneaked out of the house and went down to the corner store without permission. From an early age, Madonna didn't like anyone getting the better of her, and—no surprise—also hated to be told what to do and how to behave, even by her parents. "When I was a child, I always thought that the world was mine," she has explained, "that it was a stomping ground for me, full of opportunities. I always had the attitude that I was going to go out into the world and do all the things I wanted to do, whatever that was."

Certainly no child likes to be given rules but, repeatedly, people from Madonna's past remark on her particularly rebellious nature as a child. She herself often talks about the defiant personality she possessed from an early age. She started out, and would remain, outspoken about people and matters that rubbed her the wrong way—even well-meaning children. For instance, one of Madonna's earliest memories is of sitting in her parents' front yard in Michigan, punished by her father as a result of some youthful misdeed. A two-year-old neighbor, wanting to befriend the adorable little girl, waddled up to Madonna and presented her with a dandelion she had picked. Madonna's response was to stand up, face the child, and then push her to the ground. "My first instinct," Madonna said years later, "was to lash out at someone who was more helpless than I. I saw in her innocent eyes the chance to get back at authority." The fact that the young visitor offered a dandelion apparently did not help matters for her. The adult Madonna would go on to explain that she detested dandelions because "they're weeds that run rampant and I like things that are cultivated."

Even though she was the third of six children, Madonna soon learned how to keep a certain amount of attention focused upon her. For instance, she would use tricks inspired by the movies she voraciously watched on television in order to remain the focal point in a busy household—such as jumping on top of a table at a moment's notice and performing a Shirley Temple–type number. At the end of her impromptu act, she would add "a personal touch"—she would lift up her dress and flash her panties. This bit of naughtiness was always a success, delighting everyone, young and old. The youngster seemed to be learning that a little flash, mixed with a bit of exhibitionism, could go a long way toward pleasing people. Of course, years later, the adult Madonna would combine these talents to great effect in her professional career.

*

Almost certainly, the defining moment of Madonna's childhood—the one that would have the most influence in shaping her into the woman she would become—was the tragic and untimely death of her beloved mother at just thirty years of age.

After her mother was diagnosed with breast cancer, little Nonnie and her siblings watched as she slowly wasted away over a period of about a year. Many months before her mother would die, however, five-year-old Nonnie began to notice changes in her behavior and personality, although she didn't understand the serious reasons for such changes. Her mother had always been greatly attentive to detail as a homemaker, but after her diagnosis she grew tired easily and was unable to keep up with housework she had previously maintained with such diligence. Madonna has remembered her mother sitting exhausted on the couch in the middle of the afternoon. The young girl, wanting to play with her parent, just as she always had in the past, would jump on her back; her mother, too tired to move, would be dismissive. The little girl—sensing that something frightening was in the offing— would respond by pounding angrily on her mother's back and sobbing, "Why are you doing this? Stop being this way! Be who you used to be. Play with me!"

Madonna's mother was, no doubt, at a loss to explain to her frightened daughter the reality of her dire medical condition. Probably scared and feeling helpless, she would just begin to cry, at which point her daughter would respond by wrapping her arms around her tenderly. "I remember feeling stronger than she was," Madonna recalled. "I was so little and yet I felt like she was the child. I stopped tormenting her after that. I think it made me grow up fast."

Eventually Madonna's mother had to be moved to a hospital. Once there, she attempted to maintain a cheery demeanor, always appearing upbeat for her visiting children and cracking jokes for them. Though she knew she was dying, she didn't want her offspring to realize it. "I remember that right before she died she asked for a hamburger," Madonna has said. "She wanted to eat a hamburger because she couldn't eat anything for so long. I thought that [she chose a hamburger for her meal] was very funny." Later that day, though, Madonna's father broke the news to her that her mother was dead. At first, she couldn't comprehend the enormity of the tragedy that had occurred and, as she put it, "I kept waiting for her to come back. We [she and her father] never really sat down and talked about it. I guess we should have."

Madonna was just five when her mother died on December 1, 1963, and the impact this loss had on her is almost certainly immeasurable. She lost her mother at a time when, as a young girl, she was forming her personality, her ideals. She needed a mother then, and she would need her evermore.

One theory about childhood loss is that the earlier the age the more profound the influence and the longer lasting the impact. Five is a formative age. A child of five could easily feel victimized by events, and maybe even think that he or she should have been able to influence them in some way. Certainly, the anger Madonna would feel at losing her mother would be extremely difficult for a five-year-old to handle. Some people never reconcile themselves to such a loss at so early an age, at least not without a great deal of therapy.

After she became famous, Madonna would say, "We are all wounded in one way or another by something in our lives, and then we spend the rest of our lives reacting to it or dealing with it or trying to turn it into something else." For Madonna, the anguish of losing her mother "left me with a certain kind of loneliness and an incredible longing for something." She has also said, "If I hadn't had that emptiness, I wouldn't have been so driven. Her death had a lot to do with me saying—after I got over my heartache—I'm going to be really strong if I can't have my mother. I'm going to take care of myself."

As they grew older, Madonna and her sisters would feel deep sadness as the vivid memory of their mother began drifting farther from them. They'd study pictures of her and would come to think that she resembled Anne Sexton, the 1960s Pulitzer Prize–winning poet who wrote about depression and suicide in books like *To Bedlam and Part Way Back* and *Live or Die*. This may have led to Madonna's intense interest in poetry. (Madonna has also cited Sylvia Plath as a poet she admires—an intellectual reference that goes beyond most people's image of Madonna as being shallow. Actually, many of her songs have roots in art, poetry, philosophy and different religions.)

Not only did the young Madonna learn to take care of herself, she also cared for her brothers and sisters. As the oldest girl, she was happy to take on the maternal role with her siblings. In fact, her brother Martin remembers that Madonna not only fed the younger children but she always made sure that they were properly dressed for school. "I didn't resent having to raise my brothers and sisters as much as I resented the fact that I didn't have my mother," Madonna confirmed. Actually, she didn't have to raise her siblings alone since her father did hire a series of housekeepers . . . all of whom eventually ended up quitting rather than having to endure the behavior of the unruly Ciccone brood. Madonna and her siblings invariably rebelled against anyone brought into the home ostensibly to take the place of their beloved mother. If it meant she could keep other women out of her father's life (and have him to herself), Madonna was happy to continue in the role of surrogate mother. "Like all young girls," Madonna would say, "I was in love with my father and I didn't want to lose him. I lost my mother, but then I was my mother . . . and my father was mine."

"I see a very lonely girl who was searching for something," she once said in an interview with *Vanity Fair* in describing her youth. "Looking for a mother figure. I wasn't rebellious in a conventional way; I cared about being good at something. I didn't shave under my arms and I didn't wear makeup. But I studied hard and got good grades. Rarely smoked pot, though I'm sure I did from time to time. I was a paradox, an outsider and rebel who wanted to please my father and get straight As. I wanted to be somebody."

The death of her mother had left such deep emotional scars on her, the young Madonna was terrified that she would lose her father, too. As she had done a couple of years earlier with both her parents, she would now crawl into bed in the middle of the night with just her father. The young girl suffered constantly from recurring nightmares and it was only with the assurance that her father was with her could she fall soundly and safely asleep. In time, no doubt because of the devastation she felt, she would never again allow herself to feel as abandoned as she had felt when her mother died. Madonna would have to remain strong for herself because, from an early age, she feared weakness—particularly her own.

☦

Confusing Times

In 1966, three years after the death of Madonna's mother, Tony Ciccone became romantically involved with Joan Gustafson, one of the Ciccone's many housekeepers. Much to Madonna's resentment, the two were soon married. It was, perhaps, at this time that Madonna began to express unresolved feelings of anger toward her father that would last for decades.

Repeatedly, biographies about Madonna have proffered the notion that, because of her mother's death, Madonna has always yearned for her father's approval, and that his apparent lack of approval had been the source of ongoing tension between father and daughter. It's true that Tony Ciccone's lack of understanding of Madonna's artistic vision has certainly not enhanced their relationship over the years, and she has definitely sought his approval. However, a close study of Madonna's life clearly shows that another factor in the instability of her emotional relationship with her father has to do with anger. Tony's courage in moving on with his life after his wife died did nothing to elevate him in the eyes of a daughter who felt strongly that her mother could—and should—never be replaced. Or, as one close relative put it, "It was as if, as a young girl, she was so filled with rage because of her mother's death and the way her father handled it, she had to direct it somewhere . . . and so she directed it at the one person she loved the most, her father."

Is it possible to be angry with a person and also to seek that person's approval? Most mental health professionals would agree that major characteristics of the human experience are ambivalence and contradictory feelings. Whereas in logic a thing can't be a chair and a table, it has to be one or the other, it's not an either/or situation in human nature. It's entirely possible that Madonna was angry at her father for going on with his life after the death of his wife, but underneath that rage she still longed for his approval and acceptance. It was as if she put him to a test she knew he would fail: would Tony accept his daughter on her own terms, even if she acted outrageously? If not, she could continue to be angry at him. If so, she would find another reason to be resentful of him. Certainly, anger just continues to recycle itself until it's finally dealt with, once and for all.

In comparison with Madonna's gentle, olive-skinned mother, the stern, blonde Gustafson was quite the contrast. Whereas Madonna's mother was easygoing and loving, Joan was a disciplinarian—or at least she tried to be one. None of the children ever listened to a thing she had to say. The young Madonna also seemed to have a difficult time adjusting to no longer being the female head of the household. She refused, for example, to refer to the new Mrs. Ciccone as "Mother," which her father had requested.

When Madonna's career was just beginning to gain momentum in the early 1980s, she talked a great deal about how her life had changed when her father remarried. She didn't hate her stepmother, she explained, she simply could never accept her in the place of her real mother. True to her sensational nature, Madonna would later embellish any tension between stepmother and stepchild for the press by saying she always felt unwanted and unneeded, "always like Cinderella."

Madonna would also tell how the new Mrs. Ciccone once bloodied her nose in a physical altercation—although Madonna professed to be delighted by this turn of events since it enabled her to miss Sunday church for a change. ("I most certainly do not remember that," Joan Gustafson Ciccone says today. "It never happened. Do you think her father would have allowed such a thing?") Another indignity often recounted by Madonna is that her stepmother supposedly refused to let her wear a tampon when she started menstruating (which, according to Madonna, occurred at the age of ten) because, in Joan's opinion, tampons were the equivalent of sexual intercourse and should not be used until after marriage. ("Oh my God! That *never* happened," an incredulous Joan says today. "How awful! Did she say that? No, she did *not* say that. Did she?")

According to Madonna, it seems that another major "wicked stepmother" indignity perpetrated on her by Joan was that she insisted Madonna and her sisters dress in matching outfits, thereby stripping Madonna of the individuality she so valued. Wearing school uniforms was bad enough for Madonna, she said, but dressing exactly like her sisters was pure torture. ("What are you talking about?" Joan asked when told of Madonna's claim. "I never did that. Why would I do that? Are we talking about the same Madonna here?")

Even at this young age, Madonna learned to be innovative with her wardrobe while attempting to assert her own personality—whether it meant wearing her clothes in an unconventional manner by ripping them or turning them inside out once Joan wasn't around. Madonna would also wear old rags in her messy hair—anything that would enable her to stand out from her younger sisters. (This quest for fashion individuality would carry itself into later years when Madonna found herself struggling in New York, trying to be a dancer. She would often dress flamboyantly, cutting up her leotard and holding it together with only safety pins. Then, as now, she remained fascinated with the idea of individuality.)

No matter how much Madonna might have resented the situation, it seemed that the new Mrs. Ciccone was in her life to stay. Joan and Tony went on to have two children together, Jennifer and Mario.

Tony Ciccone did his best to make sure his growing family stayed on the right track in life. A hardworking man, he tried to teach his children to follow in his footsteps and focus on their school lessons. There were rules to follow, he would tell them, and they were expected to live within those rules. It was especially important to him that his children attend church regularly. "I wouldn't call it strict, I'd call it conservative," Madonna said. "My father was a stern believer in excelling toward leadership. Maintaining a competitive edge. And be proud of yourself and do good in school and you will reap the rewards of your investment." Years later, Madonna recalled that her father would tape a "chore chart" to the wall, assigning each child a task. She never forgot which chores appeared under her name: "Washing out the diaper pail. Defrosting the freezer. Raking the leaves. Washing the dishes. Babysitting. Vacuuming. Everything."

Perhaps recognizing the obvious correlation between her ability to achieve success, keep a competitive edge and observe her father's own work ethic, Madonna would often speak of Tony Ciccone with admiration: "One thing my father was with us was very solid," she has said. "Very dependable that way; he didn't confuse me. He didn't preach one thing and live his life another way. He always stuck to his word. He had a lot of integrity. And that consistency, especially not having a mother, was extremely important."

Always, Madonna enjoyed reaping the rewards of hard work; she liked to win. Tony had a practice of awarding each of his children fifty cents for every A grade they received on their report card; Madonna always got the most As. She was naturally intelligent, a good student who always seemed to have an eye on the importance of preparing for her future. "That bitch never had to study," her brother Martin laughs. "Never. She got straight As. I used to get up there and study all the time but my mind wasn't on it. I did it because I was supposed to, but I didn't like it. She did it because she knew it would take her to the next phase." Madonna also remembered the rewards she received for her A grades and laughingly added, "I was really competitive and my brothers and sisters hated me for it. I made the most money every report card."

As well as their academic studies and household chores, all of the Ciccone children were encouraged to play a classical instrument.

Madonna was designated the piano, though she genuinely hated it. The neighborhood in which she was raised was racially mixed and, with that cultural influence at work, she was more interested in the local Motown sound than she was in classical piano. Her idols were Diana Ross and the Supremes, Ronnie Spector and Stevie Wonder.

"When I was a little girl, I wished I was black," she said. "I was living in Pontiac, Michigan, some twenty-five miles northwest of Detroit. All of my friends were black and all the music I listened to was black. I was incredibly jealous of all my black girlfriends because they could have braids in their hair that stuck up everywhere. So I would go though this incredible ordeal of putting wire in my hair and braiding it so that I could make my hair stick up."

Madonna soon convinced her father to allow her to give up her boring piano lessons and, instead, take on more exciting (for her) activities, such as dance—tap and jazz—as well as baton twirling.

"She was a smart girl, always motivated," remembers her stepmother, Joan. "Brilliant. Manipulative, I guess so. Yes. But you knew she would survive. You knew she would never be weak. And you were glad about that."

*

It isn't surprising, especially given the religious convictions Tony Ciccone shared with his late wife, that all the Ciccone children were educated at Catholic schools. In the sixties, the strict rules and regulations of these parochial schools were stringently observed by the nuns in charge, many of whom used tactics that today would be considered child abuse.

"They'd smack you around, for sure," Madonna has said. "It was an environment of fear, mixed with these contrasting images of the holy."

In 1966, she had her First Communion and, when confirmed a year later, she added the name Veronica to her birth name. "I took the name of Veronica," she explains, "because she wiped the face of Jesus. You weren't supposed to help Jesus Christ while he was on his way to the Crucifixion. She was not afraid to step out and wipe the sweat off him and help him. So I liked her for doing that, and took her name. There was also Mary Magdalene," she says, when speaking of biblical women who had influenced her. "She was considered a fallen woman because she slept with men. But Jesus said it was okay. I think they probably got it on, Jesus and Mary Magdalene."

Catholicism gave her a foundation of faith upon which, she has said, she was always able to fall back, even as an adult. However, the religion's strong emphasis on the notions of guilt and forgiveness has, she's said, "screwed up many a Catholic person. How many Catholics are in therapy, just trying to get over the idea of Original Sin. Do you know what it's like to be told from the day you walk into school for the first time that you are a sinner, that you were born that way, and that that's just the way it is? You'd have to be Catholic to understand it."

Early in her career Madonna would playfully make use of religious icons as part of her sexy wardrobe and then distribute juicy comments to journalists, such as the oft-quoted "crucifixes are sexy because there's a naked man on them." As an adult, Madonna would employ one of her most frequently used and successful "shock" formulas: taking a respected, sacred image and imbuing it with completely inappropriate sexual connotations, thereby making even the mere thought of the total package completely taboo. She quickly found that making startling statements—such as "crucifixes are sensual because Jesus was so sexy, like a movie star, almost"—raised eyebrows, got her noticed and made people talk about her as a sexual revolutionary. Combining these elements of religion and sex was a successful recipe for controversy. While easy to prepare, after the second or third time, it was also a relatively transparent gimmick. Yet, since the public continued to act shocked, and even to express delight and amusement at her observations, Madonna repeated the formula often—on talk shows, in music videos and in some of her songs. (It wouldn't be until nearly ten years into her career, when she published her steamy book *Sex*, that most people would catch on to what she was up to . . . and then begin to reject it.)

One story in her arsenal may or may not be true: "When I was a little girl, I was at church by myself on a Saturday afternoon going to confession. No one was there, and instead of going out the main entrance, I went through this vestibule off to the side with a swinging door. I opened the door a little bit, and there was this couple standing up, fucking in the church. I thought, 'Oh my God!' and shut the door really fast. That's the only sex I've seen in a church. Seems like a neat thing to do, though."

In fact, many of Madonna's tongue-in-cheek takes on Catholicism (which have been considered blasphemous by some more devout observers) have to do with an intense bitterness toward the church. Perhaps she had such a strong feeling that the orthodoxy that surrounded her had let her down, she acted provocatively as a way of thumbing her nose at it. It appeared to some that she had rejected God because He had done a terrible thing to her—taking away her mother. Through the years, she seemed to continually dare Him to retaliate against her as she continued to act out in ways that could be considered, at least to a religious person, sacrilegious.

As an adult, Madonna would also blame the church's stringent, puritanical, suffering-based teachings for many of the problems the Ciccone children experienced in life. "My older brothers were incredibly rebellious," she said. "They got into drugs and into trouble with the police. One of my brothers ran off and became a Moonie. Me? I became an overachiever. I had it programmed in my mind—'I don't care if I have to live on the street, and I don't care if I have to eat garbage. *I'll do it.*' "

Adding to Madonna's ambivalence about religion must have been the way she was influenced by the somewhat fanatical—and confusing—devotion she witnessed in her mother. "Catholicism is a very masochistic religion," the adult Madonna would declare. "And I saw my mother doing things that really affected me. She would kneel on uncooked rice and pray during Lent. She would sleep on wire hangers. She was passionately religious. Swooning with it, even. If my aunt came over to my house and had jeans that zipped up front, my mother covered all the statues so that they couldn't see such a display. She then turned the holy pictures toward the wall."

When Madonna was about ten, the family moved to 2036 Oklahoma Street in Rochester Hills, Michigan, an affluent community not far from the exclusive Detroit suburb of Bloomfield Hills. It was then that she began to think she might one day like to become a nun. "I wanted a pious way of life," she told the author in 1983. "But I was at odds with the whole thing. The more it repelled me, the more I wanted it, as if I was trying to conquer something. I think the church really screwed me up. It made me competitive. It made me afraid to fail. It caused all kinds of problems, some I probably don't even know about. I'm actually afraid to go into hypnotherapy for fear of what I will learn about my Catholic upbringing!"

Indeed, her rebellious nature being what it was, she couldn't help but turn against the moralistic and conservative school system. In the playground, for instance, the young Madonna would hang upside down from the monkey bars, acting oblivious to her "performance" but quite intentionally making sure her underpants were exposed for the enjoyment of all the boys. Constantly, she was being chastised by the nuns for flashing her underwear.

Those nuns at St. Andrew's Elementary School were always a source of great fascination for Madonna. She would try to sneak glances at them through the convent windows to catch them in their informal, "natural" setting. She wondered what they looked like sans habits and if, indeed, they even had hair. Childhood friend Carol Belager recalls peering through convent windows with Madonna.

"Oh my God, they *do* have hair," Madonna whispered to Carol as the two girls spied on the unsuspecting Sister Mary Christina.

"Let's go now," Carol said, nervously.

"No, she's getting ready to strip," Madonna said, excitedly. "I want to see what she looks like naked."

Carol pulled Madonna away before she had the opportunity to see her first nude nun.

These strange, humorless and immensely powerful nuns were, to the young Madonna, beautiful and mysterious. As an adult she would remember, "I saw them as really pure, disciplined, sort of above-average people. They never wore any makeup and they had these really serene faces." Then, in typical Madonna fashion, she added for good measure, "Plus, they were very sexy."

The ambivalence Madonna still feels for the teachings of the Catholic Church is especially ironic given that it would seem that Catholicism did empower her with the ability to transcend her own insecurities. The philosophy encouraged her to confront moments of great self-weakness, those times when she suspected that she really wasn't good enough, or talented enough, or pretty enough . . . those times when she most needed to fall back on a foundation of faith in order to conquer feelings of inadequacy. It also imbued her with the strict sense of self-discipline so necessary to challenge the many difficulties she would, no doubt, encounter on the road to stardom.

"I don't talk about it much," she said in another interview with the author in 1985, "but, yes, I pray. I pray when things are going wrong, like most people, I guess. The key, I think, is to pray when things aren't all screwed up. That's when you know you have a relationship with God. Coming from a Catholic school, though, it's so ingrained in me to pray, that now I do it without even thinking about it. To me, when I say, when I'm pissed off, 'Oh my God,' well, that's a prayer, in a sense. Even if people don't agree with me that it's a prayer, I don't care. When you're angry and you call out for God's intercession, that's a prayer. And, also, I tend to pray when there's so much bullshit going on that I just need to stop and remind myself of the things I have to be grateful for. So, yes, I pray."

✝

Losing Her Virginity

Though feeling almost smothered by a strict religious environment, Madonna's talent still somehow managed to blossom and, on occasion, she would find imaginative ways to unleash it. For instance, in a fifth-grade talent show, the eleven-year-old scandalized the school audience when, clad only in a coat of fluorescent green paint and a revealing bikini, she did a knockout imitation of a go-go-dancing Goldie Hawn (à la Hawn's early performances on the classic television program, *Rowan & Martin's Laugh-In*). Madonna's father smoldered at the sight of his pubescent daughter bumping and grinding for all to see. Afterward, he grounded her for two weeks. "I don't know what she was thinking," he says today. "Besides the fact that she wanted to shock everyone."

Once in Rochester Adams High School, Madonna found various activities with which she could keep herself in the public eye. As a cheerleader, she got a taste of what it was like to be in front of enthusiastic crowds. She then had the opportunity to test some of the tricks she had used as a child in front of her appreciative family, but on a bigger, and maybe even more critical, audience.

Karen Craven, who was on the cheerleading squad with Madonna, recalls the day the squad was to form a typical "human pyramid" during a break in a game. Madonna "vaulted up to the top and did a little flip," she remembers. A collective gasp erupted from the crowd when the teenager's skirt flew up. Guidance counselor Nancy Ryan Mitchell recalls, "From a distance, it looked like she was nude. However, she was actually wearing a pair of flesh-colored tights. It was shocking, I must say. But that was Madonna.

"I remember that she would also dance vigorously during some of the plays she was in, using a lot of body movement. It was pretty controversial for the times. Her father wasn't pleased. Anything she could do to shock people, that's what she would do. But, to her credit, she was a bright student, involved in a Big Brother/Sister program, a thespian group. She was very positive thinking. She was taking dancing lessons after school when a lot of other kids were drinking Cokes. She worked hard."

Madonna was also involved in the theater department, starring in productions such as *My Fair Lady, Cinderella, The Wizard of Oz* and *Godspell.* On the high school stage, she would learn what it was like to please an audience, to stand in the spotlight and accept a crowd's warm applause. "She liked it," says Clara Bonell, a former classmate. "I saw her in *Godspell,* and I remember that when the audience stood for the curtain call, she was crying. The sense of acceptance, I think now that this is what she most appreciated, most craved. I think she felt that she didn't get it at home from her father, who was just not supportive at all, as I recall it. So, if she could get it from an audience, then that was good for her."

Beverly Gibson, her drama teacher, adds, "When the spotlight came on her, she was pure magic. People paid attention to her; you couldn't take your eyes off of her. You often hear about people who become famous being wallflowers. You hear their friends and teachers say, 'Oh, I would never have expected her to become famous.' Not so with Madonna. There was no way she could ever be anything other than famous at something. I would watch her on stage with that vibrant personality and charisma, and think to myself, 'Oh, my, it is inevitable, isn't it?' "

"In high school, Madonna was a nonconformist," says her former classmate Tanis Rozelle. "Unlike the other girls, she didn't shave her armpits, and neither did her sister Melanie. That was considered pretty weird. Both had thick tufts of hair growing out from underneath their armpits. It caused a minor controversy, but after a while people just accepted it. Madonna explained that she didn't shave because she didn't want to be a typical suburban American girl. She said she didn't want to remove something from her body that was natural. It didn't stop her from raising her arms high while cheering, even when she wore a sleeveless uniform," recalls Tanis. "And it certainly didn't stop her from being popular with the boys. She was very pretty and the guys really liked her."

It was during her first year in high school, at the age of fifteen in December 1973, when Madonna lost her virginity to seventeen-year-old Russell Long. Actually, she says she had some sexual encounters prior to this time, when she was eight, but not intercourse. "All of my sexual experiences when I was young were with girls," she says. "I mean, we didn't have those sleepover parties for nothing. I think that's really normal, same-sex experimentation. You get really curious and there's your girlfriend, and she's spending the night with you, and it happens."

"She wanted her first time having real sex to be something special," Russell Long now recalls. "We had a date—a movie and burgers—and afterward we drove my very cool, blue 1966 Caddy back to my parents' place."

While Long recalls being nervous about the signals he says Madonna was sending—it was clear that she wanted to be intimate with him—he didn't have to worry about initiating anything. She was the aggressor. "Are we going to do it, or not?" she wanted to know as she removed her bra.

"I guess so," Russell said, breathlessly.

"Well, then, c'mon," she urged. "Do it!"

Years later, she would observe, "Even after I made love for the first time, I still felt like a virgin. I didn't lose my virginity until I knew what I was doing."

After that first time at the home of Long's parents, he says, they chose the backseat of his Cadillac for future rendezvous. "My friends called it 'the Passion Wagon,' " he recalls.

"She didn't have a problem with people knowing we were having sex. Lots of girls of that age would have been embarrassed by it, or would at least not have wanted people to know. Not Madonna. She was proud of it, said that it had made her feel like a woman. She was comfortable with her body, didn't mind being seen naked. She just seemed comfortable with all of it."

"I liked my body when I was growing up," Madonna once said in a press interview, "and I wasn't ashamed of it. I liked boys and didn't feel inhibited by them. Maybe it comes from having brothers and sharing a bathroom. The boys got the wrong impression of me at high school. They mistook forwardness for promiscuity. When they don't get what they want, they turn on you. I went through a period when all the girls thought I was loose, and the boys thought I was a nymphomaniac. The first boy I ever slept with was my boyfriend and we'd been going out a long time."

"She wasn't like most other students," Russell Long recalls. "There was a group of kids who were just the odd ones, the ones most of the students thought were sort of creepy. Madonna was in that bunch. She didn't assimilate into the student body, rather she was one of those kids on the fringe, sort of on the sidelines smirking at everyone else.

"However, I found her to be quite sensitive," he continues. "We had long talks about her mother, and how much she missed her. Also, we discussed the tension that existed between her and her father. By the time she was in high school she was rebelling against him in every way, she seemed so angry at him, though I didn't understand why. She would say, 'What do you think he'd do if he knew we were having sex? Do you think it would freak him out?' And I would say, 'Hell, yeah, it would freak him out.' Then she would come back with, 'Well, then, maybe I should tell him.' I would say, 'Madonna, no! He'll kill me.' But my safety, or her privacy, wasn't on her mind. If she could blow his mind, shock him, she wanted to do it. Even more than that, if she could piss him off, she wanted to do it." Long and Madonna continued their relationship for six months.

Russell Long, now a trucker for United Parcel Service, still lives in Michigan and is married with children. "I wonder if he still loves me," Madonna once mused. Then, as if coming to her senses, she answered her own question. "Oh, of course he does!"

"Sure I do," says Russell Long today. "Even if she had not become famous, there's no way I would ever have forgotten her. She was one of a kind."

✟

Christopher and Whitley

In the ninth grade, Madonna joined a high school jazz-dance class. However, with determination and dedication uncommon for a four-teen-year-old, she soon outgrew it. A friend then recommended that she consider the Christopher Flynn Dance School at the Rochester School of Ballet. Once accepted as a student, she was quickly exposed to students who were serious about the art of classical dance, "which was a real turn-on for me," she has said. In his studio Christopher Flynn stressed hard work and discipline, concepts Madonna had some-times felt the need to rebel against in her home and at school, but which she now embraced as a dance student. "He was very Catholic and all about rules," she recalls. Because she worked up to five hours a day in his class, Flynn was quickly impressed with his new student's remark-able progress. Soon, she quit cheerleading, began to watch what she ate in order to trim her figure, and spoke of little more than her love of dance. Her enrollment at the Christopher Flynn Dance School was the first of several years of serious dance study.

Flynn the dance instructor, thirty years Madonna's senior, was one of the first people to notice the budding "star quality" in the teenage girl and, as a result, the first to push her in the direction of a career as a performer. His enthusiasm for Madonna quickly gave her a boost of self-confidence that even the most self-assured youngster needs at that age.

Once, after a particularly grueling dance routine, a sweaty and ex-hausted Madonna wrapped a towel around her head "swami-style," and then gazed moodily out of the window, deep in reflection. Flynn observed his student, so lost in thought. Years later, he would recall the moment with vivid clarity.

"My God," he said to her, "you really are beautiful."

"What?" Madonna asked, wide-eyed and perhaps wanting to hear it again.

"You have an ancient-looking face," he told her, "a face like an ancient Roman statue."

"Why would you say that to me?" she asked.

"Because it's true," he answered. "It's not physical beauty I'm talking about, it's something deeper. Know it."

"I already know it," she said, speaking frankly. "I just wasn't sure anyone else did."

Years later, she would recall, "I was fourteen, maybe fifteen, and feeling horribly unattractive and unpopular and uninteresting and unfabulous. And Christopher said 'God, you're beautiful.' Well, no one had ever said that to me before. He told me I was special. He taught me to appreciate beauty—not beauty in the conventional sense, but rather beauty of the spirit."

Actually, Christopher Flynn's influence on Madonna's life and career cannot be overstated. "My whole life changed," Madonna has said. "Not just because studying dance with Christopher was so really important, but because he gave me a focus. He took me out of what I considered to be a humdrum existence."

Flynn was happy to help encourage Madonna to her next level of her growth as a performer. After she became a star he would say of her, "Madonna was a blank page, believe me, and she wanted desperately to be filled in. She knew nothing at all about art, classical music, sculpture, fashion, civilization—nothing about life, really. I mean, she was just a child. But she had a burning desire to *learn*, that girl. She had a thirst for learning that was insatiable. It was something that would not be denied. She was a very positive young girl, always focused on what she could do to be better. She had this tremendous thirst and, really, it was insatiable."

Christopher Flynn was also the first homosexual man with whom Madonna became close. Although she was still underage, he allowed her to accompany him to gay bars and clubs. It was there that her education began to expand beyond the scope of classical music, art and sculpture. With Flynn as her guide to the more provocative aspects of Michigan nightlife, Madonna learned a great deal in a short amount of time about eroticism and, as she later put it, "pushing the envelope to the point where it screams out: 'stop!' " It was much more of an education than she could ever have acquired from her home life or at school. Because of her completely uninhibited way of expression through dance, Madonna won over crowds of gay men with her campy, sexy and energetic moves. Her appreciative "fans" filled her with a sense of self-confidence and energy, making her truly believe that her aspirations to be a dancer were not unwarranted.

Her French teacher, Carol Lintz, recalls that Madonna was so influenced by her experiences at the gay bars, she no longer even needed a partner to dance. "Something happened to her at this time, and it caused her to no longer think of dance as a social act, but rather an artistic one. There she would be, in the middle of the dance floor at one of those teen dances, by herself, dancing. People would ask me with whom she was dancing. I would answer, no one. Herself. She was dancing with herself, just for the experience.

"I started seeing technique. I started seeing showmanship. It was a fascinating evolution.

"When she graduated, she was given the Thespian Award for her work in the many school plays she did—so many, I can't even remember how many, and she was always the lead . . . she wouldn't have it any other way. She was very proud of that award. I remember, she said, 'I always knew I'd get this award one day,' as though it was an Oscar. But I never thought of her as an actress. I thought of her as a dancer."

Christopher Flynn once remembered another conversation he had with Madonna at his dance studio that, he says, "really clued me in on the kind of entertainer she was becoming."

While doing stretching exercises in her black leotard, she asked Flynn, "Why do you think you like men?"

He answered the question by saying his sexuality was something that "just happened, nothing I can control."

"Well, I wish I understood it," she said.

"Why?"

"So that I can tap into it," she said. "Look at women like Judy Garland and Marilyn Monroe. These women are gay favorites, aren't they? I wish I knew what it is about them. Is it the glamour? Is it their behavior?"

"I think it's because they're so tragic," offered Flynn. "I think that's what it is. You see them and you want to slit your wrists. Every gay man has wanted to slit his wrist at one time or another. So yes," he decided, "it's because they're so tragic."

Madonna stopped stretching. "Well, then, forget it," she said, looking at her dance teacher seriously. "I will never be tragic. If it takes being tragic to have gay fans, then fuck it. I'll appeal only to straight people, I guess."*

*

By the time seventeen-year-old Madonna graduated from Rochester Adams High School in 1976—a half semester early due to her exceptional studies—Christopher Flynn had became a dance professor at the University of Michigan. Wanting to bring his young protégée with him to the new school, he agreed with Madonna's high school guidance counselor, Nancy Ryan Mitchell, that she should audition for a scholarship there. She applied, she got it and so, in the fall of 1976, Madonna enrolled at the University of Michigan in Ann Arbor.

"Our dad was pretty damn proud," says Martin Ciccone. "I'm not sure that Madonna knew it, though. Their relationship was strained. If she was in trouble, of course he would be there. But she was never one to admit when she was in trouble, and definitely she would not turn to our father. They argued a lot, there was such anger there from her. She was his daughter; he was an old-fashioned Italian-American man, and family meant a lot to him. But there was always this great divide between him and Madonna. He never understood her. 'Break rules?' he would say. 'But why? What's wrong with the rules?' When it was time for her to go off to college, I think they were both ready for a break from each other.

"Our father had always stressed education, though. He raised his kids to appreciate a good education. When Madonna went to college with that scholarship, we all knew she was going to really come into her own."

* Christopher Flynn died of AIDS at the age of sixty on October 27, 1990, in Los Angeles. In a statement, Madonna said, "I really loved him. He was my mentor, my father, my imaginative lover, my brother, everything, because he understood me."

It was then, when she enrolled at the University of Michigan, that Madonna Louise Ciccone, middle child of a strict Catholic family, began her metamorphosis into "Madonna," free-spirited artist.

"I guess my immediate impression of her was a combination of fascination and intimidation," says Whitley Setrakian, a young and aspiring choreographer who became Madonna's first roommate at the University of Michigan's Stockwell Hall, and then later at the University Towers. "She was beautiful. Articulate. Very, very thin. Her hair had been chopped off in a sort of odd way with little bits sticking out on the sides. She wore lots of heavy, dark eyeliner and interesting clothes, baggy T-shirts and tight pants. She was startlingly brilliant, with a quick, incisive type of mind. She was very spontaneous, driven and unafraid. She had a way of owning a room when she came into it. I've never met anyone quite like her. Also," she adds with a laugh, "her front extensions [a dance technique] were very high, which meant a lot at the time. She was a good dancer with strong technique. She took chances. She was raw, but we were all raw then. However, if one dancer got a lot of attention and she didn't, that made her angry and she would talk to me about it. 'What does she have that I don't have?' she would ask. She would think it was unjust that anyone got more recognition than she got. It drove her crazy that others were as good, or better, as if there was a mad race to the finish."

Setrakian continues, "She worked well with Christopher Flynn, though a lot of other students didn't. He was a delightful person, and yet scary in ballet class because if he thought you were lazy he would pinch you really hard and leave little blood blisters on you. I had some trepidation about that, but Madonna didn't. She liked it, actually. He was flamboyant and sarcastic, like her."

Setrakian—who worked at the same ice-cream parlor as Madonna to earn extra money—was struck by the way the seventeen-year-old Madonna gave her all to everything she did, whether it be partying or rehearsing: "She'd drag me out of bed. I couldn't keep up with her," says Madonna's former roommate. "She was up in the morning and out the door, in class before everyone else, warming up. We'd go out dancing on Saturday nights, up all night dancing very late. She'd be up early warming up if she had a rehearsal on Sunday morning. She was not easy on herself. She lived hard and worked hard.

"She embarked on what seemed to be a calculated campaign to be my friend," Setrakian recalls. "I resisted it at first but she won me over. She was determined to break down whatever limits and boundaries I put up. I felt she was being real with me when she would reveal herself in vulnerable ways. But yet, in the back of my mind, I would always think, 'Maybe not.' I felt that there might be an element of exploitation going on, that she was using our friendship to meet her emotional needs. I felt there was something mercenary about it, but it was vague and unclear to me then. I just knew that she would expect a person to be there for her, unconditionally. However, if you had a problem and you needed her, well, she wasn't always there.

"We had many long talks about her mother," Setrakian says, "and about how much she missed her. She envied the relationship I had with my own mother. My mother called a lot and, when I would speak to her on the telephone, I would be aware of Madonna standing around and listening. We also talked about her father, but not much. I sensed anger from her whenever I brought up the subject.

"We became closer after a few months. She was huggy, very touchy. I got used to it. After a while it became a part of the way we related to each other."

In December at the Christmas break, Whitley Setrakian went to the Bahamas on a vacation with her boyfriend. Madonna spent the holiday alone at their apartment, pining for her. When Whitley returned from her trip, she found on her bed a six-page handwritten letter from Madonna. In it, Madonna wrote that she "missed the hell" out of her. "I've realized how much I've grown to depend on you as a listener, advice giver and taker and general all around most wonderful, intimate friend in the whole world," she wrote. She mentioned that she and a female friend had gone to a bar and, because of the way they were dancing, were "verbally accused" of being lesbians. In fact, wrote Madonna, she wished that she had been dancing with Whitley, not Linda. She also indicated that her rent was due, that she didn't have the money, and didn't know what she would do about the problem. She was so poor, she wrote, that she had taken to rummaging through garbage cans for food. She would just continue dreaming of a career in show business, she concluded, and hope for the best.

Those who knew her best at this time agree that Madonna had already made up her mind to be famous for doing *something* and so, as a means to that end, she was completely focused on her dance curriculum. Her inborn instinct for what was right for her, and for finding people who not only believed in her but could also assist in bringing out the best in her, led her to dance professor Gay Delang's "technique class." Delang remembers her as a standout from the very beginning. "She had many qualities that young dancers desire. She was lean. She had a nice edge to her muscles. She was hungry. Great appetite. She was sassy, kid-like. Chewed gum. Lived on butterscotch candies. She was disciplined, hardworking. A pleasure to be with. She was young. Just a kid."

"All these girls would come to class with black leotards and pink tights and their hair up in buns with little flowers in it," Madonna has remembered of her days as a dance student. "So I cut my hair really short and I'd grease it so it would be sticking up, and I'd rip my tights so there were runs all over them. Anything to stand out from them and say, 'I'm not like you. Okay? I'm taking dance classes and everything but I'm not stuck here like you.' "

In college, Madonna sometimes worked off campus (as in the ice-cream parlor) but, to her, survival meant getting by any way she could. Roommate Setrakian remembers: "She taught me how to shoplift. One of us would make a diversion at the counter and the other would place her dance bag under the counter. Then, you'd sort of lean casually over the counter and at the height of the diversion you'd sweep your arm over the counter. Finally, the item would be in your dance bag. We got a lot of cosmetics that way, and lots of food, too. Whatever we needed. She would say, 'Who needs it more than we do? When we get famous, we'll give a lot of money to charity to make up for stealing this stuff. It all balances out with God in the bigger picture, don't worry.' "

During her year and a half at the University of Michigan, Madonna received decent grades; she was satisfied with her work. However, the notion of graduating soon became less important to her than the idea of finally launching her dance career. She had been studying dance intensely for five years and the response to her work had been positive. Having gone as far as the university could take her, she now yearned to go farther. Christopher Flynn's enthusiastic encouragement, along with the admiration of her friends and roommates, served to validate her inner voice, the one that assured her that she had something special, unique, to offer. When she sensed that it was time to move on, she saw no reason to waste time finishing her formal studies. Whitley Setrakian remembers that Madonna "saw better things for herself if she moved on quickly, without so much as a glance back. She wanted to be a dancer. She wanted to go to New York and get into a good company," she recalls. "It was time. She never said she wanted to be a cultural icon or anything like that. She just wanted to dance."

From childhood, Madonna had wanted to be an actress or, to be clearer, a *movie star*. Now, according to what she would later explain, she reasoned that as a dancer she would eventually find an entrée into the world of dramatics. Of course, in making these decisions, she was working completely on gut instinct. Certainly, she could have migrated to the West Coast, to Hollywood—the so-called entertainment capital of the world. However, she sensed that her immediate opportunities would be found in New York, a city known for its frenetic energy and diverse cultures.

Predictably, her father, Tony, was most unhappy when Madonna told him that she was forsaking her scholarship to run off to New York and focus on a dancing career. "He was very, very upset," says Madonna's brother Martin. "Our stepmother backed him, of course. They both agreed that she was making a huge mistake, and they did everything they could think of to talk her out of it. There were some big battles, yes. I recall some pretty bad scenes."

"You drop out of school, you'll no longer be my daughter," Tony told her one night over a family meal, according to a later recollection.

"Fine," Madonna said, angrily. "But when I'm famous, will I be your daughter again? Is that how this works?"

"We'll cross that bridge when we come to it," Tony countered. "*If* we ever come to it."

"Oh, we'll come to it, all right," Madonna said.

Contrary to what has been reported in the past, however, Tony never discouraged Madonna's show-business aspirations. Rather, he just wished for her to graduate from college first, and then, as he puts it now, "do whatever she wanted to do, but with an education."

"He would never tell her she was untalented," says Gina Magnetti, one of Madonna's cousins. "He wasn't the kind of father to do that. Italian parents, they generally don't do that anyway, especially if they came from the Old Country. They support their kids' ambitions.

"Silvio—Uncle Tony—he wanted the best for her, big things. And, to him, that meant a college degree. Then, after that, she could have done whatever she wanted. She didn't see it that way, however. So they fought. Madonna was so angry all the time.

"I was at their home one night when, right in the middle of dinner, she threw a plate of spaghetti across the room. 'Stop trying to run my life,' she screamed at him. The plate smashed against the wall, spaghetti and meatballs dripping down all over the floor. Everyone was shocked. Martin was there. I remember his eyes were wide, like saucers.

"I thought Uncle Tony would have a stroke. His face got red, his blood pressure shot up and he looked like he was being stricken. Madonna got scared and ran to him.

"Down on her knees in front of him, she started crying and apologizing. 'I'm so sorry,' she kept saying. 'I didn't mean it. I didn't mean it.' An apology to her father? Why, that was a major concession on her part.

"And then he started crying, patting her head, and saying, 'No, I'm sorry. I'm the one who's sorry.'

There was always big drama between them, and she was the one who always instigated it. It was as if she felt that she and her father had to have these big scenes in order to validate their love for one another."

✝

Finally . . . New York City!

Whether it's all true or not—and with the always imaginative Madonna one can never really be certain—the story, or legend, of Madonna's arrival in New York City on that morning in July 1978 is a good one. Intent on her easily-salable image as a modern-day Cinderella, she has often recalled leaving Detroit Metropolitan Airport— her first flight—and arriving in the city with nothing but thirty-five dollars in her pocket, a winter coat on her back, a duffel bag full of ballet tights slung over her shoulder . . . and a determination to do something significant with her life, to succeed. "Ten summers ago," she announced in 1988 to a cheering crowd at the premiere of her film

Who's That Girl?, "I made my first trip to New York. My first plane ride, my first cab ride. I didn't know where I was going. I didn't know a soul. And I told the taxicab driver to drop me off in the middle of everything, so he dropped me off at Times Square. I was completely awestruck."

Around the time Madonna arrived in New York City, the play *Evita* was making its initial impact on Broadway. The heroine of the show is an ambitious woman who, with unflappable self-confidence, leaves her hometown to make her first trip to the big city, in her case Buenos Aires. She doesn't know anyone there. She is dropped off "in the middle of everything." Then, she takes over . . .

One can somehow imagine the five-foot-four-and-a-half, nineteen-year-old Madonna (she would turn twenty in a month) clad in her out-of-season winter coat, walking past the porno theaters and peep shows in Times Square and stopping to admire the billboards and placards dis-played in front of the theater featuring *Evita,* starring Patti LuPone. Did she ever imagine how closely her life would parallel the Argentin-ian icon's? Certainly she never considered that she would one day play the leading role in the movie version of this same play, some fifteen years in the future. Or did she?

New York, one of the toughest, most unforgiving cities in the world, did not intimidate Madonna in the least. Always with an eye to-ward the future, Madonna would manage to survive on her wits. As legend has it, she roamed the strange, frenetic city on that first day until finally ending up at a street fair on Lexington Avenue, where she no-ticed a man following her. Instead of fleeing, as most young women in a new city might, Madonna greeted him. "Why are you wearing that coat?" he asked her, giving her a cue to launch into her "story."

"Hi! I just arrived in town and I don't have a place to stay," she said. It was a story that had had some rehearsal time; she had already tried it on other disinterested strangers. Still, Madonna's intensity must have made it seem compelling to this particular passerby because she ended up moving into his apartment and, according to her, sleeping on his couch. Home at last.

Madonna soon learned, however, that a young woman could not al-ways be so trusting of people, particularly of men she might meet on the streets of New York. Years later, when she was famous for contro-versial anecdotes about herself, Madonna revealed that she had been attacked in New York at this time. "I have been raped and it is not an experience I would ever glamorize," she revealed. The subject came up while she was discussing scenes from her controversial book of nude studies entitled *Sex*.

"I know there are a lot of women who have that fantasy of being overpowered by two men or a group of men." One photograph in her book depicts Madonna dressed in a schoolgirl's uniform while being attacked by two boys. She insisted that the photograph, however, was pure fantasy. "It's obviously completely consensual," she said. "Everybody wants to do it."

Madonna did not give any date or details of her own experience, saying only that, "It happened a long time ago, so over the years I've come to terms with it. In a way it was a real eye-opening experience. I'd only lived in New York for a year and I was very young, very trusting of people."

"I remember her saying something about it," her longtime friend Erica Bell recalls. "But it wasn't something I felt she wanted to discuss openly. I think it was a date rape, meaning I think she knew the guy. It was someone who betrayed her confidence, her faith. It must have been devastating."

Says another friend—a woman who still knows Madonna today and in whom she often confides—"The date rape was something she never wanted to talk about. But when it did come up, you could tell that she was deeply affected by whatever happened. She cried when she spoke of it, as if she had been traumatized. She said, 'I wanted to call my father and tell him about it, maybe go home for a while. But he would have killed me.' I felt that she needed her father at that time, but was afraid to turn to him. I know she could have used a mother, as well. These were lonely years."

Her former manager Freddy DeMann adds, "I remember a time, long after her first taste of fame, when a girl in one of her audiences was being pushed around by some guys in front, trying to get closer to her [Madonna]. Suddenly, the girl went down, into the crowd. It was as if she was going to get stomped. Then, a couple of guys went down after her, and none of them came up. Madonna was watching the whole thing. She stopped the show, stopped singing, and called security out and told them to help that young girl. 'I know what it's like to feel powerless,' she said from the stage. 'And it doesn't feel good.' I'll never forget that night. I felt that she had great empathy for that girl, and a certain amount of fear, too."

"I don't want to make it an issue," Madonna has said about the rape incident. "I've had what a lot of people would consider to be horrific experiences in my life. But I don't want people to feel sorry for me because I don't." Madonna said that the experience had made her "much more street smart and savvy. It was devastating at the time but it made me a survivor."

✝

Pearl

After a few weeks, Madonna moved out of her benefactor's home—for reasons as unknown now as her destination was then—and she was on her own, again. She moved into a dilapidated fourth-floor walk-up at 232 East Fourth Street between Avenues A and B, truly just barely fit for human occupation. "I moved here from the Congo," she told one neighbor, very seriously. "I've been studying the collective behavior of apes for the last year. I'm just now reacquainting myself with civilization. Do you have any money you can loan me?"

She survived by taking any odd job available, such as working in a series of fast food chains, or simply by taking the easy way out: asking her friends for handouts. Later she would tell the press that she ate from garbage cans, though some close to her at the time have disputed this memory. Food did not concern her, anyway. She preferred to eat at irregular hours, a banana for breakfast, an apple for lunch, perhaps some yogurt as a snack. Any hardships she experienced at this time were, in her view, just annoying distractions. After all, as she would explain it, she was in New York to dance—not eat. She didn't waste time on unrealistic planning ahead, or optimistic dreaming, either. She had a goal, and she went after it.

In November of 1978, Madonna auditioned for the highly respected Pearl Lang Dance Company. On that day, she brought with her the emerging "Madonna persona." Immediately, Pearl Lang—a former dance soloist with Martha Graham—recognized her as being

37

unique. "She came in wearing this T-shirt that was torn all the way down the back," Lang recalls. "And she had this enormous safety pin—it must have been a foot long—holding it together. I thought if she doesn't poke her partner's eye out, she'll do something with her dancing one day."

Madonna was one of several people chosen from those who had auditioned for Lang's company. Her freestyle dance was impressive simply by virtue of its wild abandon. After the audition, Lang recalls walking over to Madonna until her face was just inches away from the young girl's. It was as if the instructor wanted to get a closer look. Then, studying her carefully, she stroked Madonna's face: "My dear, you have something special," she whispered to her, taking her hand.

"I know," Madonna replied.

As Madonna pulled away, Pearl relinquished her hold unwillingly, as if she wanted another moment to study the young woman before her.

"She was an exceptional dancer," Pearl Lang recalled. "Many dancers can kick and exhibit acrobatic body control, but that is just run-of-the-mill, taken for granted. Madonna had the power, the intensity to go beyond mere physical performance into something far more exciting. That intensity is the first thing I look for in a dancer, and Madonna had it."

Clearly, Madonna had won over choreographer Lang just as she had already won over others—such as Christopher Flynn—who would assist her in shaping her talent, guiding her toward her goal and becoming her mentors. As her skills broadened, she became an assistant to Lang. "I actually started to rely on her quite a bit," says Lang. "She was organized, professional and very serious, at first. But then, after a few weeks, I noticed that she was feeling stifled by the regimen of my teachings. She was annoyed when I pushed her for more."

One day, after Madonna completed a complex dance routine, which she performed to jazz music played by a frantic pianist, Lang stood before her, looking unhappy. Clapping her hands once, she ordered, "A-*gain.*" ("Again," but with pretentious upper-crust enunciation.)

Madonna danced until the routine was over.

"A-*gain!*"

More dancing.

"A-*gain!* And don't land in position, Madonna," the teacher said, impatiently. "Now," she added, clapping her hands loudly, "a-*gain!*"

More dancing.

"A-*gain!*"

More dancing.

"A-*gain!* And move it along, Madonna," she said, her tone sarcastic. "I'm in my late fifties, you know?"

Suddenly, Madonna bolted toward Pearl Lang. "I can't do it a-*gain,*" she said, almost in tears. "Stop pushing me. Why are you being so mean?" Going into her bag, she rummaged through its contents and took out a pill—perhaps an aspirin, but maybe something stronger—and washed it down with a sip from a plastic water bottle. Afterward, she pitched the bottle to the floor, uttered an expletive and glared at her instructor.

"That's when we had our, shall I say, little scene," Pearl Lang remembers. "When I accused her of not wanting to work hard, she lashed out at me. I knew she would have trouble being a dancer in any troupe because she was such an individual. It wasn't really a matter of working hard; she worked hard. But not in a way that gave me hope that she could blend with others.

"When she continued questioning me, well, that was it, really. At one point, after I gave her some advice, she curtsied and, in the most spiteful tone I had ever heard from a student, said, 'Why thank you ever so, *Lady Hateful.*' I believe it was then that I asked her—told her—to leave."

Soon after her experience with Pearl Lang, Madonna was accepted for a brief workshop at the world-renowned Alvin Ailey Dance Company. However, despite this happy coup, it was becoming clear that all of the determination, desire and pizzazz she could muster would not immediately guarantee her a place in the highly competitive world of New York dance. Though completely dedicated to her craft—mind, body and soul into dancing—Madonna found herself once again counting out change behind the counter of a local doughnut shop in order to make ends meet. She also worked in the prestigious Russian Tea Room restaurant in Manhattan as a hatcheck girl.

Gregory Camillucci, former manager of the restaurant, recalls, "She was a frail girl, very thin. I often thought that the meals she had at the restaurant were probably the only meals she was eating. But she was upbeat, never rude, always on time. At the beginning of her short time there, I caught her staring at the customers. 'I watch rich people eating and drinking,' she explained, 'so that when I can afford to, I can do it right.' However, it wasn't long before she became bored by rich people's eating habits. You then had a sense that she wasn't going to last long. 'This is not what I came to New York to do,' I once heard her grumble.

After Madonna had been in New York for several months, living in one of the East Village's bleakest neighborhoods in her dilapidated walk-up apartment on Fourth Street and Avenue B, she was paid a visit by her father, Tony Ciccone.

"I didn't want him to come," Madonna remembered years later. "The apartment was crawling with cockroaches. There were winos in the hallway. The entire place smelled like stale beer."

"What is going to happen if this fool's dream of yours doesn't work out?" Tony asked her, he recollected many years later. Father and daughter were sitting in an Italian restaurant on Eighty-first Street. Madonna was eating spaghetti and clams, and with such fervor it was as if she hadn't enjoyed a good meal in many months. "Please come back home," Tony said. "I miss you so much, Nonnie."

"I love you, Dad," Madonna said. "But I just can't come home."

"Look at how you're living," he told her, trying to reason with her. "In a roach motel. Like a bum, you're livin'."

"No," she said, correcting him. "Like a dancer, Daddy. *Like a dancer, I'm livin'*. Now, just leave me alone."

Cousin Gina Magnetti recalls, "Still today, when Tony talks about that visit, he gets tears in his eyes. I know his heart was aching. He cut the trip short, I remember. He said, 'She's so smart, why is she doing this? I don't understand it.' He begged her to go back to Michigan with him, telling her that he would never fight with her again, he would let her have her way, if she would just go back with him. 'If you want me to have my way, let me do it my way,' she told him. He tried to give her money before he left. She wouldn't take it. The fact that she refused his help somehow seemed like she was punishing him.

" 'She never listens to me,' Tony said when he got back to Michigan. 'No, she wants to live like a pauper. She wants to starve herself so she can be a dancer. *A dancer!*" He was always amazed that Madonna wanted to be a dancer, saying that there was no future in it."

The hard fact, of course, was that dancing jobs were really scarce, even in—and maybe especially in—Manhattan. Competition was stiff from agile, talented dancers whose own intense hunger and drive most certainly matched Madonna's.

"I'd go to Lincoln Center, sit by a fountain and just cry," she once recalled. "I'd write in my little journal and pray to have even one friend. I had been used to being the big fish in the little pond and all of a sudden I was nobody. But never once did it ever occur to me to go back. Never."

"Oh, please, she never sat by a fountain and cried," says her brother Martin. "She never wrote in some diary about her loneliness and pain. And she had loads of friends. She took those years, hard as they were—I mean, she had a lot of despair and I don't want to say she didn't, you know? But she later made it all just a part of the glamorous legend that is my sister. That's what she does best, she creates legend.

"I remember that after my father visited her, he said, 'Either she will be the greatest dancer who ever lived, or she will be the biggest fool.' She turned out to be neither, of course."

✟

Busting Out

By the beginning of 1979, Madonna—who would turn twenty-one that year—realized that it could take five more years for her to be accepted into a major touring dance company. She knew that the solution to her dilemma was obvious: she would have to diversify, expand her horizons, maybe even change her vision if she was going to survive in New York.

Ever true to her character, Madonna would not waste much time strategizing her next move. She needed a vehicle that would showcase her extraordinary charisma. She needed a forum, a venue. In order to earn extra money, Madonna began posing in the nude for art classes.

She had heard that it was an easy way to make money and, as she later recalled, "I was so broke and desperate, I would have done almost anything. And I thought it might give me a new thing, that maybe I might become a model. Who knows?"

Anthony Panzera, one of the artists for whom she posed, recalls that he was unhappy with Madonna's appearance when she showed up at his studio on West Twenty-ninth Street in New York after having answered an advertisement.

"I was hoping for someone a little less boylike," he said, as he got ready to send her on her way.

Perhaps sensing imminent rejection, Madonna unbuttoned her blouse and exposed her breasts. "Do boys have these?" she asked. Then, without hesitation, she slipped out of her jeans. Once naked, she blithely asked, "Now, just tell me where to pose."

"What's your name?" he asked.

"Madonna."

"No last name?"

"Do I look like I need a last name?" she said as she stood before him, unclothed. She grabbed her breasts and pushed them up, then out toward him.

"Her answer made no sense," the artist now recalls, "but yet, somehow it made all the sense in the world.

"It was basically seven dollars an hour in those days, and that was a lot for her. She needed the money, that's for sure.

"What I most remember about her is that she never seemed to have a place to live that she could call her own. So if you wanted to find her, you'd have to call a series of numbers she had left. 'In the morning,' she said, 'you can reach me here' and she'd hand you one number scribbled on a piece of paper. 'Then, at night, try this number,' she'd say, and then stuff another piece of paper in your hand. 'But sometimes, I'm staying here, and other times, there,' and she'd hand you two more numbers. It was absolutely impossible to find her. She was a vagabond. But when you did find her, she was a good model, very cooperative, always willing to do energetic, enthusiastic poses."

In order to continue making extra money, Madonna then decided to pose nude for photographers who had advertised in the magazines and newspapers she read to find work. Martin Schreiber, who was teaching a course for the New School in Greenwich Village at the time, paid her thirty dollars for ninety minutes on February 12, 1979, to pose naked. Upon her receiving her payment, she signed the release form with the name Madonna Louise. "What I recall of that session was that she really wasn't into it," says Schreiber. "Whereas some models come in and are raring to go, strip down and pose, I sensed that she was really just doing it for the money, that she really didn't want to give it much thought, and wasn't going to dwell on it. I thought to myself, after she leaves here she will never again think about these pictures."

Meanwhile, Madonna's combination of style, daring and charisma continued to draw influential people to her like a magnet. While at a party and spinning around in the middle of the dance floor, she was spotted by graffiti artist Norris Burroughs. "It was the winter of 1979," Burroughs recalls. "I remember she had leopard tights on, and there were people all around her, but she was getting center stage even though it was a house filled with dancers. It was like some kind of ritual, as if she was dancing in a ring of fire. So there we all were, me and my friends and everyone else, singing and dancing to the Village People's 'YMCA,' and Madonna was in the middle of it all, holding center stage. She was this amazing and exciting-looking creature with wild hair and loads of sexual energy just waiting to bust out, to make an impression. I was completely taken aback. So I had to approach her.

"If I could rearrange the alphabet," Burroughs told her, "I would put U and I together."

"Screw you," Madonna said, sizing him up. "You remind me of a guy on Fifth Avenue who tried to sell me his comb earlier today." Then, having delivered her sharp dig, she began to walk away. After a beat, though, she turned around and asked, "Does that offer come with dinner?"

"It does."

"Fine. But it'll have to be Italian," she said, "or the deal is off."

Still, despite the tentative date, the two didn't get together until a few weeks later after Burroughs finally telephoned Madonna. "You get your gorgeous Brando body over here," Madonna told him.

"How could I resist?" Burroughs now asks. "It was then that our affair began."

Though the tall and slim "dirty blond" Burroughs was not

Madonna's usual physical type—she preferred darker, more muscular types—she seemed happy in the relationship. He remembers her as a sexual being. "It was just an animal kind of sexuality," Burroughs said. "She wasn't coquettish, or shy, that's for sure. It was all raw, but fun. Lots of disco dancing to Gloria Gaynor's 'I Will Survive,' her favorite song at the time. She was incredibly self-involved. Everything was all about her, her wants, her needs, her thoughts, her desires . . . but, still, you got swept away by it. She was just so fascinating to watch and to be around.

"During one lunch date, Madonna ordered an ice-cream sundae for dessert, with bananas and chocolate syrup. Then, she poured maple syrup over the whole thing. I was nauseated just watching her lick the bowl clean. Her whole chemistry was always on overdrive; she could never get fat with that metabolism of hers.

"She acted like she didn't care at all about her looks, but I think now that it was all an act, that her whole thing was to make people think she didn't care so that she could be as outrageous as possible," Burroughs observes. "I remember giving her a pair of jeans with a thirty-four waist, way too big for her. She couldn't wait to wear them. She had sweaters and shirts with holes in them, and she'd stick her thumbs through the holes, posturing and posing. She always looked cool. She always *was* cool."

Burroughs says that during the time he dated Madonna there was always a sense of the temporary about the romance. "I knew it wasn't going to last," he said. "She never said it to me directly, but I sensed that she believed that she was going places . . . and that I wasn't. I knew that she wasn't going to be around very long."

After one lovemaking session, Burroughs turned to Madonna and said, "In a year, we'll look back on this time and appreciate it even more, won't we?"

"Hmmm," Madonna said in her most noncommittal tone. "Interesting," she concluded with an evasive smile.

Burroughs lay quietly with his arms around her, knowing—he would later admit—that there would not be many more of these tender moments in the future.

So far, the momentum of Madonna's career had been pushed along by a series of random circumstances that had exposed her to certain influential people who could help her achieve her goals. She eagerly took advantage of the opportunities that had been presented to her, then, without much apparent gratitude or sentimentality, she moved onward and upward, never once looking back. It was the way it had been up until now, and a pattern of her life that would continue for years to come. Though her relationship with Norris Burroughs lasted only three months, it did take Madonna to the next chapter of her life story. At a party at his home on May 1, 1979, Burroughs introduced her to friends Dan and Ed Gilroy, who had formed a band called the Breakfast Club.

Madonna hit it off immediately with Dan Gilroy. As the evening wound down, she asked him, "Well, aren't you going to kiss me?" While he pondered the question, she grabbed him by the tie, pulled him close and kissed him fully on the lips. Then, she smacked him lightly, twice and on the same cheek. After winking at him, she walked away.

Years later, Norris Burroughs would say, "Before I knew it, she was done with me and was with Dan. Immediately, Dan began teaching her how to play instruments. She learned to play the guitar, she learned to play organ. They put her behind the drums for a while . . . but eventually she wanted to sing."

Soon, Madonna was living with Dan and his brother in a rundown and boarded-up synagogue in Corona, Queens, which they would use as a rehearsal hall as well as a living space—for she was now a member of the Breakfast Club. Says Whitley Setrakian, "I remember walking for a long time through what seemed like a bombed-out area of Queens until I finally came to a crumbling synagogue. And I thought to myself, 'Oh my God, this is where she is living now?' But when I met with her, I saw further evolution in her personality, more self-confidence about her decisions. I heard the band she and Dan were trying to form, and it was good. It was loud, but it was good. She had the microphone firmly in hand and gyrated a lot. I sat in one of the chairs of the synagogue and watched her and saw that she was really in her element. I knew that she was finished with dancing, even though she never said it. I could tell that she loved this side of performing, as a singer, an entertainer. She and Dan had become romantically involved, and they seemed happy."

Dan was fascinated by Madonna. "You make love like a man," he told her, according to a later recollection. "You're so aggressive. Uninhibited."

"Does that scare you?" she asked him.

"No," he told her. "It turns me on."

"I always wanted to be a guy," she confided. "I want to just take my shirt off in the middle of the street, like a construction worker. I like the freedom."

"I like *you*," he told her.

"I know," she said as she kissed him.

"Dan and Eddie both sang and sometimes she sang, and then they would sing behind her," Norris Burroughs recalls. "Eventually she wanted to sing more. She had pretty much given up the idea of dance, I think, once she got into the band, once she got involved with Dan. She just wanted to do less as a dancer and more with the band. She soaked it all up, learning everything Dan could teach her about rock music, about playing it and singing it. She just wanted more . . ."

"More" was something Madonna always wanted "more" of, and it now seemed that she was beginning to wonder if singing was not the way to get it. Producer Steve Bray, who had known Madonna in Michigan and met up with her again in Manhattan at around this time, recalls, "With the Breakfast Club, she found her muse medium, she found the best vessel for her drive as a rock performer. She played guitar and fronted the band. I always thought she could have had a great career as a rhythm guitarist. She'd dance on the tabletops and break things all around her. She'd pour champagne all over herself. She was just a fabulous, wild child.

"Dan taught her a lot. He loved her. I thought they got along great. But I knew it would just be temporary."

Each week, Madonna continued to scour the pages of industry publications such as *Backstage, Show Business* and *Variety* for job opportunities. She told a writer for *Playboy* (in September 1985): "I saw an ad in the newspaper for this French singing star, Patrick Hernandez. He had this record called 'Born to Be Alive.' His record company [Columbia Records] was trying to put together an act to go on a world tour with him, and they wanted girls to sing backup vocals and dance. It was going to be a big gala performance. I thought it would be great; I'd be dancing and singing and traveling around the world—I'd never been out of America. So I went to the auditions, and after they were over they said they didn't want me for Patrick Hernandez, they wanted to bring me to Paris and make *me* a disco star."

"But you hate disco," Dan Gilroy told her when she told him the news.

"Who cares?" Madonna said, packing her bags. "This could be my big break."

"But you're a *dancer*, "he argued.

"Since when?" she asked. "When was the last time I danced?"

Dan didn't want her to leave Queens. Not only was he afraid of what trouble she might get into in Europe, he didn't trust the people financing her trip . . . and was also nervous that she wouldn't come back to him. He cared about her deeply.

"Well, now I'm a dancer who sings," Madonna said, flatly, "if that's what I gotta do to make it in this damn business."

Madonna explained that she hated to leave Dan so suddenly, and said that he had been one of the most generous men she'd ever known. "I learned a lot from you, Dan," she said. "However, it's time for me to go. And if that makes me a bitch, then I'm a bitch," she concluded. Hurt, Dan readily agreed with her self-assessment: yes, she was a bitch, he said. He loved her, he would later admit, and thought they had "somethin' goin' on." He couldn't fathom that she would leave him, "especially after all we shared."

In May 1979, twenty-year-old Madonna was off to Paris with producers Jean Vanloo and Jean-Claude Pallerin, who had promised to treat her well, feed her "fabulous foods," and "get me a vocal coach." To one reporter, she recalled, "They did all of that. It was a blast. I had a great apartment. I never had it so good. I was chauffeured all over. They were going to develop my talent, find a vehicle for me."

To another reporter, she changed the story a bit: "They took me to Paris and introduced me to awful French boys, took me to expensive restaurants and dragged me round to show their friends what they had found in the gutters of New York. I would throw tantrums and they'd give me money to keep me happy. I felt miserable."

In an interview with the author, she continued the story: "After a couple of weeks, I got bored. They were focusing on Patrick Hernandez and wanted me to wait. Me? Wait? Meanwhile, they were trying to mold me into Donna Summer. I kept telling them, 'I am *not* Donna Summer.'

"So I went into my rebel mode and gave away my money and

started hanging around with bums," she said. "Oh, how I missed New York. I hated France and everything French. If they weren't going to do anything for me, then I wanted to go back to New York where I felt I could do something for myself. I didn't have a contract, so I told them I wanted to go home to see a sick friend. They said that was fine, called a limousine and had me dropped off at the airport. When will you be back, they asked. I told them two weeks. Then, I just never went back. I heard [in 1985] that they're still waiting for me. Poor dears." (For years, Madonna collectors have been frustrated that no recordings of any kind have surfaced from this period in her career. There's actually no evidence to suggest that anything was ever recorded.)

It says a lot about Madonna's personality that, even though she had nothing going on for her there, she would eagerly return to New York where she, at least, felt in control of her destiny. In France, it would have been left up to a couple of record producers she didn't even know very well to make her dreams a reality. However, in New York it was up to her. She was willing to take the gamble, to wager that her own creativity and ingenuity would take her to the next phase in her career.

Before she left Paris for her "brief stay" in New York, Madonna ran into Patrick Hernandez at the rehearsal hall in which he was putting together his disco act. "Success is yours today, honey," she told him, "but it will be all mine tomorrow."

"What the hell ever happened to Patrick Hernandez, anyway?" Madonna asked a reporter in 1999.

✝

Certain Sacrifices

In August 1979, three weeks after she returned home from Europe, Madonna and her friend Whitley Setrakian talked about her exciting journey overseas. "She was living in a real hellhole in New York," recalls Whitley. "But she called it home, and so we laid on the floor on a futon and she told me this amazing story about how she had gone to Paris on the Concorde, how she hated it there, and turned around and came back. She was telling it to me in such a matter-of-fact manner, I was startled by it. To me, this was such a big deal. But she was nonchalant about it.

"I was so amazed that she was suddenly entering another world and was quite separated from the world that we once shared. However, she really saw it all as a natural evolution, and expected more trips to Europe, more opportunities to do more wonderful things. The trip may have been an unhappy one for her in some ways, but it did inject her with a new confidence, I think. She seemed even more self-assured when she returned from it. It was soon after I left New York during that visit that she saw another ad in *Backstage* for a film role that interested her."

After having already auditioned for the movie *Footloose* and the television series *Fame* (and not being cast in either), the twenty-one-year-old Madonna sent her photographs and a handwritten letter/résumé to amateur filmmaker Stephen Jon Lewicki. She was responding to his advertisement in *Backstage* which said, in part, "Wanted: Woman for low-budget movie. Dominatrix type."

Recalls Lewicki, "I was looking for a fiery, sexy, dominant girl in her early twenties who could act. I got about 300 responses, most of which were 8×10 glossy photos with résumés boasting of summer stock experience, and all of which were incredibly boring. And as I was getting completely discouraged by the process, I came across this one, last envelope."

When Lewicki opened the envelope, he found Madonna's résumé, two 3×5 color photographs, one black-and-white 8×10, as well as a handwritten three-page letter, which he still treasures. Madonna, who began by mentioning that she had just "returned from Europe," further wrote, "I was born and raised in Detroit, Michigan, where I began my career in petulance and precociousness. When I was fifteen, I began taking ballet classes regularly, listening to baroque music, and slowly but surely developed a great dislike of my classmates, teachers and high school in general. There was one exception, and that was my drama class."

He recalls, "Suddenly, here was a girl who I thought had some interesting possibilities." He also noticed that they shared the same birthday, to the year. But it was more than just that particular coincidence—or, perhaps, omen—that interested him in her. Lewicki explained, "There was something about her photos that made me want to meet her. In them, she was sexy, but not lewd. I had received all kinds of pictures and letters from girls who looked like they were whores who wanted to be actresses, and actresses who wanted to be whores. However, Madonna's photos were different. In one, she was putting on lipstick with her pinkie finger while sitting, I believe, in a bus station. There was something seductive about it, yet it had a certain fragility, an innocence that really fascinated me. I knew I had to meet her. So we set up a meeting in Washington Square Park."

Madonna showed up in a tight red miniskirt, and with her cocky, self-assured attitude in tow. "You would have thought she had a great résumé with a lot of experience, judging from the way she acted," Lewicki recalls with a smile. "She was tough."

"Look, I'll do your movie," Madonna told Lewicki, nonchalantly. "But there'll be no screwing."

"Who said anything about screwing?" he asked.

She took out her compact and began applying a pink blush color to her lips with her pinkie finger, as she had been doing in the photograph that had so fascinated the producer. "Just know," she said, seeming bored, "that you and I will not be screwing. Got it?"

"I didn't realize it then, but now I think she was auditioning for me right then and there," says Stephen Jon Lewicki. "I knew she was perfect for the role. She was *doing* the role."

Lewicki hired Madonna for his low-budget, one-hour movie, the plot of which involved the strange goings-on between a downtown dominatrix named Bruna (Madonna) and her suburban, outcast boyfriend, Dashiel (Jeremy Pattnosh). When Bruna is raped in the bathroom of a diner, she and her boyfriend employ her "sex slaves" to perform a satanic human sacrifice on her rapist. "At no time did I ever ask her to take her clothes off," recalls Lewicki. "It just evolved as she was doing the scene. She was very comfortable with her body, with nudity. Far from being pornographic, it's very passionate and interesting," he says. "We started the movie in October 1979, and we had a lot of fun, she was always up, had a lot of energy, able to improvise. I had a crush on her, actually. We cut each other down a lot, insulted each other. That's sort of how you relate to Madonna. She insults you, you insult her back . . . then, she knows you love her.

"She talked a lot about her life, the death of her mother and how it had affected her," he recalls. "I knew that she felt she had to take care of herself because she would never allow anyone else to do so for fear that she would depend on that person, and that he would leave. So, I understood her brash nature. Also, she had a father who she believed disapproved of her. There was a certain scene in the film which was racy, and I remember her saying, 'Oh my God, my father will freak out when he sees this.' I asked her, 'You'll let your father see this?' And she said, 'Oh, absolutely.' I had the feeling that she wanted to be rebellious just for the sake of rebellion, that she wanted him to see that she had a mind of her own. She was driven by this need, she had to prove she was independent of everyone, her deceased mother, her disapproving father."

The first low-budget films made by many actresses are seldom memorable, and Madonna's is no different, with its finale featuring a human sacrifice. The script is muddled, the sound mediocre and the acting by everyone, including Madonna, overwrought and amateurish, though perhaps unintentionally prophetic ("Do you think for once that any lover of mine could be tame?" she asks at one point. "It's not possible.") Still, the movie is well-intentioned.

Despite the low-budget nature of what she was doing, leading lady Madonna—with her natural brunette hair cut in a close-cropped style—was already acting like the star she would become in just a few short years. Co-star Russell Lome, who appeared in a steamy love scene with Madonna, was struck by the novice actress's brimming self-confidence. "She was acting as if she had a makeup person, a wardrobe person and a whole entourage—yet there was no entourage," Lome remembers. "She was this attractive, unknown young woman who seemed to command a great deal of attention. She had already adopted the practice of using one name, thinking of how the great stars of yesterday would become known by a single name at the height of their fame. Marilyn, Dietrich, Gable, Garbo, Liz, Brando. I guess Madonna wanted her name added to the list of one-name legends." *

* Lewicki's film, *A Certain Sacrifice*, was actually filmed in parts, the first in October 1979, the second in November 1981. A twenty-four-second outtake of *A Certain Sacrifice* features Madonna singing the song "Let the Sunshine In" from the musical *Hair*. A short audio clip of this performance has, for years, been circulating on CD in the collectors' bootleg market. Also, the film itself contains an ensemble chant, "Raymond Hall Must Die." "Sunshine" and "Raymond Hall" are considered by Madonna historians to be two of her earliest recorded vocal performances.

By the beginning of 1980, Madonna's instincts were telling her that her future was most definitely not in film, at least not yet, and not in dance, either. At this time, she realigned herself with her ex-boyfriend Dan Gilroy, who couldn't resist taking her back . . . into his life, and also into the Breakfast Club. However, before long, her growing ambition caused conflicts with both Gilroy brothers. While they viewed her as just a group member, she saw herself as the main attraction and thus wanted to sing more leads—especially after another female (Angie Smits) was added to the group as a bass player. Though she liked Angie, she couldn't help but think of her as competition; she didn't like sharing the stage with another woman. As weeks turned into months, Dan became frustrated by Madonna's constant habit of upstaging him and the other band members. "You're all naked ambition with no talent," he told her during one particularly bitter argument in front of the band.

"Oh yeah?" she countered. "Well, screw you, Dan. Screw you."

"That's when she quit the band. It was pretty tough being her boyfriend, to say the least," said Dan Gilroy in what seems like a great understatement, "mostly because you knew there was no way she was going to be faithful. She always had a lot of other guys lined up, and each one had a purpose in her life. When she was done with me that time, well, she was done with me for good."

Again, it seemed time for Madonna to move on. From Dan Gilroy she had been given a place to live, the security of being in a relationship with someone who truly loved her, knowledge of certain musical instruments as well as a sense of what it was like to sing in front of an audience accompanied by a backup band. She now had the idea to start her own band, develop her own sound, and promote her own persona . . . and without Dan Gilroy.

"I know he was pretty brokenhearted," says Norris Burroughs, the man responsible for introducing Dan to Madonna. "He wasn't the type of guy who invested in relationships heavily, but Madonna did a number on him. There was a sense of destiny about them, the way she went off to Paris and you thought it was over, then she was back and you realized that it wasn't over at all, that maybe it had just begun again. I don't know if she was using him, or not. Only she would know that. But at the time, it all seemed very star-crossed to me."*

Soon after moving out of the Gilroys' synagogue/studio/living quarters, Madonna partnered with her Michigan boyfriend, drummer Steve Bray. The two had met at the University of Michigan in 1976; at the time, Bray was a waiter at the Blue Frogge club on Church Street in Ann Arbor, which was frequented by many of the university's students. He was also a drummer for an R&B band and, says Madonna of the dashing African-American Bray, "the first guy I ever allowed to buy me a drink [a gin and tonic]. He was irresistibly handsome." After becoming romantically involved with her, Bray allowed Madonna to travel with him across Michigan as he and his band performed in small clubs. When the romance ended, they remained friends. Bray then moved to New York. (In years to come, Steve Bray would write, co-write and produce many of Madonna's greatest hits, including "Express Yourself," "True Blue," "Into the Groove," "Papa Don't Preach" and "Causing a Commotion.")

Now that Madonna had determined that she would have a musical career in New York, she wanted to be immersed in that business twenty-four hours a day. Feeling herself bursting at the seams with imagination and creativity, she would spend the next year writing songs and performing locally around New York with a small backup band, which included Steve Bray on drums. Because Bray also needed a place to live, the two agreed to move into a West Side Manhattan conglomerate of offices and rehearsal studios on Eighth Avenue called the Music Building, and simply sleep in the studios of any of the tenants there who would agree to such a thing—and some actually did. "The Music Building," Bray explains, "was near Port Authority Bus Terminal. There were a lot of singers and bands working in rehearsal halls and studios there, just trying to figure out their music. It was a good place, very artistic. You could just taste the creativity there. We loved

---

* It was at about this time that Madonna recorded bizarre backing vocals for Otto von Wernherr, including "Cosmic Club," "We Are the Gods" and "Wild Dancing." These songs would be released in 1986 on independent labels. That same year, to capitalize on Madonna's fame, Otto would record an answer video to "Papa Don't Preach," entitled "Madonna Don't Preach."

it, just being in the atmosphere was intoxicating. Our band was hot, and getting hotter all the time."

There were some problems, though, not the least of which was the solution to a disagreement involving the group's name. Bray recalls, "We had a lot of names. First, we came up with 'Emmy', meaning 'M' for Madonna. Emmy was also my nickname for Madonna. Then, we were 'the Millionaires.' Then, 'Modern Dance.' " (It should be noted that, in a separate interview, Steven Bray recalled that the name "Emmy" was actually short for "Emanon," "no name" spelled backwards.)

Despite the uncertainty of the group's name, Madonna's self-confidence and outlook for its future remained unshakable. However, for someone who was not a known performer, she had already developed the ego of a major—and, in some ways, difficult—star. Bray continues, "She wanted to call the band 'Madonna.' Well, I thought that was just too much."

"But it makes a lot of sense," Madonna told Steve Bray during lunch at Howard Johnson's in Times Square. "See, there's this group that was called Patti LaBelle and the Blue Belles. And when they reinvented themselves, they called themselves Labelle, after the leader of the group."

Bray digested this piece of information. "So, what are you saying?" he asked her. "That you're the leader of this band?"

"Why, no, not at all," Madonna answered, her tone sweet. "You're the brains, Steve. You're the musical genius. Me? Why, I'm just the star."

"Forget it, Emmy," he told her. "It sounds too Catholic, anyway. 'Madonna?' No, I don't think so."

Even today, Madonna has to admit that she was perplexed by the group's reluctance to be named for her. Why didn't her colleagues recognize the clear reality—at least her reality—that she was their meal ticket? While she may have felt she had their best interests at heart as well as her own, it didn't appear that way to the rest of the band, who thought she was just being selfish. In the end, the group did settle on the name "Emmy," with Dan and Ed Gilroy as front men, Madonna on lead vocals, former Breakfast Club member Gary Burke on bass, Brian Syms on lead guitar and Steve Bray on drums. Madonna recalls, "We played, we sang, we went all over New York just trying to make money, which never happened. It got to be less fun than I had hoped."

Frustrated, Madonna decided that the restrictions of being a member of a band had begun to erode her true identity as a performer, anyway. "It was too confining," she would later recall. "I had ideas. In a band, you can't have ideas. Without being able to express myself, I felt, well, why bother?"*

☩

Camille

In early 1981, a woman entered Madonna's life—again the result of happenstance, coincidence and sheer luck—who would go on to become her mentor and, in many ways, her savior. Her name was Camille Barbone, at the time a musical talent agent with the Gotham Agency and Studios (writing rather than recording studios) at the Music Building. Barbone—who describes herself as "a tough-talking New Yorker"—is an extremely attractive woman with short, wavy brunette hair, soulful brown eyes and a flawless complexion. Her personality is contagious and her memory for detail vivid, especially when it comes to Madonna.

"Madonna and I kept running into each other in the elevators and the hallways of the Music Building," Camille recalls. "She flirted with me constantly. For instance, she once opened a door for me when my hands were full, and when I thanked her, she said, 'Oh, don't worry. Someday you'll be opening doors for me.'

* Some material recorded during this time has surfaced on a bootleg release, *Emmy and the Emmys Live, First Time Out of Manhattan,* including live (and punk-rock-sounding) performances of "Bells Ringing," "Love for Tender," "Are You Ready for It," "Nobody's Fool" and "Love Express." Alternate versions of other Emmy songs have also appeared on various bootleg collections over the years. On November 30, 1980, Emmy recorded four songs at the Music Building in New York for a demo tape—"(I Like) Love For Tender," "Drowning," "Bells Ringing" and "No Time," all hard-edged rock and roll.

"She was about twenty-two. She was homeless at the time, living in one of the studios in the Music Building. She had just left the group Emmy, saying that she wanted to do other things. She had cut some music, and eventually, I got to hear a demo, which I thought was fair-sounding. I was supposed to see her show at a Manhattan dump called Max's Kansas City, but I got ill and couldn't go. The next day, she came raging into my office screaming at me."

"How dare you not show up?" Madonna hollered at Camille, a woman she barely knew. "This is my *life*. What happened to you? You promised you would be there."

"I had a terrible migraine headache," Camille offered by way of explanation. "I'm sorry. I just couldn't make it."

Madonna gave Camille a dramatic stare. Then, she asked, "What? You had a headache? What an excuse! What kind of talent manager are you?"

When Camille promised that she would be in the audience for Madonna's next performance, Madonna told her the date, time and location of that show. Camille began to write the information in her appointment book. Suddenly, Madonna grabbed the book from her and smacked Camille across the chest with it. "If it's important enough to you, you'll remember," Madonna said. "You won't have to write it down because it'll be important enough for you to remember."

"I should have been outraged," Camille says with a smile. "But, instead, I was intrigued.

"Then, after I saw the show, I knew in an instant what she was about: potential stardom. Her hair was red when I met her but, in a day or so, she had dyed it brown. Onstage, she was wearing men's pajamas, and had this completely original appearance. She had great body-mind coordination. She knew how she looked, and when she was onstage she gave the audience the feeling of being inside her and of knowing what she was feeling. It's a rare quality. She was beautiful, really. What a face."

Awed by Madonna's raw talent—she was performing a combination of dance and rock and roll music at this time—stunned by her colorful imagination and even a little startled by her brazen chutzpah, Camille Barbone's fascination resulted in the quick signing of a management contract between herself and Madonna. In another amazing coincidence, the twenty-nine-year-old Barbone—seven years Madonna's senior—shared birthdays with her new protégée. It certainly seemed like the stars, karma, the universe, God or simply Lady Luck were always on Madonna's side during these formative years, in perfect alignment with her personal goals and professional ambitions. Over the next twenty months, Barbone and her business partner, Adam Atler, would exhaust most of their company's funds in promoting and developing the burgeoning career of Madonna, whom Camille referred to as "a nobody who was about to be a somebody."

During the course of their relationship, Madonna and Camille would become players in a confounding game of wills and emotions. Years later, Camille Barbone would confess that she had probably fallen in love with Madonna. Though Barbone did not admit her feelings to Madonna at the time, surely the instinctive young performer was able to sense their intensity. She would not be able to resist this tantalizing turn of events. After all, by now every step of her career was a seduction—one person after another being seduced by her to do her bidding—and it had been that way for some time.

The truth was that—talent, luck and cunning aside—Madonna was just an extremely ambitious person in a city overcrowded with extremely ambitious people, all of whom were jockeying for the best position to get noticed. Was it wrong for her—she must have reasoned—to realize that she needed people in her corner, pulling for her, pushing her, making the right contacts for her?

In the particular circumstance in which she found herself with Camille Barbone, Madonna would play the role of little-girl-lost to Barbone's sensible and influential mother figure. The older Barbone was more than happy to accept her part in Madonna's real-life drama, first by paying for her to have four wisdom teeth extracted and then letting her recuperate in her Bayside, Queens, house. Soon, Camille was loaning—giving—her money, food and, perhaps most important, a sense of security.

"I thought that the first thing I needed to do was to make her feel safe," Camille now recalls. "So I needed to find a place for her to live. She had found a small place that she adored, a one-room apartment across the street from Madison Square Garden on West Thirtieth Street. The building was called—ironically enough—the Star Hotel. So I moved her in there, paid for it for a few months in advance—sixty-five dollars a month—even though I was frightened to have her live there, it was such a dump. She was there for about two weeks when she got robbed. They only took her photographs, but it was still very upsetting to both of us.

"So I moved her out of there and into a much bigger apartment on the Upper West Side, on Riverside Drive and Ninety-fifth. My business partner knew a middle-aged guy who lived there, and convinced him to let Madonna move in as a roommate. We also gave her a hundred bucks a week to live on."

Because Madonna said that she wanted to act, Camille sent her to an acting coach, a Russian émigré named Mira Rostova, who had taught such notable actors as Montgomery Clift and Roddy McDowell. It didn't go well. After one session, Mira refused ever again to work with Madonna. "I doubt that this girl will ever be taken seriously as an actress," she told Camille. "First of all, she's vulgar. Second, you can't tell her anything because she's already decided that she knows all there is to know, about everything. Third, she doesn't listen, and if she doesn't listen now, she never will. If I were you, I'd reconsider representing her."

*

It was spring 1981. "You are so goddamn selfish," Camille Barbone was telling Madonna.

As Camille recalled years later, she had been experiencing personal problems with a member of her family and wished to talk to Madonna, as a friend, about what was happening. However, Madonna—often preoccupied and seldom really paying attention when it came to listening to other people's problems—seemed disinterested in Camille's ordeal. It hadn't taken long for Camille to understand that, at this time in her life, Madonna was too self-absorbed to truly care about anything other than her career. "When you have a problem, I solve it," Camille said, frustrated. "But when I have one, you couldn't care less."

"Look. I pay you to solve my problems," Madonna shot back, as if Camille was actually making money from her career.

"But what do *you* give, Madonna?" Camille asked, she would recall years later. "You give nothing," she observed, answering her own question. "You're selfish."

"But I give my all," Madonna said.

"Bullshit. You give your all to *you,*" Camille said. "It's all for your career, isn't it? You don't care about me or my life."

It was then, as Camille remembered it, that Madonna went on the attack. "Look at me," she said, practically screaming, her face instantly red with rage. (She could raise the level of an argument to a full-scale fight in a nanosecond.) "I'm getting old," she continued, her eyes blazing. "And nothing is happening for me. I'm ready to do something with my fucking life, can't you see that? And you promised to help me, Camille. So help me, goddamn it," she concluded, angrily. "If you're my friend, *do something for me.* If you love me, *do something for me.*"

Camille reached out and stroked Madonna's face. With an index finger, she wiped away a tear. "Okay. I'll do what I can," she told her, trying to calm her down. "I do love you. Relax. Adam and I have meetings set up next week with record people. I have lots of ideas."

Taking a dramatic breath, Madonna put the finishing touch on the fight. "Why, oh why, must everything be such a big deal with you?" she asked, exasperated. "Now," she said, shaking off the drama with a shrug, "tell me, what kind of meetings?"

Years later, Camille would say, "When the line became blurred between management and friendship, that's when trouble became inevitable. Of course, I knew she was using me. But what could I expect, really, under the circumstances? I tried to set up some boundaries, some rules, but . . . well, forget it . . . Try giving Madonna rules."

One of Camille's "rules" was that if any member of the band she had organized to support Madonna musically onstage ever had sex with her, he (or she) would be automatically fired for such indiscretion. Barbone felt strongly that romantic relationships within the band would serve only to complicate matters for everyone involved. Also, no doubt, she just didn't want Madonna being intimate with anyone else. She couldn't help but be jealous, her feelings for her were that strong. However, the cunning Madonna decided to use Camille's regulation to her own advantage. Because she wanted her ex-boyfriend, Steve Bray, to replace the band's drummer, Bob Riley, she decided to seduce Riley. "If you were any more delicious, I'd have to spread you on a cracker right here and now," she told him with a smack of her red lips. Then, she tumbled into bed with him.

"Now you *have* to fire him, Camille," Madonna said at a meeting with Riley in Barbone's office the next morning. "I mean, that's your rule, isn't it? Whoever screws me gets fired, right? And we can bring Steve in now, can't we?"

"My God! I'm not firing Bob just because he screwed you, Madonna," Camille said, incredulous. "You set him up!"

"I did not set him up," Madonna said. "He came on to me. And I told him what would happen if we made it together. But, no, he wanted to do it anyway. Now, you have to fire him. Or *you're* the one who will look weak and indecisive."

Riley looked at Madonna as if he was looking at garbage. "No one has to fire me," he decided. "I quit."

Madonna blew a big, pink bubble with her gum. "Fine with me," she said. "Suit yourself."

"I wondered what kind of person would do something like that," Camille recalls years later, still seeming astonished at just the memory of it all. "I had created a monster who, I knew, would eventually turn on me. I just couldn't believe she would be so crafty, so mean. Sex, to her, was really just a means to an end, it meant nothing more. I actually became a little afraid of her when she did that to Bob."

"I love you," Barbone remembers Madonna telling her one day. The two had just had a meeting with a record industry executive that went well. It seemed that a record deal for Madonna was imminent.

"In what way?" Camille asked, suspiciously.

"Well, in every way, of course," Madonna said. They embraced. "How can I thank you for what you've done for me?" Madonna asked. "I think you're the most wonderful woman in the world."

There was a beat. Just as it seemed they might kiss, Madonna abruptly pulled away. "Oh my God," she exclaimed with girlish enthusiasm. "I just had the most brilliant, fucking *idea*. Let's you and I call that record guy back and tell him . . ." She had deftly moved the conversation back to business. The mood now altered, the two then began brainstorming about Madonna's "great idea."

"She seduced me, psychologically," Camille Barbone says today. "I put her first. And, really, that would be my downfall because it was all about her, not about us and certainly not about me.

"There were lots of mixed messages, strange moments . . . and also great ideas as to how to promote her career. There was such imagination and fire between us, such great creativity. We never got together without a notepad because there were so many ideas flying back and forth. I had to keep notes just to keep track of all of the stuff we discussed twenty-four hours a day. She was brilliant, really. Constantly, we had this mad banter about what to do, how to do it, and where we would end up.

"I often felt like Chicken Little running around saying 'The sky is falling, the sky is falling' because there were people telling me 'I don't get it. I don't understand. What's with that girl? What do you see in her?' I would say to them, 'I promise you, one day you will understand. She has a vision. She's got something no one else has.' I so believed she would one day be a star. I knew that she was destined to be a great entertainer, a pop star, and I invested everything in her . . . my mind, my heart, my soul, everything."

"You know what? I promise that we'll always be together," Madonna told Camille one day over breakfast. Just the night before, she and a female dancer named Janice had had sex with a recording engineer from Queens, much to Camille's chagrin. Madonna looked exhausted, a rag tied into her ratty, short, brunette hair, her eyes sleepy.

"Sure, you say that now," Camille told her, annoyed. "But wait until you get famous. You won't even remember my name."

Madonna sighed, shaking her head. "It's a lousy business, I know," she said. Her voice was weary with experience, as if she was a seasoned performer.

Years later, Camille would recall, "I had a feeling then that we both knew my time was coming, that I would be gone soon. We just knew how she was . . . and maybe we just hoped she would change. Meetings, demos, rehearsals, whatever it was . . . she would do it. Except true friendship. That, she had a hard time doing."

✟

"Drama Queen"

In August 1981, Madonna recorded a demo tape of four songs, under Camille Barbone's tutelage, at Media Sound (also known as Master

Sound), a converted church on West Fifty-seventh Street in Manhattan in which Barbone had leased studio time. In performances that sound reminiscent of rock singer Pat Benatar's style, Madonna performed "Love on the Run," "High Society (Society's Boy)," "Take Me (I Want You)" and "Get Up." The recordings—known by Madonna fans as "the Gotham Tapes"—were produced by guitarist Jon Gordon, who would go on to produce Suzanne Vega. According to Madonna's contract with Camille (signed on July 22, 1981), Madonna was to receive $250 for each unreleased master, and twice that amount for every one that was released, as well as a 3 percent royalty on the sale of every record.

Notes Madonna historian Bruce Baron, "To this day, the original mixes of these Gotham songs have not yet seen the light of day, though slightly different mixes have leaked out to various collectors in the past few years. Those versions are different, however, and the sound quality on them is poor. It is highly unlikely that the original, perfect-sounding mixes of these four tracks will ever surface. For collectors, these four recordings are probably the rarest, and most sought-after Madonna tracks of all time."

(After Madonna became famous, Camille Barbone offered her the opportunity to purchase the original studio master recordings, but no deal was struck. Ownership of these songs would eventually become the subject of bitter lawsuits between Madonna and Barbone, in litigation that would drag on for many years. In March 1993, Camille Barbone played bits of three of the songs during Robin Leach's television special about Madonna, "Madonna Exposed," on which the author also appeared as a guest.)

It took some doing, but Camille Barbone eventually convinced her friend Bill Lomuscio, a band manager and promoter, to give Madonna a break and book her into some local clubs for necessary exposure. Barbone hoped to interest other record company executives in the singer in the hope perhaps of starting a bidding war for Madonna's services. Without having had the benefit of seeing Madonna perform, Lomuscio says he at first wasn't interested in her. "Camille let me listen to Madonna's tape [of "High Society (Society's Boy)"]. It was not anything at all impressive to me," Lomuscio remembers. "But she wanted a place to try out her live act. I agreed to let her be the opening act for a band I was managing."

Whenever Madonna got up onto a stage, the result was predictable: all of her pent-up yearning to do and be something wonderful—her energy, drive and talent, not to mention her need to be the center of attention—burst forth in a rush of sheer spectacle. "It wasn't so much about the music as it was the personality behind it," Camille Barbone recalls. "I found that the best way to have a meeting with a record label or a booker was to bring Madonna with me. Once you met her, you either loved her or hated her, but you knew she was fascinating. She was really her own best advertisement."

"The band I managed was the house band at this particular club, and they were pretty popular," Lomuscio recalls. "But out came Madonna, and the band and three break dancers that Camille had picked up in Times Square, and that was the end of anyone's interest in my band. With her act, Madonna proceeded to blow my band off the stage. She really was phenomenal. A great talent. You could see it immediately. And after three songs, she was being called back for encores. My band was having a hard time even getting on the stage." When the deeply impressed Lomuscio asked Barbone if she'd like a partner in the handling of Madonna, the two began working together as a team.

While her new managers were excited about Madonna's successes onstage in front of live audiences, attempts to impress record executives with her demo tape did not go as well. As with Lomuscio, most people failed to be sold on Madonna's voice alone. She was a visual performer. The whole package was important, certainly not just the voice, which was, at best, no more than average. "There was a lot of talk that the tape was no good," Lomuscio says, "and she'd never go anywhere—one person said she sounded like Minnie Mouse on helium on a song she had recorded called 'Get Up'—but that was just not true. All you had to do was come down and see her perform live . . . and that was it."

Over the next year, as Madonna continued to grow in her New York stage act, she began attracting a cult following, not only of her music but of her funky image (complete with the secondhand street clothes she now enjoyed wearing on stage). Before she even had a record played on the radio, groupies who dressed just like her had begun following her from gig to gig. She didn't have much of a career . . . but she actually had fans!

"These people love me," she told Camille of her "fan club." Then she giggled. "You know what?" she asked. "I think I will always be nice to my fans. I think they deserve that."

Camille smiled. "Well, that's a nice thought," she said. "We'll see how you feel in about ten years."

Later, in another conversation, according to Camille, Madonna said, "Some awful person told me today that I was crass, vile, rude and disgusting. What do you think about that?"

"Well, I think that's absolutely true," Camille said, frankly.

"I know," Madonna agreed, enthusiastically. "It is, isn't it? Don't you just love the fact that people know that about me! I mean, that is so *cool*, isn't it?"

"It is," Camille said. "It certainly is."

"Here, I want you to have this," Madonna said, reaching into her pocket. She pulled out a turquoise rosary. "It was my grandmother's," she explained, tears welling in her eyes. She extended her palm to Camille, the rosary in it. The two women sat down over a cup of coffee, and Madonna then told Camille touching stories about her mother.

After about half an hour, Camille was overwhelmed with emotion. "I can't take that," she said, closing Madonna's hand around the rosary. "I could never take that from you. It's too precious."

"But I want you to have it," Madonna insisted. "I don't want you to think I'm just an ungrateful little bitch. I don't have anything else to give you."

Camille embraced her. "Keep your grandmother's rosary," she told Madonna as she ran her fingers lovingly through her hair. "You've just given me the best present in the world, and you don't even know it." *
Playing out a sexless seduction, Madonna continued to take Camille into her world, teasing her—maybe unintentionally, maybe not—with sentimental stories about her and her family.

It was inevitable that word of Madonna's popularity would continue to spread; soon, those same record company talent scouts who had ridiculed her voice were lining up outside her dressing-room door

---

* Years later, during a costume change for a photo session, the crucifix slipped off Madonna's neck and down her jeans while she was zipping up. "You see that?" she said with a squeal. "Even God wants to get into my pants!"

and waving business cards in her face as she left the club. Geffen and Atlantic Records both passed on Madonna's demo, but it seemed as if Camille had interested an executive at Columbia Records in the songs. However, storm clouds were brewing—though Camille didn't know it yet.

"Unbeknownst to me, Madonna had also started working with another set of people in the record business," Camille Barbone recalled. "She had others doing for her what I was doing for her. My company was just four years old, and we weren't moving as fast as she wanted to move. Plus, we were arguing about the direction of her music. She wanted to do more of a black sound, I think. We were doing Pat Benatar–sounding material on her, but we could have changed, and we would have suited her . . . if she had just given me some time to make back some money so that I could reinvest it in new material."

Suddenly, Camille Barbone's world began to crumble. Just when it seemed certain that Madonna would sign the Columbia deal, she decided that she wanted to end it with Camille. Madonna said that she wanted to terminate the Gotham Agency as her representatives, explaining that she wasn't happy with the music she had recorded while under contract to Gotham. She no longer respected Camille as a manager, she told her, "because it's taking too long for you to do anything for me."

"But I won't let you out of your contract," Camille Barbone told her while engaged in a tense meeting with Madonna in the recording studio. "I invested everything in you," she said angrily, according to later recollections. "I was doing just fine in my life until you came along. Now, look at me. I'm flat broke. I spent it all on you, Madonna!"

"Oh, fuck you, Camille," Madonna said, her tone icy and detached. "That was *your* choice, now wasn't it?"

"Why, you *bitch,* " Camille said, practically sputtering. As she now remembers it, she was so angry she could barely speak. Instead, she plunged her fist into a wall, fracturing her hand. Though Camille was clearly in terrible pain, Madonna walked away from her, shaking her head. "What a drama queen," she muttered as she walked out of the studio.

✝

"You know what you have?" Madonna asked Camille Barbone on one of the last occasions they saw each other. Madonna tapped her mentor on the chest. "You have heart," she said, "and you really don't need me."

It was a confusing moment, one that Camille recalls vividly to this day. Her eyes red from crying, she put her palm on Madonna's chest and said, "If *you* had heart, I don't know that you'd do this to me."

Tears began to splash onto Madonna's cheeks. "I have to go," she explained. "I love you, Camille. You're such a bitch, like me. We worked well together. But now it's over. So . . . good-bye."

Madonna then walked away, never to look back.

"Sometimes I feel guilty because I feel like I travel through people," Madonna has said. "That's true of a lot of ambitious people. You take what you can and then move on. If someone can't go with me—whether it's a physical or emotional move—I feel sad about that. But that's part of the tragedy of love."

"She seduces people," her longtime friend Erica Bell observes. "She'll tell you what you want to hear, she flatters you, kisses your ass, makes you feel a part of her life. She's a smart girl. She knows how to get her way," says Bell. There is no acrimony in Bell's seemingly harsh assessment of Madonna. "Then, after she has you set up the right way, she sucks it all out of you."

"Oh, she's a sponge, all right," Camille Barbone concurs. "She soaks up what she can and drains you in every way and then goes on to her next victim.

"I risked my entire career on Madonna and she nearly destroyed me. I begged, borrowed and stole to do what I could do for her. But rules of loyalty and decency that apply to the rest of us didn't apply to her," she continues. "She wasn't intentionally malicious, but just incapable of seeing life from anyone else's point of view. She wanted what she wanted, and if you didn't give it she turned her back on you.

"I lost everything in the process because I had focused only on her and spent every dime on her. I ended up losing my studio."

Camille Barbone says she feels no malice toward the woman whose eventual success she had helped create—even though she would not be around to share in any of the rewards. "I don't hate her," Barbone sighed years later. "On the contrary, I miss her. And I understand her. It all has to do with her mother, it all goes back to her death. It has to do with Madonna feeling so beat up by what she felt when her mother died, she never wants to connect to her emotions. So, she leaves people before they can leave her, the way her mother did. I knew that when I was going through it with her. And I know it even better now, having had years to think about it. Her mother," Camille concluded, firmly, "that's what it's always been about." *

Madonna would say that she left Camille Barbone because "she had gotten too attached to me." Also, she said, it was worth it for her not to take advantage of the Columbia recording contract offering because, as she put it, "the songs they wanted me to sing were crap, and I wasn't going to build a career on them. No way."

In another interview she further explained, "I've always been into rhythmic music, party music, but Gotham wasn't used to that stuff, and although I'd agreed to do rock and roll, my heart was no longer in it. Soul was my main influence and I wanted my sound to be the kind of music I'd always liked. I wanted to approach it from a very simple point of view because I wasn't an incredible musician. I wanted it to be direct. I still loved to dance and all I wanted to do was to make a record that I would want to dance to, and would want to listen to on the radio."

So, while she waited for what Camille may have called "her next victim" to come along, Madonna and Steve Bray moved back into the Music Building where they slept on cots, sat on crates and sustained themselves on popcorn. (Their relationship at this point was platonic, not romantic.) Meanwhile, Madonna again survived by taking odd jobs around the New York City area. This time, though, her "odd jobs" were music industry related. For instance, she sang back-up vocals for a number of recording artists, including heavy metal superstar Ozzy Osbourne. She could also be seen dancing wildly as an extra in a music video for the group Konk.

* At the time of writing, Camille Barbone was still in the entertainment business, involved in recording and management.

Says actress Debi Mazar *(GoodFellas)*, one of Madonna's best friends who has known her since those early days (and who appears in the video for Madonna's 2000 hit, "Music"), "Neither one of us had any money. We were just young girls trying to do interesting things in New York City. People weren't dying yet of AIDS, and here was a small community of artists and musicians—[Jean-Michel] Basquiat, Keith Haring—and everybody was together: black, white, Spanish, Chinese. It was the beginning of rap, and white people and black people were all together making music . . . [Afrika] Bambaataa was sampling Kraftwerk. Madonna and I used to run around and go to the Roxy, go dancing and to art shows." She adds, "At the time, we both had a taste for, you know, Latin boys."

Without a manager to advance her ambitions, Madonna had no choice but to promote herself. After she and the multitalented Steve Bray recorded four new songs—"Everybody," "Stay," "Burning Up," ("She has a Joan Jett kind of thing going on with this one," Bray recalls) and "Ain't No Big Deal" ("We didn't have access to the vocoder that we wanted for the vocal effect, so Emmy just pinched her nose and pretended," says Bray)—she began taking the tape to the hottest nightclubs in the city, her goal being to get disc jockeys to play them so that one of her songs would catch on and become a club hit. In the early 1980s, DJs wielded tremendous power on the dance circuit. The songs they chose to play nightly could make an artist. Once a song caught on in the New York dance club scene, its success could easily encourage a major label into signing the artist.

In 1981, one of the hottest clubs in Manhattan was called Danceteria, where Madonna was a regular patron. Madonna had her sights set on the trendsetting DJ at Danceteria, the darkly handsome Mark Kamins. With her eye-catching dancing and sexual aura, she had already become a star in the local club scene. Kamins, who had watched her dance from the DJ booth, was intrigued. He wanted to know her. Apparently, she felt the same way.

One evening, while Mark was playing music from his booth, Madonna strolled over to him, handed him her demo and asked him to play it that evening.

"This is a great song," she told him. "It's called 'Everybody.' People will love it."

Kamins shook his head negatively. "What if it's not good?" he said, warily.

She got closer to him. "Would I just give it to you like this if it wasn't good stuff?" she said. "Oooh, baby, you are so *fine,*" she added as she stroked his face.

He would remember feeling an urgency as she approached him. Then, as she kissed the disc jockey full on the lips, he was hers.

While he now says he was "impressed by her moxie," Kamins still decided that he wanted first to listen to the demo before playing it for an audience. He took the tape home that night, and when he heard it he was impressed.

"The following night I threw 'Everybody' on and got an amazing response," Kamins remembers. "I mean, it was a great song. It was the kind of thing that caught your attention. That voice was so unique, and so perfect for that kind of fun record."

While Mark Kamins was a DJ by profession, he had hopes of one day becoming a record producer. Although he had already dabbled in music production, he saw in Madonna a chance to further his career, and perhaps further hers as well. He proposed a partnership: he would do the legwork to secure a record contract for her and, then, when the deal was set, she would allow him to produce her first album. Madonna, who craved a record deal and was actually surprised that she hadn't gotten one by this time, immediately agreed to the partnership. On the edge of tears, her voice faltered: "Maybe this might work," she said. "Or, at least I hope so." As confident as she was about her future, clearly there was vulnerability beneath all of the bravado.

It seemed only natural—predictable as her life was, in this regard anyway—that the partnership between Madonna and Mark would become intimate: the two became lovers. "She was always sexually aggressive, and it wasn't just her image," Kamins said. "She used her sexuality as a performer, but it's also how she got over offstage. We started hot, and it just got hotter. She was hard to resist."

With his new lover in tow, Mark Kamins brought her demo tape to Michael Rosenblatt, a young, aggressive executive at Warner Bros. Records who was eager to sign new talent. As Kamins and Madonna sat and studied his reaction, Rosenblatt listened to the four songs on the tape. He then rewound it, and listened again. "The tape was good," he now remembers but, echoing others who had shared his view, he adds, "but not outstanding. However, here was this girl sitting in my office, radiating a certain *something*. Whatever it was, she had more of it than I'd ever seen. I knew that there was a star sitting there."

Much to Madonna's exhilaration, Michael Rosenblatt decided to offer her a record deal: $5,000 as an advance, plus royalties and publishing fees of $1,000 for each song she would write. It had all happened so fast. All of the years gone by, years of struggling and hoping and plotting and scheming and wondering and worrying . . . and, suddenly, Madonna Ciccone had a record deal. However, there was one signature needed on the contract before it could be finalized and that was Seymour Stein's, President of Warner's Sire Records, the division to which Madonna would be signed.*

Unfortunately, Stein was in the hospital, recovering from heart surgery.

Undaunted—and certainly not willing to sit and wait for someone to recover from a major operation, not after all she had been through up to this point—Madonna pressed Rosenblatt to get the demo to Stein in the hospital. Reluctantly he agreed, probably knowing that there would be no point in challenging his new young artist on this matter. When Rosenblatt told Madonna that he would make sure Stein heard the demo immediately, Madonna took his face in both her hands and kissed it—which must have seemed a little inappropriate but was certainly endearing, just the same.

"I was in the hospital when [Rosenblatt] called me and said, 'Seymour, I think you should listen to a one-song demo ["Everybody"] by this girl. Her name is Madonna. I listened to it, and I flipped out,' recalls Seymour Stein, who was in his early forties at the time. "I said, 'I want her to meet with me at the hospital.' I had my barber come in and cut my hair and shave me—I didn't want her to think she was signing a contract with someone who would be dead in six months. Let me tell you, she was so anxious to do a deal that she couldn't have cared if I was

* Sire Records was formed in 1966 by Seymour Stein and Richard Gottherer. After a decade, the label became a part of Warner Music Group—and Stein helped shape popular music in the 1980s and 1990s, not only with Madonna but also with the Ramones, Talking Heads, the Pretenders, Depeche Mode, k.d. lang, Erasure, the Cult, the Replacements, Ice-T and Barenaked Ladies. Today, Stein is still president and CEO of Sire Records and also president of the Rock and Roll Hall of Fame.

lying in a coffin. She was twenty-three, and I believe she was very poor, but she put herself together great. It was only one song, 'Everybody', but there was just a drive, a determination—she was going places."

Seymour, like so many others, was taken aback by Madonna's aggressive nature, as well as her apparent star quality. "The thing to do now," Madonna said, seeming oblivious to the fact that she was talking to a man who was sitting in his underwear, a drip feed in his arm, "is to sign me to a record deal. Take me," she said, arms extended, "I'm yours." She was being facetious, but the sentiment was genuine.

"Oh, I don't think so," Stein remembers saying.

Madonna took a step back, looking confused. After a beat, perhaps to reconsider her strategy, she appeared to marshal her thoughts before jumping back into the game—but now with less aggression. "Okay, look," she said. "Just tell me what I have to do to get a fucking record deal in this fucking town. That's all I want to know."

"Well, you had one before you even walked in the door," Stein said, good-naturedly.

"Then why screw with me?" Madonna asked.

"Why not?" asked Stein. It would seem that Madonna had finally met her match in Seymour Stein. Probably relieved, she stepped toward his bed, extended her hand and said, "Nice doing business with you, *Mr.* Stein." To her delight, he took her hand and touched it with his lips. Their eyes met. There was something conspiratorial in the moment, a suggestion of intimacy, as if they both knew something about Madonna's future that nobody else knew.

"If the shortest way home was through a cemetery, she would take it, even at midnight on Friday the thirteenth," observes Seymour Stein. "She had an almost ruthless edge to her. I mean that in all the best ways. You could just tell this woman would go far."

"This is it," Madonna later told her friend Erica Bell. The two had become the closest of friends at this time, after Erica hired her to work as a bartender at her New York nightclub, the Lucky Strike, on Ninth Street off Third Avenue. (The job lasted two days.) "With this record deal, I think I'm finally on my way," Madonna said. "I can't believe that it's happened just as I thought it would. This is how I charted my life, for this to happen in it."

"Tell me. What do you want most in life now?" Erica asked. It was a lazy Sunday morning and she and Madonna were lying on the couch together after a boozy night on the town. Years later, Erica would remember the conversation as if it had just occurred.

"I want to be famous," Madonna said, quickly. "I want attention."

"But you get so much attention now," Erica said, snuggling closer.

"It's not enough. I want all of the attention in the world," Madonna said, dreamily. "I want everybody in the world to not only know me, but to love me, love me, *love me.*"

"Well, I love you," Erica said.

"That's nice," Madonna said while gently stroking Erica's hair. "But it's not enough."

✝

Roller Coaster Ride

After Madonna was assigned to Warner Bros. Records' dance division at Sire, her first contract was not for an album but rather for two twelve-inch dance singles. It was decided that the first release would be "Ain't No Big Deal," backed with "Everybody." However, when the time came to determine who would produce the songs, Madonna wanted her good friend Steve Bray to do the honors. Mark Kamins, though, felt strongly that, since he had brought Madonna to the label, he should be allowed to produce the single. Both men had been her lovers, so Madonna had a dilemma. "The arrangement we had was that, if I got her a deal, I got to produce the album," Kamins now says, "and, damn it, I wanted her to honor the deal. I knew that if I let her, she would walk all over me."

An argument ensued, but by the end of it Mark Kamins had the distinction of doing something most people at that time never managed to do when in hot debate with Madonna: he won. Feeling that he had become the latest casualty in Madonna's quest for fame, Steve Bray was so angry with her that he would not speak to her for almost two years. "It's a shame when stuff like that happens between friends," he now says. "But even though I knew her and understood the way she operated, I just never thought I would be next on the list. But I was."

"Well, it's not like I had a choice in the matter," Madonna has said in her defense. "Everyone wanted to work with me by that time. I remember when nobody wanted to work with me, and when it changed everybody got pissed off at one thing or another."

At this same time, Steve Bray—who got the sole writing credit for "Ain't No Big Deal"—sold his publishing rights to July Fourth Music. Then, a disco act called Barracuda recorded and released their own version of the song on Epic Records before Warner Bros. Records had selected which Madonna version to release. Consequently, the song was then dropped from consideration. (Years later, a Reggie Lucas production of "Ain't No Big Deal" would be released on the B side of the "True Blue" single. The other original versions, however, remain unreleased.)

Instead, Warner Bros. issued "Everybody" (with different mixes on both sides of the record—and a surprising hint of a British accent on the verse vocal) in October 1982, produced by Mark Kamins (Strangely, the original version of "Everybody" has never appeared on any of Madonna's own albums; a rare remix by Rusty Egan was used on the vinyl twelve-inch for the UK release only.) When it charted on *Billboard*'s dance chart on November 6, "Everybody" marked the beginning of her "new life," or, as she put it most succinctly to Mark Kamins, "The old me was broke. The old me had no place to live. The old me was someone my father wasn't proud of. The old me was Madonna Louise Ciccone. The new me is *Madonna.*"

Aware that they were sitting on potential dynamite, Sire Records sent Madonna on the road to polish her act. At this same time, Madonna also began expanding her knowledge of the music business. Instinctively, she realized that no manager, producer, agent or record company would ever have her best interests in mind, not the way she did. No one worked harder for Madonna than Madonna. So, her first order of business would be to strike up friendships with people at the record company who were in positions to assist her. She soon discovered that one of Sire's key dance music promotion men was Bobby Shaw, whose job it was to take the company's dance records to important clubs and promote them there. Madonna understood the importance of Shaw's position because she, of course, had done it herself with "Everybody" when it was still in its earliest, unreleased form.

On Fridays, Shaw customarily held meetings in his office where he played and discussed current music with the local disc jockeys. Madonna convinced Shaw to allow her to sit in on these meetings, which was practically unheard of in the business. "Leave it to Madonna to break tradition where this kind of thing was concerned," says Shaw. "I couldn't say no to her, now could I? Well, I could have," he added, answering his own question, "but eventually she would have convinced me otherwise." Along with the industry experts in the room, Madonna was able to listen to the latest records, learn who produced the hits, what was selling and in which direction the trends in music were headed.

It was at this time that Madonna met John "Jellybean" Benitez, a disc jockey at the Funhouse in Manhattan. Benitez and Madonna became fast friends, and then lovers. On his arm, she attended record industry functions and, as he recalls, "for about a year and a half, I loved her very much. She was everything to me—my woman, my favorite artist, the bitchiest, funniest smart-ass I had ever known.

"Yes, she used me to 'network' into the business," he says, objectively. "But I did the same for her. I think one of the biggest misconceptions is that the people Madonna used along the way didn't also get something out of the deal for themselves. But just by being associated with her, if you played your cards right, you could advance your career. Her position was that if you could get something out of exploiting her—the way she would you—then go for it."

With more than ample proof that the record company had a moneymaker on their hands, Warner Bros. was finally ready fully to exploit Madonna's talents; she was given the go-ahead for her first album. While Mark Kamins thought he was going to produce the album, as earlier agreed, he was to be disappointed. "Madonna decided to go with Reggie Lucas at Warner, which was a bummer," he recalls. "I was so pissed off. After all, we had a deal. But that's the way it goes. She went a different way, and that was the end of that."

With her first album now the task at hand, Madonna could no longer represent herself. There was too much work to do, and she was so busy dealing with her recordings and concert act there was little time to focus on the business end of "show business." It was time for her to find a manager. Experienced at handling her own career, she decided that she would only pass the baton on to someone she considered to be the best in the business. After some research, she set her sights on forty-one-year-old Freddy DeMann of Weisner-DeMann Entertainment, an aggressive and well-respected entertainment manager who, at the time, had the distinction of having represented perhaps the biggest music star in the world: Michael Jackson. Seymour Stein arranged an audition for DeMann. Afterward, DeMann had to admit that he wasn't knocked out by Madonna's act. He asked one of his assistants, "Who is this girl? And who in hell does she think she is?" Ultimately, it was on Stein's recommendation that DeMann finally agreed to manage Madonna. Again, her timing was impeccable: just before she signed the contract with DeMann, the manager had had a falling out with Michael Jackson and was no longer working for him.

When he heard that DeMann and Jackson had parted ways, Seymour Stein thought Madonna would be disappointed that she would not be sharing a manager with the world's top hit maker. "I was afraid she would be upset about it, but she wasn't," he recalls. "Quite the contrary. She said, 'Good. Now he's free to devote all of his time to me.' Of course, he had other artists at the time, but . . . that's Madonna."

✝

Madonna: The Debut Album

Madonna's debut album, released in July, could have belonged to any number of dance acts that came and went through pop music's revolving door of 1983. Certainly, the eight-song collection didn't offer even a glimpse of the massive superstardom to which it would be the introduction, but it certainly did give a strong indication as to what the pioneers in the Madonna movement, such as Camille Barbone and Steve Bray, saw in her.

Producer Reggie Lucas had made a name for himself in the R&B music business with songwriting partner James Mtume, producing a series of hit records on such acts as Roberta Flack and Donny Hathaway ("The Closer I Get to You"), Phyllis Hyman ("You Know How to Love Me") and, most notably, Stephanie Mills ("Whatcha' Gonna

75

Do with My Lovin," "Put Your Body in It" and "Never Knew Love Like This Before").

Under the band name Mtume, Mtume and Lucas wrote and produced one 1980 album *(In Search of the Rainbow Seekers)* for the Epic label before going their separate ways. While Mtume the band was creating their 1983 R&B hit, "Juicy Fruit," Mtume's ex-partner was producing an unknown white girl who didn't possess the voice of Stephanie Mills or any of the other artists he'd worked with in the past: Madonna. When Madonna and Reggie Lucas began working on songs for her first album, the process became frustrating. "She had her way of wanting to do things," says Lucas. "And I understood that. So we had to have a meeting of the minds, from time to time."

Madonna had written a song called "Lucky Star" (plus two others), which, along with Reggie's composition of "Borderline," seemed the perfect foundation for the album. However, after recording the three songs, Madonna was unhappy with Lucas's production. "It's just too much," she complained at the time. "Too many instruments, too much stuff going on."

"You have to let me do what I do," Reggie told her, according to what he would later remember saying.

She made a long face. "But I have *ideas*. I have *concepts,* "Madonna argued. "I've been doing this for a long time, too."

"I know that," he said. "But, Madonna, when you bring in a producer, you have to let him do his job."

"Well, just don't get in my way," Madonna told him, her tone threatening.

The next day she apologized.

After he finished the album, Lucas didn't seem interested in redoing it to Madonna's specifications. Instead, he went on to another project as quickly as possible, leaving Madonna to figure what to do next with her record. She decided to bring in her boyfriend, the talented Jellybean Benitez, to remix many of the cuts, including the fluffy, danceable (but forgettable) "Lucky Star." Also on the album would be a song Jellybean would add to the album at the last moment, "Holiday" (which was written by Curtis Hudson and Lisa Stevens from the group Pure Energy), and produced by Benitez.

"She was unhappy with the whole damn thing, so I went in and sweetened up a lot of the music for her, adding some guitars to 'Lucky Star,' some voices, some magic," says Jellybean. "The thing about Madonna is that she has good instincts. You have to listen to her vision. I'm not sure Reggie did. We put together a great album, and I didn't even get co-producing credit for it. But I didn't care. I just wanted to do the best job I could do for her. When we would play back 'Holiday' or 'Lucky Star,' you could see that she was overwhelmed by how great it all sounded. You wanted to help her, you know? As much as she could be a bitch, when you were in the groove with her, it was very cool, very creative."

At first glance, Madonna's album looked like a rebound project for Reggie Lucas, the kind of job a record producer of some note accepts for the money, and just to stay busy. It especially seemed that way when word got out that he didn't want to finish the album Madonna's way. Upon closer inspection, though, it was clear that the album was armed with hit records. Even if the songs had never become popular, no one could have denied that they were terrific, well-crafted pop songs that deserved to find an audience. However, one would never have known as much judging by the chart performance of the album's first single, "Everybody." The rhythmic call-to-party did reach Number 1 on *Billboard*'s dance chart—a chart driven more by a song's popularity in dance clubs than by commercial sales—but languished at Number 103 on the trade magazine's pop chart, the one, as they say in the industry, "that really counts."

The double-sided twelve-inch single that followed—the yearning "Burning Up" backed by the droning but urgent "Physical Attraction"—didn't make *Billboard*'s pop chart at all, but earned another Number 1 position on the dance chart, seemingly defining this young new singer as just another disposable post-disco dance act.

Then, along came "Holiday."

Written once again by young journeymen Chris Hudson and Lisa Stevens, the festive, infectious anthem caught fire almost immediately, first soaring in dance clubs across the country—where audiences were already hip to Madonna—and then working its way onto R&B and pop charts. Ultimately, the song made it to Number 16 on that coveted *Billboard* pop singles chart—a triumph for a new act.

Just when the marketplace had gone on watch for this new "dance act," Sire mixed things up and released "Borderline." Written by Reggie Lucas, the song was a sentimental track with a particularly strong melodic lyric about a love that's never quite fulfilled.

Maybe it was Madonna's fluid, loving way with lyrics that had more to say than "shake your booty," or the fact that listeners had become familiar with her tangy voice; regardless, on "Borderline," her vocals sounded refined, capable, expressive. The combination—a not-so-great but affecting voice at the center of Lucas's full, twinkling instrumentation—made the track as close to an old Motown production as a hit could get in the dance-music-driven eighties.

Arguably, "Borderline," along with "Holiday," were two of the most important records in Madonna's formative years, and not simply because they reached Number 16 and Number 10 respectively on the pop charts. Rather, the singles were pivotal because, musically, they supplied Madonna with two distinctively different platforms within the dance music structure. Most important, they delivered the one-two punch that allowed "Lucky Star," so ingenious in its simplicity and danceability and the fourth single from the album *Madonna,* to glide into the Number 4 position.

Later Madonna, who co-wrote five of the album's eight songs, would refer to this first effort as an "aerobics album," but the songs were in perfect alignment with the times. In spite of a slow start, the album eventually climbed the charts and, after a year in release, finally found its way into the Top 10. It went on to sell four million copies in the USA, eight million worldwide.

Shortly after the album broke the Top 10, Madonna and Erica Bell toasted her new success with a bottle of champagne. Years later, Erica remembered the conversation as if it had happened just days earlier.

Seeming contemplative, Madonna said, "I feel badly about some of the people who aren't with me, the ones I met along the way."

"You mean, like Camille?" Erica asked.

"Yeah, like her and the others."

"Well, this is a tough business," Erica observed. "It's the people hangin' around the moment you become successful who get to celebrate with you . . . not the ones you met along the way."

Madonna agreed. "I guess so," she said, clinking her glass of champagne against Erica's. "Anyway, sentimentality is a weakness, don't you think?"

Erica didn't respond.

"People hate me," Madonna observed.

"I know they do," Erica said.

"Oh well," Madonna shrugged. "I did what I had to do. At least I still have you."

"That you do," Erica concluded as she hugged her friend.

Perhaps the most perfect timing of Madonna's career was in the seemingly magical way her recording career coincided with the growing popularity of the music video art form. Teenagers at this time seemed to be longing for idols. In the seventies, the disco era had spawned many hit records but very few memorable artists. Several music performers in the early eighties, however, would gain popularity for the unique images they showed the television-watching public in videos of their songs: Cyndi Lauper with shocking, orange hair, crazy makeup and thrift-store clothes; Boy George with heavy-lidded mascara eyes and woman's wardrobe; Prince with his androgynous sex appeal and *Purple Rain* ruffles. All three, and so many others, including Michael Jackson—who really helped to pioneer the medium, and even expand it with his long-form "Thriller" video—benefited from the three-minute star vehicles in which videos allowed them to shine.

No one took better advantage of the medium, though, nor to greater effect, than Madonna. Borrowing liberally from the downtown street scene, from nighttime clubbing and from icons such as Marilyn Monroe, she added a dash of her own brand of simple sexiness for an early image that was simply unforgettable. Even with her bubble gum–sounding first album, her look fueled ample controversy as she co-mingled sexuality and religion, belly button–exposing T-shirts and rosary beads. Many observers felt her use of crucifixes to be sacrilegious, but the religious symbol became a crucial part of the Madonna fashion craze. "I don't think that wearing the crucifix was an attempt to seek out controversy," says Mary Lambert, herself a controversial director who would direct several of Madonna's music videos. "I think that it had meaning for her—religious significance, mystic significance. Madonna is a very religious person in her own way."

At the time, Susan McMillan of the Pro Family Media Coalition declared of Madonna's image, "Underwear as outerwear is only there to titillate men. And believe me, some sicko seeing a fourteen-year-old girl walking down the street in nothing but a lacy bra isn't going to stop and say, 'Excuse me, before I grab you, can I talk about what kind of statement you're trying to make?'"

Of course, Madonna loved the outrage she generated in zealots like Susan McMillan. It was what she wanted, what she worked for . . . and what she knew would make her a pop sensation just as much as any music she could ever hope to record. She believed that the more the press dubbed her style "trashy," the more vociferous the parental objection to her look—which in turn would only encourage rebellious children to emulate her. Young girls, who were soon dubbed "wannabes" by the press (as in "wanna be Madonna"), began wearing cross earrings and fingerless gloves. They tied scarves and stockings in their wild hair—again, all introduced to popular culture by Madonna in her videos. Her success most certainly validated the blueprint for attention drawn up by Madonna as a child: do something to shock people and, if it's outrageous enough, it will get them talking. She didn't care what they were saying, as long as they were saying *something* about her.

The image Madonna projected was selfish, vulgar and sexual. More than anything else, the statement she was making with her image and attitude had to do with a hunger for fame and notoriety. It wasn't phony or contrived, that's for certain. It was organic—she just threw her costumes together, she has said, from whatever she had in the closet, from whatever cheap clothing she had picked up at thrift stores—and very timely, as well.

"Do you think my mother would be proud of me?" she asked Jellybean Benitez after her first album was released.

"Oh my God, Madonna, yes," he remembers answering. "Look at what you've achieved. Look at all you've done. Any mother would be proud."

Madonna smiled. "And my father?"

"Absolutely," Jellybean said. "Tony's happy. You know it."

"Yeah, well," Madonna concluded, "not that it matters."

✝

While Madonna and Jellybean Benitez enjoyed their newfound success as a result of "Holiday," the romantic relationship between these two immensely creative and emotionally explosive people soon became combative. "Egos, man," Jellybean observes when trying to explain the problems he had with Madonna. "It happens in show business. She was getting to be huge, and, now, I had my own success going on. Slowly, things changed between us."

"I never saw fights like the kind they had," Erica Bell recalls. "Jellybean is five feet, six inches, a little guy. He wore his hair shoulder length, he was cute. Not a muscle guy, but Madonna didn't go for muscle types anyway. Mostly Latin guys. Still, he was pretty wild, temperamental . . . like her.

"I remember one time he walked out on her, and she just went crazy. She was a heap on the floor, sobbing and moaning, writhing on the floor as if she was having some kind of a breakdown. 'What is this about?' I wondered. I know for a fact, because she told me, that she had three abortions, Jellybean's kids, along the way. She wasn't secretive about it. All of her friends knew. She loved Jellybean, but didn't want children at that time. 'I can't wreck my whole career by having kids now,' she told me. 'I'm way too selfish. The only other person I think about is Jellybean.' "

While she may have told Erica Bell as much, it seems unlikely that Madonna would have had three abortions in two years. Those who knew her at this time have said that she did use contraceptives. However, in press interviews over the years, Madonna has noted that the press "knows every time I have an abortion," implying that she has had more than one such procedure.

Melinda Cooper, who worked as an assistant to Madonna's manager Freddy DeMann, confirms at least one abortion during these early years. "Madonna loved Jellybean very much," she recalls, "but she wanted a career and so did he. So the abortion was necessary."

Cooper says that Madonna called Freddy to tell him that she was pregnant and had decided not to have the baby. Freddy agreed that the timing was probably wrong for a child in her life, and so he had

Melinda make the necessary arrangements. Melinda remembers the pregnant Madonna as, "scared to death, and I also recall that she definitely did not want her father to know that she was going to have this abortion, or any family member for that matter. I drove her to the doctor's office myself, a long, difficult ride in which she was very quiet, sometimes crying. I know that she had made a conscious decision that the mature thing for her to do at this time in her life was not to bring a baby into her world. 'I'm not cut out to be a mother,' she told me. 'At least not yet.' Still, she definitely wanted to be a wife. Jellybean's."

"We were going to be married along the way," concurs Jellybean Benitez when speaking of his two-year romance with Madonna. "But there was no way [this would happen], when you really think about it. I don't know that she could be monogamous, though, at least at this time. I mean, no, to be frank, she couldn't be."

Says Melinda Cooper, "Definitely, Jellybean was the man for her. She was crazy about him. I think that the reason she started playing around behind his back was to get his attention. She would do anything to get him to treat her the way she wanted to be treated, even if that meant inciting his jealousy."

Indeed, while engaged to Benitez, Madonna began dating Steve Newman, the editor of a small-time magazine in New York, *Fresh 14*. After he featured Madonna on the cover of the magazine, the two began their own romantic relationship.

"I told her that I wasn't going to be into it if she wasn't going to be committed to me," he recalled many years later. "And she said, 'Oh yeah, definitely. I want this relationship more than anything in the world.' So I was cool with that, even though I knew she still had a lot of unfinished business with Jellybean. I figured, well, she knows what she's doing. He was out and I was in . . . or so I thought."

One morning, a frustrated and enraged Benitez broke into Newman's home, where he found the woman he'd been searching for the entire previous evening. It seemed clear that his girlfriend and Steve Newman had just made love. Jellybean turned toward Madonna in a cold fury. He dragged her into another room and became engaged in an argument with her that was so vicious, Newman was stunned by it: "She was screaming things like, 'If it wasn't for me, you'd be nobody today. I *made* you, Jellybean. You were just nothing until I came along and fucking transformed your life.' And he was saying the exact same things to her. And it was all about who made who a star.

"I knew then that she was still obviously involved with him, but I loved her. Sure, she was an incredible sexual partner, very imaginative, wild. But more than that, she was seductive, just in her personality. There's something about being with a woman who is that aggressive, and who you know is going to make a success of her life. It's intoxicating to hear her talk, to watch her do the things she does on a daily basis."

When Benitez finally left Newman's home, Madonna saw Steve Newman standing at a window and looking out at the city, probably wondering about his fate in the relationship. She walked up to him and touched his arm. When he turned around, she fell into his arms, tears streaming down her face. "She hugged me tightly," he recalls, "and it was as if time stood still. I was in love, I told her she was not going to ruin me emotionally. I said, 'Listen, don't think you are going to do to me what you are doing to Jellybean.' And she said, 'Oh, no, Steve, you're different.' "

She cried and begged for his forgiveness. "I love you," she told him, "and only you."

"I looked into her beautiful eyes and I saw reflected there all the love we shared," he now recalls. "She looked so lost and awful, I felt that I needed to take care of her. So what could I do? Just wait and see how it would turn out, that's all I could do."

The predicament Madonna has said she faced in her personal life at this time was that, because of her runaway success, she felt she would not be able to find a mate among the men who had been in her circle— all of whom were really still struggling to attain their own measure of success. Even though Jellybean Benitez was now making a good living as a result of the success of his song "Holiday," she didn't think he would ever be able to equal her financial status. Steve Newman, she felt, would probably never even come close to Benitez's financial status. Simply, she was a practical woman who didn't want to be in a relationship with a man who had less money than her. "I want to be taken care of," she had said. "I don't want to be the one doing the taking care of."

While she may have thought she loved Steve Newman, in a matter of months Madonna no longer felt that way about him, just another example of her mercurial nature. One evening during a date, Madonna and Steve Newman were enjoying martinis in an intimate bar in New York. Steve took the moment to address the fact that he sensed her lack of commitment. Many years later, he would recall the conversation. "I really love you, Madonna," he told her. "I mean, I swear to God, you are the woman for me."

"I know I am," Madonna said, matter-of-factly. "That much is clear."

"So why not just drop that Jellybean character? Let's you and me get together," Newman said, pushing.

Madonna thought it over for a moment and, toying with the slice of lime in her drink, looked at her boyfriend with a serious expression. "Steve, face facts," she said. "You're this nobody writer making no money. Right? But I'm *Madonna*. I mean, I'm making, what? A quarter million a year? And next year, I'll be making ten times that much. And you? Well, you'll *still* be this nobody writer, making no money, won't you?"

Ignoring the hurt expression on his face, she continued, "In fact, your magazine will probably even be out of business in a year. So, I'm afraid that this will never work. You and I, we're over, Steve. I'm so sorry," she concluded, "but, really, it's over."

"Is that all it's about for you?" Newman asked, incredulously. "Success and money?"

"Yeah, it is," she answered, nodding her head. "Now that you mention it, it is."

*

Anyone who knew her well knew that Madonna—who would turn twenty-six in August—wasn't the kind of woman one might consider a particularly nice person. However, she was also objective about herself and her shortcomings. She would be the first, for instance, to call herself "a bitch." In an interview with the author in June 1984, she said, "Yes, I admit it. I'm tough. And I don't use the fact that I'm a woman as an excuse like a lot of other bitches. They say, oh, poor me, I'm a woman, so I have to fight harder. That's true. But that doesn't mean you have to be a bitch."

She also had a sense of humor about herself.

"How did you get this reputation?" I asked. "Is it because you want attention, and so you push people around?"

"No, that's not it," Madonna said.

"Well, then, what is it?"

She mulled over the question. "Basically, I think it's this: people just tend to *piss me off*. Therefore, I hate them."

The two of us dissolved into laughter. She was wearing a black lace bodysuit with a plunging neckline. Three crucifixes dangled from her neck: "one for each of the sins I committed just in the last hour," she explained.

Later in the interview, Madonna openly admitted that she has been intimate with both men and women, and that often they were people who could advance her career. "True," she said. "And they fucked me to advance their careers, too. Let's face it. It has worked both ways. How many people used me to get ahead? You're a reporter. Make a list and get back to me later."

I wondered how she felt about Cher's recent comments that she was "tacky"?

"Now, that's in the eye of the beholder, isn't it?" she answered. "And who knows tacky better than Cher?"

"She also said that you are 'vulgar, aggressive, even mean-spirited.' "

"Oh, puh-leeze," Madonna said, giggling. "Of course I am."

*

As her musical career continued to thrive, Madonna turned her sights on one of her earliest obsessions: the movies. She still wanted to be an actress, that ambition had not changed. Obviously, her musical career had begun to be rewarding, financially and creatively. Now, she was seeking a movie role. Once again, timing and Lady Luck conspired to make Madonna's dreams a reality.

At this time, movie producer Susan Seidelman was in the process of casting a relatively low-budget ($5 million) film for Orion Pictures. The script, entitled *Desperately Seeking Susan*, was a good one—a modern, screwball comedy with a New Wave feel about a suburban housewife who, bored with her upper-middle-class existence, starts following romance through the personal ads. Enter the "Susan" of the title, a kooky, scatterbrained "street girl" who disrupts the sex lives of all concerned and causes the housewife (Rosanna Arquette), to shed her inhibitions and, after a temporary loss of memory, to "become" Susan. The character was perfect for Madonna's brash image and in the late summer of 1984 Madonna turned her attention to landing the role, letting Seidelman know she was interested.

Seidelman was also interested in Madonna. She had been having problems casting the role of Susan with an actress who could convincingly convey the character's combined qualities of sexiness, brashness and self-confidence (actresses who were tested included Jennifer Jason Leigh, Melanie Griffith, Kelly McGillis and Ellen Barkin). After Madonna's screen test, it was quickly agreed by everyone involved that she was perfectly suited for the part. She began filming the movie in November 1984.

Though the film had been a vehicle for Rosanna Arquette, it wasn't long before *Desperately Seeking Susan* was being referred to by the media as "the Madonna Movie" . . . much to Arquette's dismay. The movie was soon structured to showcase the inexperienced pop-star-turned-actress. A song by Madonna, "Into the Groove," was even worked into the thread of the story line, which prompted Arquette to complain later, "It was completely unfair. As soon as Madonna came into the picture, the script was changed to suit her. I told them that if *Susan* was going to be nothing more than a two-hour rock video spotlighting Madonna, well, I didn't want to be a part of it. A disco dance movie isn't what I signed on to do. However, I couldn't get out of it . . ." (Ironically, it would largely be because Madonna, described by former *New Yorker* film critic Pauline Kael as "a trampy, indolent goddess," was in the film that it would go on to become one of the top-five-grossing movies of 1985.)

✟

Like a Virgin

Back on the pop music scene, Madonna's second album, *Like a Virgin*, was released on November 12, 1984.

Like A Virgin is really a portrait of Madonna's uncanny pop instincts empowered by her impatient zeal for creative growth and her innate knack for crafting a good record. With the unqualified success of her debut album, just who and what fueled the Madonna persona was now clear: she was a street-smart dance queen with the sexy allure of Marilyn Monroe, the coy iciness of Marlene Dietrich and the cutting (and protective) glibness of a modern Mae West. Madonna's first album succeeded in introducing that persona and, now, with the new album she set out to solidify and build upon the concept. The work, the dedication—the stubbornness—had paid off. Now, it was time to solidify her future.

"Warner Bros. Records is a hierarchy of old men, and it's a chauvinist environment to be working in because I'm treated like this sexy little girl," she said at the time. "I have to prove them wrong, which has meant not only proving myself to my fans but to my record company as well. That is something that happens when you're a girl. It wouldn't happen to Prince or Michael Jackson. I had to do everything on my own and it was hard trying to convince people that I was worth a record deal. After that, I had the same problem trying to convince the record company that I had more to offer than a one-shot girl singer."

Taking control as the record's primary producer, Madonna chose Nile Rodgers, a man of great experience when it came to creating personas in the recording studio. With production partner Bernard Edwards, Rodgers had formed the seventies band Chic, essentially a studio rhythm section (including two female vocalists and drummer Tony Thompson) which had a string of disco-era dance hits, including "Dance, Dance, Dance," "Everybody Dance," "Le Freak" and "Good Times."

Because pop and R&B music is a producer-driven medium, Chic's hits quickly put Edwards's and Rodgers's sound in demand. Soon, the duo had written and produced hit records for others, including the sibling act Sister Sledge who found commercial success with Edwards's and Rodgers's "We Are Family" and "The Greatest Dancer," and Diana Ross, who did the same with "Upside Down" and "I'm Coming Out." Indeed, when guitarist Rodgers split with Edwards to work separately, his inventive ability to meld rock and rhythm is what made his production of David Bowie's 1983 hit "Let's Dance" so spectacular . . .

and probably what attracted Madonna to him as a producer. Theirs was—and still is—a mutual admiration society.

"I'm always amazed by Madonna's incredible judgment when it comes to making pop records," says Nile Rodgers. "I've never seen anyone do it better, and that's the truth. When we did that album, it was the perfect union, and I knew it from the first day in the studio. The thing between us, man, it was sexual, it was passionate, it was creative . . . it was pop."

Their collective energy—Madonna wanting to score with a smash second album and Nile Rodgers wanting to be the producer to give it to her—drove the production of the *Like a Virgin* collection with great precision. The album's title track, and first single, offered the perfect continuation of the Madonna persona with sexy double entendres, every step along the way: "Like a virgin . . . touched for the very first time." The expensive, lavish video—featuring Madonna with a wild lion—was filmed in Italy. When she sang the song on the 1984 MTV Video Awards show—the public's first taste of her in live performance—she wore a knee-length, white wedding dress, veil, bustier, garter belt and plenty of clunky jewelry. She worked the stage like a panther in heat, crawling on the floor seductively, playing right to the camera and flirting all the while with what she knew was an international audience. Recalls Melissa Etheridge, "I remember thinking, 'What is she doing? She's wearing a wedding dress. Oh my God, she's rolling around on the floor. Oh my God!' It was the most brave, blatant sexual thing I've ever seen on television."

Since Nile Rodgers brought musicians from Chic with him to the studio with Madonna, many Chic fans felt that *Like a Virgin* was actually just another Chic album. If that was true, it was certainly armed with better, more durable singles. However, neither Madonna nor Rodgers had a hand in writing the song "Like a Virgin." Tom Kelly and Billy Steinberg penned it, and it was middle-aged Mo Ostin (then president of Warner Bros. Records) who found it, then passed it on to the label's fledgling artist. Madonna and Rodgers, who brought the song to life, created a sparse, anxious groove, driven by a big, mechanical snare drum. Madonna crafted a coy vocal that suggested she really was a virgin—excited, sexy and willing. It all worked: "Like a Virgin" became Madonna's first Number 1 pop single, and stayed in that position for six weeks. (Nile Rodgers remixed "Like a Virgin" for the twelve-inch dance single; however his version was rejected in favor of the remix produced by Jellybean Benitez.)

With the success of the single "Like a Virgin," the album only then began to show its true worth. Behind the title track, Warner Bros. Records released "Material Girl," an even funkier musical sound with a New Wave accent. Armed with a great melody and semi-biographical, tongue-in-cheek *ironic* lyrics about a girl's love for cash, "Material Girl" was propelled to Number 2 in the pop charts.

In the meantime, two songs from movie soundtracks would further raise Madonna's popularity to fever pitch. "Crazy for You," a sassy ballad written by Jon Lind and John Bettis and produced by Jellybean Benitez (from the movie *Vision Quest*) would become Madonna's second Number 1 single. Then, the up-tempo "Into the Groove," co-written and co-produced by Madonna and ex-boyfriend, musical mentor and cohort Steve Bray (from the soundtrack of *Desperately Seeking Susan*), went to Number 1 on the dance charts (even though it was just the B side of "Angel," the third single from *Like a Virgin*). Both tracks were vital to the public's growing fascination with Madonna, "Crazy for You" because it provided more proof that she was vocally capable of delivering a serious ballad, and "Into the Groove" because it demonstrated her continual ability to create infectious dance music. "Dress You Up," the next single from *Virgin*, added to the successful, commercial streak when it went to Number 5 in the pop charts.

Though *Like a Virgin* became Madonna's first Number 1 album (and one of the biggest-selling albums of 1985), it generated less than enthusiastic reviews ("A tolerable bit of fluff," *People* magazine observed). It's true that, today—and especially when compared to Madonna's body of work since that time—the album seems a bit repetitious and immature. Nile Rodgers confesses, "As a fan, it wouldn't be what I consider my favorite Madonna album compositionally."

However, the mere fact that at the time of its release so many couldn't resist commenting on the record was testament to the continuing, growing fascination with the artist who created it. Mick Jagger even threw his hat in the ring by commenting that Madonna's songs were characterized by a "central dumbness."

Indeed, maybe it was Madonna's so-called central dumbness that sparked the interest of much of her public, fans hungry for a sexy and provocative star who actually conveyed that she enjoyed the limelight and her celebrity. There really hadn't been a pin-up phenomenon since Farrah Fawcett's reign in the late seventies, and her reign as one of "Charlie's Angels" had been relatively short-lived before she tired of her bathing-suit-blonde image and sought recognition as a serious television actress.

Madonna, though, had been fantasizing about fame and fortune for years and was more than happy to give to the public the provocative, double-entendre female image that had been absent from the spotlight since the days of Marilyn Monroe. Her new album taunted, with song titles like "Dress You Up," "Angel," "Material Girl," and of course the title tease, "Like a Virgin."

Further to fuel Madonna mania and the success of *Like a Virgin,* Warner Bros. Records sent her on a heavily promoted tour. Not surprisingly, the tour was a smashing success; at Radio City Music Hall it broke all attendance records when the show sold out in a breathtaking twenty-four minutes. It certainly seemed that by the mid-eighties there was no stopping her—Madonna's albums were selling at a staggering 80,000 a day. Although she was looking to the future with declarations such as "I want longevity as a human being. I want it to last forever," critics like Robert Hilburn of the *Los Angeles Times* were already predicting her rapid decline. "It's like having a new toy," Hilburn stated. "Everyone wanted the Cabbage Patch Doll for Christmas. She's the Cabbage Patch Doll this year." Other critics were placing their bets that Cyndi Lauper, with her pure and powerful yet quirky voice, would be the pop diva who would endure. *Billboard* magazine editor, Paul Grein, predicted that "Cyndi Lauper will be around for a long time; Madonna will be out of the business in six months."

"In the beginning, I was called everything from a Disco Dolly to a One-Hit Wonder," Madonna recalled in 1999. "Everyone agreed that I was sexy, but no one would agree that I had any talent, which really irritated me."

In fact, if she was going anywhere, it would be straight up. After all, this was the 1980s. In many ways, Madonna was exactly what people wanted at this time. During the previous decade, Andy Warhol had made the statement that in the future everyone would be famous for fifteen minutes, and many seemed intent on making that prediction come true. Many people not only wanted fame, they wanted money, name brands and everything else in excess. On television, ordinary citizens were discovering talk shows as a viable forum to indulge in exhibitionism by exposing their most intimate secrets to a worldwide audience. Cable television brought sex and violence into America's homes as never before. On Wall Street, brokers in their early twenties were becoming rich by selling junk bonds to yuppies eager for overnight millions.

In a sense, Madonna became the human embodiment of a junk bond. People were willing to exploit and sell her in order to make as much money as possible—and she was happy to be exploited . . . if it meant money in her pocket, too. The public, fascinated with fame, was happy to watch.

Not to denigrate Madonna's talent—because she certainly had a great deal of it (most of which hadn't even been explored yet)—but the notion of "celebrity" has never had much to do with what special abilities a person has, or what he or she has accomplished in terms of artistry. It's always had to do with personal marketing—and never was this more true than it was in the 1980s. With burgeoning cable TV, videos, magazines, billboards, radio and film media, a celebrity could now be exploited twenty-four hours a day: in living rooms, at clubs, in supermarkets or on the streets, the same image projected from every direction, at every turn. Madonna was one of the first artists to understand this cultural twist; Michael Jackson also got it. At the beginning of her career as a singer in the 1980s, she always made sure she had all areas covered for total media saturation. She would gladly appear on any television show, magazine cover, splashy video, whatever it took . . .

☩

Meeting Sean Penn

Perhaps one of Madonna's most popular videos is the one she filmed for "Material Girl," a modern-day reworking of Marilyn Monroe's most famous vocal performance, "Diamonds Are a Girl's Best Friend." Madonna said at the time, "Marilyn was made into something not human in a way, and I can relate to that. Her sexuality was something everyone was obsessed with, and that I can relate to. And there were certain things about her vulnerability that I'm curious about and attracted to."

When the time came to film the video (two days in Los Angeles in February 1985), Madonna decided on a clear and obvious homage to her blonde inspiration, Monroe. The video featured Madonna wearing an exact replica of Marilyn's shocking pink gown from the film *Gentlemen Prefer Blondes* (she hated the dress, however, complaining that it constantly slipped down her bosom), singing on a reconstruction of the film's set, complete with staircase, chandeliers and bevy of tuxedo-clad chorus boys. ("I can't completely disdain the song and video, because they certainly were important to my career," she said later. "But talk about the media hanging on to a phrase and misinterpreting the damn thing as well. I didn't write that song, you know, and the video was all about how the girl rejected diamonds and money. But God forbid irony should be understood. So when I'm ninety, I'll still be the Material Girl. I guess it's not so bad. Lana Turner was the Sweater Girl until the day she died.")

Freddy DeMann's assistant Melinda Cooper drove Madonna to the sound stage where "Material Girl" was to be filmed. A photograph taken that day shows Madonna wearing a pink bodysuit and a black velvet shirt, unbuttoned enough so as to reveal her black Chantelle bra. She also wore large dark sunglasses and a wide-brimmed red hat, lest she be recognized.

Because of the enormity of the video production—and the Marilyn Monroe association that was bound to cause a sensation—Melinda Cooper sensed that Madonna's life and career were about to be transformed. It was an exciting notion. "Do you realize how much things are going to change for you now?" she asked her as they drove to the set.

"What do you mean?" Madonna responded. She had her compact mirror out and was inspecting a pimple. "Jesus Christ. Of all the days to get a zit," she said, preoccupied. "I ask you, can anything else go wrong in my fucking life?"

"I mean, your whole world is going to change after this video," said Cooper, ignoring Madonna's rhetorical question. "Do you know that?"

Madonna snapped the compact shut. "I know that, Melinda," she said, perturbed. "Now can we please just get there!"

On that first day on the set, while Madonna was standing at the top of the staircase and waiting for filming to begin, she gazed down and noticed a guy in a leather jacket and dark sunglasses striking what seemed to be a deliberate pose in a corner, looking back up at her intently. He was twenty-four-year-old actor Sean Penn—born on August 17, 1960—at the time considered the most moody and brooding (and probably most talented) of the young Hollywood actors who made up what was known as "the Brat Pack." (Others in the so-called Pack included young actors Charlie Sheen and Emilio Estevez.) Because he hailed from a privileged background, having been raised in Beverly Hills with both parents in show business (his father is television director Leo Penn, his mother actress Eileen Ryan), Penn didn't have to struggle much to break into the business. However, his privileged lifestyle didn't make him any less angry. He had a reputation for being an intensely private, sometimes violent and extremely jealous young man—and he was also thought of as a proficient actor thanks to roles in *Fast Times at Ridgemont High*, *Racing with the Moon* and *The Falcon and the Snow Man*. After having expressed an interest in meeting Madonna, Sean Penn had been brought to the set of "Material Girl" by the video's director, Mary Lambert.

"He was somebody whose work I'd admired," Madonna has said, "and I think he felt the same way about me. I never thought in a million years I would meet him."

As soon as Madonna, still at the top of the stairs and waiting to start her descent, realized that the stranger below was Sean Penn, her heart skipped a beat. Though she fancied actor Keith Carradine at this time (who appeared in the video and with whom she was seen making out in between takes), she knew that she had to meet Penn. Even at first glance, he seemed self-confident and cocky—just her type. When they finally did meet at the bottom of the stairs, he didn't disappoint.

"Well, just look at you," Sean Penn said to her as he motioned to the gown and wig. Full of swagger, he hooked his thumbs in the belt loops of his jeans. "You think you're Marilyn Monroe, don't you?" He was joking, but Madonna didn't appreciate his brand of humor.

"What's the matter with you?" she asked, annoyed. "You don't even say hello? You just go straight for the insult? Is that what you do? You don't even say, 'It's nice to meet you?'

"Oh, I'm sorry, *Marilyn*," Sean Penn said, his voice dripping with phony sarcasm. Sean's eyes were a bit glazed, a cigarette dangled from his mouth. He extended his hand to shake hers. "It's nice to meet you," he said with a warm smile.

Madonna had to laugh. She took his hand and, putting on a whispery Marilyn Monroe voice, cooed, "Nice to meet you, too . . ."

Later, she recalled, "I had this fantasy that we were going to meet, fall in love and get married. Suddenly it's what I was wishing would happen. Why I fell for him that day, I can't say. I have no idea. I just know I wanted him."

✞

The Affair with Prince

Soon after their first meeting on the set of the "Material Girl" video, twenty-six-year-old Madonna and twenty-four-year-old Sean Penn began dating. "After the video shoot, I was over at a friend's house," he explains. "And he had a book of quotations. He picked it up and turned to a random page and read the following: 'She had the innocence of a child and the wit of a man.' I looked at my friend and he just said, 'Go get her.' So I did." Complicating matters a bit for Sean, however, was the fact that Madonna was also dating the rock star Prince at this time, whom she had met backstage at the American Music Awards earlier, in Los Angeles on January 28, 1985. He wasn't her type, and it's difficult to know why Madonna was even interested in him, except for the fact that she respected him as a musician and probably just wanted to know what made him tick.

Prince (real name Prince Rogers Nelson) was—still is—an eccentric man known for strangely shy demeanor in private and outrageous sexuality—prancing about in bikini briefs and high heels—on stage. During an interview with the author the same year he met Madonna, Prince refused to speak. Instead, he sat silently in his chair in front of a dinner of Chinese food and spent the entire evening playing with shrimp fried rice, all the while with a grim expression on his face. In response to any question, he would either nod affirmatively or shake his head negatively. When the interview was over, he departed without saying good-bye. "And that, my friend, is Prince," said his publicist by way of explanation.

As their first date, Prince invited Madonna to accompany him to one of his performances in Los Angeles. Though she was scheduled to leave for New York to begin rehearsals for her own concert tour, she decided to delay that trip a few days so that she could spend some time with the rock star. The night of his concert, he picked her up in a white stretch limousine and took her to the Forum, where he was performing. Madonna later said she was amazed to find that the diminutive rock star smelled so strongly of the scent of lavender, "Like a woman," she observed. "I felt like I was in the presence of Miss Elizabeth Taylor. He reeks of lavender. It turned me on, actually."

Once in the limousine, recalled T. L. Ross, who was a friend of Prince's, "I heard she was pretty aggressive, that the poor little guy had to fight her off. She was strong. He told me that she had the strength of ten women." Because he had a performance that evening, Prince didn't want to exhaust himself with Madonna. He suggested that they wait.

After the show, the two ventured out into the Los Angeles night and eventually ended up at the Marquis Hotel in Westwood for a party with Prince's entourage. The gathering turned rowdy when Prince leaped up onto a table and began to undress. Joining him on the table, Madonna engaged him in a sensual bump-and-grind, her shoulders bouncing up and down, her body undulating. The party broke up at five in the morning, after which Prince and Madonna—arm in arm and practically holding each other up—retired to Prince's private suite.

For the next two months, the couple continued seeing each other, though they didn't seem to have much in common other than their status as superstar performers. While she was honest and forthright, he was secretive and bashful. Luckily, they both idolized Marilyn Monroe. When he told her that his home was filled with posters of the blonde movie goddess, Madonna said that she couldn't wait to see his collection of memorabilia.

One romantic evening, Prince leased the entire Yamashiro moun-taintop restaurant overlooking Los Angeles, with its breathtaking view of the city lights. Madonna wore a lacy purple skirt with trademark black bra peeking out from behind a sheer white blouse. At the restau-rant, they ate Japanese food and then, after three hours of what ap-peared to some observers to be little conversation, they departed for a nightclub called Façade.

"I've been nibbling around the edges of this thing long enough, because I didn't know where to start or how to tell you," Prince told Madonna once they were at the club with friends. He was being much more courageous than he'd ever been with her, and in front of witnesses, which made it even more surprising. "Madonna, I think we should hook up, you and I. I want you to be, you know . . . my girl."

Seeming surprised, Madonna let the request linger as if anticipat-ing a punch line. But he wasn't joking. He waited for her response. "Hmmm," she said while frowning and looking as if she was trying to figure out just how to handle the moment. "Now, *that's* food for thought, isn't it?" Her words didn't hold much conviction.

When Prince look deflated, Madonna grabbed his hand. "C'mon, let's dance!" she said cheerily as she walked him out onto the dance floor.

After about two months, when there really wasn't anything left for them to say to each other, Madonna became bored with Prince. They had recorded a couple of songs in his Minneapolis studio, and one would even be released later. But her friends recall that, while she com-plained about his passivity, he griped about her aggressive nature.

Says T. L. Ross, "Prince is way too cosmic for Madonna. For him, making love is a spiritual experience. For her—at least at that time—making love was just a physical expression. While he wanted to savor every second of the experience, she was into multiple orgasms. After two months, he cut her loose. Then, she did the scorned woman act.

"After he stopped acting interested in her, that's when the phone calls started. Madonna pestered him for weeks. He said later that she screamed at him, 'How dare you dump me. Don't you know who I am?' She was definitely not used to getting dumped."

Madonna would have the last word on Prince, though, with the *Los Angeles Times* years later, in October 1994: "I was having dinner with

Left: Madonna Louise Ciccone in 1963 at the age of five, the year she suffered the loss of her mother, also named Madonna. *Paragon Photo Vault*

Right: In 1966, the First Holy Communion girl. *Globe Photos*

✝

Left: Madonna at twelve. *Paragon Photo Vault*

Right: As a cheerleader at Rochester Adams High School, 1975. *Globe Photos*

Clockwise from left:

Straight-A student Madonna graduated from high school at the age of seventeen in 1976. *Globe Photos*

After graduation, Madonna enrolled at the University of Michigan where she studied for a year and a half before moving to New York in pursuit of her dream . . . to be a dancer. Here she is, age twenty in 1978. *Michael McDonnell/Archive Photos*

Early New York days, spring 1979. *Michael McDonnell/Archive Photos*

Left: An early publicity photo, taken to secure work as an actress. *Oscar White/Corbis*

Right: Though many people along the way felt she had used them to attain stardom, "they got as much out of it as I did," Madonna said. It wouldn't be long before she would find her niche with her first, self-titled album in July 1983. Here's the "Lucky Star" at the 1984 MTV Video Music Awards. *Richard Corkey/Sygma*

✝

The first low-budget films made by many actresses are often not memorable and Madonna's *A Certain Sacrifice* is no exception . . . with its finale featuring a human sacrifice number. *Pictorial Press, Ltd.*

Madonna's romance with talented record producer, John "Jellybean" Benitez, was serious enough for them to consider marrying . . . but monogamy really wasn't a priority in her life at this time. Here they are in Los Angeles, January 1985. Madonna was twenty-six. *Scott Downie/Celebrity Photo*

The love Madonna felt for the emotionally complex Sean Penn was strong and resilient . . . though a successful relationship with him was but an elusive dream. *Cooper Cunningham/Retna Ltd.*

A production still from Madonna's 1985 film, *Desperately Seeking Susan*. *Orion/Motion Picture and Television Photo Archive*

Madonna performing for a throng at Philadelphia's JFK Stadium in July 1985. ©*1985 Ken Regan/Camera 5*

One of the many big arguments before the couple married in August 1985 occurred when Madonna's attorneys tried to persuade Sean to sign a prenuptial agreement—which he refused to do. Here they are, trying to get away from it all on the Malibu beach. *Barry King/Corbis Sygma*

Young, glamorous and exciting to watch, Madonna and Sean did have happy times—if only a few!—before the relationship ended when Sean was arrested in December 1988, amid accusations of domestic violence. *Laura Luongo/Liaison*

With her short-cropped blonde hair, Madonna spent the summer of 1987 on the "Who's That Girl?" tour. A diva of the first order, she demanded that road managers hold a barrier of sheets around her while backstage so as to shield her from the eyes of those who couldn't help but stare because . . . well, look at her! *Ross Marino/Corbis Sygma*

At a table reading for her first Broadway show, *Speed-the-Plow*, with Joe Mantegna *(left)* and Ron Silver. By this time, Madonna was dating John Kennedy, Jr. Though Jackie Kennedy Onassis attended opening night (May 3, 1988 at the Royale Theater), she opted not to meet Madonna for fear of validating John's relationship with her. *Photofest*

✝

Madonna and Sandra Bernhard became good friends in 1988. Here they are with artist Keith Haring at an AIDS benefit. Their friendship, however, ended in tears a few years later because of envy and jealousy. *AP/Wide World Photos*

Left: After Sean, the older and more sensible Warren Beatty seemed a breath of fresh air for Madonna. Whereas Sean was emotional and explosive, Warren was resigned and even philosophical about her daily defiances. *Trippett/Sipa Press*

Right: Unfortunately, Madonna continued an explosive relationship theme with Warren—though the couple did manage to make *Dick Tracy* film history in 1990. *Sunset Blvd/Corbis Sygma*

When Warren ended it with Madonna—after giving her a cheap brooch for her thirty-second birthday—the sexy Tony Ward became a difficult rebound relationship. *Christophe Robert/Corbis Sygma*

In June 1992, Madonna's father, Silvio (Tony) Ciccone appeared with her on the *Arsenio Hall* television show. Not until Madonna had her own children would she fully understand Tony's determination live a full life after the death of his first wife, Madonna's mother. *AP/Wide World Photos*

In March 1991, the King and Queen of Pop—Michael Jackson and Madonna—attended the Academy Awards together. They made a striking, if odd, couple. (Never had she spent time with a man with whom she had less in common.) *David McGough/DMI/TimePix*

In October 1992, Madonna released her notorious *Sex* book, marking the beginning of serious career concerns. Here she is in Florida, naked from the waist up—of course!—being positioned by photographer Steven Meisel.

Madonna at the (blessed) end of her S&M phase, with dancers for the "Human Nature" video. By this time, her controversial antics had worn thin; it was time for a change . . . *Online USA Inc.*

Facing page, clockwise from left:

In Madonna's love life, Carlos Leon turned out to be one of the "good guys," at her side unconditionally even—and especially—when she became pregnant with his child. Here they are in April 1997, jogging in Central Park. *Marcel Thomas, Sipa Press*

Secretly pregnant while filming *Evita* in Buenos Aires, Madonna waves to fans, providing a very Eva Peron-like moment from her balcony. *AP/Wide World Photos*

With Carlos gone from her love life—by mutual consent—Madonna continued on, content with their daughter, Lourdes Maria Ciccone Leon, but starved for true intimacy. Here are mother and child in Paris in February 1998.

✝

After a brief and unsatisfying relationship with basketball star Dennis Rodman in 1995, Madonna was appalled to learn that he wrote about it in his memoirs. *splashnews.com*

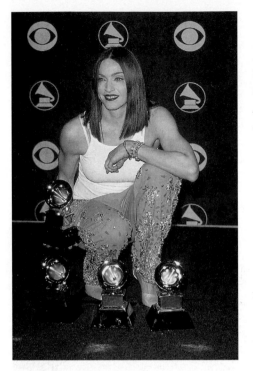

Madonna poses with her four well-deserved Grammys for the critically acclaimed *Ray of Light* CD in February 1999. *Fitzroy Barrett/Globe Photos*

As a practical joke, Guy Ritchie borrowed photographer Richard Young's camera and took this picture of the unsuspecting Madonna. *R. Young/Ritchie/REX*

Clockwise from left:

Pregnant with Guy's baby, Madonna's priorities changed—and so did some of her personal aspirations. "I finally figured out that if you want to have the right kind of man in your life," she said, "you have to be the right kind of woman." *Dave Benett/Apha/Globe Photos*

Madonna and Guy leave Dornoch Cathedral in Scotland after the christening of their four-month-old son, Rocco, on December 21, 2000. Though the couple would marry the next day at Skibo Castle, this would be the only photo opportunity for the paparazzi. It was the determined groom's decision—not the bride's!—to prohibit the release of any photos of the wedding. *Jeff J. Mitchell/Reuters*

Here's a rare photo of seven-month-old baby Rocco, with his dad, Guy, in New York. *Arnaldo Magnani/Liaison*

Make no mistake about it: she's his, and she likes it that way—Madonna makes as much clear at the January 2001 premiere of Guy's film *Snatch* in Hollywood. This was their first public appearance as husband and wife.
Fred Prouser/Reuters

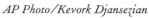

With more than 100 million records sold and an estimated worth of $600 million, what Madonna has so far achieved in her lifetime is hard-earned and well-deserved. Still, as she proved with her *Music* CD, she remains contemporary, on the cutting edge. Here she is performing the title track at the 2001 Grammys.
AP Photo/Kevork Djansezian

Prince and he was just sipping tea, very daintily. I was stuffing food down my face and I was, like, 'Aren't you going to eat?' She mimicked a delicate, whispered no. Continuing, she concluded, "And I thought, 'Oh my God!' I have this theory about people who don't eat. They annoy me."

✝

"Madonna: A Lonely Life"

After her brief romance with Prince, Madonna began to concentrate on Sean Penn as a potential mate. In spite of her fanatical need for the spotlight and Sean Penn's obsessive desire for privacy, the two began a passionate and exciting courtship that, if nothing else, certainly proved that opposites do attract. Impressed as much by his tough guy reputation as by his acting credentials, Madonna would later admit that she was, as she put it, "completely unable to resist him, not that I ever tried. He was the sexiest, smartest man I had ever known." Sean was equally fascinated by her. He had been a fan of Madonna's, which is why he had wanted to meet her. Once he got to know her, he quickly realized that she was fun to be with, and also the kind of woman who would, when necessary, meet him at his own level of arrogance. "I admit it, I was a smart-ass," he says. "And so was she. It was a relationship made in heaven, two smart-asses going through life together. How romantic."

Of course, the paparazzi were delighted at the pairing of the unpredictable Penn and his exhibitionist girlfriend, Madonna. They were even photographed on their first dates: in New York at a club called Private Eyes, and in Los Angeles where Penn had accompanied Madonna on a pilgrimage to Marilyn Monroe's crypt at Westwood Memorial Cemetery. (Madonna was shaking with nervous tension during the visit to Monroe's grave. When she spotted a red rose left there by her ex-husband Joe DiMaggio, she was heard to murmur "Oh, my. He really loved her.")

At this time, with everyone trying to get a piece of her—or at least that's how it probably felt to her—Madonna had said she wanted someone in her life she believed truly loved her. "She was lonely, the classic victim of stardom in that she was the popular and well-loved celebrity who went home alone at night and cried her eyes out," said her former producer and boyfriend Jellybean Benitez. While she certainly wasn't lacking in sexual experiences, missing in her life was a sense of true intimacy with another person. Of course, those in her circle at this time admit that Madonna wasn't an easy person to get to know or to be intimate with on an emotional level. "She had a lot of barriers up," says Tommy Quinn, a New York studio musician who dated her shortly before she met Sean Penn.

While Quinn had heard the charge made against Madonna that she was cold, selfish and aloof, he disagreed. "I found her to be very guarded," he says. "Of course, she was brash and—oh, man!—she could be a royal bitch. But beneath it, if you really got to know her, she was a different kind of person, a very insecure girl.

"I remember one night in particular: she was at my place and we made love. It was pretty intense, and afterward, as I held her in my arms, I noticed that she was sobbing. When I asked her why, she refused to open up to me. But every time we made love—which was about a half dozen times—she seemed sadder than she was before. I thought to myself, either I'm pretty bad in the sack or this girl has a problem with intimacy. It was more than she could take when she allowed herself to be vulnerable."

"What's wrong?" he asked Madonna, touching her tenderly on the cheek.

"Nothing," she responded quickly. "I'm fine. Leave me alone, will you?" As he recalled it, she took a deep breath and then let it out slowly, as if being pushed down by an excruciating weight. Then, she pulled away from her lover and slept at the foot of the bed in a fetal position.

"At first, I thought she was crying because she thought having sex made her vulnerable, and then that made her feel weak. But, after knowing her a little better, I decided it was because she was just afraid of being hurt, of letting down her guard, of being truly intimate."

A few nights later, Quinn decided to ask the question that had been on his mind but for which there had never been an appropriate time.

"Why do you hate your old man so much?" he asked "Every time you bring up your father, it's always to say some horrible thing about him. I think that's the source of your anxiety."

"What are you talking about?" Madonna said, now crying. "How dare you say that to me?"

She then bolted out of bed, ran into the bathroom and slammed the door behind her.

The next morning, Madonna—her eyes red-rimmed and watery—put on her black fishnet tights and hip-slung miniskirt in preparation for leaving. She slipped into a hand-painted jacket with no shirt underneath. As she was putting on her spike-heeled boots, she looked up at Tommy Quinn and said, "You know, just because I was crying doesn't mean anything. So don't think you have some kind of hold over me, or that I care about you." She didn't mention anything about Quinn's having brought up her father.

As he tried to figure out how to respond, she walked across the room and out the door, without saying good-bye.

A week later, Quinn found her staring out the eleventh-story window of his brownstone on East Seventy-second Street in New York. She looked fetching, wearing his T-shirt and nothing else, certainly putting on a fairly indecent show for the neighbors. "A penny for your thoughts," Quinn said to her as he brought her a glass of chilled white wine.

"They'll cost you a lot more than that," Madonna said with a weak smile. Then, after a sip, she thoughtfully observed, "It's all a fiction, you know that, don't you, Tommy? I'm just a character in a novel. None of this is real. None of it."

"What's the novel called?" Quinn asked, intrigued.

"It's called *Madonna,*" she answered. Then, after a thoughtful beat, she added a subtitle: *"A Lonely Life."*

No different from a lot of other people, she wanted to be loved—but she was also afraid to be loved. Or, as her sister Paula observed, "She was a woman, like any woman. She needed someone to hold on to. But it scared her."

Sean Penn had his own insecurities. His mania for privacy was obsessive, and those who knew him well claim it was because he was never satisfied with the way he looked, always feeling awkward in his own skin and not wishing to be seen by anyone, let alone *everyone*. His bravado and bad temper, according to those who knew him well, was—not surprisingly—a camouflage that masked a litany of other emotional issues the explanations of which are probably best left to Sean Penn biographers. However, when he and Madonna began to date, they found something in each other that felt like, as Madonna put it, "a sense of personal completion." Also, their sexual chemistry was explosive. After their first date, he threw her to the floor and stripped off her clothes and his own in such a hurry he left his boots on. Then he made love to her. Later, she said, "We reached orgasm together, and it was as if time stood still."

"Who's to say how the heart works . . . it just does," observes Meg Lowery, an actress friend of Sean's who lived in Los Angeles at the time and attended acting classes with him. "Sean told me he was crazy about her. But he was worried about it. 'She's nuts,' he told me. 'And I'm nuts. The two of us together? Man, that's trouble.' Plus, he sensed that she wasn't going to be faithful to him. 'She's out there, wild and free,' he told me. 'And I don't think any man will be able to tame her. In fact,' he said, 'I think the last thing she wants is to be tamed.' "

Along with his brooding nature, Sean Penn was also a talented actor and an intelligent man. When she found that he was a voracious reader and wrote poetry, Madonna was even more attracted to him. Soon, she was announcing to any friend, foe or reporter that Sean Penn was her hero, her best friend and the "coolest guy in the universe." She could tell him her problems, she said. Somehow, he had the instinctive understanding of a man who had suffered himself and knew all there was to know about loss and grief, even though his parents were both still alive. She could talk to him as she could talk to no one else.

The couple soon announced their engagement. As word of this big event spread, publicity about Madonna's life and career reached a new fever pitch. A surprising declaration for some of her fans—but not so surprising for those who knew her—came when the men's magazine *Penthouse* announced it would be publishing nude photographs taken of Madonna years earlier. Not to be outdone, *Playboy* announced its own imminent publication of similarly scandalous photographs. As a media sensation ensued over the idea that photographs of Madonna would expose her in a new and revealing way, it was just as it had been thirty-five years earlier with the news that Marilyn Monroe had also posed nude.

Some observers suggested that these nude photographs of Madonna would somehow damage her career. Reporters pointed to Vanessa Williams who, a year earlier, had been forced to turn in her Miss America crown. It had been discovered that she had posed nude years before she won her title. (Of course, Vanessa Williams would ultimately turn the scandal to her advantage. She is now one of the only Miss Americas whose name anyone can even remember.) The existence of nude pictures, the race between two men's magazines to beat each other to publication, and Madonna's bold declaration, "I'm not ashamed of anything," only fanned the flames of red-hot publicity.

Tommy Quinn had not seen Madonna in more than a year when, he says, he received a telephone call from her. She asked if they could meet. When he invited her to his apartment, she said, "No. I'm a trapped animal now. If I come to see you, everyone will know where you live, everyone will know that I know you, and they'll never leave you alone." He now recalls, "In order to protect me, she wanted us to meet in a small Italian restaurant on Second Avenue near Seventy-first Street."

When he showed up, he found Madonna in a back booth wearing large sunglasses, a floppy hat and an old, worn, flower-print "house-dress." He recalls, "She looked like a bag lady. I was astonished."

"What the hell happened to you?" he asked as he sat down.

"My life. That's what's happened to me," Madonna responded glumly. She leaned over to kiss him on the cheek. "So, how do you like my outfit? I'm a millionaire, but this is what I have to wear in public just so that I can have some peace and quiet."

After ordering spaghetti, Madonna got to the point of why she wanted to see her friend. "I need your advice," she said. "Have you heard about these pictures?"

"Who hasn't?" Quinn answered.

She took off her sunglasses. She looked as if she had been crying. "I just don't know how to be with this goddamn thing," she said, sadly. "I mean, I don't know how to *be* . . . how to act."

Quinn would recall years later, "I was astonished. When I first heard about the pictures, I thought she would probably take the position that they didn't matter, that she was above worrying about them. But, sitting with her, looking at how distressed she was, I saw that the existence of these pictures had really bothered her."

"Oh, screw it, Madonna," Quinn told her. "You have to act like you don't care. What choice do you have?"

"But I do care," she said. "What about my father? Why should he have to see those pictures? And Sean! What will Sean think?" Her temper rose. "Parasites!" she said, referring to the media. "I feel so . . . *misunderstood*."*

For the next forty-five minutes, over two plates of pasta with meatballs and a bottle of Merlot, Madonna remembered the time not so long ago, in 1979, when she decided to pose in the nude. "He was a nice guy, actually," she said of the photographer, Martin Schreiber. "Or at least I thought so at the time. He flattered me. He said I had a good body. He wined and dined me in his loft studio. I trusted him. And I was an idiot for doing so, I guess."

Madonna and Tommy finally agreed that she had no choice but to act completely unaffected by the existence of the photographs, just as Marilyn Monroe had done before her. The tale of Marilyn Monroe's naked session in front of the camera is the stuff of Hollywood legend. A few years after posing, when she was arguably the most famous actress in the world, the photographs were released. The naysaying press predicted that if the luscious young woman sprawled naked on red velvet was, indeed, *the* Marilyn Monroe, her career would surely be over as a result of the scandal. However, undaunted by the media's histrionics, Marilyn did not deny the photographs. Instead she turned the publicity to her advantage by declaring to reporters, "Sure I posed. I was hungry." When asked what she had on during the sessions, she quipped, "the radio."

"If they [presumably the public and press] know that I'm unhappy about them, they'll just love that," Madonna concluded, sounding defeated. "Oh, who cares, anyway," she added, with forced cheerfulness. "I have press agents now, you know?" she added. "Let them figure the

* "*Penthouse* did something really nasty," Madonna would complain, years later. "They sent copies of the magazine to Sean."

whole thing out. I'll use this thing to my advantage somehow. You know that, don't you, Tommy?"

"Hell yeah, you will," Quinn agreed, nudging her. "You're bigger than this, anyway, Madonna."

He recalls that she forced a sad smile and then, facetiously, made a sign of the cross.

"Are you happy, Madonna?" he asked her. As she rose, hugged him and said good-bye, it didn't seem as if she intended to answer the question. She threw fifty dollars onto the table. "Look at my life," she said, arching a brow. "Who wouldn't be happy?"

✝

"Oh My God! Look at Me!"

Was Madonna really as upset about the nude photographs as she had indicated to Tommy Quinn? Perhaps an example of her mercurial nature was that she could later make light of the predicament in which she had found herself.

"I remember when we were both broke and living in New York, Madonna showed me some of the nude shots," recalls Erica Bell. "We were just sort of being lazy, and a little drunk, and she brought out this envelope and spread the pictures on the floor. 'Look at me, Rica,' [Madonna's nickname for Erica Bell] she said. 'I'm as flat-chested as you are!' And we just laughed and laughed, for some reason, thinking the pictures were hysterical. She said, 'One day I will be world famous, and *Playboy* will publish these photos, and it'll be the greatest scandal of all time.' I asked her, 'My God, won't you be embarrassed?' And she laughed and said, 'What do *you* think?' "

When the photographs were published many years later, Erica received a telephone call from Madonna.

"Oh my God," Madonna said, nearly hysterical with laughter. "It's happened, just as I predicted."

"I know," Erica said, giggling. "I can't believe it, after all of these years."

"But I'm so flat-chested," Madonna said. "Just like you," she added, joking.

Years later, Erica said, "I don't think she was that upset about the pictures. If she was, I didn't know it. I just know we laughed a lot about them. We thought it was pretty damn funny, the whole thing."

More of Madonna's past was excavated when filmmaker Stephen Jon Lewicki decided to exploit his association with her by releasing a home-video version of *A Certain Sacrifice,* the low-budget movie they had made in 1979. Perhaps hoping that Madonna would pay him to keep the film from commercial distribution, Lewicki was dismayed when her people offered him a measly $10,000, which he flatly rejected. Although Madonna took him to court in an effort to keep the film out of circulation, Lewicki ultimately won the right to release it, making him a millionaire in just a short time—not bad for the producer of a movie made six years earlier on a $20,000 budget.

"I think Madonna tried to stop the movie more as a publicity stunt than anything else," says Lewicki today. "It was also an interesting use of her power, really, to get the kind of exposure she wants when she wants it. The *New York Post* had huge headlines on the front page, 'Madonna Seeks Nude Movie Ban.' I mean, the hysteria she whipped up over this film was amazing. But in the end, when it came right down to it, she really didn't put a wholehearted effort into suing me. I think even the judge realized that all that was happening was a certain amount of posturing, and just for publicity. So he threw the case out, and I released the movie."

At this point in her career, Madonna really didn't need to seek out publicity—it came to her in tidal waves. She had a love/hate relationship with the press—for the most part, she loved seeing herself in the media, but at the same time she pretended to hate the attention. Once at a birthday party in her honor she stood up to model a green silk pants ensemble. "I like it," she told her guests, "because it's green, the color of envy. I envy all of you," she continued melodramatically, "because you all have your privacy . . . and I don't." Madonna, however, did nothing to stop the media's attention—on the contrary, she almost always courted it.

In May 1985, Madonna made the cover of *Time,* with the accompanying headline: "Madonna—Why She's Hot." Though she seemed to some observers to be blasé about much of her newly acquired fame, this particular tribute from such a well-respected publication was not one that she took lightly. According to one of her manager Freddy DeMann's assistants at the time, "Madonna waited by the front door for the messenger to arrive from Freddy's office with a first copy of the magazine. I remember the day so well. She was wearing black mesh stockings, a short skirt and brief top, with four crucifixes around her neck. Because she was working, she also had on her herringbone glasses. When the magazine arrived, she ripped the envelope apart trying to get to it. Then, when she saw it, she let out a shriek."

"Oh my God, look at me!" Madonna said, dancing around the room in her Gucci flip-flops, magazine in hand. "I am on the cover of *Time* magazine! Can you believe it? Just look! Can you imagine it?" Earlier in her career, she had said, "I won't be happy until I'm as famous as God." Maybe now she was beginning to feel that she was on her way to that goal.

Truly awed by Madonna's appearance on the cover of one of the most respected magazines in the world, the incredulous assistant said, "No, I just can't believe it."

Suddenly, Madonna stopped dancing. Whipping around to face the employee, she said, "What do you mean, you can't believe it? Why shouldn't I be on the cover of *Time*?"

"I didn't mean . . ." the secretary began to stumble over her words. "What I meant was . . . I'm sorry."

"Oh, stop your groveling," Madonna said, exasperated. "You're so *weak*. Just get Sean on the phone. I want him to see this."

When the assistant telephoned Sean to ask him to come by Madonna's home to see the magazine, Sean indicated that he was busy. He asked that she send the magazine to his home, by messenger. Madonna, pacing the room and staring at the magazine cover, overheard the conversation between the assistant and her boyfriend. She went to the employee and grabbed the phone from her. "You get over here, now, Sean," she said into the phone. She had an angry, imperious edge to her voice. "How many girlfriends have you had on the cover of *Time?* One! Me! Now, get over here."

Penn showed up thirty minutes later.

The fact that Sean Penn was also such a combative person only added fuel to the bonfire of publicity that seemed to erupt on a weekly basis for Madonna. On June 30, 1985, he was charged with assault and battery after he beat up a couple of journalists outside a hotel in Nashville, Tennessee, where he was filming a movie.

That morning, he and Madonna had received a bouquet of balloons delivered to their room, sent by someone in the media and with a card that read, "Madonna and Sean. Congratulations, Mom and Pop. How about an exclusive?" Penn, who was annoyed by the constant scrutiny, as well as rumors that Madonna was expecting, bolted out of the room, heading towards some waiting journalists.

Lori Mulrenin, who witnessed the ensuing attack, recalls, "He was screaming at them like he was going to break open their heads. Then, when one of the journalists took his picture, he blew up. He picked up a rock and threw it carefully and precisely at the photographer. Then he ripped the cameras off the photographer's back and slammed them against the photographer, who fell down. He then picked up the rock again as the other newsman tried to step in. Sean hit that one in the eye with his fist, and also hit him on the head with the rock. Madonna, who had been in the background when the fight started, pulled her hat over her eyes and then ran back into the hotel."

Sean Penn would enter a no-contest plea to charges that he assaulted the two journalists. He received a ninety-day suspended sentence and was fined fifty dollars on each of two misdemeanor charges.

*

While some of Madonna's publicity ploys seem fairly unsophisticated in retrospect, they always worked. For instance, when the time came for the planning of her wedding to Sean Penn, she insisted that she wanted it to be a private affair with no publicity. She acted as if she did not want the kind of international attention she knew was bound to be generated by such an event. Besides simply going to Las Vegas where she and Penn could have quietly and quickly married, there were any number of ways Madonna could have ensured an intimate wedding, if such a thing was what she really desired. However, savvy as she is, she no doubt realized that the air of secrecy she pretended to foster only made the press more determined to cover the event . . . and the public more determined to read about it. Of course, to make matters even more tantalizing, Madonna banned the press from the wedding.

The only thing Madonna could not control was Sean, and his ambivalent feelings about the impending nuptials. Two nights before the ceremony, he threw his bachelor party in a private room above Hollywood's Roxy nightclub. Among others present at the party were his brother, Chris, actors Harry Dean Stanton, David Keith, Tom Cruise and Robert Duvall. Stripper "Kitten" Natividad, who entertained at the party, recalls, "Those guys were pretty drunk. They had a good time. But Sean didn't fall on his face, or anything. When he talked, he made sense. Sort of."

Sean told his friend Isaac Benson, also at the party, "Man, I don't know that I can go through with this thing."

"Do you love her?" Benson asked.

"Hell yeah, I love her," he said, sipping a Bacardi and Coke. "But we're gonna tear each other apart. We're nuclear, together, man. Nuclear."

"So maybe you shouldn't marry her," Benson suggested.

"Oh yeah? And then what?" Penn asked, raising an eyebrow. "She'll kill me for embarrassing her in front of the whole world, that's what. No," he decided after tilting back a beer. "I love her. So, I'm marrying her. God help me. Look, if the whole thing falls apart," he offered, trying to be optimistic, "at least I'll have acting, right?"

Then, the two friends toasted the upcoming nuptials. "Hopefully, no one will find out where the wedding is gonna happen," Sean said. "That's what Madonna wants. A nice, quiet ceremony."

✝

The Remaking of *Apocalypse Now*

It would seem that Sean Penn actually believed that Madonna wanted "a nice, quiet ceremony," the location of which was to be kept a closely guarded secret, even though such a concept was at odds with everything everyone else believed they knew about the publicity-hungry superstar. No address, location or telephone number was printed on the invitations, written by her brother Michael and printed on shocking pink paper. ("Please come to Sean and Madonna's Birthday Party. The celebration will commence at six o'clock. Please be prompt or you will miss their wedding ceremony." Those on the select list realized that the bride would turn twenty-seven on her wedding day; the bridegroom twenty-five the day after.) Guests were to be informed of the location by telephone at their homes or hotels less than twenty-four hours before the ceremony. Only key employees at the caterer, chair rental firm and florist were to know of the location of the ceremony. Delivery drivers were to be given the address only when their trucks were loaded and ready to go. Also, supervisors were to follow the trucks just to be certain that no driver stopped on his way to the ceremony to make a telephone call that (for a few bucks) would tip off any press people to what was happening, and where.

Of course, it didn't take long for word to get out that the Penn/Madonna wedding would take place outdoors on the very visible Point Dume, Malibu, hilltop property of real estate developer Don Unger on August 16, 1985, at six P.M.

Four days earlier, the couple took out a marriage licence. Sean Penn listed his middle name as "Justin," born August 17, 1960. His residence at the time was at 6728 Zumirez Road in Malibu. Highest school grade completed was twelfth. His father was listed as Leo Penn, mother Eileen Annuci. Occupation: actor.

Madonna filled in the same address as Sean's—they were living together at the time. Her occupation: entertainer.

In the days before the ceremony, there was a great deal of acrimonious discussion regarding Sean's refusal to sign a prenuptial agreement. Madonna's handlers were adamant that she should not marry without first having a "prenup" in place with her fiancé, and they pestered her until she finally—and, one might speculate, with some hesitation—asked Sean to sign one. He was adamant that he would do no such thing. "I equated it to a death warrant in a marriage," he explained, years later. Perhaps he knew that the request wasn't coming from Madonna; it was coming from attorneys and managers (whom he later referred to as "a bunch of pathetic idiots who were accusing me of trying to cash in, move in on Madonna's money. It was completely ridiculous, and it really pissed me off.") Sean must have quickly become concerned about what would be in store for him as Madonna's husband. "She had become a one-person megacompany," he said, "and all of those people were on the telephone with her every day, to make sure I wasn't looking for cash, as if I didn't have my own career. Buncha' chumps."

"Look, Sean, just sign the goddamn papers," Madonna told him in front of one of her attorneys.

"Fuck you, Madonna," he said, his tone acrid. "I ain't signing nothing."

"Then, I ain't marrying you," she told him.

"Fine," he said. "Fuck you, anyway."

"No," she countered. "Fuck you, Sean."

"No," he responded. "Fuck you, Madonna."

And on it went . . .

In the end, after all of the screaming and shouting, Sean did not sign a prenuptial agreement. The wedding plans were finalized, though to some observers it seemed that these two people barely liked each other, let alone loved one another. There wasn't much warmth between them. Sean was distant, Madonna aloof. They seemed to annoy each other. Still, the marriage was on. Perhaps in their quiet moments alone, out of the public eye, they shared something no one else was aware of, something that they may have interpreted as genuine love and trust: a foundation for a life together.

There was simply no way to ensure that the news of this marriage ceremony wouldn't somehow be leaked, despite the "precautions." Some of her friends joked that Madonna probably sneaked into a guest room and called the *National Enquirer* herself. In a matter of an hour, it seemed that practically every tabloid reporter in the Los Angeles area—more than a hundred of them in any case—congregated in front of Unger's $6.5-million estate, scheming to find ways to get a closer look, bribing caterers so that they could sneak onto the property. Media outlets began making deals with the locals to rent neighboring houses so that cameras with telephoto lenses could be implemented for exclusive photographs.

The wedding ceremony—complete with a celebrity-driven guest list of more than two hundred (including Andy Warhol, Tom Cruise, David Letterman and Cher)—turned out to be a highly publicized fiasco. Not only was the property surrounded by press, but photographers were hanging from the trees. Earlier, Sean had tried to convince

Madonna to allow the press a few quick photographs in private just to let some of the steam out of the event, but Madonna would not allow such a "photo op."

At first, the helicopters stayed five hundred feet above the wedding. However, as soon as Madonna walked out of the house, they came dangerously close to the ground, whipping the hair of the female guests with the power from their rotating blades. A cursing Sean Penn ran around the perimeter of the seaside mansion with a gun, shooting at the eight helicopters circling above. Madonna looked stunned. The naked hatred etched on her groom's bitter face must have been a startling sight. "I would have been very excited to see one of those helicopters burn and the bodies inside melt," he later declared. "They were non-people to me. I have never shot a firearm at anything I considered to be a life form."

"I realized then," Madonna would remember years later, "that my life would never be the same."

Madonna looked stunning in a strapless, white (!) $10,000 wedding gown (created by her "Like a Virgin" tour designer, Marlene Stewart), on the arm of her father, Tony, who gave her away. For some unknown, odd reason, under her veil—which she had to hold down to keep it from flying away—Madonna wore a black-rimmed hat. Under the hat, her hair was spun into a French twist. Sean wore a double-breasted $695 Gianni Versace suit. His tie was clumsily knotted. He had missed a few patches while shaving.

With their long dresses flying up, female guests began screaming as Madonna furiously shook her fists at the helicopters. "Welcome to the remaking of *Apocalypse Now*," said Sean Penn to the windswept guests. Then, the angry-looking bride and groom began shouting out their vows to Malibu judge John Merrik over the roar. In the middle of "I do take you," Madonna jabbed her middle finger upward. Sean's mouth was grimly set throughout the service.

The ceremony lasted five minutes, during which time the couple exchanged plain gold rings. Penn then lifted his wife's veil, and to the accompanying theme from *Chariots of Fire*, he kissed her as the guests stood and applauded. Afterward, on a balcony a few feet above the guests, Sean toasted "the most beautiful woman in the world." Then, he was to remove his wife's $700 custom-made garter. Delicately,

Madonna raised her gown so that Sean could find it. But, just as indelicately, Sean completely disappeared under the billowing skirts, where he acted as if he was scrambling about and having a difficult time finding the garter. Finally, he emerged with it. Madonna, her eyes twinkling, threw it out to the crowd, where it was caught by her sister Paula, who was also her maid of honor. (She handed it over to the young daughter of Madonna's manager.)

The wedding dinner—lobster in a white cream sauce, swordfish and a mixed vegetable side dish—was then held under a large tent on the front lawn of the home (of course!), catered by Los Angeles chef (and owner of the famous Spago restaurant) Wolfgang Puck. Three fully stocked bars, each eight feet long, kept the guests distracted from the continual noise of the circling helicopters. No live band played at the wedding reception—much to the amazement of some of the guests such as Cher who, in shocking purple spiked wig, said, "What? She couldn't afford live entertainment? We have to listen to records? I could listen to records at home! And without helicopters!"

At the reception, Madonna danced with the guests to records by Prince and Michael Jackson. Meanwhile, Sean seemed glum and depressed, much as he had seemed at his bachelor party.

Later, acting as if she was in a sour mood, Madonna called the wedding a "circus," as if that were a bad thing—a thing she hadn't counted on. "Damn them," she told one associate when speaking of the press's intrusion. "Damn them all to hell for ruining my special day."

"Really?" the associate asked her. "You didn't expect all of this to happen?"

"I didn't say that," Madonna answered, sheepishly. "But damn them, anyway," she concluded, with a smile. (Later, demonstrating either her sense of humor about the ceremony, or the fact that she really wasn't that upset about the way it turned out, she spoofed it hilariously on a *Saturday Night Live* sketch.)

In fact, Madonna had staged the ultimate press event. "What better to get on the cover of *Time*. And *People,* and *Life.* And every other magazine," Madonna's brother Martin Ciccone said. "It was all calculated. She's a marketing genius, no question about that."

"I thought it was a lovely affair," observed her father, Tony, fifteen years later. Perhaps only a father would be able to overlook the fracas in order to see the beauty of his daughter, in white, marrying the man of her dreams. He recalled that, just before she married Sean, Madonna asked him, "Are you proud of me, Daddy?"

"I have always been proud of you," he told her.

"Daddy, that's not true," she said. "Just be honest with me, for once."

"But why won't you just believe that I am proud of you," he asked her.

Tony would later recall that Madonna had tears in her eyes as she answered, "Because you never wanted any of this for me. You didn't even want me to be a dancer, let alone what I became. You just wanted me to stay home, go to college, get married and have children."

It was difficult for Tony to comprehend the reasons for his daughter's statements. While it was true that he had wanted her to go to college, he had simply never shown as much indifference to her career as she had repeatedly maintained he had. It was clear that something else was wrong, that Madonna had feelings of anger toward him about another matter. However, because father and daughter had never truly communicated their emotions in an honest, direct manner, the real source of Madonna's resentment toward Tony would have to remain unaddressed.

"Well, you're getting married now, aren't you?" Tony Ciccone concluded. "That's gotta count for something, doesn't it?"

✞

Shanghaied

After the wedding, the newlyweds moved into a Spanish-style canyon villa in Malibu with a stunning view of the ocean. The estate chosen by Penn sat on fifty acres; surrounding hills shielded it from prying photographers. Just to be on the safe side, Penn hired contractors to build a wall around the property, topped with spikes. "We're also going to have gun towers," Sean said, and only half joking.

Ensconced in her safe haven, Madonna then tried her hand at married life, even making halfhearted attempts at doing housework. Sean was bemused to come home with friends and find the queen of pop washing dishes. Laughingly, he would introduce his sponge-wielding wife as one of the richest women in America.

Like most young couples, the Penns had their share of first-year challenges. Of course, the difference between their relationship and those of most others was that Sean's and Madonna's was played out in the public eye. Because they were, arguably, the most famous young couple in the world, their spats—many of which took place in front of strangers outside the privacy of their home—always made for splashy headlines. Young, glamorous and exciting to watch—and unpredictable in every way—they were constantly followed by the press, spied on in restaurants and reported about as they went about the business of screaming at each other in public, which seemed to be a commonplace occurrence. Madonna, accustomed to the attention and even used to courting it, seemed to take the scrutiny in her stride. "Well, you have to expect a certain invasion," she said, "such as people walking up to you on the streets. But I draw the line when I get to my house. People hang out at the bottom of our driveway a lot and ring our bell constantly. They want to see us. They think we're going to invite them in for a cup of tea or something." Such intrusions drove the fiercely private Sean Penn to exasperation. In one interview, he scornfully observed, "I hate it. I hate those people. I hate the whole goddamn thing."

At this time, Sean entertained several ideas that would team him up with Madonna in a film. She wanted to be a movie star; he was already one. It seemed natural that he would help her to achieve her goal. Eventually, the couple settled on ex-Beatle George Harrison's movie *Shanghai Surprise*. The film—about a missionary in China—seemed doomed almost from the start. The script was lousy, and soon after filming began (Madonna and Sean had to fly to Asia for the production) the Penns started making changes to the story. At first they had great faith in their director, but they soon grew to despise him.

"We had the wrong script, the wrong director [Jim Goddard] and the wrong stars," George Harrison now says of the film. Of the Penns, he says, "Don't ask."

There was trouble off the set as well as the Penns continued to engage in almost daily battles with the press. Although they were both highly paid stars who relied on the public's interest and support for their livelihoods, Sean Penn seemed determined to keep himself and his wife from the media—he regularly brawling with and spitting at reporters and photographers, she looking on, beaming and seemingly bemused. They were already being tagged "the Poison Penns" by the time they flew to London for more work on the film.

Once back in America after the movie's completion, and against a backdrop of anger and hostility—toward each other as well as the outside world—the couple attended the premiere of Sean's latest movie *At Close Range* (for which Madonna wrote and recorded a song for the soundtrack entitled, "Live to Tell'). At the premiere, Madonna sported a new, gamine look: short hair, softer makeup and a short black cocktail dress. As they rushed into the theater, a reporter asked Penn, "Does your appearance tonight have anything to do with you trying to sort of patch things up with the press. Is that part of why you're here?" Sean stopped walking. He watched with a disgusted face as photographers jockeyed for position to get the best shot. Meanwhile, Madonna smiled broadly . . . this way . . . then that way . . . then, this way again . . . at the cameras that were pointed toward her. All about her, fans cheered and waved. "To the press that slams me," Sean suddenly announced, as his wife lapped up the attention, "I say, fuck you."

Considering the hoopla and interest surrounding the couple who had starred in it, the real surprise of *Shanghai Surprise* was that no one was interested in seeing it. *Rolling Stone* declared the film "Madonna's first flop," after the $17 million film grossed an embarrassing $2.2 million. Producer George Harrison blamed Penn and Madonna for the film's failure. Both of the movie's stars had refused to breathe life into the anemic box office by doing any publicity for it, and Madonna had even badmouthed it. "The director turned out to not know what he was doing," she complained. "We were on a ship without a captain and we were so miserable while we were working on it that I'm sure it shows . . ."

"I had just gotten married," she would say years later when talking about *Shanghai Surprise*. "It was still really new to me, and my ex-husband was really kind of railroading his way into the whole project. Because I was in such awe of him, I kind of let him make a lot of the decisions that I shouldn't have allowed him to make. I was so green. I just found myself in a situation where I felt completely bullied and out of control, and I didn't know what was going on, and it was not pleasant."

Of George Harrison, she observed, "He's a sweet, hapless kind of character without a mean bone in his body."

Sean was blunt about the experience, telling *Playboy*'s David Rensin, "[During filming] I just said, 'I don't give a fuck.' I just stayed drunk the whole fucking time. I was so pissed off and preoccupied with other things that it's the one time I took a movie entirely for the paycheck."

Friends noted that the failure of the movie marked the beginning of Madonna's ambivalence about her marriage to Penn. "The fights were incessant," says Todd Barash, a friend of Penn's at the time. "She stuck around, I think, because she thought there might be an 'up' side with the movie. But when the movie tanked, she began wondering what she was doing married to a temperamental guy who hated publicity."

What Sean didn't know at the time—but found out many years later—is that Madonna would often have her press agents call the media ahead of time to alert them of dinner or movie plans the couple had made. Then, when they arrived at their destination to find themselves surrounded by photographers, Madonna would act chagrined.

"My understanding of the direction that Madonna was choosing was a misunderstanding," Sean told David Rensin, choosing his words carefully. "And to the degree to which she would be choosing, and chosen for, such an intense spotlight was not something that I had seen in the cards. So that was a surprise. It was a big surprise. I started to get the idea very shortly after we were together, but by then there's that heart thing that gets involved, you don't walk away so easily just because something is a little difficult. And you don't know how long certain things are going to last. That might have passed. It could have just neutralized itself."

"When it all would blow up into a physical altercation between Sean and the media, she would become infuriated with him," said Todd Barash. "I was at their home the day after Sean had spat on a reporter, and he was still fuming about the incident. He was going on and on and, at one point, he said, 'What I don't understand is how the hell these guys know our every fucking move. Everywhere we go, there's a sea of fucking cameras!' "

Madonna was preoccupied with something else, on her knees organizing books on a bottom shelf ("They must be in alphabetical order," she had said, "or how will we find anything?") when, under her breath, she observed, "Well, look at who we are." The tone of her voice was distant and bored, as if she had said these words to Sean many times in the past. "We're stars, Sean. People take our picture. So, what's the big deal?"

According to Barash, Sean turned on Madonna. Standing above her, his face instantly crimson, he shouted, "And you love it, don't you, Daisy? [His nickname for her was "Daisy Cobb," which he had tattooed on one of his toes.] You can't get enough of it. You don't care how much it interferes with our lives, do you?"

Never one to back away from a good fight, Madonna stood up and faced him. Immediately, she seemed to be trembling with rage; it never took long for her to meet Sean at his level. "Look, I worked hard to get to a place where people care about me, and damn it, I'm going to enjoy every moment of it. So what? Get used to it, or get the fuck out!"

"One of these days, you're gonna have to choose," Sean countered, glaring at her. "It's gonna be me. Or them."

Her eyes blazing, Madonna reached out and grabbed Sean's arm. She dug her nails into his skin. He twisted away from her and yelped. "Jesus Christ, Madonna!" Then, he raised his hand. For a moment, it seemed as if he might strike her. Rather than recoil, though, Madonna took a step towards him as if daring him to smack her.

Perhaps because a witness was present, Sean took a breath and just shook his head. "You bitch," he said, massaging his arm. "I'm bleeding here. Look at this."

Ignoring his small wound, Madonna narrowed her eyes and opened her mouth to say something, but then checked herself. She returned his angry look with a steady, unblinking gaze. Suddenly, the mood changed. Madonna sidled closer to Sean and ran her finger down the side of his cheek. She nuzzled his neck. "I'm sorry, Sean," she said. "I choose you. Not them. You. I will always choose you." She dropped her voice to a confidential whisper, her manner unexpectedly conciliatory, and said something in his ear. His face lit up with a grin. They embraced.

✝

True Blue

It's been said that the third album is actually the most important one in an artist's career. Generally, recording companies aren't run by sentimental people. If a label asks an artist to record a third album, it is usually only because the first two were a success, not out of a sense of duty or loyalty. The debut album that finds an audience creates the need for a second album, which then serves to feed a suddenly acquired appetite. The role of a third album, however, is tricky and not so easily defined. The third time around, the artist can simply give his or her audience more of what was found on the last two albums and risk boring them, or explore new musical terrain and risk alienating them. Or, the artist can do what Madonna did with 1986's *True Blue:* build on the musical theme she'd already established in such an honest and creative fashion that the results actually reflect legitimate musical growth and maturity. She was getting a lot of attention because of her exploits with Sean Penn. However, there was more to Madonna than her headlines, and she wanted people to know as much. She was an artist and not a tabloid cartoon, though it was admittedly sometimes difficult for some of her public to reconcile the two.

In creating the recordings that were included on *True Blue*, Madonna again turned to Steve Bray, who obviously knew his ex-girlfriend's musical tastes well, in part because he actually helped to develop them. Of course, she knew his musical strengths as well, which is why she turned to him when she wanted to create up-tempo songs with a classic Top 40 commercial sensibility.

Madonna's other collaborator on the album was keyboardist/songwriter Patrick Leonard. Leonard had collaborated with her on "Live to Tell." Pleased with the outcome of that track, she decided that Leonard would be a great new musical voice with which to work. For the most part, Madonna worked with Bray and Leonard separately, with the three minds meeting on only one track.

One could sense that *True Blue* was a vehicle of growth for Madonna simply by looking at the cover artwork. The washed-out color photograph of Madonna with her head tossed back and eyes closed in seductive meditation is understated, especially when compared to the sexier poses with which she had been associated in the past. The album's inner sleeve didn't feature any photographs at all, devoted instead only to song lyrics and production credits, an indication that Madonna may have wanted to be best represented by just her work.

"Papa Don't Preach," the album's opening track, began with an odd, classical-sounding synthesized string arrangement that gave way to an urgent, driving beat. The song was written by Brian Elliot with additional lyrics by Madonna. How incredible it must have been for an unknown songwriter like Elliot to one day answer the telephone and hear that Madonna wanted to record one of his songs. Even though she contributed some lyrics to the tune, according to the credits she didn't even take a percentage of the song's lucrative publishing points.

"Papa" tells the story of a young girl who suddenly finds herself pregnant and insists to her stern father that she is "keeping my baby" and marrying her teenage lover. (The staid string arrangement at the beginning of the song might have been specifically designed to symbolize the parental authority of this girl's strict, doting father.) "Papa Don't Preach," as produced by Madonna and Bray, succeeded in telling a dramatic tale in the time-honored tradition of Top 40 tragic songs from the 1960s—such as Diana Ross and the Supremes' "Love Child" and "I'm Living in Shame," or either of pop/country artist Bobbi Gentry's hard-luck songs "Ode to Billie Joe" or "Fancy" (later recorded by country artist Reba McEntire). These kinds of records were usually about working-class people faced with simple but dramatic circumstances, songs that have the listener sitting on the edge of his seat while following the story and hoping for a happy ending. Madonna was rewarded for her skill at delivering such an intriguing tale—"Papa Don't Preach," the first single from *True Blue* went to Number 1 in the pop charts. ("Live to Tell," also featured on the album, had gone to Number 1 before "Papa," but was from the movie soundtrack.)

Before "Papa Don't Preach" was even issued, Madonna alerted the media that the song was bound to be an eyebrow-raiser by announcing that it was "a message song that everyone is going to take the wrong way." The storm of publicity that Madonna had predicted occured, of course, but in a way that may have surprised her. Conservative groups who had previously spoken out against Madonna's image, now applauded her for what they thought of as an antiabortion song. Meanwhile, her liberal supporters blasted her. Other groups, like NOW, attacked the song for (as they saw it) condoning teenage pregnancy. Magazines put her on the cover with headlines asking "Should Papa Preach?" and "Does Madonna's Hit Encourage Teenage Pregnancy?"

After two rather solemn singles, Madonna and Warner Bros. Records brightened matters for the fans by releasing the album's title song, "True Blue," one of two light-hearted, fun tracks for the project written and produced by Madonna and Bray which had a retro 1950s feel to it ("Jimmy Jimmy" was the other). "True Blue" soared to Number 3 on the pop charts, clearing the way for another Number 1 for Madonna, Leonard's big, anthemic production of a song she penned (with writers Gardner Cole and Peter Rafelson), "Open Your Heart."

Madonna may not be remembered in the annals of pop music history for having the greatest singing voice ever to grace a recording. That voice, however, will most certainly be noted for its emotional quality. In her own way, Madonna sold "Open Your Heart" as convincingly as Aretha Franklin sold "Respect"; as heartfelt as Barbra Streisand rendered "A House Is Not a Home." The record couldn't help but go to Number 1; it was a tune people could understand and latch on to, which is what makes a pop song memorable—when audiences adopt it and apply it to whatever they're going through every day.

Nevertheless, the pride of *True Blue* would turn out to be another collaboration with Leonard (and Bruce Gaitsch), the exotic "La Isla Bonita." An enchanting, up-tempo Spanish-themed song with an equally enchanting melody, "Bonita" was unlike any song Madonna had written or recorded before, its tropical attitude able to bring warmth even to the synthesized production. This romantic number went to Number 4 on the pop charts. (The music track for this song, composed by Leonard, was originally intended for Michael Jackson, but he rejected it.)

For her "True Blue" video, Madonna displayed a new look—leaner and blonder than ever before. Always searching for ways to improve herself, she had hired a personal trainer to assist her in a relentless exercise program. With trainer and bodyguards in tow, she would run ten miles a day, no matter what the weather conditions, in the hills when in Los Angeles and through Central Park when in New York. After the run, she would continue her exercise regimen by working out for another hour. She also took her diet seriously, sticking to a strict vegetarian menu with pasta and nuts, no junk food. Because of her grueling schedule, her trainer tried to include foods in her diet that allowed a protein and carbohydrate base.

In the end, *True Blue,* which went to Number 1 on *Billboard*'s album chart and would go on to become Madonna's most internationally successful album (selling seven million copies in the USA alone, and another thirteen million worldwide), wasn't a great album. A less intriguing artist might not have survived it. Even the organic percussion work of the legendary Paulinho da Costa could not help the record's musical identity rise above the cold, synthetic sound so typical of the "drum machine records" of the era. Nevertheless, several of its songs showed considerable artistic growth and fortitude on Madonna's part, keeping the Madonna phenomenon musically humming along.

✝

Trouble in "Paradise"

By mid-1986, twenty-eight-year-old Madonna's musical career was nothing if not monumentally successful; she couldn't have been happier with the results of her *True Blue* endeavor—artistically and commercially. Her personal life, however, was not as stellar; her marriage had fallen further into disrepair. The couple seemed to argue over everything, including her refusal to be tested for the HIV virus. At this time, there was much less known about HIV, and also a great deal of discussion about the pros and cons of being tested for it. Today, Madonna—an AIDS activist—would most certainly suggest that a sexually active person be tested for the HIV virus, and often. However, in 1986, she seemed just as confused about the dangers of deadly HIV as most of the population.

"But why should I get tested?" she asked Sean in front of two people from her management company. She was preparing to take "test shots" of the wardrobe that would be seen in a new video. Frustrated, she ran her hands through her new platinum pixie cut. "What if I'm positive?" she asked. "What then? I'm dead, right?"

"Well, if you're positive then at least I'll know, won't I?" Sean said, clearly annoyed at her.

"So, what are you saying?" Madonna pushed on. The two witnesses present became more uncomfortable with the exchange. "Are you saying that you won't make love to me if I'm [HIV] positive."

"Hell yeah, that's what I'm saying."

Madonna vanished. A few minutes later, she reappeared wearing a black corset tied tightly in the back with gilded breast cups, mesh stockings and high heels. She looked stunning. She could always manage to make the trashiest of outfits look classic. A designer's assistant walked out clutching what appeared to be a Norma Kamali fake leopard-skin coat. "Is this what you wanted?" he asked her, his tone tentative. Madonna ignored him.

"Well, then, all the more reason for me *not* to get tested," Madonna said, picking up the argument as if she had never left the room

Sean Penn took a beat to stare at his wife in her unusual wardrobe, perhaps admiring her elegance, her elusiveness, her impeccable style. She studied him, as well. Then, without releasing her gaze on him, Madonna snapped her fingers twice. A subordinate ran to her and placed a freshly lit cigarette between her lips. She puffed away. Sean smiled. "That's my wife," he said, dismissing the futile discussion in a tolerant fashion.

"Oh, screw you, Sean," Madonna said from the corner of her mouth.

"Yeah, well," he muttered, "not until you get tested."

In the summer of 1986, the epidemic hit home when artist Martin Burgoyne, a good friend and former roommate of Madonna's from her New York days, was diagnosed with AIDS. Madonna was devastated. Earlier, as a surprise, Sean had flown Martin and Erica Bell out to Malibu from New York for a party to celebrate the release of "Papa Don't Preach." Madonna immediately noticed that Burgoyne was not well. A few weeks later, he called her with the tragic news.

"She was beside herself," says Melinda Cooper. "From that point on, whenever Martin's name was mentioned, she would just begin to cry. She leased an apartment for him on West Twelfth Street, so that he could be closer to St. Vincent's Hospital, where he was being treated. She also arranged to take care of all of his medical bills, which would come to more than $100,000."

As a last-ditch attempt to save Burgoyne, Madonna asked Sean to fly to Mexico to purchase an experimental drug there, one that was not available in the United States. She hoped the drug would "cure" her friend. Of course, it didn't. Martin, only twenty-three, died in November 1986, just before Thanksgiving. At his bedside, Madonna held his hand until he passed away. She paid $4,000 for his memorial service.

Sean did what he could to console Madonna after Martin's death, demonstrating a tender, sympathetic side. However, his all too frequent jealous outbursts had become a significant problem.

One of the first signs that Sean's sometimes violent temper could be directed not only toward photographers but also toward his own wife had occurred before their wedding when he learned that she had once dated Prince. An argument about the rock star resulted in Sean punching a hole through the wall. Madonna has since said that she was stunned and frightened by the incident. "That's when I first saw the appearance of the demon," she said. "I should have known then that there would be trouble."

However, Freddy DeMann's assistant, Melinda Cooper, remembers a different story. "I went over to their apartment one day to pick her up for a recording session, and there was this huge hole in the wall," she says. "So I asked Madonna what happened."

Madonna told the story as if she was recounting the plot of an exciting soap opera on television. "Oh my God, Melinda," she said. "Sean found out about me and Prince, and we had this amazing fight. I told him to fuck off, that I can do whatever I want. He was so mad, he left the house, and then I slammed the door behind him. Then, he came back in," she continued, breathlessly, "and, I swear to Christ, Melinda, he was so mad at me, he punched this hole in the wall. Look at that? Is that cool, or what?"

"That's cool?" Melinda asked, examining the hole. "Madonna, that is not cool. That's scary."

"What are you talking about?" Madonna enthused. "I mean, how much must he love me, to punch a hole in the wall like that." (A couple of days later, Madonna telephoned Prince and told him to come to her home and fix the hole, "because you're responsible for it, after all." As instructed, Prince showed up with plaster, and repaired the hole.)

Now that they were married, Madonna didn't think Sean's violent streak was so "cool." When he became angry, he would grab one of his guns and fire off a string of shots at rabbits or birds. He walked around the house with a loaded .22 tucked into the back of his pants, which seemed to Madonna's concerned friends, if not to the lady herself, a form of emotional abuse.

One close friend of Sean's recalls what happened at a dinner party at the Penns' home. "We were at the pool. Sean had a little too much to drink. Madonna did, too. There was a guy there who had been eyeing her all night. Madonna went over and started flirting with him."

"What's this all about?" Sean said bitterly as he walked over to them.

"Oh, get lost, Sean," Madonna told him. "We're just talking."

Without a second's hesitation, Sean picked up his wife and, in one quick motion, threw her into the pool. The crowd of about thirty seemed stricken. As they watched, Madonna swam leisurely to the shallow end of the pool and then climbed its few steps. Dripping wet and without saying a word, she walked across the patio and into the house. "She never came back out," recalls the friend.

Earlier in 1986, Madonna and Penn were dining at Helena's, one of their favorite restaurants in Los Angeles, when an old friend, David Wolinsky (from the group Rufus featuring Chaka Khan), approached her at their table, bent over and gave her an innocent kiss in greeting. Immediately enraged by the gesture, Penn leaped from his chair and attacked Wolinsky, beating and kicking him. The attack ended only when shocked onlookers managed to restrain Penn. Madonna was humiliated. "She looked like she wanted to crawl into a hole," recalled one witness. "I remember watching her as she glared at Sean and thinking to myself, she's starting to hate him."

"He was a hothead," says David Wolinsky. "I did nothing but greet his wife, someone I knew before he had married her. It was completely unprovoked. I wondered what she was doing married to that creep."

Though her marriage with Sean seemed to be falling apart, she wasn't able to focus completely on repairing it for she was a busy woman with a thriving career. Constantly, she was distracted by the business at hand. "There's no time to figure out how to handle Sean," she despaired. "I barely have time to sleep."

Sean Penn had bounced back after the *Shanghai Surprise* fiasco and was busy at work on a gritty cop film, *Colors,* with Dennis Hopper. Meanwhile, Madonna was considering several scripts for herself. Influenced by her love for old Hollywood, she was keen to do a remake of Judy Holliday's smash 1950 comedy *Born Yesterday,* or Marlene Dietrich's star-making role in the 1929 drama *The Blue Angel.* As for new scripts, she was offered something called *Blind Date* and an early version of *Evita* (which would remain in development for years). However, she was most eager to appear in a film that had a Carole Lombard screwball-comedy flavor to it. Called *Slammer,* it was about a madcap blonde, Nikki Finn (Madonna), who, after being released from jail for a crime she did not commit, sets out to find the man who framed her. The usual screwball complications ensue, including chase scenes, mobsters and a 160-pound cougar. A deal was made; filming began in New York. Perhaps because Sean was now awaiting sentence on the assault charges, the name of the movie was changed from *Slammer* (which, her handlers reasoned, was where Penn was destined) to *Who's That Girl?*

Meanwhile, in Los Angeles, Sean's volatile temper continued to get him in trouble when he attacked a thirty-two-year-old actor on the set of *Colors.* As the young extra knelt on the sidelines with a camera, hoping for a good shot, Sean appeared from seemingly nowhere. He knocked the camera from the extra's hands. "You bastard," Sean snarled, "don't take any pictures of me between takes." Then, he punched him in the face.

✝

Who's That Girl?

Although Madonna would publicize the movie heavily, posing for many magazine covers à la Marilyn Monroe, *Who's That Girl?* would go on to become another box-office bomb, no doubt because its star was trying so hard to be so many different things she was not. By appropriating a Judy Holliday voice, along with Marilyn Monroe's hair and makeup for a movie that seemed somehow designed for Carole

Lombard, Madonna proved she was not up to any of the tasks at hand. *Variety* called the film "a rattling failure," while most of the other reviews were no better.

So far on the screen, Madonna had been most successful in *Desperately Seeking Susan,* a film in which she had exploited so many of her own personal characteristics—in essence playing herself. Had she continued to brand her performances with her own unique and, by now, identifiable persona (at least until she was more skilled at developing characters), her movie career might have ignited in the same way as her musical career. However, in trying to create a popular character for *Who's That Girl?* by imitating her movie idols rather than using her own personality, Madonna just came across as annoyingly cloying. "I don't like that movie," she would say in February 2000. "Don't like my performance in it. Any other movie I did, I would say there are things in it that are good. Or I think my performance was good, but the movie wasn't. *Who's That Girl?* I think all of it was pretty bad."

If Madonna was worried that the failure of the movie meant that her star was fading, she needn't have been concerned. After all, she still had that amazing recording career.

As soundtracks go, 1987's *Who's That Girl?* was not much of one in the conventional sense, but rather a collection of nine songs from the movie. While Madonna only had four tracks on the album, each was important because, conceivably, it meant the album could sell on the strength of her presence alone. Still a fresh commodity and successful at her career, twenty-nine-year-old Madonna was not only one of the hottest artists in popular music, but one with obvious and incredible staying power. *Who's That Girl?* was a relatively low-budget film with a cast of actors who weren't going to be receiving Oscars anytime in the near future, so to Warner Bros. Records, the soundtrack was at least as important as the film.

When Madonna was presented with the challenge of writing and producing the film's title song, she got together with Steve Bray and Patrick Leonard, her co-writers/producers, and went to work. Meanwhile, other slots in the album were filled mostly by obscure Warner Bros. Records' acts, like Club Nouveau, Michael Davidson and Scritti Politti.

It was of course Madonna who delivered the hits that kept the *Who's That Girl?* soundtrack out of record-store bargain bins. The title track and first single, written and produced by Madonna with Leonard, were quintessential Madonna music—funky, sassy and melodic, with a Latin accent. It wasted no time in going to Number 1 on the *Billboard* singles charts.

The soundtrack's second single, Bray's party "groove," "Causing a Commotion," did just that on both international dance floors and the U.S. singles chart, climbing all the way to Number 2. The other two Madonna tracks—"The Look of Love," an exotic Madonna/Leonard ballad, and the uptempo dance number, "Can't Stop," another Madonna/Bray creation—were strategically left on the soundtrack album to induce LP sales. It worked. The *Who's That Girl?* album ended up selling more than a million copies in the United States and five million worldwide.

Riding on Madonna's coattails proved profitable for everyone involved, including Warner Bros. Records, which notched up big sales with a compilation that was basically a showcase for its marginal artists; the artists and producers themselves, most of whom were never involved in a project as successful, before or since; and Peter Guber and Jon Peters, the film's producers, for whom the album's brisk sales served as the bright spot in a film enterprise whose overall success could be deemed modest at best.

Meanwhile, it was during 1987's "Who's That Girl?" tour that the public first saw Madonna's new updated, sleek look in concert—a look uncluttered by bangles, jewelry and other accessories (although Mr. Blackwell would still add her to his infamous list of worst-dressed women that year).

The "Who's That Girl?" tour was musically and technically superior to Madonna's first concert appearances in that she incorporated multimedia components to make the show even more compelling. For example, huge video screens projected images of the Pope and Ronald Reagan as she belted out "Papa Don't Preach." She had more confidence in her stage presence, her music was showing a deeper maturity, her voice was fuller, and the show was expertly choreographed with complicated numbers. She was mobbed in London, and in Japan a thousand troops had to restrain a crowd of 25,000 hysterical fans who turned up to greet her at the airport.

Many female artists behave like a diva for a period when they reach superstar status, and the "Who's That Girl?" tour marked the beginning of Madonna's. For instance, she wouldn't allow crew members to talk directly to her; they had to talk to her representatives lest they distract her from the business at hand. She has, to this day, a difficult time giving names to faces and so, rather than struggle to do so, she'd rather not meet anyone she's not going to have to know for a long period of time. (Early in her career, there were times when she wasn't able to remember the names of lovers the morning after. One assistant who accompanied Madonna during evenings on the town would be sure to place a note on her kitchen counter with the consort's name written on it, just in case she forgot.)

Her dancers too were told never to address her, a far cry from the rapport she would establish with her troupe later, on the "Blonde Ambition" tour. Her musicians were not permitted even to look at her, unless they were onstage with her. Moreover, when coming on and off the stage, Madonna demanded that road managers hold sheets around her in order to shield her from the eyes of those who couldn't help but stare at her because, after all, she was Madonna. Her dressing room at each stop along the way had to be redecorated to her specifications with new carpeting, fresh paint (always pink), new furniture . . . and so much Mexican food it would have taken an army to eat it all. "She has a way of demanding that compels you to give her your undivided attention," Freddy DeMann says, diplomatically.

One evening, at a very late hour, Freddy DeMann's assistant, Melinda Cooper, received a telephone call from Madonna. She was expecting a limousine to take her to a party, and it hadn't yet arrived.

"The goddamn car isn't here yet," Madonna said, fuming. "It's, like, fifteen minutes late, Melinda."

"It'll be there soon," Melinda recalls replying patiently.

"Why, you idiot," Madonna screamed at her through the telephone. "It's your job to get the limousine here on time, Melinda. Do you know how much I have to do?" she asked, her temper rising. "I have a lot to do, Melinda, and all you have to do is get the car here on time. And can you do it? No you cannot. What in the world is wrong with you, Melinda?"

"But, Madonna . . ." Melinda began.

"Don't 'But, Madonna' me," she said, interrupting her. "Look, here's the deal: if the fucking car isn't here in five minutes, you're finished."

Madonna hung up.

Melinda Cooper burst into tears.

✝

You Can Dance

In November 1987, Warner Bros. Records quickly followed *Who's That Girl?* with the one-two punch of *You Can Dance*.

In any business, there's nothing quite like the windfall created by being able to sell something to somebody twice and, in the recording industry, popular music is the gift that keeps on giving. At the major record labels, greatest hits and catalog sales packages (the various albums in an artist's career) have always accounted for a good portion of annual profits. In the 1980s, something else came along to enhance the companies' bottom lines: the "remix album." Thanks to the popularity of post-disco dance music, many fans now wanted to hear how some of their favorite songs would sound if the music was reworked, or "remixed," to enhance the song's danceability.

Remix albums—collections of already popular songs enhanced in the studio to alter their tempo and sound—are common today, but in the 1980s it was a revolutionary concept. The remix process itself was a holdover from the days of disco, when producers would remix pop/R&B recordings specifically for the disco market and then issue long-playing, twelve-inch dance singles of the songs in addition to the original, shorter versions. At first, the labels would supply these disco versions only to the DJs spinning records in clubs across the country. However, soon fans wanted to own the versions of songs they'd danced to the night before, so the labels made the versions available in record stores. Suddenly, the disco—and the club DJ—became a great catalyst for labels to promote dance music, in the way Top 40 radio (and later MTV) sells pop, rock and soul. The most skillful club DJs were often hired by the labels to remix the disco tracks, and, for some, remix assignments eventually led to them actually producing records.

By the eighties, with post-disco dance music in full swing, the remix concept had truly come into its own. By then, several artists' tracks were being remixed and compiled to make up an album. Madonna, the most important dance artist of the period, led the charge with *You Can Dance,* a compilation of remixes of seven of her more uptempo songs.

How does one bring more "danceability" to songs that were crafted specifically to get people onto dance floors in the first place? Probably by hiring remixers who are most familiar with the material, in this case, Jellybean Benitez. Also on board was Shep Pettibone, a popular remixer who'd earlier engineered more dance rhythm into Madonna's single "True Blue."

You Can Dance made one point clear about Madonna. While she was evolving into a serious pop star, musically she still knew how to host the best party. The new and pumped-up versions of "Holiday" (two different versions), "Everybody," "Physical Attraction," "Over and Over," "Into the Groove" and "Where's the Party" took *You Can Dance* to Number 14 on *Billboard*'s pop album chart. To further entice music fans, *You Can Dance* also featured "Spotlight," a previously un-released track recorded during the *True Blue* sessions. The album's performance both in the charts and in the clubs served as a testament to the quality of the material and the enduring appeal of Madonna.

With *You Can Dance,* Madonna may not have initiated a trend but she certainly played her part in jump-starting it. Soon, major acts of the day were following suit with remix LPs of their own, including Bobby Brown's *Dance . . . Ya Know It!* and New Kids on the Block's *No More Games/Remix Album.*

"I don't know that I like it," she would say, "people screwing with my records, remixing them. The jury is out on it for me. But the fans like it, and really, this one was for the fans, for the kids in the clubs who like these songs and wanted to hear them in a new, fresh way."

*

At the time of the release of *You Can Dance* in November 1987, Sean Penn had disappeared from Madonna's life for a number of days. She was frantic with worry. Then, he turned up unexpectedly at her New York apartment, expecting to spend Thanksgiving with her there. She probably didn't know whether to be furious or relieved. She chose the former. "You're not spending Thanksgiving here," she told him. She then informed him that she had already instructed her lawyers to draw up divorce papers. (Her attorneys filed those divorce papers on December 4, 1987. Twelve days later, though, Madonna would withdraw them.)

"She was completely distraught," said a friend. "She could see that the marriage was over, and she was really starting to get scared. 'I don't want a divorce,' she told me, 'but I don't know what else to do. I'm starting to really hate him. You know that saying that there's a thin line between love and hate?' she asked. 'Well, I think I've crossed it. It's very ugly on the other side, too.' "

Perhaps one of the reasons Madonna had such a particularly strong reaction to the problems caused by Sean was that her nerves were frayed by the discovery of a lump in her breast shortly before Thanksgiving. Because of her mother's death, Madonna has always been conscientious about self-examination for signs of cancer. When she found the lump, she feared the worst and called Dr. Jerrold Steiner, a respected Beverly Hills specialist, to make an appointment. She was so upset that she was unable to drive herself to his office and asked a secretary to take her. After examining her, the doctor told her to watch the lump and look for any changes in texture or size. He also suggested seeing her in two weeks to conduct tests. Madonna couldn't help but be frantic. Two weeks seemed an eternity to wait to handle something that so frightened her. Yet, she was so scared that she canceled the appointment and decided just to, as she put it to one friend, "sit still and try to figure out how to handle this."

No doubt, her troubled marriage did little to ease her nerves at this time. Madonna spent Thanksgiving with her sister Melanie in Brooklyn while Penn flew back to Los Angeles, where he indulged in a drinking binge. While she didn't say much about the scary lump during the holidays, Madonna did confide to friends that she was confused as to how to handle Sean and his erratic temper. Neither was really mature enough to be able to understand, or help, the other deal with the anger, hurt and insecurities that had turned them into the so-called Battling Penns. "I'm ashamed of how we turned out," Madonna told her friend. Then, perhaps romanticizing the past, she added, "I think back on our wedding and how wonderful that was. Then, I look at today, and I think, it's all turned to shit, hasn't it?"

✝

John Kennedy, Jr.

All artists are inspired by others, but perhaps no modern-day entertainer has borrowed as much from so many and with so few alterations as Madonna. Although her hard-as-nails personality, ambition and canny sense for publicity and business are all her own, her "reinventions" of her persona are more often than not inventions created by someone else and then borrowed for a Madonna makeover. In various points in Madonna's videos, movies, interviews and photo sessions one can see heavy traces of Marlene Dietrich, Judy Holliday, Twiggy and Lana Turner in her looks and attitudes. Even lesser-known performers such as Edie Sedgwick, Andy Warhol's decadent star of the sixties who starred in his underground films and died of a drug overdose at an early age, seem to have had a big influence on Madonna's various projects. But perhaps the biggest influence on Madonna's career has been Marilyn Monroe, the sex symbol from a generation earlier. Fans of both stars can't help but notice the impact Monroe has had on Madonna's career, in everything from hair and makeup, expressions and poses for the camera, all the way to paraphrased quotes in interviews. (In fact, some of Madonna's most famous photo sessions are exact replicas of Monroe's.)

Some critics commented that during the filming of *Who's That Girl?* Madonna looked as if she had stepped right off the set of *The Seven Year Itch,* one of Monroe's most famous movies— although Madonna did add a contemporary element to the look with a leather jacket. Sandra Bernhard, who was at one time extremely close to Madonna, went as far as saying that "she thinks she *is* Marilyn Monroe." (One of Madonna's funniest and most clever moments on television occurred in 1993 during a sketch on *Saturday Night Live* when she spoofed Marilyn's "Happy Birthday" song to President

John F. Kennedy, complete with skin-tight gown and bouffant blonde wig.)

Through the years, John F. Kennedy, Jr.—son of the late president of the United States—had also expressed his own interest in and passion for Marilyn Monroe. As he was growing up, it became well known that his father had indulged in an extramarital affair with Monroe, which, say his friends, seemed to fascinate John. As an adult, when John Jr. started his own magazine, *George,* he astonished many observers by featuring Drew Barrymore on the cover of one of the issues—dressed as Marilyn in a replica of the gown Monroe wore the night she sang "Happy Birthday" to his father at Madison Square Garden in 1962. Most people were amazed that Kennedy should pay homage to a woman who had indulged in an adulterous affair with his father.

Either they met at a party in New York in December 1987, as John had said, or at a "fitness salon" that same month, as Madonna has recalled. After one date, the dashing, dark, muscular Kennedy gave her a set of keys to his apartment. According to what Madonna once told a friend, John walked into his home shortly thereafter to find her lounging on the couch wearing nothing but sheets of clear plastic wrap, the kind purchased in the supermarket. He said later that he couldn't believe his eyes. After a beat, Madonna smiled lasciviously at him and purred, "Dinner's ready, John-John." (The press always referred to him as John-John, but family or friends never did.) That night, they laughed and danced and drank great quantities of wine.

Later, one oft-told story would have it that, while making love to her, John would apply peanut butter to her legs, and then lick it off. "Nonsense!" Madonna has said when asked if this story was true. "Do you know how many calories are in peanut butter? Low-fat whipped cream, yes. But not peanut butter."

*

Madonna may have found him fascinating, but she was not yet close enough to John Kennedy, Jr., to discuss the troubling lump in her breast that had ruined her holidays. No doubt it was on her mind. To whom could she turn?

One lonely evening, according to a later recollection, she picked up the telephone and called the one person she felt closest to, despite the shattered state of their relationship. Though there was such acrimony between them—and had always seemed to be, even before they were married—she still sensed that the one person who knew her best and could tell her what to do about this dizzying scare was Sean.

"Sean was distraught to hear about the lump," says his friend actor Stephen Sterning. "He told her that she simply had to have it looked at, have a biopsy done. He later said that she was crying on the telephone, saying she was frightened and didn't know what to do. So he offered to go with her, and that's what he did. They went to the doctor together. She had the biopsy. A few days later it came back negative. She was fine."

Said Sean at the time, "Nothing sobers a man like knowing your wife might have cancer. I finally got the message that I had to get serious about my life, about Madonna's life, about our marriage." He now believed that if they could only recapture the sexual passion they had felt for each other at the beginning of their relationship, she might change her mind and not divorce him. Still, he was not naive. He knew they had problems. "Ultimately, we had different value systems," he would say to writer David Rensin.

However, for Madonna, it was too late in 1988 to recapture anything with Sean. As much as she appreciated his support during a tough time—perhaps one of the most difficult in her recent memory—she felt that it would take more than the occasional medical crisis to keep them together. He had been the only real love of her life, but she was no longer comfortable being with him. She understood him all too well. Says Sterning, "She told Sean that she loved him still, but because of their differences, there was no way they should be together. She said that the cancer scare made her see even more clearly that life was too short not to be completely happy. Sean had to agree, actually. I think that little crisis made them both see the light . . . and, ironically, maybe in seeing that light it somehow brought them closer together as it pushed them closer to divorce."

*

"Will you look at how handsome Johnny is," Madonna told a friend over a martini lunch. She was holding a color photograph of Kennedy—a close-up—which she had carefully clipped from a gossip magazine. His face was raw-boned and lean. If ever a person had "bedroom eyes," this was the guy. "Have you ever seen a man this hand-some? Look at his face. Look at his hair."

Many years later, her friend ("Don't use my name or Madonna will kill me") would recall Madonna saying, "He's unbelievable. A perfect specimen. And look at that body. Who has a body like that? He's a god," she concluded with a sigh.

Again, her friend had to agree.

"Finally, I'm dating someone respectable, someone the public loves, someone I can be proud to be with," Madonna said. She signaled the waiter to bring her and her friend another round. "Can you see John Kennedy beating someone up and humiliating me in public. Now *that* would never happen."

"But what about Sean?" her friend asked. "You're still married."

Madonna's smile quickly faded. She folded the magazine photo-graph into quarters and put it away safely. "I don't know what to say about Sean," she said with a frown. "I love him. I'll always love him. He's the one person who knows the real me. But it's over. Oh," she concluded, wistfully, "to be a Kennedy. Do you think they have the kinds of problems I have?"

It seemed that "Johnny" felt the same about her. After a few months, as the relationship continued, he pinned posters of Madonna onto the walls of his Manhattan bachelor apartment, and even began to shed his Ivy League wardrobe for a look that he thought was more punk, and one that she would prefer: leather jackets, ripped jeans, spiked hair. He grew a goatee, which looked terrific and just a bit edgy. He told his friends that he was "crazy" about her. After a few months, John seemed to become all but consumed by his fascination with Madonna. He told Thomas Luft, a college friend from Hyannisport, that he couldn't stop thinking about her. "It's like she put a spell over me," he said. "I'm a little obsessed with her."

Madonna acknowledged that she now couldn't help but fantasize about divorcing Sean Penn and marrying into the affluent and influen-tial Kennedy family (a fantasy that the troubled Marilyn Monroe had often related in the last few years of her life). "To have a Kennedy baby was a goal Madonna had set for herself," says a former associate of hers, "and I heard from good sources that she did what she could to in-terest John in the proposition."

Sean had been a lot of trouble. She loved him, but how much more could she take, she must have reasoned. Kennedy was smart, sophisticated and . . . sensible. However, there would be one major stumbling block to the continuation of any romance between her and the heir to Camelot—and, as it happened, it would come in the form of the same woman who had put the kibosh on the president's affair with Marilyn Monroe: Camelot's queen, Jackie Kennedy Onassis. Indeed, any woman in John Jr.'s life prior to this point had always been measured by a formidable standard: his mother's.

In spite of the married Madonna's rather startling suggestion that John father her baby—an offer he chose to decline—his feelings for her continued to grow unabated. Steven Styles, a good friend of John's who attended Brown University with him, recalled John's fascination with Madonna:

"He telephoned me one day and sounded uncharacteristically depressed. He eventually confessed that he had fallen in love with a married woman who was a very celebrated personality. Conflicted, he said he didn't know what to do. He was torn by his desire for this woman and his need to conform to societal pressure that he find the so-called 'right girl', someone whom his mother and the other Kennedys would approve. And he said, 'Believe me when I tell you that this is not the right girl.' I asked him who she was. When he told me, you could have knocked me over with a feather. It was Madonna.

"He asked me if I wanted to be with him when he told his mother. I told him, 'John, I actually would prefer to be almost anywhere else.' "

"I know that she wants the best for me," Kennedy told Styles of his beloved mother. "But sometimes, that means I have to keep secrets from her . . . otherwise, I'd never be able to date. Let's face facts: no woman will ever be good enough for her. Unless she's royalty . . . but even then . . ."

☩

Jackie Kennedy Onassis, America's revered former First Lady, was already well aware of the whisperings of something romantic going on between her only son and Madonna. She used to purchase all the tabloids and other papers at a newsstand in the lobby of the publisher Doubleday's Fifth Avenue offices (where she worked as an editor) to keep up on current events, and that's where she first read the news about the growing romance. She quickly made it clear to John that she did not approve.

Thomas Luft, whose mother was close to Jackie, said, "He couldn't decide if he was intrigued by her because he liked her, or because Jackie *didn't* like her—not that Jackie ever met her. He said, 'I don't want to string her along if I'm really just rebelling against mother.' His therapist had told him that Madonna represented insurrection to him, not romance."

For her part, what most fascinated Madonna about John was his complete lack of pretense. "We were exercising with her, running through Central Park one day," recalled Stephen Styles. "She had four bodyguards trailing her. John, of course, had none. It was so ludicrous, I said to him, 'Why is it that she needs all of that security and you don't need any?' He laughed and facetiously answered, 'I may be a Kennedy but, hey, man, she's *Madonna!*'"

"He always introduced himself as just John, never John Kennedy," another college friend, Richard Wiese, remembers. "The word 'Kennedy' never came willingly off his lips. He downplayed it as much as possible . . ."

"Johnny, do you know how big a star you could be if you only acted like a Kennedy instead of just any other person?" Madonna told him. She was nearly unrecognizable in a baseball cap, scruffy hair, and a T-shirt belted outside cycling shorts. She was chewing gum, as John liked to say, "like it's going out of style." She said, "I mean, my God! You could be absolutely huge!"

"Oh, don't worry about me. I'm huge enough," John said with a grin. He, too, was in tight biking shorts and a simple white T-shirt. A baseball cap was turned boyishly backward. His chiseled cheeks were shadowed by two days' growth of beard. "I don't want to be a star," he said, dark eyes dancing. "I'm just me."

Madonna seemed stunned. "But how could anyone not want to be a star?" she asked.

"Count me out," John said, still jogging. "You can be the star in this family." Then, with a grin back at her, he sprinted off.

While dating Madonna, John moved into a two-bedroom apartment near his mother's penthouse on Fifth Avenue. As a surprise, Jackie hired a maid to help him organize his belongings. In the process, the maid apparently disposed of love letters Madonna had written to John. When John discovered the loss, he was angry because he thought that the maid had actually been following instructions given her by Jackie. However, those close to the family say Jackie had no idea what he was talking about when he confronted her about what had occurred. Also, she couldn't believe that her son would accuse her of such behavior. She chalked it up to Madonna's "bad influence on him."

When John finally told Jackie that he had fallen for Madonna, she made it clear that she was unhappy about this turn of events. Jackie had been concerned about her children's social status since they were young. Always protective of them, she was suspicious of most of their friends and unyielding in her demand that both John and his sister, Caroline, remain single until after graduating from law school.

"Jackie wanted her son to be with a woman of a certain breeding," said a Kennedy family friend, Senator George Smathers of Florida (who was also very close to President John F. Kennedy). "She wanted both of her children to be with a person of class. But John always gravitated toward movie stars and flashy types, a lot like his father. Jack Kennedy ended up with Marilyn Monroe and, somehow, John ended up with Madonna. I don't know which scenario most upset Jackie: her husband with Marilyn, or her son with Madonna."

If Madonna had been single, perhaps Jackie would have been better able to deal with the relationship (though, no doubt, she would still have been unhappy with Madonna's sexually charged image). She didn't want to have to deal with the scandal it would have caused if word had gotten out that John was dating a married woman. Also, according to those who knew her, she had heard stories—many of which were probably accurate—about Sean Penn's temper. She feared for her son's safety. But, says Thomas Luft, who witnessed the scene, John told

Jackie, "Mother, I can take that loud-mouthed little punk Penn blindfolded and with one arm tied behind my back." "And he could have, too," said Luft. Jackie shivered at the thought. "Oh, great! That's all I need, John," she said, "seeing you led away in handcuffs for getting into a fight with that hooligan. Don't you dare!"

Also, Jackie feared that Madonna might influence John to reconsider a future as an actor, something she definitely did not want to occur. He had appeared in a couple of plays in college and, though she attended the performances to demonstrate her support, she asked him not to become an actor. Her dream was to see her son as an attorney.

"I was there at her home on Martha's Vineyard when Jackie told John, 'I need you to think about this, carefully. Madonna may be a nice girl, but until she is single, she will be nothing but trouble,' " says Thomas Luft.

"But I like her," John said, trying to reason with Jackie. "She's quite intelligent. You should know her, Mother. You're an editor! She's just the kind of woman you would find fascinating."

Luft says that Jackie rolled her eyes and shook her head in what appeared to be complete dismay.

"My goodness, there are millions of intelligent women on this planet, John," she told him. "And you have to go out with the only one who calls herself a 'Material Girl'? I just don't understand it. I mean, really!"

"John got angry," says Luft. "Even though I was standing right there, and he never talked back to his mother in front of others, he shot back, 'Mother, let me ask you this: who in this world has been more materialistic than you?' "

Luft recalls that Jackie shot him a look. Then, without warning, tears came to her eyes. She rushed from the room. John was immediately overwhelmed by regret. "Mother, please, I didn't mean that," he said, following her. "I'm sorry." Then, for the rest of the day, he was angry with himself. "How could I be so stupid and mean," he said. "Stupid, stupid, stupid," he muttered, chastising himself. "But I like Madonna," he told Thomas Luft, "and, damn it, I'm going to date her."

One wonders if Madonna ever imagined the impact she had on these denizens of so-called Camelot . . . and if ever she would have believed any of it possible just a few short years earlier.

*

With Sean Penn in Asia filming *Casualties of War,* Madonna was free to explore a number of life options. In her personal life, there was the possibility of a long-term relationship with John Kennedy, Jr., though that seemed a long shot. As adorable as he may have been, she would later have to admit that something was "missing." She liked strong-willed, powerful men. John seemed too reliant on his mother, his family, for strength. She needed time to marshal her thoughts, but it did seem that her future with Kennedy had certain limitations.

Professionally, Madonna was considering a Broadway show which, she hoped, would allow her to shine so brightly that she would be able to eradicate the memory of the many bad reviews generated by her last two films. She wanted to prove that she could act. Film director Mike Nichols had mentioned to her a part in David Mamet's *Speed the Plow.* Madonna was a huge fan of Mamet's earlier works and has said that she went after the role in his new play "with a vengeance." She personally called Mamet and requested an audition.

The plot of *Speed-the-Plow* involved a plain, seemingly naive secretary, Karen (Madonna), who comes between two movie moguls (Joe Mantegna and Ron Silver) known for their production of surefire, commercial Hollywood films. Mantegna bets Silver $500 that he can bed Karen. However, she turns the tables by seducing him. She then tries to convince him to put up the money to turn a brainy, pretentious book she has been reading, one with absolutely no commercial appeal, into a film. Mesmerized by the dynamic woman masquerading as a plain office worker, he agrees to her request—almost enabling Karen to destroy the commercial deal that Mantegna and Silver virtually have in the bag. Madonna described her character as, "honest, sincere and naive, and hungry for power, like everybody else." Her observation proved that, at first, Madonna didn't even realize that her character was not what she seemed to be; she was anything but naive. "It was a real mind-fuck of a script," she discovered midway through rehearsals. "Little did I know that everyone else involved saw me as a vixen, a dark evil spirit."

Whether or not Madonna agreed with the interpretation of the role, her name on the marquee meant big business for the show. It sold out for six months in advance, which meant millions of dollars in ticket sales. Although the three-character play did much to confirm Madonna's drawing power, it did little to reverse critical reaction to her acting skills. Madonna's opening night on May 3, 1988, at the Royale Theater in New York City attracted celebrities such as Brooke Shields, Jennifer Grey, Jennifer Beals, Tatum O'Neal, Christie Brinkley and Billy Joel.

While the critics praised the play, they panned Madonna. "She moves as if she were operated by a remote control unit several cities away," said Dennis Cunningham of CBS, adding that "her ineptitude is scandalously thorough." John Simon of *New York* magazine complained that "she could afford to pay for a few acting lessons." The *Washington Post*'s David Richards said simply, "she's the weakest thing in it." Madonna, though, was happy with her performance. "It's like having really good sex," she said of the experience.

"I hated to love it and I loved to hate it," she said, later. "It was just grueling having to do the same thing every night, playing a character who is so unlike me. I didn't have a glamorous or flamboyant part. I was a scapegoat. That's one of the things that attracted me to it. Still, night after night, the character failed in the context of the play. To continue to fail each night and to walk off that stage crying, with my heart wrenched . . . it just got to me after a while."

Also in that first-night audience, perhaps to check out her son's latest romantic interest, was Jackie Kennedy Onassis.

"John told me that Jackie thought she was 'fascinating'," said Stephen Styles. "I asked him, 'What does that mean?' and he laughed. 'That's Mother's way of saying that Madonna isn't her cup of tea,' he said."

"Madonna didn't know Jackie was in the house [the theater]," said Diane Giordano. "If she had known, as fascinated as she was with Jackie, she might have had trouble going on, she would have been that nervous."

After the show, when Madonna *was* told that Jackie had been in the audience, she waited backstage for an hour, hoping the former First Lady would come back and say hello. She had applied a pale, almost white foundation to her face, which contrasted dramatically with her bright red lips. Carefully she penciled in her eyebrows and then shaded her beauty spot. She pulled her dark hair back severely and dressed in a natty, gray, pinstriped Armani trouser suit with a white silk blouse—buttoned all the way to the top. Three friends joined her. Someone fixed martinis. Then they waited . . . and waited. Jackie never showed up.

Later, Madonna would say that Jackie's absence backstage "ruined" her opening night. "The only reason a person doesn't come backstage after a show is if they didn't like what they saw and don't know how to tell you that," Madonna said, sadly. "If I had only known she was out there, I swear to God, I would have been much, much better. I would have tried so much harder. Why didn't Johnny tell me she was coming?"

Madonna loved a good icon, always had. She was such an admirer of Jackie, she desperately wanted her approval, especially now that she was dating her son. She was certain, she told friends, that she would be able to convince Jackie that she wasn't as notorious as the former First Lady believed her to be. However, Jackie steadfastly refused to meet her. "How can she not take my calls?" a perplexed Madonna was reported as having said. "Doesn't she know who I am?"

Privately, Jackie told a colleague at Doubleday, "I don't want to validate the relationship by meeting her. I'm not going to have her going around saying that she and I are friends." If circumstances had been different, no doubt Jackie would have wanted to meet Madonna and discuss with her the writing of her memoirs for Doubleday, just as her son had observed. In fact, she asked certain people in the publishing company's editorial division if they thought Madonna had a compelling story to tell. She was told that such an autobiography would definitely translate into a best-seller. When she asked for details, she was duly intrigued but also more sure than ever that this woman was not for her son. "Yes, she has had an amazing life," Jackie said to a source, "but I simply don't want my son to now be a part of it."

In July 1988, Madonna pleaded with John to arrange a meeting with his mother. Two other people were present at John's Upper West Side apartment in New York with John and Madonna while they engaged in a conversation about meeting Jackie. John was in red sweats and a black T-shirt with the words "Man Power" emblazoned across his chest in big, white letters. In an odd contrast of fashion, Madonna wore a slinky, short black dress that appeared to be designed by Yves Saint Laurent, with heels. She was smoking. John never smoked. He asked

Madonna why she was so certain his mother would be interested in meeting her. His tone, the witnesses recall, was sarcastic and inconsiderate.

Madonna, as per usual, was unruffled. "She'd want to meet me because I'm Madonna," she said, exasperated. "Who wouldn't want to meet me? After all, John," she concluded, "your mother is probably the only woman on earth more popular than I am."

"Can't happen," John declared. "Mother would make sure we never see each other again if she meets you. I can guarantee it."

No doubt, the fact that Jackie Kennedy Onassis refused to meet her tapped into Madonna's deep inferiority complex. Beneath all of the bravado, she has always been insecure—it doesn't take a psychiatrist to discern that much about her. During this time, she kept saying to friends, "His mother would love me, if she gave me a chance." Jackie's refusal even to give Madonna "a chance" quickly became a source of hurt for her. Then, as often happened in her life, hurt turned to anger. By the end of 1988, Madonna told friends that she was bored with John.

Besides the Jackie factor, another issue in her relationship with John was her communication with him. One had to know how to deal with John Kennedy, Jr., when he was angry. John was a shouter. If he was upset, he'd scream at full volume, his own face just inches from the object of his aggression. Though such a thing could be daunting to some people, it certainly was not to Madonna. She was equipped with the skills to handle this kind of explosive personality, simply because of who she was married to and what she put up with on an almost daily basis. However, for some reason, she didn't seem to be able to meet John at that hot level during a disagreement. Perhaps she was awed by him because of his family's almost regal history. Maybe she wished to appear dignified in his presence. Or, maybe she just didn't care enough about him, didn't feel passionate enough about him, to engage in the kind of fracas with him that she would customarily have with Sean.

Apparently, a defining moment in Madonna's relationship with John occurred when he thought she had told someone else something personal about him—and that this person had then gone to the press with the information. When Madonna denied having done as much, he didn't believe her. "What the hell is wrong with you?" he screamed at her at full volume in front of friends. Everyone in the room who knew Madonna held on to his chair for dear life, probably expecting the outbreak of World War III. However, instead of firing back as expected, Madonna was quiet. Her startled expression indicated that she was stunned by John's outburst. She dropped her eyes, unable to meet his accusatory gaze. Then, she ran from the room. This was odd behavior from a woman used to taking as much as she could dish out in an argument. Mystified by her conduct, John turned to his friends and sputtered, "What'd I say? What'd I say?"

After that incident, Madonna seemed to lose all interest in John Kennedy, Jr. Some intimates believed she thought he was a "hothead," and since she already had one of those at home she didn't need another. Others said that the intensity of the physical intimacy they shared had waned and it now wasn't worth her tolerating him and his domineering mother. Madonna didn't say much about any of it. To one friend, she called the situation with Kennedy "toxic and sad," and said "I needed out of it." She asked that friend, "Don't you think the need for companionship is a weakness? Because I do. And I refuse to be weak."

After a two-week cooling-off period at the end of July, John invited Madonna to dinner at a trendy West Side restaurant to discuss their relationship. According to law school classmate Chris Meyer (whom John brought to the dinner because, as he put it, "I don't want to be alone with her. She scares the hell out of me.") John told Madonna that he was sorry for all that had happened in their relationship concerning his mother. He hoped that they could still be friends. He also indicated that there could be nothing more than that between them because his mother would not approve, "and her approval means everything to me."

"Madonna was annoyed by the whole thing," said Chris Meyer. "He thought he was letting her down easy, but she was clearly finished with John. He didn't need to be gentle with her. My impression of her was that she had already given him the heave-ho in her mind, anyway. John's ego, though, would not allow him to believe that she had lost interest."

A week later, Chris Meyer had an appointment with an attorney at the same New York high-rise that houses Doubleday when he happened upon John Kennedy, Jr., in the men's room. John was probably visiting Jackie at work. As they stood beside each other at adjoining urinals, Meyer asked Kennedy about Madonna. "How's it going, buddy?" he wanted to know. "Is it really over with Madonna?"

Staring straight ahead, Kennedy smiled thinly and said, "She's great, but, yes, it's over between us, Chris."

"Because of your mother?"

Kennedy shrugged. "Not really," he said, sounding vague. "But any excuse will do, I guess. That's as good as any other when you're trying to break it off with someone gently."

"Wow," Chris said. "Too bad."

Without a reaction, John zipped up, walked over to the basin and washed his hands. As he dried off with a paper towel, he turned to Chris who was finishing up at the urinal. "We had some good times," John observed. "I like her a lot. Oh well. Easy come," John said while crumpling the towel, "easy go," he concluded as he tossed it into a trash can.*

✞

Sandra Bernhard

During the 1988 run of *Speed-the-Plow* Madonna had a dream that she and actress/comedienne Sandra Bernhard—a casual friend whom she had met a few years earlier—had survived a catastrophe and were the only two people left on the planet. Madonna had always placed importance on her dreams. She enjoyed sharing with friends the details of her nightly dreams and also recorded them in journals. So, she was astonished when, a few weeks later, she went to see Bernhard's Off-Broadway play *Without You I'm Nothing* and heard one of her monologues referring to the comedienne's fantasy that she and Madonna had survived World War III and were now indeed the last two people on earth.

Madonna had actually first met Warren Beatty and Sandra Bernhard at the same party, at Beatty's home, both of them introduced to

---

* John Kennedy, Jr., and his wife of nearly five years, Carolyn Bessette (along with her sister, Lauren), were killed when the private plane he was piloting plummeted into the Atlantic Ocean in the summer of 1999. John, Carolyn and Lauren were all buried at sea on July 22, 1999.

her by Sean Penn. "We met and got to know her when she came to see my show," Sandra now recalls, "and she really enjoyed it, so she came backstage and we really hit it off. We just started becoming friends, that's all. Before that, she was someone I just knew through Sean. I was always fascinated by her. When I would see Sean at a party and she was there, she would give me the evil eye, like she thought maybe Sean and I were fucking. But we weren't."

In Bernhard's dressing room after the show, Sandra told her, "I can't imagine being you." Unfazed, Madonna—wearing a white Chanel dress that exposed plenty of cleavage—replied, "I can't imagine being *you.*" Madonna so enjoyed Bernhard's act, she even toyed with the idea of playing herself in the movie version of Bernhard's play (which never happened).

In the five years since Madonna had first come to prominence, she had become accustomed to the fact that she could not be harmed by scandal. In fact, any controversy to which she was attached merely added another layer of intrigue to her infamous image . . . and that usually meant more money in the bank. When one of her backup dancers expressed concern that being involved in a steamy dance scene with Madonna might damage his career, Madonna lectured: "The more notorious you are, the more you're going to work. Don't you guys understand that?" She certainly understood it, and exploited it better than any other performer. Now, Madonna may have decided that her friendship with the openly bisexual Bernhard gave her a new act, something else to get her name in the papers and to start Middle America's tongues a-wagging: lesbianism.

Within weeks of their growing friendship, Madonna was immersed in a lesbian subculture, socializing in New York "girl bars" and showing up dressed in the same gay fashions as her "gal pals." Bernhard and Madonna added Jennifer Grey to their small band of carousers and, in a take-off of Sean Penn's "Brat Pack" status, they dubbed themselves the "Snatch Batch." The gals began an "in your face" promotion of their "lesbian" exploits—leading to gossip that Madonna and Bernhard were having an affair. When asked by reporters, Madonna encouraged the gossip, giggled and blinked and only halfheartedly denied the rumors. A gleeful Bernhard—getting the most publicity of her career so far—played along.

"She is probably one of the world's sexiest women," Sandra told a reporter for *Penthouse*. "She's worked hard at it and done some interesting things with it. Despite all of the mixed messages people think she gives, she's one of the smartest women in the business—and most disciplined—and I really admire her. I think what she has done is great, and that makes her sexy to me."

The witty and talented Bernhard had a reputation for her wild antics and vulgar mouth. When Bernhard was booked on David Letterman's *The Late Show with David Letterman*—taped at Manhattan's NBC studios—Madonna tagged along. Bernhard appeared first and Letterman wasted no time in asking her to "talk about your new good friend Madonna. Is there any truth to this nonsense?"

"A tad," was Bernhard's response. "A hair."

When Letterman asked Bernhard what they did when they went out, she replied, "We party and we get crazy. We drink tequila, we talk about old times, and we get to know each other a little better. What do you think you do with a girlfriend? What do you do when you go out with your girlfriend?"

Then Madonna made a grand entrance, wearing an outfit matching Sandra's—knee-length jeans, a simple white T-shirt, black shoes with ankle-high white socks. Ever impatient for a media fracas, Madonna wanted to get the ball rolling. "Let's talk about me and Sandra," she instructed Letterman.

Letterman, tactfully prying, asked Madonna for her version of what she and Sandra did when they were together, and he wondered if he could be a part of it. "If you get a sex change," Madonna shot back. Her posture was all masculine, legs spread apart, slouching. There was nothing traditionally feminine about her at all.

"We meet up," Bernhard interjected, "sometimes with Jennifer Grey, sometimes just the two of us. You usually find us at the Canal Bar or at M.K [two lesbian bars]."

Madonna pushed it farther: ". . . en route to the Cubby . . . ," leaving Bernhard to finish with "Hole."

Bernhard whipped the little act to a fever pitch by claiming she had slept with both Sean and Madonna.

While sprawled all over the set's furniture—practically reclining on it rather than sitting on it, and with their legs wide open—the two spoke over one another, laughed at each other and at Letterman, and were raucous, rude, annoying and unappealing in every way.

"We just thought it would be fun," Sandra now explains. "She had never done Letterman before, and she was afraid to do it on her own, so I said, 'Look, come on with me and we'll fuck with him, and with everyone else.' It turned out to be a lot crazier than I think either of us expected, though. I really think we were great guests, even though David looked like the whole thing confused him."

Judging by what she said and did, Madonna didn't seem concerned about what her husband, Sean Penn, still filming *Casualties of War* in Thailand, would think of her latest promotional hook as a lesbian. She realized, no doubt, that the international publicity and worldwide attention generated by such a surprising twist only served to benefit her career, which, to some observers, seemed as urgent a concern to her as anything else in her life at this time. The fact was that Madonna had never even been to the Cubby Hole. By this time, though, Madonna was well aware that many of her staunchest supporters were homosexual men, and that even a hint that she herself was gay would only strengthen their loyalty and devotion. Soon, she began appearing in gay-oriented magazines as an activist for gay rights, and was even named in the book *The Gay 100* as one of the most influential gay people in history.

According to Madonna the press "failed to get the joke." Madonna would also claim that she and Bernhard were just "fucking with people's minds," though some of her friends insist that at this point in her life Madonna was once again exploring her bisexuality, especially after seeing the odd couple fondling themselves and grinding their bodies together while singing the Sonny and Cher song "I Got You Babe" at a New York benefit. Perhaps she was so unhappy with the way matters had turned out with Sean Penn and John Kennedy that she decided to try something different. Or maybe not. Only she would know—and she has denied it. Because Madonna has been frank about her bisexual nature, one has to assume that if she and Sandra—who is open about her own sexuality—were having a romantic relationship, she would have said as much. After all, she's talked in the past about some of her other dalliances with members of the same sex.

One of Madonna's first experiences with a female was with twelve-year-old Moira McPharlin. Madonna was the same age. During a sleepover, she and Moira stripped naked and began to explore each other's bodies. Madonna says that Moira was the first to show her how to insert a tampon. She said that, prior to Moira's influence, "I put it in sideways and was walking around paralyzed one day." Of course, through the years she had many other dalliances with women. "Let me tell you this much," says Erica Bell, her close friend, "I was fascinated by her long before she kissed me. But once she kissed me, wow! When you've been kissed by Madonna, you have definitely been kissed."

When Penn returned from filming *Casualties of War* that August, he was not amused at the latest scandal his wife's actions had generated. He disliked Sandra Bernhard as much as she disliked him, but Madonna managed to placate him enough for the two of them to call a truce and celebrate her thirtieth birthday.

In September, free of her commitment to *Speed-the-Plow*, Madonna returned to Los Angeles to begin work on her next album, which she hoped would unveil a new maturity in her work. Wanting to be near his wife, Penn accepted a role in the new hit play *Hurly Burly*, but only if it could open in Los Angeles. Although friends like Sandra Bernhard advised Madonna to leave the emotionally abusive Penn, Madonna confessed, "I still love Sean." While they both worked on their respective projects, the couple had another shot at making the troubled marriage work: Sean moved back into the home he had shared with Madonna in Malibu. The reconciliation was, however, short-lived.

The author observed the two of them in action backstage at the Westwood Playhouse, where Penn was appearing in *Hurly Burly*. Madonna showed up with Sandra Bernhard, both women wearing matching black trouser suits with plunging necklines. "Eat your hearts out, ladies," Madonna said to a couple of female fans who began snapping photographs. "This one's mine," she added, motioning to Sandra.

When Sean spotted Sandra, he went into a slow burn. "I see you brought your little girlfriend with you," he told Madonna.

"Now, Sean, don't get started," Madonna said with a smile, trying her best to be sweet to him. "This is your night, after all. Be nice." She blew a puff of smoke from her cigarette into the air and then struck a pose for one of the camera-wielding fans.

Madonna and Sean never allowed the presence of admirers, photographers, reporters or anyone else to stand in the way of a noisy, marital spat. "If it's my night, then why'd you bring *her* with you?" he countered angrily, motioning toward Sandra, who stood in the background glaring at him and sipping a Diet Pepsi. The two eyed each other with disdain. Then, there was a sudden strong smell, suggesting that someone had just broken wind.

"Sean, that's disgusting," Madonna said.

"It wasn't me," he said, defensively. "It was her," he added, pointing to a sheepish-looking Sandra.

"You know what your problem is?" Sean continued, turning his anger on Sandra. "You're a little instigator. You like to start trouble, don't you? You like to see me pissed off, huh? You like the *drama*."

Sandra held up a silencing hand. She said nothing.

"And you never fail to give it to her, or to me, do you, Sean?" Madonna said, glowering at her husband. "Can't we just have a nice time? Why are you trying to pick a fight with us?"

"What are you talking about? You're the one who showed up here with your girlfriend," he said, angrily.

"Oh, forget you, Sean," Madonna countered, ignoring Sean's truculence. She took a final drag on her cigarette, threw it to the ground and dug her heel into it. Perhaps she sensed a need for a tactful resolution to the public scene. "Sandra and I are going to Crayons [a bar in Westwood]," she said. "If you want to join us, you're welcome to do so. If not, then I guess I'll just see you in the morning."

As his wife and his nemesis walked away, Sean Penn shook his head negatively and spat on the ground. "Women," he said, annoyed. "Why couldn't *I* have been born gay?"

✝

Dinner with Warren

Despite her phenomenal success as a recording artist, Madonna still dreamed of critical respect as a film actress. She no doubt realized that her stint on Broadway had done little to make her more marketable as a Hollywood actress. Typically, she kept her eye on her goal and instructed her film agents to continue the search for properties in which she could appear, roles for which she might be suited. In the fall of 1988, a part came her way in a film she knew she couldn't resist, a new

Warren Beatty movie which was in the process of being cast. The film, *Dick Tracy*, was based on the popular comic strip character and had all the makings of a top-grossing film, something Madonna wanted in her career about as badly as she wanted anything at this point in her life. Her role as the sexy femme fatale, Breathless Mahoney, seemed tailor-made for her.

The problem was that the quality of Madonna's acting work in past screen endeavors did little to warm Beatty to the idea of her playing opposite him as the film's Mahoney. He favored Kathleen Turner, whose sultry voice had added steamy dimensions to the character of Jessica Rabbit in *Who Framed Roger Rabbit?* The beautiful Kim Basinger had also been smashing in a similar fantasy movie, *Batman*, and Beatty thought she could contribute the same kind of sexual glow to the female lead in *Dick Tracy*.

When Warren Beatty wanted to go out with Madonna to discuss the movie, she put him off. "It took me weeks to get a date with her," he once recalled.

In her book *Sex*, published in the 1990s, Madonna explained that, in her view, "The best way to seduce someone is by making yourself unavailable. You just have to be busy all the time and they'll be craving to see you. Then, you don't fuck them for the first five dates. Let them get closer and closer, but definitely don't fuck them."

When Madonna allowed Warren to take her out for dinner at the Ivy restaurant in Los Angeles, she finally turned on the charm in order to get him to see her in the role. Wearing a sleek, black leather jump-suit—unzipped in a revealing manner—with a matching leather cap, she asked a lot of questions. She was clearly trying to find out new information about him, weaknesses, anything that could prove helpful. He did the same. According to Beatty's later recollections to friends, Madonna said, "I know you've heard a lot of terrible things about me, and I'm here to tell you that they're all true." She laughed. "How about you?" she asked. "I've heard a lot about you. True?" Warren didn't answer. "Just as I thought," Madonna said. "All true."

Warren later said he was instantly struck by Madonna's humor. She was entertaining, and sexy—perfect for the role for which she was auditioning. He kissed her on the doorstep, after he dropped her off. "Houston," he reportedly said, after kissing her, "we have lift-off."

"He thought she was pretty great," said a friend of Beatty's. "He hired her on the spot."

The truth is, however, that both Kathleen Turner and Kim Basinger were unavailable at this time. Beatty could have continued looking for his Breathless Mahoney or he could just hire Madonna. He clearly didn't think she was worth much as an actress, though, because he asked that she essay the role for Screen Actor's Guild scale wages of just $1,440 a week. So, in effect, Madonna's participation lowered the film's budget considerably since neither Turner nor Bassinger would ever work in a $60-million budget film for less than $2,000 a week— nor would any popular actress, except one smart enough to know that such a decision could be a brilliant career move. After all, *Dick Tracy* boasted top production values; and along with Beatty an all-star cast including Al Pacino, Gene Hackman and Mandy Patinkin, with cameos by Dick van Dyke, James Caan and Charles Durning. As a splashy summer-release Disney film, it was almost guaranteed to do big business. Madonna realized that if, by some fluke, the movie flopped, it could hardly be blamed on her since she was only one star in an ensemble piece. However, if it was a success, she would be credited with having had her first screen bonanza, and she could use it to demonstrate her box-office appeal. Also, Madonna's deal had it that, in return for her small fee, she would receive a percentage of the film's profits. For Madonna, therefore, *Dick Tracy* presented a win-win situation. She was savvy enough to see it just that way and eagerly accepted a contract that was viewed by some observers in the industry as an insult, especially considering her status in the entertainment field.

✝

Malibu Nightmare

By Christmas 1988, Madonna's marriage to Sean Penn was more than three years old. To say that the forty months since their August 16, 1985, union had been difficult would be an understatement of epic proportions. Penn's drinking and his violent temper had been more than Madonna could handle, and by the end of 1988 the marriage was all but over. She said that it was as if she had married a child in a man's body, someone who operated on the emotional level of a ten-year-old.

By this time, of course, Madonna fully understood that Sean Penn had a drinking problem, and that this made it impossible for him to focus on saving their marriage. His temper was more unpredictable than ever. For instance, after one bitter argument, he threatened to drown their dog, Hank. Somehow, Madonna managed to change his mind. The next day—at the suggestion of actor Robert Duvall—she personally drove Sean to Palm Springs to the Betty Ford Center where, she hoped, she could convince him to dry out. They signed in as Mr. and Mrs. Victor Cobb, but after speaking to counselors, they realized that the chances of keeping Sean's presence there from the press were negligible. They weren't even halfway back to Los Angeles on the two-hour drive home when calls began coming in on their car telephone from Madonna's manager Freddy DeMann, telling them they had been recognized at the Betty Ford Center. "But how did anyone know?" Madonna remembered asking Freddy. "Someone must have told someone."

"The press is psychic when it comes to you," he told her.

Once back in Malibu, Madonna didn't know what to do about Sean. "I have to help him, I know. But he doesn't want any help," Sandra Bernhard would later recall her saying. Sandra had flown to the West Coast to spend the Thanksgiving holiday with Madonna.

"I don't know what to do," Madonna continued. "His drinking is wrecking our marriage. He pushes me away. I'm miserable."

"Let me ask you a simple question," Sandra asked her. "Do you ever have fun?"

"What do you mean?"

"Fun, Madonna. Do you and Sean ever have fun?"

Madonna looked dispirited. She had answered her friend's question, and without saying a single word.

"Then he's got to go," Sandra decided.

Madonna said she agreed, even though she and Sean had been thinking about having a baby to save their marriage. She had promised him that 1989 would be the year that they would start a family. She feared having Sean's child, she said, because she didn't want a baby to be raised in a broken home, "and we are nothing if not broken," she added tearfully.

"You're crazy if you bring a kid into this mess," Sandra said. "I'm telling you, he's got to go."

After another fight, Madonna asked Sean to move out. He moved in with his father, director Leo Penn. A few days later, on the morning of December 26, Sean telephoned Madonna to discuss the state of their relationship. During the conversation, Madonna told Sean that she had decided not to have his baby. In signing a contract to appear in *Dick Tracy*, she explained, she would have to postpone a family for another year.

According to documents she would later file with the Los Angeles County Court House, Madonna said that Penn was "disgusted and pissed off" with her after that conversation, and they engaged in a heated argument.

"It's over," Madonna told Sean on the telephone, she later remembered. "I want a divorce. I *need* a divorce."

When she hung up the telephone, she must have been shaking.

That afternoon, Madonna telephoned John Kennedy in New York. Recalls Stephen Styles, "By this time, John and Madonna had cooled their own romance, but she was still depending on him for emotional support. She asked him to fly to the West Coast and help her solve some problems related to her marriage." According to Styles, Madonna further explained to Kennedy that she needed "moral support to get through this time in my life."

John decided not to fly to California. "I think he didn't want Madonna depending on him," said Stephen Styles. "He was afraid that if he came to her rescue every time she called, they would end up back in a relationship—which would only upset his mother, and he didn't want to do that. He felt badly about it, but he also felt he shouldn't just drop everything and be at Madonna's beck and call.

"Instead, what he did was track down Sean," says Stephen Styles. "He had his cell phone number. Madonna had given it to him, earlier. And John called Sean and said, 'If you lay one hand on her, I will come out there and pulverize you, you little punk.' He actually threatened him with bodily harm. Penn was furious and told him he would call the cops on him. So, John backed off. He didn't need that kind of attention."

(Adds Stephen Styles, "John told me that he ran into Sean Penn at a party a couple years later. Penn wanted him to apologize for sleeping with his wife while she was a married woman. John told him to take a hike, and then left the party before a fight could break out. Madonna apparently found out what had happened because the next day, John received a funeral wreath at his home. The message on it read; 'In Deepest Sympathy, from Madonna.' He thought that was pretty funny.")

Although Madonna was perceived by her public as strong and independent, at this point in time she was actually frightened and vulnerable, causing some of her friends to wonder what was really going on in her marriage. Doubtless, Sean Penn was angry that Madonna was engaging in what appeared to him to be an extramarital affair with Warren Beatty. "He would follow her at night and, always, they would end up at Warren's," says a friend of Penn's. "He'd sit in his car in front of Beatty's gate, waiting for her to leave. Often, she wouldn't do so until the sun rose. This was driving Sean crazy, along with her decision to not start a family with him. It was all building up in him, a fury that was bound to explode."

Madonna's telephonic declaration of independence from her husband that December morning was her first step in regaining her identity. However, it wasn't that simple. Nothing with Sean was ever simple.

In the late afternoon of December 28, 1988, Sean Penn allegedly scaled the wall surrounding the Malibu house and burst in, finding Madonna alone in the master bedroom. She had given the live-in help the night off to attend a holiday party. According to a police report later filed by Madonna with the Malibu Sheriff's Office, the two began once again to quarrel over Madonna's decision to divorce. When she told him that she was going to leave the house—at least, according to the official report—he tried to bind her hands with an electric lamp and cord. Madonna fled from the bedroom.

Sean chased her into the living room. Once there—again, according to the report—he tied her to an easy chair with heavy twine. Many other dreadful things occurred—at least according to published accounts of this incident, none of which was ever contested by Madonna—but, suffice it to say, it appears to have been a night of physical and emotional abuse.

As per the police report, Penn was "drinking liquor straight from the bottle," and his abuse of her went on for several hours, during which time he allegedly smacked her and roughed her up. After a couple of hours, Penn went out to purchase more alcohol. Several hours later, he returned and—back to that police report—continued his attacks against her.

In desperation—again, according to official documents—Madonna finally persuaded Sean to untie her by telling him that she needed to go to the bathroom. Finally free, she ran out of the house. Sean stumbled while racing after her, which gave her an edge. She got into the coral-colored 1957 Thunderbird, which Penn had bought her on her twenty-eighth birthday. She locked herself inside the car.

While Sean pounded furiously on the automobile windows, Madonna called the police on her cell phone. When she had finished speaking to them, she threw the car into reverse, and sped away—headed for the Malibu Sheriff's Office on Pacific Coast Highway.

"When Madonna staggered into the station [fifteen minutes later], she was distraught, crying, with makeup smeared all over her face," remembered Lieutenant Bill McSweeney. "I hardly recognized her as Madonna, the singer. She was weeping, her lip was bleeding and she was all marked up. She had obviously been struck. This was a woman in big trouble, no doubt about it."

Police officers, stunned by details Madonna had provided of her nine-hour ordeal, went to arrest her husband. Sean Penn was still inside the house when the officers pulled up outside. Remembered one officer, "We had to use our bullhorns. 'Sean Penn, come out of the house with your hands in the air,' we said. The suspect came out and we took him away in handcuffs."

✝

Divorce

In any incident of domestic violence, there are usually two sides to the story. Madonna charged Penn with inflicting "corporal injury and traumatic conditions" on her as well as committing "battery." However,

Sean Penn has a different version of the fracas that ensued in Malibu on that December day in 1988. He says that he never tied up his wife. He explains that, after a typical argument with him, Madonna stormed out of the house to cool off. He hollered after her that if she dared return, he would cut all of her hair off. He says that as a result of his threat, "she developed a concern that she would get a very severe haircut." If Sean's story is true, it's understandable that the image of her infuriated husband coming at her with a pair of scissors would be a terrifying one to Madonna. "So, she took this concern to the local authorities, who came back up to the house," Sean said. "She felt the responsible thing would be to inform them—since they were coming up there ostensibly to keep her from getting a haircut and to let her gather some additional personal effects—that there were firearms in the house." He admits that, indeed, he did have weapons in his home. Sean was in the kitchen eating Rice Krispies cereal when the authorities arrived, brandishing bullhorns and handcuffs. Sean says that the police, fearing that he had a gun, "suggested I come out of the house. They did what they had to do, the way they had to do it. I was cool with that."

After the Malibu incident, whatever its particulars—and Lieutenant Bill McSweeney of the Malibu Sheriff's Office does insist, "We were called to investigate an assault"—Madonna instructed her attorneys to file divorce papers. Sandra Bernhard had convinced Madonna that she should not stay in the marriage another day. Later, as Madonna would tell it, Sandra could "see my pain."

"As your friend, I can't stand by and watch this happen," Sandra later recalled telling her. "I want this to be over for you. What can I do to help? Get rid of him, once and for all."

On the same day that she filed for divorce, Madonna met with Deputy District Attorney Lauren Weiss to explain that she now wished to withdraw the charges against her husband. It was said that she feared the publicity the resulting scandal would most surely generate if there was a trial. However, the truth is that she couldn't bear to see Sean put on trial. She still felt that he was the love of her life, no matter how badly their relationship had degenerated. She cared about him, wanted him to be safe. "May God bless and keep him," she said at the time, "but far, far from me. This marriage is over."

"Madonna asked that there be no criminal charges pressed," district attorney spokesman Al Albergate now says. "There was no other evidence on which to base a criminal charge, so one wasn't filed."

The manner by which Madonna's marriage ended would reshape certain aspects of her personality. She had long ago become accustomed to being in control of her life, of her men. She prided herself on it, even boasted about it. At times she exhibited a startling lack of sensitivity and ridiculed women who appeared weak or vulnerable as a result of a relationship gone sour. She never really understood how a woman would let a man get the best of her. But Sean Penn put an end to her comfort zone of control, and not only metaphorically.

The Malibu nightmare affected Madonna in ways that only she would be able to fully explain . . . and she hasn't seen fit to do so. For the next few months, her friends say, she would have nightmares about that terrible time in December when her husband lost control of his senses. She seemed psychologically wounded by the experience, more so than she would let on to anyone but close friends.

"She would start crying for no reason," said a friend of hers who requested anonymity. "At this time, I felt that she was sad, lonely. Her fans and the press had an image of her as being strong and self-sufficient, and she had been—and would continue to be. But she was emotionally wrecked by that ordeal with Sean. She lost a lot of self-confidence and self-esteem as a result of it, and it would take years for her to get over what happened. In some ways, I think she still hasn't."

When Madonna packed her suitcases and left the Malibu home she and Sean had shared for her apartment in New York, she left behind her gold wedding ring on the vanity in the bathroom. It had been inscribed "M LOVES S."

Neither Madonna nor Sean would ever speak publicly about the incident. "Suffice it to say that Sean has a profound anger management problem," Madonna told one friend, privately. It says much about Madonna's uneasiness over what had occurred that she didn't discuss the matter with the media. Certainly, in the past, she'd been known to run to the press with many incidents having to do with her private life . . . but not this one. Those closest to her say that Madonna chose to be silent because she just didn't know what to make of Sean's actions, and simply couldn't bear to speak of them. Moreover, out of affection and respect for Sean, she didn't wish to sully his name in any way. After all, Madonna knew Sean better than did most people, and she must have realized that what had happened in Malibu did not constitute his finest moment. No doubt, she didn't want his reputation to be further darkened by publicizing what had occurred between them.

For his part, Sean was said to have been grateful for Madonna's silence. He felt terribly sorry, he told one friend, explaining that whiskey had led him into a dangerous error of judgment.

Sean didn't want any of Madonna's money, though by California law, he could have been entitled to half of her fortune. Instead, he wanted Madonna to keep the entire $70 million her career had generated for her in the three years she was a married woman. "I could have gone any way I wanted," he said later. "There's community property in California. But I would never, even under the worst of circumstances, take a penny of somebody else's change."

Instead, Sean Penn walked away from the marriage with the approximately $5 million he had earned (while being paid $1 million a film), as well as the couple's $2-million, three-bedroom, Spanish-style villa. Because Penn's personal investment in the joint property was only $880,000, he made $1.2 million on it. He also got to keep the Southwestern and Santa Fe–style furniture in the home, including a log-built four-poster bed. Madonna took all of the art deco and art nouveau paintings and sculptures. Oddly, she did leave behind, at least according to one court document, a mutilated doll with pins through it. Madonna kept their New York apartment, but gave Penn $498,000— the equivalent of his investment in that property. (She purchased for herself a $2.9-million, seven-bedroom home in the Hollywood Hills.) According to legal papers filed, she also handed over $18,700 in "short-term paper" investments and another $2,300 in cash (both sums from a joint financial account).

The divorce was finalized on January 25, 1989. Because the necessary documents had been prepared and then filed away so many times in the past, they were updated and ready to be signed by Sean Penn within days. Madonna had loved Sean and truly intended to honor her marriage vows, so she was deeply affected by the divorce. She hadn't been happy for some time, so she may have thought that she wouldn't miss Sean. She was wrong. She was actually surprised at the sense of loss she felt in the months after the final decree, as she would later admit. On a deep level, as she would explain to friends, she felt that she and Sean were "soul mates." It was difficult for her to fathom the way it had all turned out for them.

Today, according to those who know her best, she still looks back on the union with Sean with great regret. She can't help but romanticize her marriage to him, retrospectively viewing it through a filter that obscures the darker aspects of the relationship. Perhaps to her credit, she only seems to want to recall the happier times with Sean—certainly not the Malibu nightmare. Of course, some of her friends have wondered when those happy times occurred since most people never actually witnessed her and Sean being happy, at least not after their wedding ceremony—and Sean didn't seem too thrilled that day, either. However, it's true that no one really knows what happens in a marriage when two people are alone, other than the two people to whom it's happening.

Madonna also feels, or so she has said privately, that perhaps she could have been more tolerant of Sean's feelings where Sandra Bernhard was concerned. Also, she wonders if perhaps she should have been more proactive in forcing him to stop drinking. She has said that she felt guilty because, "I should have made him stop. Every time we ever had a drink together, I felt guilty about that."

Perhaps some of her guilt stemmed from her Catholic upbringing. "Once you're a Catholic, you're always a Catholic—in terms of your feelings of guilt and remorse and whether you've sinned or not," she explained in an interview. "Sometimes I'm racked with guilt when I needn't be, and that, to me, is left over from my Catholic upbringing. Because in Catholicism you are a born sinner and you're a sinner all your life. No matter how you try to get away from it, the sin is within you all the time."

Actually, there was nothing Madonna could have done for the deeply flawed Sean Penn. The truth, it would seem, is that Penn was a coward. For whatever reasons, he wanted to break up with Madonna and end their union, but he didn't have the courage to do it. Rather, he created an appalling scene that he knew would force her hand and cause her to file for divorce. "You can't change a person, or control their demons," Madonna later said of Sean Penn. "That's one of the things I learned from that relationship."

It could be argued that Sean and Madonna did the best they could with what they had available to them, in terms of common sense and maturity. The fact that both were so famous at such a young age did nothing to enhance their marriage, either. Certainly, today, Madonna would never be as publicly antagonistic to her partner as she was with Sean. While still a complicated, often temperamental and sometimes difficult person to understand, she's obviously not the same woman she was a decade ago.

Madonna would also later admit that the breakup with Sean made her "more suspicious of people. You imbue men with characteristics you want them to have," she observed. "Then they're not what you expect, at all. But it's your own fault too for not having done the homework, the investigating. I'm more cautious now. But I'm still a hopeless romantic."

Since his marriage to Madonna, Sean Penn has worked to clean himself up—he's not "sober," still drinks, but hasn't had a display of public drunkenness in years. He has gone on to be a contented and productive person—though, by some accounts, is perhaps still not the ideal mate. He and his second wife, actress Robin Wright, mother of his two children, have had their own difficulties since their marriage in 1996.

When asked if he thought the marriage to Madonna could have worked, he replies, "No fucking way. Not with what we had to deal with." Constantly, reporters ask for Sean's opinion of the latest public relations' sensation generated by his ex-wife, thinking him an authority on the subject. He usually has no opinion about any of it. "Look, I'm not any better an expert on her than anyone else," he says. "I don't know her any better from having been with her. I was drunk most of the time, anyway."

In years to come, he and Madonna would continue to hold strong feelings for each other, though they would seldom speak to one another. "It's too painful," Madonna told writer Kevin Sessums when asked if she and Penn were in touch. "It's horrible," she said, tears welling in her eyes.

Some years later, in 1995, Sean suddenly appeared on stage unexpectedly before a stunned audience as Madonna was receiving a VH1 Fashion and Music Award. While Madonna enjoyed shocking others, but rarely—if ever—enjoyed it when the tables were turned, she seemed genuinely happy to see Sean. The two embraced lovingly.

When he left the stage, she walked to the microphone and said to the audience, "Now, that was really dirty."

Perhaps her brief 1995 reunion with Sean Penn stirred something in Madonna that had lain dormant for some time. The next day, she tucked her hair under a hat, threw on a leopard-skin coat and rendezvoused with the low-key, baseball-cap-wearing Penn in Central Park. "I miss you so much, baby," she was overheard saying to him. "Don't you miss me, too?" The ever-present and stirred-up paparazzi feverishly snapped pictures of the couple formerly known as "the Poison Penns." This time, Madonna and Sean, lost in each other's company, didn't seem to mind.

✝

Like a Prayer: The Album

In March 1989, the commercially prudent thing for Madonna to do would have been to release another dance album of new material. After all, based on the sales performance of the recent *You Can Dance,* her public would have been happy just to keep dancing. However, Madonna—who was now thirty—had certain matters on her mind, personal thoughts about her troubled relationship with her ex-husband, her family, the world and even her God. So while she still wanted her fans to party, with her fourth album she also wanted them to think. To that end, Madonna began to develop lyrical ideas that, until then, were personal meditations never to be shared with her public so openly and pointedly. Thoughtfully, she sifted through her personal journal and diaries and began considering her options. "What was it I wanted to say?" she recalled. "I wanted the album to speak to things on my mind. It was a complex time in my life."

As Madonna considered her alternatives, producers Steve Bray and Patrick Leonard individually began to tinker with various instrumental tracks and musical ideas to present to her for her consideration. Though the two producers knew one another well and had even worked together on songs with her, there was always quiet but fierce competition between them as they vied to see who could get the most songs on one of her albums. Since Madonna had become a franchise, songwriting royalties from albums that sold millions of copies globally had already made Bray and Leonard wealthy men. The stakes remained high.

Both producers brought their own special style to the project that would go on to become the *Like a Prayer* album. Though Bray had a penchant for kinetic pop-dance songs, while Leonard was more melodic in style, both proved indispensable to Madonna's ever-developing sound. In fact, the versatility of both producers unwittingly saw to it that there was no real Madonna "sound" to speak of, no way for critics or fans to pigeonhole her. Thus, while Madonna was well aware of the sometimes contentious dynamic of the relationship between Bray and Leonard, she never did much to deter them—the tension was good for creativity and business. "I like it when people go up against one another," she has said. "I even like it when they go up against me. If you want creativity, you have to have sparks. I'm all for that."

Moreover, Madonna's own musical tastes and ideas have as much to do with who she is artistically as anyone else's. Ultimately, she's the one who decides for which tracks she'll write lyrics.

When *Like a Prayer* was released, music journalists took note of Madonna's artful, mature way of expressing herself. She had become a proficient song writer and was credited with co-writing ten songs on the album, and writing one on her own.

"Like a Prayer," written by Madonna with Leonard, deserved every bit of the curiosity it generated. Like the startling music video that would accompany it, the song is a series of button-pushing anomalies. It is filled with references to both the spiritual/religious and the carnal—a joyful celebration of love . . . but for whom? In a twist so typical of Madonna's clever way with words, the lyrical theme of devotion could either be for a lover, or for God. For instance, throughout Madonna sings "Prayer" with a measure of devotion and reverence, as if to a higher power. Yet the lyric about being "down on my knees," and wanting to "take you there" evokes distinct images of . . . something else.

Indeed, double entendres and ironies abound in "Like a Prayer." While devilishly danceable, the music is interrupted by a quiet break during which Madonna offers a loving homage against a backdrop of heavenly angelic voicings. While the song feels distinctively religious, the underlying sexual tension is undeniable. The jubilant voices of a gospel choir conducted by André Crouch heightened the song's spiritual nature while a stingingly secular rock guitar kept it dark and mysterious. Like the legendary Marvin Gaye (whose music she greatly admired), Madonna has the uncanny ability to inspire strong, conflicting emotions during the course of a single song, leaving the listener scratching his head for answers—and craving more. This is certainly one of the woman's great gifts.

"Express Yourself," one of two tracks Madonna produced with Bray, was a funky dance anthem urging a female call-to-arms in communication and self-respect. "I think it's one of my better songs," Madonna has said. "We had fun in the studio with it."

In three songs on the album, Madonna sought to purge herself of certain personal demons. "Till Death Do Us Part," her sad, harsh open letter to Sean Penn, revealed her feelings of hopelessness for their marriage. As would any artist intent on exposing herself through her music, she transformed personal experience into art, making clear to anyone interested how she felt about what had happened with Sean. Likewise, with "Oh Father" Madonna revisits the pain and confusion that had characterized her relationship with the most important man in her life. Some critics felt it was a love letter to Tony Ciccone, while others saw it as an indictment. "That's fine," Madonna said. "It is what the listener thinks it is, all open to interpretation. I just write the songs, it's up to others to interpret them to mean what they want them to mean."

She countered the somber moments with songs such as "Keep It Together," the other Steve Bray track, which is an up-tempo romp about the trials and tribulations—and the joys—of family.

"Cherish" was a particular triumph for the Madonna/Patrick Leonard partnership. A delightful confection of radio-ready proportions, the song had it all—strong, positive, remarkably dysfunction-free lyrics about love, a memorable, singalong vocal melody and a tight, punchy, rhythm arrangement. It remains, quite simply, one of the best songs Madonna has ever written; sweet and happy but by no means corny, it's a perfectly constructed pop song which Madonna delivered beautifully, and with undeniably sassy charm. Indeed, if "Cherish" had been released in the sixties, it would have most likely emanated from Detroit's Motown or the New York songwriting Mecca, the Brill Building, both sources for some of pop music's most enduring classics.

Madonna and Patrick Leonard created much of the *Like a Prayer* album with the exception of "Love Song," a duet co-produced and performed on the album by Prince. While they were dating, the two superstars had tried writing together, but never came up with anything that ever saw the light of day. Perhaps "Love Song" should also have been kept where light couldn't find it. A potentially fabulous collaboration is wasted on a meandering mid-tempo song that goes nowhere—an exercise in Prince excess. Though she shared production credit with him, Prince played all the instruments and Madonna's role was reduced to sitting in on her own album and trying to sing like Prince. Her guest star might have even inspired "Act of Contrition," an experimental mess that has Madonna mumbling a prayer over edgy, solo rock guitar while a choir's background chants are played backward, a recording tactic used by the Beatles and Jimi Hendrix for psychedelic effect some years earlier. Like any art, sometimes what Madonna comes up with works . . . sometimes it doesn't. (Of course, who's to say what works and doesn't, all criticism being subjective.)

Every important artist has at least one album in his career whose commercial and/or critical success becomes that artist's magic moment. For Marvin Gaye, it was *What's Going On*. For Stevie Wonder, *Songs in the Key of Life*. For Diana Ross, the soundtrack to her breakthrough film, *Lady Sings the Blues*. For Aretha Franklin, it was *Hey Now Hey (The Other Side of the Sky)*, produced by Quincy Jones and including the Stevie Wonder–penned single, "Until You Come Back to Me." Of course, for Michael Jackson it was *Off the Wall* and *Thriller*. For Madonna, *Like a Virgin* was just such a defining moment. *Like a Prayer* was another. For better or worse—usually better!—Madonna pushed onwards as an artist, using her creative wit to communicate on another level, musically. *"Like a Prayer* is about the influence of Catholicism on my life and the passion it provokes in me," she explained. "In these songs I'm dealing with specific issues that mean a lot to me. They're about an assimilation of experiences I had in my life and my relationships. I've taken more risks with this album than I ever have before, and I think that growth shows."

✝

"Like a Prayer": The Pepsi Commercial

"Like a Prayer" was notable for more than just its musicality. The circumstances under which the "Like a Prayer" single and album debuted turned out to be one of the biggest controversies in the history of corporate advertising's often uneasy liaison with pop music. It began in January 1989, when Pepsi-Cola announced that it had signed Madonna to a $5-million deal to use her and "Like a Prayer" in a television commercial. The agreement also called for Pepsi financially to sponsor a Madonna world concert tour. (The soda giant had a similar contract with Michael Jackson, and news of the arrangement alone had garnered both the company and the artist a great deal of valuable publicity.)

"I consider it a challenge to make a commercial that has some sort of artistic value," she said. "I like the challenge of merging art and commerce. As far as I'm concerned, making a video is also a commercial. The Pepsi spot is a great and different way to expose the record. Record companies just don't have the money to finance this kind of publicity. As it is, the music will be playing in the background, and the can of Pepsi is positioned very subliminally. The camera pans by it, so it's not a hard-sell commercial."

The Pepsi/Madonna deal had something conceivably great for both parties. Madonna would use the commercial to debut her single "Like a Prayer" globally before its actual release—the first time anything like this had ever been done in the music industry—thereby creating international promotion for the single and album to come. Pepsi, on the other hand, got to have its product, already a pop-culture staple, associated with the world's biggest female pop star.

While it seemed the perfect marriage of art and commerce, there were problems from the beginning when Madonna refused to put the

Pepsi name in the commercial's version of "Like a Prayer." Initially, she also balked at dancing in the multimillion dollar ad, styled to look as slick as an MTV video.

Still, Pepsi went all out with its campaign. On February 22, 1989, the company ran an expensive television commercial during the globally telecast Grammy Awards which, oddly, was actually just an advertisement for the upcoming Madonna commercial. Then, on March 2, during the most popular TV show in the country at the time, *The Cosby Show,* Madonna was seen in an elaborate—and wholesome—commercial hawking Pepsi as diligently as she could while still maintaining some measure of equity as a pop star. An estimated 250 million people around the world made it their business to see the two-minute commercial, marking the first time a new single would be debuted in almost its entirety in an ad shown around the world. Pepsi-Cola Company spokesman Todd MacKenzie said that the ad would air simultaneously "all around the globe, all across Europe, the Philippines, Thailand, Japan, in South America as well as in North America. Just about every TV set on the planet will have that commercial on." A thirty-second version of the spot would run on television during the summer months.

At least, that was the plan.

Pepsi had kept its part of the agreement by pumping up "Like a Prayer" (and thus Pepsi) via a campaign with a price tag on it worth millions. However, Madonna was, as one executive later put it, "the wild card." True to form, she shocked Pepsi executives and conservatives alike with the resulting "Like a Prayer" video. Madonna, always on the lookout to better herself, planned the video to be more provocative than anything she'd done before it. Having previously taken on the social issue of teenage pregnancy with great commercial success, Madonna now thought to tackle racism by having the new video depict a mixed-race couple being gunned down by the Ku Klux Klan. However, upon further thought and in keeping with the song's religious connotations, she decided on another provocative theme. The video's director, Mary Lambert, says, "I felt it was a song about ecstasy and very specifically sexual ecstasy and how it relates to religious ecstasy. We listened to it together and we agreed that that's what it was about. Madonna said she would like to make love on an altar in the video."

When Lambert kept Madonna's initial idea of an interracial love affair in the concept, the result was a hodgepodge of controversial images—Madonna kissing a black saint (played by actor Leon, who most recently portrayed David Ruffin in the *Temptations* miniseries, and Little Richard in that rock and roller's TV movie biography), receiving the stigmata, dancing in front of burning crosses while scantily clad in what appeared to be just a black slip and, as per her request, making love on an altar to a black man (again Leon, who, in the course of the story line of the video, had been falsely accused of murder). It was a terrific video. A brunette Madonna danced throughout the spectacle with such wild abandon—at one point singing and dancing while wearing her little undergarment in church, being backed by a black gospel choir—it was as if she knew she was about to cause a commotion, and couldn't wait to see how it would all unfold.

Religious groups around the world wasted little time protesting about what they deemed to be a blasphemous use of Christian imagery. They called for the national boycott of Pepsi and PepsiCo's subsidiaries, including their fast-food chains Kentucky Fried Chicken, Taco Bell and Pizza Hut.

With Pepsi executives on the ropes trying to explain the thin line separating advertising and artistic expression, the Pope himself jumped into the fray, calling for the ban of any appearances by Madonna in Italy. Pepsi, nervous that the idea they had counted on to generate millions was about to make the company lose that much, finally caved in to international pressure. The *Fortune* 500 company canceled the advertising campaign shortly after the two-minute commercial's debut on March 2, 1989. It also bowed out of financing Madonna's upcoming tour. So eager was Pepsi to extricate itself from the revenue-threatening venture, it even allowed Madonna to keep the $5 million she had been advanced with the signing of her contract—not that it had much choice for, most certainly, she would have sued had Pepsi demanded the return of its money.

While she said that it was never her intention that Pepsi be the fall guy in this fiasco, Madonna stayed true to herself. The fact that she didn't want to hold a Pepsi can in the commercial should have clued in the Pepsi executives to the fact that Madonna the pop star was going to do it her way, no matter what Madonna the businesswoman had agreed to do. She maintained all along that the Pepsi ad and her music video were two distinctly different entities, and that she was right to stand her ground. Of course, all the headlines only served to increase interest in

Like a Prayer. The album generated five hit singles on the *Billboard* charts—"Like a Prayer" became her seventh Number 1 single; "Express Yourself," Number 2; "Cherish," Number 2; "Oh Father," Number 20; and "Keep It Together" rallied to Number 8. The album sold some four million copies in America, and a stunning thirteen million around the world.

In the end, the events surrounding "Like a Prayer" only served to enhance Madonna's reputation as a shrewd businesswoman, someone who knows how to sell a concept. Of course, the recruitment of pop stars and athletes to sell soft drinks would become commonplace in the future. However, none of those successes would generate the excitement of Pepsi's failed deal with Madonna.

Ironically, "Like a Prayer" won the Viewers Choice category at the 1989 MTV Video Music Awards—a program sponsored by Pepsi. "I guess this means you like me," she said, spoofing Sally Field's famous Oscar-winning speech. "You really like me." Then, smiling, the now blonde Madonna added with a twinge of irony, "I'd like to thank Pepsi for causing so much controversy."

✝

Goodies

When production began on Warren Beatty's new film *Dick Tracy* in February 1989, it seemed inevitable to some Hollywood observers that a romantic relationship had developed between the longtime Hollywood rogue and pop music's current, publicity-mad temptress. Now that she was working alongside him, Madonna, a longtime movie fan, probably couldn't resist the idea of a relationship with Beatty, a film icon who cultivated women with astonishing success. Because the final and painful breakup with Sean was still fresh, though, perhaps Madonna felt as she might after having been to the dentist. Inside she was probably numb after such a dreadful ordeal, especially considering the Malibu nightmare. However, on the outside she seemed fine—and she was adamant about keeping up appearances. She told friends that she was determined to move forward with her life and remain as distracted as possible, so as not to focus on Sean, her failed marriage and the catastrophic way it had ended. What better distraction, one might muse, than a relationship with a man who had romanced many of the biggest and most glamorous names of his era, including Natalie Wood, Joan Collins, Julie Christie, Carly Simon, Cher and Barbra Streisand?

While still certainly easy to look at, at fifty-two Warren Beatty's sex-symbol status in Hollywood had long ago faded. Now, around his still-handsome face was the faint suggestion of discoloration, thin white lines that were nearly concealed by either a tan or maybe even pancake makeup. (Some who got close enough for an inspection would wonder if these marks could have been the result of cosmetic surgery.) Perhaps realizing that his "Old Hollywood" image would be bolstered by becoming linked with the young, leading sex object of the day, Warren seemed dumbfounded by his good fortune. "Sometimes I look at myself in the mirror and say, 'Man, I am with Madonna!' " he told a reporter. "She makes me young."

From the beginning, Warren provided loads of fun for Madonna. For instance, one day Madonna came home to find her living room full of packages: lingerie, perfume, makeup, and dozens of expensive dresses, both formal and informal—all her size. There were also boxes of bikini underwear in a variety of colors—again, all her size—and a dozen black lace Lejaby brassieres—her favorite. (One might wonder how Warren would have known, or even remembered, the brand name of her favorite bra.) There were also eight pairs of expensive Italian designer shoes. She was astonished when she read a card that had been propped on a large hatbox: "From Warren." Had he really selected all of these clothes just for her? Had he spent that much time making certain of the sizes? And why would he do all of this?

As she pondered those questions—and who knows how many others—Madonna and two of her female assistants enjoyed a wonderful afternoon with Warren's exquisite presents. After putting her *Like a Prayer* CD into the player, she slipped in and out of each new dress while dancing and preening in front of the mirror, admiring her reflection. She and her friends enjoyed "a silly girl's day," as one of the assistants called it. They pinned up their hair, let it back down, sampled the new lingerie—tags dangling—and tossed aside the garments Madonna decided were "tacky." At the end of the fun day, Madonna gave the two girls the clothing and makeup she thought flattering on them, and kept the rest for herself—including all of the shoes.

The next day, Madonna telephoned Warren to ask about the gifts. He explained that buying for himself was a bore since, as he put it, "a man can only wear pants and a jacket. What fun is that?" He said that he enjoyed shopping for women and, if Madonna didn't mind, he might send over an assortment of "goodies" whenever the mood struck him.

Madonna was ambivalent about such generosity. As she would later say, she was, at first, annoyed. "I'm not some little starlet that you can buy things for and control," she told him. "I'm a very wealthy person. I can buy my own underwear." However, she was also impressed. "What girl wouldn't be?" she had to admit. After what she had been through with Sean, perhaps she decided that she deserved a bit of pampering. She decided to keep the gifts, but on the condition that the next time Warren Beatty had such an impulse, he would take her along so that she could help select "the goodies."

As well as his passion for beautiful and famous women—and for buying them "goodies"—Warren Beatty's other great love was of filmmaking. On *Dick Tracy*, he would act as star, producer and director. Madonna could learn a great deal about moviemaking and screen acting from him. She needed his credibility and experience as much as he needed her youth. To her restless child, he would play the indulgent adult, slightly abashed but definitely enchanted by her whirlwind lifestyle. Some people in her circle went so far as to say that Madonna looked to Warren as a father figure.

After Sean Penn, Warren Beatty must have seemed like a breath of fresh air for Madonna. For one thing, he could be pushed around—as she would soon learn. He would take a lot, get angry, and then disappear . . . to cool off. Unlike Sean, he wouldn't lash out at her, at least not in any physical way. It had always been Madonna's nature to bully the man with whom she was romantically involved. Whereas Sean had been emotional and explosive about her daily defiances, Warren would usually just be resigned and philosophical about them. For the most part, he was tolerant of her; he thought she was amusing.

Ironically, it had been Sean Penn who first introduced Madonna to

Warren Beatty, and on the night of Penn's first date with her, "Sean took me to Warren's house," Madonna said. "I guess he wanted to show me off—I'm not sure. I didn't know L.A. at all. I remember meeting a lot of movie stars that night, like Mickey Rourke."

Warren was intrigued by Madonna from the first time he laid eyes on her. "I understand rebellion," he observed when speaking of his new consort. "So I understand Madonna. She's all about rebellion, basically." (If that's all she was "about" in his view, maybe he didn't understand her as well as he thought he did.) To *Vanity Fair* writer Kevin Sessums, though, Warren was a bit more forthcoming when asked what he thought of Madonna's artistry: "I think she's courageous in the areas that she explores artistically. I think that's what she wants to explore. If you mean what do I think are the resonances of that or the personal motivations for that, I don't know that I would address myself to that. Off the top of my head, her generous spirit would be the thing I think that informs her work the most. As she goes on, she will gain the artistic respect that she already deserves."

Diane Giordano recalled the way Madonna described a date with Warren at the Sushi Cove, a trendy restaurant in Los Angeles on Mullholland Drive, less than a mile from Warren's estate, in January 1989: "He wore a black silk suit, black shoes, a white shirt and a black silk tie. He also wore tinted glasses. She suspected that he was trying to hide crow's-feet. She said she felt awkward because he was so nattily dressed and she had on a funky jeans outfit. They had a nice dinner and then the waitress came and asked if they wanted dessert. The only choice was chocolate or vanilla ice cream. Madonna wanted both."

The next day, Warren telephoned Madonna at her home. In talking about the date, he went on about how Madonna had wanted both flavors of ice cream. "You seem to like to try everything," he told her, teasing her. "So, have you ever made it with a woman?"

At this time, with Madonna's friendship with Sandra Bernhard flourishing, she was still teasing the public with the possibility that she was a lesbian. With Beatty now apparently questioning the validity of "those stories," Madonna suddenly became the model of discretion. She refused to answer his inquiries and, instead, attempted to turn the tables. "Have you ever done it with a man?" she countered. Beatty, it is said, ignored the question.

"Do you want a woman?" he pressed on. "Because if you do, it will be my present to you. I'll get you a woman."

"And all this, just from ordering two kinds of ice cream?" Madonna asked with a laugh.

The next night, Warren and Madonna—in a black vinyl jumpsuit with high heels (strange fashion choice for beach restaurant dining)—again dined at the Sushi Cove, this time joined by Sandra Bernhard, at Warren's request. "All I remember about that date was that Madonna and I ordered one plate of sushi for the two of us. And I said something like, 'Warren, you know that Madonna and I share *everything*, don't you?' And his eyes lit up like a kid in a candy store. A wild ride, I thought to myself. A very wild ride."

✝

Differences

Although Madonna told reporters—such as one for *Cosmopolitan*—that she didn't want to "belittle the relationship by talking about it," she was intrigued enough about what was going on with Warren Beatty to want to discuss it with close friends. When the two finally made love, Madonna had confided, it wasn't the kind of passionate experience she had known with Sean Penn. Nothing could compare to what she had with Sean, she had to admit. However, Warren was much more generous as a lover than Sean had been. Warren politely apologized for the brevity of his performance in bed, and then made sure that she, too, was completely pleasured. He sought out her needs, her preferences, her desires. "He knows a woman's body better than most women," Madonna said. "He can pinpoint the day of your cycle.

"He's into all aspects of sexuality. This is why he's so perfect for me," she added. "He has no restrictions. He says to me, 'If you misbehave, I'll just have to spank you.' I love that. Everything to him is living out his sexual fantasies."

"I don't know that he's ever slept with a man," she later said to a reporter for the gay magazine the *Advocate*. "But he's certainly not homophobic. I asked him once, 'Would you ever sleep with a man?' and he said he was sorry that he hadn't but that now because of AIDS he felt it was an unsafe thing to start experimenting with."

After she felt she knew him well enough to do so, Madonna suggested that Warren retrieve his former trim and youthful shape by exercising with her. When he told her that he wasn't interested, she was perplexed as to why a person would not want to "better himself." Rather than let it go, she pushed on, suggesting liposuction. He was either hurt or insulted—only he would know which. The two then became embroiled in a heated debate about whether she had a right to have an opinion about his body, the matter playing out in front of friends at the Los Angeles nightclub, the Club Nouveau.

"You're the one who is always telling people that they shouldn't judge others by outside appearances," Warren said to her. "How dare you judge me? It works both ways, you know?"

"Oh, please," Madonna said as she sipped a cocktail, looking terrific in velvet hot pants. "You older guys are too sensitive," she said, taking a drag from a cigarette. "I'm just being helpful. If you want to be fat and flabby, Warren, fine with me. Go right ahead."

To whom did she think she was talking? Sean Penn? It was as if Madonna hadn't learned much from her experiences with her former husband, at least in terms of diplomacy, discretion and sensitivity. It now seemed to observers that she was being purposely cruel to Warren, maybe continuing an explosive theme in her relationships, whether consciously or subconsciously.

Warren's eyes turned as cold as granite. He began to say something, but stopped himself. Typical of him—he was *not* Sean Penn— he probably didn't want to make a scene in front of so many witnesses. Instead, he sniffed his brandy as if a connoisseur before quickly downing it. Nodding pensively to himself, he then walked away, careful not to make eye contact with any observers. "Now what was that about?" Madonna asked no one in particular. "I hate it when he does that to me. That is *so* like my father. He is *so* like my father!" She then began biting on her knuckles, as if suddenly nervous or fearful.

The argument may have continued the next day in a Hollywood restaurant. "Keep your stupid remarks to yourself," Madonna said to Warren in front of other diners.

"Oh, Christ! Grow up!" Warren countered, this time visibly exasperated.

"No. *You* grow up," Madonna said, petulantly. She then reached into her bag and pulled out a Snickers candy bar, which she threw at Warren's chest. Both were apparently unaware that their display had stopped all conversation around them. Finally, hockey star Wayne Gretzky charged over to them, "Hey, you two," he said, "knock it off, will ya?"

After five minutes, Warren began cutting Madonna's fillet of sole into little pieces, and then delicately placing each into her mouth with his fork. (Though Madonna was said to have been on a strict vegan diet at this time, which prohibited fish, she did indulge now and then.)

Madonna declared to a reporter, again for *Cosmopolitan*, "What I'm doing this time is starting out being good friends with somebody." She loved Beatty's self-confidence, she said. "I used to want to be president," Warren told her. "But Hollywood is better than Washington. Here, I have more power, and I don't have to put up with the bureaucracy. I'm the president of Hollywood."

Madonna also enjoyed the manner in which Warren continued to pamper her. For instance, on the set of *Dick Tracy* he paid for a masseuse to wait on her at all times. He sent her flowers every day of shooting. One night after a tough day of filming, Warren took Madonna out to dinner to an expensive Italian restaurant. Wearing a sheer black-and-red polka-dot blouse, black bra, black hot pants and a red bowler hat—and chewing on a wad of gum—she sat down and promptly demanded a Diet Pepsi, a drink not on the menu. Diet Coke, yes. Diet Pepsi, no. "Well, we're leaving," Madonna decided. Warren then asked the waiter to go to a convenience store and purchase a can of Diet Pepsi.

When the waiter returned, Warren peeled off five $100 bills from a wad and handed them to him. He then waved toward the Diet Pepsi as if he had just conjured it up out of thin air. "There you go, my dear," he said to Madonna, "the most expensive soda in the world, and it's all yours." As Madonna laughed gaily, the waiter popped open a can and poured its contents into a glass of ice. After dinner, Warren and Madonna held hands under the table. Later, Beatty would say, "Because she's surrounded by so much stuff, I don't think people quite realize how much fun Madonna is. She's an enormous amount of fun to be around and certainly to work with."

Warren thought that the fact that Madonna had tried to have her breasts insured for $12 million was "hilarious." During the filming of the movie in late winter and into the spring of 1989, makeup artist John Cuglione literally had to glue Madonna into some of the skintight gowns. "I was terrified that she'd have an allergic reaction to the glue," he recalls. "If I'd discolored a breast or inflicted permanent damage, she could sue me for a fortune. Worse yet, I'd be known as the schmuck who destroyed a national treasure." When Madonna had the idea to have her breasts insured—interesting considering the history of breast cancer with her late mother—she asked Warren for the name and number of his agent. The agent told her that the amount she was asking for her figure to be insured was too high. "But I think each one is worth $6 million, don't you?" she asked Warren. He had to agree.

Madonna tried to be realistic about the relationship with Warren. She said that she didn't want to be swept away by the excitement of being with him. "Sometimes I'm cynical," she said wistfully to one reporter, "and I think it will last as long as it lasts. Then I have moments when I'm really romantic and I think: My God, we're just *perfect* together." Indeed, hope does spring eternal . . .

Working with Warren as her director was not as difficult for Madonna as some thought it might be. Warren is known for directing his actors to film a scene twenty, sometimes thirty, times before he is finally satisfied. Many observers thought Madonna would be intolerant of such demands. "Even I thought it would be a problem," Madonna observed at a press conference for *Dick Tracy* after the film was released. "Because of our close friendship, I thought there would be problems. But there weren't. I respect him. He's been in the business for so many years, how dare I question his judgment about anything?"

While there may have been harmony on the set of *Dick Tracy*, there were growing problems backstage as Madonna and Warren hit upon important differences in their personalities. For instance, while Madonna was the ultimate party girl, Warren was a "homebody." One night in the spring of 1989, Madonna took Warren to a dance club in a seedy part of Los Angeles called the Catch One, a notoriously popular gay hustlers' hangout in the ethnic South Central district. Woefully out of place in his tailored Versace three-piece suit, Warren declined to get up and dance with Madonna.

"Hey, Pussy Man, come on out here," she shouted at him from the dance floor. Wearing a hooded sweatshirt under a blue denim jacket, shorts, boxers' shoes and a leather cap, backward, she laughed, tossed her head back and beckoned to him. "Let's have fun!"*

The author—observing Madonna for a feature about her—watched as Warren stuck out his lower lip and shook his head. "No, I'm just fine," he said with a weak smile. He then took a small bottle of allergy nasal spray from his jacket pocket and sprayed the medicine into his nose. "I can't even breathe," he complained, "let alone dance."

"Oh my God," Madonna hollered back at him. "Quit your whining, will you?"

Clearly exasperated by Warren's conservative demeanor, she danced with a couple of shapely young women. Beatty sat on the sidelines, watching, wheezing and looking as though he was truly feeling his age.

"I shoulda' come here with Rob Lowe," Madonna shouted out at Warren, referring to the young actor she was also rumored to be dating at the time. "Now, he's a guy who knows how to party hearty." (The two were not in a serious relationship.)

Warren just shrugged.

The next morning, Madonna was at the Johnny Yuma Recording Studio in Los Angeles recording the vocals to the Stephen Sondheim songs that would appear on the album *I'm Breathless* (*Music from and Inspired by the Film* Dick Tracy). Wearing a low-cut, pink satin minidress over leggings, she stood in front of the microphone and sang the song beautifully while a roomful of people, including Warren, watched, apparently agog.

Recalled one studio technician, "Madonna and Warren were happy together, but mismatched just the same. I remember the night she recorded the vocals to 'Hanky Panky'—which is about Beatty's favorite sport, spanking. The atmosphere was so charged and intimate, I felt like I was intruding on something private. She was flirtatious. He lapped it up. She definitely knows how to keep a man interested. Plus, she was proud to be there with Warren. She wore him like a badge of honor. Some people whispered that he was only using her to help pro-

* Madonna's nickname for Beatty was "Pussy Man" because, as she explained to the *Advocate*, "When I say pussy, you know what I mean. He's a *wimp*. I enjoy expressing myself, and if I think someone's being a pussy, I say it."

mote his movie. That seemed possible to me. But she was definitely using him, as well."

Later that day, in April 1989, Warren accompanied Madonna to an audition for the futuristic video of her song, "Express Yourself" (inspired by the 1926 Fritz Lang classic film, *Metropolis*). She had twenty dancers (some were only models who could also dance) in a lineup, finalists for the $1-million production (only Michael Jackson's long-form "Thriller" cost more). Marching down the line, a gum-chewing drill sergeant, she sized up each candidate. To one long-haired fellow, she said, "Now, there's no problem with cutting your hair, is there?" When he hesitated, she said, "Oh, give me a break. Yes or no!"

Then, on to the next dancer. "What's with that posture?" she asked. "Stand up straight," she ordered. "Do you want this job or not?"

Then, to the next one, "Oh my God," she said. "Look at you." She paused for a moment to scrutinize him. Then, she turned to Warren and said, "Look at the bulge in this guy's tights. What's *that* all about?"

Warren didn't respond. Instead, he just looked on with a bemused expression. "Man, she's rather a bitch, isn't she?" Warren observed to one of the choreographers.

"Yeah, well . . ." answered the choreographer, his tone exhausted.

"Or maybe she's just showing off for me?" Warren wondered aloud. Looking troubled, he took out a silk handkerchief from his breast pocket. Then he blew his nose.

✝

"Blonde Ambition"

After they finished *Dick Tracy*, Warren and Madonna would have some time away from each other while busying themselves with other career matters. As he focused on editing *Dick Tracy*, she concentrated on her "Blonde Ambition" concert tour

On Friday May 13, 1990, Madonna kicked off "Blonde Ambition" in Tokyo. With complete control over virtually every aspect of this extremely theatrical presentation, from music to sets to dancers to gowns, she would see the four-month tour through a total of twenty-seven cities worldwide. It was a truly spectacular show, the tour during which she wore the well-known gold cone bra designed by Jean Paul Gaultier (who had been designing such exaggerated bras since 1984). "With Madonna, it always comes down to clothes and shoes," says her friend, background singer and dancer on the show, Nikki Harris. "Cone bras, bustiers, platforms . . . anything she could do to make it bad, she went for it." Brazenly sexual dance numbers and moments of religious imagery commingled in a fast-paced, tightly choreographed, unforgettable extravaganza. Choreographer Vincent Paterson recalls that Madonna's goal was that the cast "break every rule we can. She wanted to make statements about sexuality, cross-sexuality and the church. She did it."

Madonna brought her sexual image to a new, more controversial plateau by casually throwing in quips relating to sadomasochism. After performing the forties-inspired "Hanky Panky," she joked, "you all know the pleasures of a good spanking, don't you?" Then, in what may, or may not, have been a double entendre, she told the audience, "When I hurt people, I feel better, you know what I mean?"

To add new life to classic numbers from her repertoire, such as "Like a Virgin," Madonna lay on a scarlet bed attended by two male dancers, both wearing the cone bras strapped to their bare chests which they lovingly caressed throughout the number, the song reorchestrated somehow to sound Middle Eastern in melody. Then, to bring the song to a rousing climax, Madonna frantically humped the furniture while rubbing her body in a frantic, faux masturbation scene. If she was a "virgin" before the song started, she seemed determined to lose her maidenhead before it was through.

At the time of the "Blonde Ambition" tour, Madonna was at the peak of her popularity. (When HBO broadcast the show on August 5, 1990, she reached her largest American TV audience: 4.3 million households tuned in, giving HBO its highest ratings ever for an original program. For those who thought the special was too racy for television, Madonna had a message during the broadcast. "You know what I have to say to America," she said, employing a tough New York accent. "Get a fucking sense of humor, okay?" Then, pointing directly to the viewer: "Lighten up!")

While she was still in rehearsals for "Blonde Ambition," Madonna decided to market a video vehicle tie-in to the concert tour. Thus far, her attempts to play different characters for the movies had failed. While the public did not seem eager to accept her in an acting role, it did seemed constantly transfixed by the Madonna character she had created. Certainly the outrageous, sensational, sarcastic and petulant side of the Madonna persona was based in truth. It's part of who she really was at the time. Her vulnerable side, though, is what she usually kept from her fans, and when she allowed that aspect of her personality to be exposed it was usually in a calculated attempt to generate sympathy. Her concept now was to produce a documentary of her life while on tour. Although she would soon be seen as the character Breathless Mahoney in *Dick Tracy*, perhaps she reasoned that if the role didn't interest her fans, they would, hopefully, enjoy seeing Madonna playing Madonna—on and off stage in the self-produced documentary. "May St Jude, the saint of lost causes, find a way to bring that girl to her senses," the privacy-obsessed Warren Beatty said when informed by a mutual friend of Madonna's new idea.

To direct the documentary, Madonna chose Alek Keshishian, a young filmmaker who had directed music videos for Elton John and Bobby Brown. A Harvard graduate, he had directed one small film—a rock opera based on *Wuthering Heights* (his Harvard senior project) which Madonna had seen and enjoyed. In all probability, Madonna's gut instincts told her that the handsome, long-haired filmmaker with fresh ideas was the kind of hip, cool artist who could lend the film the right edge. "There was a mutual attraction," Keshishian now says, "but it wasn't necessarily sexual." That attraction would soon bring Keshishian into Madonna's trusted circle; he would become one of her best friends. He flew to Japan, where she was kicking off the tour, and began filming her in March 1990 for what would become a documentary entitled *Truth or Dare* (or *In Bed with Madonna*, as it is known in Great Britain).

Madonna gave Keshishian full access to her world, complete entrée to her life during the tour's four months. He and his camera crew would follow Madonna's every move, while on stage and off, while in makeup and without, while being nice . . . and not so nice.

✝

By the time Madonna began working with Alek Keshishian on her "Blonde Ambiton" documentary, she had already finished her next album.

No doubt, Warren Beatty had realized that hiring Madonna as an actress would be an added bonus attached to *Dick Tracy:* the possibility that she would participate in the soundtrack of his movie. To a film studio, the release of a Madonna record several weeks in advance of a film in which she is involved would automatically amount to millions of dollars' worth of promotion. When Warren Beatty gave Madonna the role of the gold-digging Breathless Mahoney, Disney (the film's distributor) got the benefit of a hugely popular pop star on the soundtrack, and Warner Bros. Records a good reason to release Madonna's seventh album, *I'm Breathless (Music from and Inspired by the Film* Dick Tracy) in May 1990.

Once upon a time, a soundtrack album was just that: a theme or love song from the film among a collection of incidental music also heard in the movie. They were usually only marginally successful in the marketplace. It was the unprecedented seventies success of the biggest selling of all pop-music movie soundtracks, *Saturday Night Fever,* that ultimately inspired film producers and record labels to rethink the notion of the soundtrack album as a viable, money-making concept. By the eighties, and into the nineties, record labels had embraced a different kind of "soundtrack" LP, one on which just a couple of songs from the film were heard. The rest of the music was provided by various artists not heard in the movie, singing songs that had absolutely nothing to do with the film. The concept became a cash cow for the labels—the opportunity to release an album with the promotional distinction of being associated with a film—and in most cases, a corny, blatant misuse of the term "soundtrack" for the rest of us.

Madonna's album would feature three songs she recorded from the film. However, her real challenge would be to write and produce new songs for the collection as well, songs that would have an authentic lyrical/musical connection to the film. Hence, the album's subtitle, *Music from and Inspired by the Film* Dick Tracy. It would be a difficult job because the three songs Madonna would record were written by theater legend Stephen Sondheim. So, the new songs Madonna chose to record would have to be at least comparable in style to his. In Madonna's favor, she would have a hand in producing the entire album—including the Sondheim songs—and her participation would at least ensure some measure of continuity. To help her with this ambitious project, Madonna brought along Patrick Leonard (who had become her most reliable ally in the studio), and recording-engineer-turned-producer Bill Bottrell (whose work with Madonna would serve him well in securing production jobs with Michael Jackson and pop rocker Sheryl Crow).

Madonna and Leonard toiled to create music that would fit the style and attitude of the film, set in *The Untouchables* days of prohibition. They were successful, as Warren Beatty put it, "beyond my wildest dreams." On the album, Madonna and Leonard set the pace with the opener, "He's a Man," a big, intense, vamping bluesy song which Madonna sings as if she's a hooker stalking the boulevard. Vocally, she's magnificent. "I want people to think of me as a musical comedy actress," she said at the time. "That's what this album is about for me. It's a stretch. Not just pop music, but songs that have a different feel to them, a theatrical feel." Indeed, she tackled the Sondheim selections— the moody, determined "Sooner or Later," the modified ragtime of "More" and the quiet, sentimental wonder, "What Can You Lose"— with the verve of a Broadway veteran. Particularly during "What Can You Lose," a duet with Mandy Patinkin, Madonna holds her own, her voice making its first appearance on the song like a flower opening at dawn, warming to the mission at hand. One might wonder what a singer like Barbra Streisand would have brought to the production that Madonna didn't, but such musing doesn't detract from the fact that Madonna's performance truly is sublime.

Comparably, Andy Paley's "I'm Going Bananas" is sweet taffy, a Ricky Ricardo kind of song that Madonna performs totally in Breathless character. Then, as if to say, "Hey, I can do that, too," she and Leonard crafted "Cry Baby," a playful, Roaring Twenties ditty which Madonna sings as Betty Boop. Both tracks, pure fun and games, are left seeming like so much filler when Madonna and Leonard roll up their sleeves to create "Something to Remember." Complex and bittersweet, the ballad sails on a wave of gorgeous, melancholy chords and rambling melody that quietly make it the most compelling thing to which Madonna has ever lent her voice. Should anyone ever query the lady about musical integrity, she can always point to the composition for "Something to Remember"—it would silence even the most accomplished composer.

Madonna also managed to bring a certain dimension to what seemed like the lightest moments. The steamrolling "Hanky Panky" simply sounds like a silly innocent romp until you realize what she's going on and on about is ("Warren's favorite pastime") . . . being spanked! It's difficult to listen to the songs on *I'm Breathless* and not be compelled to try and find the real Madonna in each song. She is, no doubt, more intelligent than Breathless Mahoney, but both possessed the drive and tenacity required to get exactly what they wanted. Consider: in 1983 Madonna was just a fledgling dance-music star looking to do great things. In less than ten years, she was the co-star of a major movie, performing on its soundtrack album, singing a playful duet— "Now I'm Following You"—with Warren Beatty!

As fine as *I'm Breathless* turned out, it still needed a musical hook: a hit song. To that end, Madonna and Shep Pettibone (the brilliant engineer/songwriter/producer still standing in the shadow of Madonna's steady cohorts Steve Bray and Patrick Leonard) dreamed up a sleek song which Madonna would co-write and produce, "Vogue." It's a funky, uptown anthem celebrating the art of "voguing"—a then-popular dance that was more about posing like a high-fashion model than breaking a sweat. Actually, voguing had been around long before Madonna sang about it; like Michael Jackson and his "Moonwalk," dance, Madonna simply introduced to the rest of the world another hot urban trend. The knockout pulsating track was a masterful dance tribute to "Ladies with attitude, fellows who were in the mood" (with an accompanying memorable black-and-white video that was, no doubt, inspired by classic photographs taken by Horst of Hollywood legends). The "Vogue rap" is still one of Madonna's greatest camp musical moments ("Greta Garbo and Monroe, Dietrich and DiMaggio. . .").

Madonna historian Bruce Baron notes that "Vogue" was first planned as the B side of the "Keep It Together" single. When Warner executives heard the song, however, it was decided to issue it as an A side. Baron points out that Madonna had to alter some more suggestive lyrics because the song was to be included on an album connected to a Disney movie.

"Vogue" did what Madonna and Shep Pettibone hoped it would do: it went to Number 1. (Her grand performance of the song on the MTV Video Music Awards in 1990, dressed as Marie Antoinette in a giant hoop-skirt outfit with lots of cleavage, a bouffant wig and white-powder makeup, was a classic camp show that elevated the standards of future performances on that program.)

Then, after "Vogue," "Hanky Panky" did a respectable climb to Number 10. Both singles served to push *I'm Breathless* to Number 2 on *Billboard*'s album chart. It sold two million copies in the U.S. and five million globally.

I'm Breathless is one of Madonna's greatest musical moments, a fairly heady proclamation considering her prolific recording career. "I worked so hard on that record," she later said. "In its time and place, it's important to me." Also, Warren Beatty could not have been more pleased with it and, as her friends have recalled, she wanted nothing more than his approval when it came to all of her work in the film, acting and singing. "He meant a lot to her," confirms Freddy DeMann. "She wanted him to be proud."

Perhaps an indication of Warren's feelings about the album came when he co-hosted a party at his home with Madonna shortly after its release. He asked her to "dress down" for his Hollywood friends such as Jack Nicholson, Michelle Pfeiffer and Al Pacino, as well as the studio heads of various movie companies, the so-called movers and shakers of the business.

Madonna had often commented on Warren's "people skills." It was true in 1990—and is still true today—that his warm, firm handclasp the moment he turns his attention to someone often leaves that person with the feeling that he or she has been touched by something special. Madonna noticed the way people felt quickened by any encounter with Warren, sincerely happy to be in his presence. With her, it was a different story: unless they were real fans, most people were generally fearful of her upon meeting her, worried about what she might say or do to them. Indeed, usually when she walked into a room, people swarmed about her not because they wanted to touch her, but rather because they wanted to see what outrageous event might occur as a result of her presence, who she might insult, what swearword she would utter while doing it. She said that she wanted to learn from Warren how to be more gracious. Therefore, parties at Warren's were always thrilling for Madonna; she enjoyed the company of his influential show-business friends, and appreciated the way they treated her, accepted her as one of their own.

For the *Dick Tracy* party, Madonna wore a simple, bare-back black gown by Halston, her golden hair in a sophisticated twist. She appeared feminine, tailored, graceful and elegant. Smiling, touching, kissing and moving through the crowd, she looked like an experienced socialite. She was breezily conversational with people who usually bored her. She laughed gaily at Warren's jokes. She didn't swear. Did she ever dream she'd come so close to the magic, power and glamour of true Hollywood, and fit in so well? Probably, yes. "She was delightful," recalled a guest, "the perfect hostess."

During the party, Warren played "Something to Remember," from the *Dick Tracy* soundtrack and asked his guests to stop talking long enough to listen to the song. Everyone obliged. Certainly, during these few minutes, Madonna must have felt at least a little awkward as she stood with a martini in one hand, a cigarette in the other . . . and all eyes on her. Even the platoon of tuxedo-clad waiters, stationed like toy soldiers with trays of crudités, pâtés and other appetizers, stopped serving long enough to take notice.

When the song was over, Warren walked over to Madonna and said something to her. She responded with a surprised smile and a nod of what seemed like appreciation. Then, with a flourish, he turned from her and began to applaud. Following his lead, his guests joined in, showering Madonna with cheers, smiles and words of congratulations. For her, it must have been a moment like no other. As Jack Nicholson later remembered, "She stood there and just accepted it all graciously . . . this beautiful, unpredictable, amazing young woman with tears in her eyes, and I thought—Jesus! What a star."

✝

Warren Asks Madonna's Hand in Marriage?

It was 1990. In a few months, Madonna would turn thirty-two. Her career up until this time had been astonishing in many ways. However, her personal life—her romantic relationships with men, in particular—had been less than satisfying. For the most part, each had been fueled by great and overwhelming passion—either intense lovemaking or heated arguing. There was no middle ground. Just as with her father, and then with Sean Penn, Madonna seemed, at least on some level, to feel that a relationship wasn't valid unless it involved screaming and shouting. Even in public, she could not refrain from picking fights with her boyfriends. She seemed unable to understand that it was possible to love a man and still disagree with him without engaging in an endless and loud battle about it.

In the past, no one with whom Madonna had ever been romantically involved did much to support her emotional needs. Many, of course, had assisted her in her quest for stardom. After she was finished with those men, she inevitably tossed them aside. The ones who had tried to help her deal with her emotional problems were also pushed away. Seemingly incapable of true intimacy she, somehow, always managed to attract men like Sean Penn, John Kennedy and now Warren Beatty, all of whom were equally incompetent.

Her love life was about to become even more entangled . . .

On May 16, over a romantic dinner at a Hollywood restaurant after a hard day's dubbing in the studio, Warren Beatty made a surprising move. Either he asked for Madonna's hand in marriage (which is what she told her friends) or he asked her to agree one day to become engaged to marry him (which is how he vaguely described the offer to his friends). Whatever his proposition, he presented her with a six-carat, $30,000 diamond-and-sapphire ring.

Madonna—wearing a long straight blonde wig parted in the middle and what appeared to be a man's classic pinstripe suit with a bustier—slipped the ring on the middle finger of her left hand, ostensibly to conceal the fact that it signified a promise of marriage. After Warren signaled the waiter to refill their glasses of Cristal champagne, the couple toasted the moment. So excited was he that Madonna had accepted his ring, Warren tipped the waiter—one of the sources for this story—$500.

Most of their friends had to agree that the promise between Madonna and Warren—whether it was an actual engagement or, rather, an agreement to one day become engaged—didn't seem to bring them any closer as a couple; they continued in their argumentative way.

"Keep your stupid opinions to yourself," Madonna said to Warren over dinner one night at the Ivy in Los Angeles just days after the "engagement." The reason for the fight remains unclear. Appearing somewhat angry, Beatty tossed a handful of bills onto the table. He got up. He walked out. A chagrined Madonna was left to sit alone and stew—with about fifty bemused patrons gawking at her. "Stop staring at me," she loudly called out before storming off.

When the couple went to San Antonio, Texas, to fulfill a weekend studio publicity commitment, Warren and Madonna stayed at the expensive La Mansion del Rio Hotel. In between press responsibilities, Warren let off steam by golfing while Madonna enjoyed daily facials and other such pampering. Bill Hollerman, a golfing buddy of Beatty's, remarked, "Warren spent the weekend on the telephone to Jack [Nicholson] complaining about Madonna, that she and Sandra Bernhard were planning a big wedding, that Sean Penn was calling him every fifteen minutes screaming at him to leave his ex-wife alone. It went on and on. Beatty said that she wasn't happy unless she was fighting with him. He told me, 'She's a nice girl, but you can't take her out. You don't know what she's going to say, or do, next. You don't know what the next big fight will be about. I'm too old for this.'"

"But you're not old," his friend told him.

"Well, I'm old enough to not want to look foolish," Warren said.

Hollerman also reports that Barbra Streisand, one of Beatty's ex-girlfriends, was also on the telephone to Texas telling him that he was "crazy for falling for a young floozy." A former business associate of Barbra's concurs, "When she heard about Warren and Madonna, she became a great instigator. She and Warren had little to do with each other prior to that news, then suddenly she was his great protector, telling him that Madonna was only using him to advance her film career.

"Also, his elderly mother, Kathleen, still a big influence on his life, did not approve of Madonna. No matter how much Madonna tried to impress the older woman, she was not able to do so." ("It's no wonder," Madonna said, privately. "Look at how many women she has seen with her son. She probably didn't approve of any of them, either.")

An unpredictable breaking point came when Madonna presented Warren with an expensive oil painting as a gift. After politely thanking her, he stashed it behind the couch where he probably intended for it to remain, because it did not match his decor. After three days, Madonna took it upon herself to hang the painting on a wall in his living room. When he saw it displayed without his permission, Warren exploded at her, accusing her of trying to "control" him. The battle raged on from there. It was a small incident but, as often happens, it triggered something in Warren and Madonna that caused a fight big enough to lay ruin to any future plans they may have had.

*

Dick Tracy premiered in June 1990 and, after all the attendant hype, it seemed as if it would be the success Disney had anticipated. It opened to big box-office receipts. (In the end, though, the film would prove to be a financial disappointment, with U.S. sales of only $104 million.)

Madonna was unhappy with the way her production numbers were edited; she has said that she refused to watch the entire movie because she couldn't bear to see the way her routines were cut (she still hasn't seen it). Warren thought she was being silly, which only inspired more arguing between them. Matters became especially tense between the couple when Warren would only agree to a cover of *Newsweek* magazine on the condition that he be featured alone. When *Newsweek*'s editor-in-chief Rick Smith informed Disney studio head Jeffery Katzenberg that without Madonna there would be no cover profile, he ordered that a photograph that included Madonna be immediately sent to the magazine. Still, Madonna thought it disloyal of Warren to try to cut her out of a major magazine cover, and the two engaged in yet another argument, this one about that matter of publicity.

One business associate and friend of Beatty's says, "I was in Florida with Warren [for further *Dick Tracy* promotion] when a call came in from Madonna. 'I'm working,' he told her. We were golfing. That, to me, told the story."

"Do you love her?" Warren's friend asked as the two played golf.

Warren seemed confused by the question. "She's fun," he said. "But what is love, anyway? I really don't think I know. My problem," he admitted, "is that I'm easily bored."

His associate now says, "I wasn't encouraged by his answer. I knew then and there that they would not be getting married, though he did tell me he had asked Jack Nicholson to be his best man if he ever married her. He also said she had asked Sandra Bernhard to be her maid of honor. I thought to myself, well, that sounds like a pretty good show, but maybe not such a good marriage. I knew it would never happen, just by his attitude."

It seemed to some observers that Warren had been worn down by Madonna's insolence. Perhaps the fact that he gave her a symbolic ring said more about his confusion when it came to matters of the heart than it did about his feelings for Madonna. He was like an impulsive, foolhardy schoolboy trying to impress his girlfriend with an expensive, showy gift. However, when the time came to live up to the promise represented by that ring, Warren was unable to meet the challenge—he couldn't commit, just as he had not been able to commit to so many other women in his past. If anyone was going to change Warren Beatty's course in life, it wasn't going to be Madonna. If anything, her behavior only sent him running in the other direction.

"Where have you been?" Madonna demanded to know of Warren, according to Bill Hollerman. The two had just walked into her suite after a day of golfing. Madonna was sitting at a desk facing a wall, sipping tea. She wore a white cottony terry-cloth robe. A wrapped matching towel covered her hair. She had on no makeup, apparently having just showered. "She looked about twelve," recalled Hollerman. "Thirteen, tops."

"Oh, we were golfing," Warren answered. He seemed nonplussed that he should have to respond, given her demanding tone.

"But we were supposed to have lunch," she said, standing up to face him. She was in a foul mood.

"Well, that's what I'm here for now, to have lunch."

Madonna took the towel from her head and began drying her hair.

"And who is this?" she wanted to know. She nodded in the direction of Bill Hollerman without ever looking directly at him.

"He's joining us. Do you mind?"

She made a sour face. "Yes, I mind," she said, flatly. "I don't eat with strangers. You know that, Warren." Turning from them, Madonna went into the bathroom and slammed the door. After a beat, from inside the other room she shouted, "For all I know, he works for the fucking *National Enquirer,* and you want me to fucking eat with him?"

"Charming, isn't she?" Warren said to Bill. The two men left her suite.

The next day, as Beatty's friend observed, Madonna called Warren on his cell phone while he was on the golf course. Beatty held the phone about two feet from his ear and cringed. It was as if her voice scratched on his nerves, like chalk on a blackboard.

While the relationship was clearly doomed, Madonna seemed determined to hang on to Warren Beatty anyway. At the time, she was known by people in her circle to have an addictive personality when it came to men. She seemed to become "hooked" on the drama of whatever relationship she was in at any given time. The fact that she and Warren engaged in such terribly acrimonious fights is what, apparently, tied them together. It was the same kind of drama that had kept her linked to Sean Penn long after their relationship should have been history. While it may not have been a good relationship, it was, at least, still some sort of relationship . . . her way of hanging on to Sean. Now, Madonna wanted to save whatever she had with Warren.

While talking to her about some of her "issues," her friend, millionaire entrepreneur David Geffen, suggested she see a psychiatrist and, after a few visits, Madonna seemed as if she was on the verge of exploding with psychoanalysis when she gave an interview to *Vanity Fair.* "I admit that I have this feeling that I'm a bad girl and I need to be punished," she said. "The part of me that goes around saying, 'Fuck you! Fuck you! I'm throwing this in your face!' is the part that's covering up the part that's saying, 'I'm hurt. And I've been abandoned and I will never need anyone again.' I have also not resolved my Electra complex," she added, without provocation.

"The end of the 'Oh Father' video, where I'm dancing on my

mother's grave, is an attempt to embrace and accept my mother's death." Then, in a moment of astute self-examination, she observed, "I had to deal with the loss of my mother and then had to deal with the guilt of her being gone and then I had to deal with the loss of my father when he married my stepmother. So I was just one angry, abandoned girl. I'm still angry."

✝

The End of Warren

In August 1990, after *Truth or Dare* was finished, Madonna showed Warren Beatty and some other friends of hers a rough cut of it in the screening room of Beatty's home. One friend of Beatty's who was present recalls that she brought popcorn for everybody—a dozen people—and served it with sodas saying, "I want this to be like an old-fashioned movie." (For her own enjoyment, Madonna brought a bottle of soy milk along with Cheddar Lites—fat-free cheese crackers.) Then, as the movie got under way and it became clear that Madonna's salty language would be as it is in real life, Warren said to his friends, "My definition of old-fashioned and her definition of old-fashioned seem somewhat at odds."

"Oh, Christ, when did you get to be so stuffy?" Madonna asked Warren while the film played on and he winced and grimaced at certain scenes. "Don't you remember when you were young and free, and re-bellious? Don't you remember when you walked a thin line?"

Beatty smiled wearily. "Barely," he said.

"My old man," Madonna said lovingly as she put her head on his shoulder. "He'd rather be home looking at his 'Hollywood Ladies of the Eighties' girlie calendar."

Beatty turned away in dismay while watching Madonna teach her dancers how to give oral sex by using a water bottle as a prop. During another scene, when Madonna calls Warren an "asshole" and hangs up on him, he shook his head with disapproval. Perhaps he was wondering if his girlfriend could tell the difference between her personal life and show business. Certainly, to a man as conscientious about privacy as

Warren Beatty, the delineation must have seemed blurred in this documentary.

Later in the film, a conversation between Madonna and Beatty over a room-service meal was caught on camera. "It was completely innocuous," says the friend of Beatty's who was present at the screening. "It wasn't so much what the two of them were saying, it was the way they were saying it. Madonna was being bitchy, as usual, and Warren was tolerant, as usual. You could see him tense up as the scene played out in front of everyone, making him look as if he allowed her to walk all over him. There were other scenes with Warren, too, that I suppose he was unhappy about.

"Afterwards as the credits rolled, there was a lot of applause for Madonna. Warren seemed happy but, if you knew him, you knew he was just acting. She kept prodding him, asking what the problem was. 'What's the matter? You didn't like my movie?' she kept asking, like a child wanting Daddy's approval. Finally, he said, 'You know what? I just have a headache. I'm fine.' Then, she started rubbing the back of his neck saying things like, 'My poor daddy, so tense. So much on his mind.' I thought to myself, my goodness, either she really loves this guy, or she thinks he's her father."

The next day, Madonna received a letter by messenger from Warren Beatty's attorney. In it, the demand was made that certain scenes with Warren be deleted from the final version of the film, or she would be sued. Most of her friends would have predicted a volatile reaction from Madonna. However, there wasn't one. If there was an argument between Madonna and Warren about the legal threat, no one heard about it.

"She didn't say anything to anyone about any of it," said Nikki Harris. "However, I felt a deep sadness in her. But one thing about Madonna that people around her well know is that if she doesn't bring up a sore subject, you don't bring it up, either. The fact that she didn't say a word about the matter said, at least to me, that she was very bothered by it."

In the end, the scenes in question were excised from the movie.

Later, Madonna complained to writer Don Shewey, "There were phone conversations I thought were really moving and touching and revealing, but Warren didn't know we were recording. It wasn't fair, plus it's a federal offense. He, more than anybody, was reluctant to be filmed. Ultimately, I don't think he respected what I was doing or took it seriously. He just thought I was fucking around, making a home movie."

Upon the film's release (in May 1991), some viewers were amazed that Madonna had left intact another surprising and genuinely candid moment. Because she was having throat problems, she visited a throat specialist. When Madonna was asked if she wanted the consultation filmed, Warren Beatty, also present, observed, "She doesn't want to live *off camera*, much less talk." Upon the movie's release she explained, "I think what Warren was trying to say is that he is very shy and private and he doesn't understand my lack of inhibition because he's the opposite of me. What's so intimate about my throat? I mean, my God, everyone knows when I'm having an abortion, when I'm getting married, when I'm getting divorced, who I'm breaking up with. My throat is now intimate? Anyway, the cameras didn't follow me around twenty-four hours a day. They weren't in the room when I was fucking."

There were some incidents, however, that Madonna decided should not be seen by her public. For instance, during the three nights of concerts in Boston, she caused so many problems for the staff of the Boston Harbor Hotel, she's not likely ever to be forgotten there. She and her entourage had taken over thirty rooms on floors nine to eleven, at a cost of $48,000. Making matters difficult for the kitchen staff was that all of her food had to be flown in from Hong Kong.

"She would be absolutely infuriated if she had to wait more than twenty minutes for a specially cooked order," said Diane Demitri, who worked in guest relations at the hotel at that time. "We didn't know how to cook those foods, and so the poor chefs were in the kitchen frantically looking up directions in Asian cookbooks while Madonna was phoning down every ten minutes screaming, 'Where's my fucking noodles? Where's my fucking noodles?' "

Madonna also insisted that none of the staff ask her for autographs, or attempt to chat with her if they saw her in an elevator.

"No employee who came into contact with her was allowed to address her or even act as if they recognized her," said Diane Demitri. "She had registered under the name of Kit Moresby [a character from one of her favorite books, *The Sheltering Sky*] and, even though you knew it was Madonna when she called for room service, you had to address her by the other name.

"Housekeeping called me one morning and said, 'Ms. Moresby is upset because she says her bathwater is a funny color.' I told them to send someone up to her room right away. When he got there, he found 'Ms. Moresby' in a white robe, pacing the floor, livid. Sadly, she was right. The pipes had apparently rusted and the water was slightly off-color. When he apologized, 'Ms. Moresby' took the towel that had been wrapped around her head, rolled it into a ball and hurled it at him. 'How is a woman supposed to bathe in that muck,' she screamed at him. 'I have a show to do tonight. Do you know how much stress I am under? Do you know how torturous my life is?'

"After she and her staff checked out of the hotel, everyone breathed a sigh of relief," said Diane Demitri. "When we went into her suite, she had left on the room service tray a card with her name embossed on it. On it, she wrote, 'What a dump!' "

*

After Warren Beatty's warning that he might litigate against Madonna over her documentary, nothing seemed the same between them—not that it had been good between them prior to his threat. He had already begun to distance himself from her and, despite her apparent desire to do so, Madonna was powerless to salvage the relationship. It was actually Warren's decision that they end it. Madonna had no choice in the matter.

Most of the public seemed unaware of the particulars of the romance between Madonna and Warren, and why it was that she seemed to be so angry whenever asked about him. It was difficult to separate the sensational reports from the truth, and there were so many conflicting tabloid reports that most sensible people simply disregarded all of them.

Madonna spent a couple of days crying over Warren, about how cruel he had been to lead her down this road only to drop her. He again explained that the ring he had given her had been only a friendship ring, not one that signified an engagement.

To Madonna, it may have been like losing a father, as well as a lover, and for no reason she could understand. Warren simply could not commit to a relationship—which is why he stayed single for so long, until Annette Bening finally tamed him. Madonna had her issues, but he had his, too. It could never have worked.

Moreover, Warren Beatty had shown Madonna a side of elite Hollywood she'd never before known, and one that she didn't yet want to abandon. His was a rarefied, exclusive world, one in which he encouraged standing ovations for his girl from big stars at glamorous cocktail parties. It wasn't easy letting go of all of that. How she had enjoyed melting into the elite company of his friends, if only a few times during parties at Warren's. She told intimates that she hated him for having aroused not only emotion in her, but for introducing a new way of life, as well—one in which people carried themselves with grace and dignity rather than with rock and roll arrogance—only then to force her to have to walk away from it. True to her often melodramatic nature, she felt cheated and used. Also true to her personality, Madonna privately said that she was annoyed at herself for not having had the strength to be the one to end it with Warren Beatty before he ended it with her. Everyone in her circle, though, viewed her relationship with Warren for what it had really been: a simple dalliance between two film stars that was not meant to amount to much—one that would probably end up a footnote to the *Dick Tracy* entry of some dreary book about movies of the 1990s.

After it was all over, Madonna attempted to downplay the significance of her romance with Warren Beatty in press interviews, probably because she was truly hurt by him and does not like to portray herself in the public eye as ever having been sad or vulnerable. For his part, Warren has never said a word about how or why the relationship ended.

"I guess I meant nothing at all to Warren Beatty," Madonna said sadly to one person on her management team. "He used me and then tossed me aside like a piece of old meat."

"I don't know about all of that," says her friend Erica Bell. "I always wondered how serious she really was about him. They didn't have much in common, let's face it. But the heart wants what it wants, I guess. And she wanted him. Was it really that Warren was just a big conquest for her? Could be," Erica Bell concludes, answering her own question. "I think she went after him because she could, because he was good prey. But then, as it sometimes happens, the hunter got captured by the game."

The Tony Ward Epiphany

On August 16, 1990, Madonna's thirty-second birthday, she received a package at her home, a gift from Warren Beatty. When she opened the box, she found a brooch that probably cost about $300. It seemed like a cheap present; unimpressed, she dismissed it with a quick flick of the hand. "I need to take a drive," she said, looking somber. She then got into her car with a friend who happened to be with her when the package was delivered. "If Warren and I weren't finished before, we sure are now," Madonna said. She kicked off her high heels and began driving barefoot. As she steered her black Mercedes 560SL around a sharp curve of Mullholland Drive, she tossed the brooch out of the window.

Annoyed by the way her romance with Warren Beatty had turned out, Madonna began to take stock of her life. At thirty-two, she looked back on the years—as she would later recall—and began to realize that she could only remember her life by what she was doing in her career at the time. She enjoyed her fame, still, and her career was thriving. She couldn't stop now. She wouldn't think of it. However, she was beginning to feel pangs of regret. "What had she given up to get where she was now? That was the question," recalled one of her brothers. Though not ready to address such concerns fully at this time, Madonna did what many unhappy people do when they feel desperate and lonely . . . especially at the end of a relationship—even a mediocre one, such as the one she had with Warren Beatty: they transfer their emotions to another person in what is then known as a rebound relationship.

Young, handsome Tony Ward was Madonna's rebound from Warren Beatty. While smoking a Marlboro cigarette and, perhaps, looking for love, Madonna spotted the twenty-six-year-old Tony on Malibu

Beach. His body was slender and coltish. His eyelashes were long and dark. His skin translucent. Though he had appeared as an extra in her "Like a Prayer" and "Cherish" videos, Madonna paid him little attention then. Now, it was her thirty-second birthday, and she knew immediately that Tony should be her special gift. She went over to him and—who knows why—proceeded to grind out her cigarette on his back. She then reached around him and pinched one of his nipples so hard, he cried out, "Fuck!" Rather than be angry, Ward was fascinated. His good-looking face broke into a grin. "I think I can balance my glass on your ass," she told him. "You know, I just love a man with an ass like yours." She patted his butt softly; he closed his eyes, like a puppy. Then she traced his lips with her fingertip. The attraction between them was immediate.

After they got to know each other, Madonna found Tony to be kind, gentle and understanding. Though she didn't speak much about what had occurred with Warren Beatty, Ward would later say that he sensed an underlying unhappiness in Madonna's personality. "I'm not a woman who likes to admit to needing anyone or anything," Madonna told him. "I've always thought of that as being a weakness." It was as if she needed someone in whom to confide. However, any shared confidences would have to wait because, that night, Madonna and Tony shared her bed.

Afterward, Madonna couldn't stop talking to friends about Tony's body, so hard and firmly muscled. "A nice change from Warren," she cracked.

Says Erica Bell, "Madonna was essentially holding casting calls for a boyfriend, and this was the guy she chose. Physically he was perfect for her. If you had a computer dating service, and you fed all her preferences into the computer, Tony Ward is what would come out. Five foot six, about 170 pounds, dark and sexy with the most beautiful brown eyes."

The couple didn't waste much time in moving forward with their relationship. They actually had a lot in common, including their love of movies. "When I fell in love with film as a kid, I was emotionally affected," Tony Ward, today an actor who has appeared in a number of independent films, now says. "When I was a kid, I watched *Grease* fifty-plus times. I watched *Hello, Dolly!* fifty times. I watched endless Lucille Ball and I was addicted to Danny Kaye movies, Abbott and

Costello, Katharine Hepburn and Jimmy Stewart. I wish I could have done a film with Danny Kaye," he says. "He was my favorite actor, the one I most related to."

Tony moved into Madonna's Hollywood mansion in September 1990.

"It was so weird because he always fantasized about making love to Madonna," recalls fashion designer Jayme Harris, who was one of Tony's many girlfriends at the time. "He also used to wish that he could have sex with me and have Madonna there watching. Tony wanted to do everything—to play my love slave and, also, my maid. For instance, he wanted to cook, do the dishes, take the trash out and make the bed. He liked high heels and thigh-high boots."

Not surprisingly, given that both had a penchant for the outrageous, Madonna and Tony had an unusual, unconventional relationship. They enjoyed playing "role games," and, she later admitted, few men were as accommodating as he was when it came to making her fantasies come true. Tony was bisexual, a cross-dresser and a nude model for homosexual magazines and leather pinups. Using the name Anthony Borden Ward, he was most known by some factions of the gay community for his nude six-page layout in a magazine called *In Touch for Men* in 1985. "He was such a hit with our readers that the issue completely sold out within a few weeks," recalled Keith Saltar, an editor at the magazine.

To entertain herself, Madonna would make up Tony and dress him in women's clothing—including underwear—and then go out on the town with him as her new "girlfriend." Ward also enjoyed playing a subservient role in Madonna's fantasies. For instance, when she took him to a birthday party for photographer Herb Ritts, she told him that she wanted him to wear jeans, and nothing else. When he insisted on adding a black leather vest to the ensemble, she allowed it. (For her part, she wore a black Chanel jacket, black tights, black sunglasses and black ankle boots.) She then proceeded to "humiliate" him in front of the guests by forbidding him to speak even a word in her presence. He seemed to enjoy the game. When she demanded that he shave off his Fu Manchu mustache in front of the partygoers, he obeyed. Later, Madonna organized a game of Truth or Dare. During it, she dared Ward to strip for the crowd. He eagerly complied. When she further dared him to pull down his briefs and expose himself to the guests, he did that as well. That night, the two went back to her place—perhaps excited by their party antics—and enjoyed another "wild ride" together. If she felt powerless about the way in which her relationship with Warren Beatty had ended, she was certainly balancing the scale with Tony Ward. In *this* relationship, she was the one calling the shots.

"I don't like being controlled," she told him one day. "To be free, you need a lot of money, and power, which I have" . . . and which Tony didn't have.

On September 18, Tony accompanied Madonna to a New York City screening of the film *GoodFellas* at the Museum of Modern Art. Recalls journalist Kelly Winters, "I asked Madonna who her date was, and she said his name was Nick Neal. He [Tony] looked at her with a confused expression, and she turned to him and snapped, 'Your name is Nick Neal now, so just deal with it.' "

Madonna then ran her fingers through Tony's thick, dark hair, seeming to luxuriate in the feel. Suddenly, she grabbed a tuft and pulled hard, making him cry out, "Fuck!" With that, she bit his ear. "Fuck!" he cried, again. Madonna looked pleased.

Recalls Kelly Winters, "Later, I heard someone ask her about Warren Beatty. She laughed in his face. 'Who?' she asked. 'Oh, you mean that guy I did that movie with? The last I heard, he was in a [retirement] home somewhere.' "

On December 10, 1990, Madonna learned that she was pregnant with Tony's child. As she had been feeling queasy for a few days, she had told him that she suspected she was expecting, and asked him to accompany her to Cedars-Sinai Medical Center for the necessary tests. She had hoped it was true that she was pregnant. He wasn't sure what to hope for, "except to just hope for the best." When her physician, Dr. Randy Harris, confirmed that she was expecting, Madonna was jubilant. "I want this child more than anything else in my life," she told a friend the next day on the telephone.

"Will you marry Tony?" the friend wanted to know.

Madonna sighed deeply, as if acknowledging defeat in the marriage department. "I doubt it," she said, sounding weary. "But I guess I can raise the kid on my own. In fact, I know I can do it."

She must have realized that Tony was not husband material for her.

Still, she was happy about the pregnancy. Perhaps she reasoned that if she could not have a satisfying relationship with a man, at least she could have one with her own child.

However, just a few days after the good news, came the bad. Because of gynecological complications, the health of Madonna's baby was already in jeopardy. In what must have been a heart-wrenching consultation, Harris recommended to Madonna and Tony that she terminate the pregnancy. This was crushing news. Madonna had undergone a number of abortions in the past, and had vowed to bring to full term any other baby she conceived. However, it was not meant to be. On December 14, Tony accompanied her to Cedars for a dilation and curettage (D&C), which took just fifteen minutes, but which also took a toll on Madonna.

Tony, who had been pacing the floor while the surgery was taking place, recalled, "When I came back to the room, she was crying. It was very upsetting. She wanted that baby, and it seemed unfair that she couldn't have it."

Madonna was impressed by the way Tony Ward cared for her. He was supportive in every way, determined to show her that he could be a good mate. He loved her, that much was clear to any observer, and hoped for a future with her. Tony, for whatever his faults, was different from the men Madonna had recently known. He seemed really to want to be with her, and to have no ulterior motives. "I've been with a great many men and women," he told her. "But none that I've really loved. Until now." For her part, she said she felt "safe" with him. However, there were problems: Ward was confused and immature in ways that were impossible to deny. He had a secret: he was a married man.

Four days after Tony met Madonna, he and his girlfriend Amalia Papadimos were wed in Las Vegas. After the ceremony, Tony was ambivalent; he didn't know if he wanted to be with his wife, or with Madonna. Two weeks later, he told his wife that it wouldn't work out between them.

"We never really spent time together," Tony explains of his marriage. "She was shocked that I would change my mind like that. But I love her, still. She's my buddy. Obviously, being married for two weeks and then saying, 'I can't do this,' put her in a really bad spot."

He also didn't know whether or not to tell Madonna of his marriage, and opted not to do so immediately. Instead, he moved into her home and, perhaps, hoped "for the best."

"It was just before Christmas, I believe, that Tony told Madonna that he was a married man. I guess that was a big hurt for her," says Tina Stanton, who also dated Tony at this time. "I once overheard Madonna tell him, 'Guys like you usually bounce right off my radar screen. I'm not even sure why I ended up with you, except that I couldn't resist you.' Plus, she saw something in Tony, a naiveté, an innocence, a good heart."

The fact that Madonna would tell Tony Ward that a man such as himself would "bounce right off" her "radar screen" indicates that she didn't understand herself as well at this time as she may have thought. If anything, she was *attracted* to men like Tony, welcomed them into her world . . . and, inevitably, paid the price for such poor judgment. Not only was Tony emotionally unavailable—like Sean Penn, John Kennedy and Warren Beatty—he was married.

It was at a Christmas party at her home in December that Madonna and Tony became embroiled in an argument that would be the subject of discussion among her intimates for years to come.

Dressed for the festive and formal occasion in a black Gaultier halter-top dress, Madonna's hair that evening was short and blonde. One would never know from her easy composure that she'd had such a bad day. A household employee had poured the wrong bath essences into her hot tub at home, turning her hair green while she relaxed in it. (One can only imagine her reaction upon making this discovery in the mirror on the morning of a big party!) It took her hairdresser four hours to restore her "natural" blonde color, at a cost of $750. Now, she looked terrific. White-coated waiters circulated among the guests—the usual relatives, friends and business consorts mixed with the publicity seekers and hangers-on who hoped to be mentioned in the gossip columns the next day—with trays of chilled champagne and warm hors d'oeuvres.

A pretty girl who couldn't have been more than sixteen—her eyes heavily veiled by drugs—threw herself into Tony's arms, asking to be taken. Madonna glared for a moment, then shrugged and turned away.

Later, Tony spotted Madonna dancing with a man he had long viewed as a rival for her affections. As he watched them cuddle on the dance floor, he seethed until he could take it no more.

"Hey, you're *my* woman," Tony suddenly hollered. "Knock it off."

"Oh yeah?" Madonna countered as she broke away from her dance partner. "You have your nerve. I'm my *own* woman."

Angry, Tony grabbed an expensive Chinese vase and threw it to the floor, shattering it.

In retaliation, Madonna hurled an antique lamp at him. He ducked. Everyone watched with horrified fascination as the lamp hit the wall and smashed to bits.

In response, Tony took a silver tray of crudités, pâtés and olives and threw it to the floor with a crash.

Then, in the finest tradition of melodramatic frustration and rage, Madonna said, "Out! Everyone, get the fuck out. The party's over." Turning to Tony, she further clarified, "And that includes you. Get out!" Then, she turned and walked out of the room, leaving everyone to fetch their wraps and jackets.

The next day, Ward apologized profusely and presented Madonna with a new vase filled with white roses. It was a sweet gesture, yet one that would not change anything. After all, how many more hair-raising scenes could she tolerate in affairs of the heart?

Bingo. It was at this time that she had an epiphany.

Unwittingly, the existence of Tony Ward in Madonna's world had provided a transformative catalyst, one that would alter her life. Something in her had been adjusted by the holiday confrontation with Tony. Who knows what spurred it—maybe it was the flying vase?—but, finally, she had made a decision about what she expected from the men in her life. It probably wasn't just the experience with Tony Ward. Rather, it was likely the cumulative experiences of Madonna's doomed romances up until this point, all of which, finally, brought into clear focus what she wanted in a relationship . . . and—bless his heart—it wasn't Tony Ward, or anyone like him.

"Look, I need more," Madonna told Sandra Bernhard, "than melodramatic nonsense." Friends like Sandra say that the final conflict with Tony marked a defining moment for Madonna, but, like many such moments in life, it wasn't thunderous. It wasn't monumental. It was just a simple moment of clarity, yet one important enough to inform everything that would follow it. Or, as Madonna put it to Sandra, "I feel as if my disorganized mind has just been organized."

"Tony, you're just not enough for me," Madonna said to him, as

Tony later recalled. "I'm finally at a stage in my life where I realize that I have to have more than what you can offer. I see that now." Tony was thrown. It was startling, he would later say, to hear Madonna suddenly so certain about what she wanted, what she deserved. The pain of it, of course, was that her newly painted picture didn't include him.

"If that's how you feel about it," he told her in a crushed voice, "then I guess there's nothing I can do but leave."

"It was really hard for me to take, to hear her say that to me," Tony recalls. "It was a very powerful statement. I was feeling very hurt, very abandoned and all of these 'poor me' things. It took me a long time to understand. I still have a very strong love for Madonna, and it doesn't matter to me whether she's here with me, or somewhere else. If I never see her again, I will still always love her. I know that if she's in a pinch, if the chips are down and she needs a friend, that she realizes she can call me and I'll be there."

"I don't want us to hate each other," Tony Ward remembers Madonna telling him as she hugged him good-bye. "I'm just so exhausted," she said, perhaps referring to her most recent romances. "After people break up, they say terrible things about each other. I'm not going to do that to you, Tony," she concluded. "I'm not going to let anyone else do it, either."

"Madonna, if people knew the real you, I think they'd be surprised," Tony Ward told her.

"Well, let's just hope they never find out," she said. "After all, I have an image to protect."

✝

The Immaculate Collection

By the end of 1990, a new greatest hits album from Madonna was ready for release from Warner Bros. Records, *The Immaculate Collection*. Actually, this was much more than a mere collection of Madonna's biggest-selling and most popular songs. It served as a proud landmark for a career that, from its professional inception, had moved in only one direction: up.

Released in November with its title a clever play on the biblical reference to Mary's immaculate conception of Jesus, the album contained more genuine hits than a Top 40 radio station usually plays in an hour. It was an audio chronicle of Madonna's wild ride thus far, starting at the beginning with three of her first singles—"Holiday," "Lucky Star" and "Borderline"—and moving on to the present day. Detractors could say what they wanted about the woman being a flash in the pan with little talent (and, believe it or not, there were actually sceptics, both fans and members of the music industry, still expecting Madonna to have a short-lived career), but *The Immaculate Collection* crystallized the reality of the Madonna success story: "Like a Virgin," "Material Girl," "Crazy for You," "Into the Groove," "Live to Tell," "Papa Don't Preach," "Open Your Heart," "La Isla Bonita," "Like a Prayer," "Express Yourself," "Cherish" and "Vogue"—fifteen hit records in all. Some of the most successful pop stars in the world have come and gone without ever having even a single Number 1 record. It is the ultimate goal of any pop artist to top the record-selling charts—*The Immaculate Collection* contained eight of Madonna's chart-toppers.

Madonna's success as a recording artist wasn't really difficult to fathom if one understood what she represented. Someone like Pat Benatar was cool, but she was a rocker, not a pop star. Madonna was the kind of female artist who didn't come along often in pop culture—a white girl with attitude who could keep a beat. (Nancy Sinatra personified her generation's version of it in the sixties when she recorded her hit, "These Boots Were Made for Walkin'," but the jig was up when it was soon discovered the attitude belonged to the record and not to Nancy.)

Madonna's music always had something for everyone. While not too funky for the white kids in suburbia to embrace, it was still rhythm and blues and hip-hop enough for inner-city kids—her core black audience—also to endorse. After all, several million records ago, Madonna was a dance act, an artist whose energy and inspiration emanated from the streets. If Madonna debuted in the twenty-first century, she'd most likely be considered a hip-hop act—too spunky and independent-minded to be the next Britney Spears and too cutting edge to be the next Jessica Simpson or even the next Mariah Carey. She would still be unique, even if she was a new artist.

Before Madonna, the last singer to meld so effectively dance and pop influences was Donna Summer and her songwriters/producers Giorgio Moroder and Pete Bellote (and later just Summer and Moroder), whose brand of Europop successfully transcended mere disco. But Summer, however successful, was not armed with Madonna's uncanny musical sense of self and of the marketplace—instincts integral to creating the hit records that were compiled for *The Immaculate Collection*. By 1990, the production on some of those hits might have sounded a little dated (the drum machine was both one of the best and worst inventions of twentieth-century pop music), but the songs themselves were timeless.

Unlike most young artists who came along when she did, Madonna could redefine her identity at will. While she could easily create party music such as "Into the Groove" and "Express Yourself," she could also appreciate a cute pop ditty like "Cherish." She could also completely relate to serious, soul-bearing love songs such as "Live to Tell" and "Crazy for You," and do so without exhibiting even a trace of the cynicism required to make smart, self-deprecating records such as "Material Girl" and "Like a Virgin." (Prince could also be as versatile, but not until much later in his career was he able to take himself less seriously on records. Michael Jackson could never do it. To him, record making is such serious business, there's no room in it for irony.) For Madonna, the reward for such versatility came in the form of a string of enduring hit records. *The Immaculate Collection* reached Number 2 on *Billboard*'s album chart. It eventually sold an amazing eighteen million copies worldwide, nine million of that number in the United States and five million in the United Kingdom. The marketplace spoke loud and clear in its acknowledgment that the music was as enjoyable the second time around as the first.

Of course, *The Immaculate Collection* had assistance in getting the attention of record buyers with the inclusion of two new Madonna songs. "Justify My Love," which would serve as the album's first single, was written and produced by fledgling rocker Lenny Kravitz with keyboardist André Betts serving as associate producer. (Later, Ingrid Chavez, a muse of Prince's signed to his Paisley Park label, came forward to claim—and also end up receiving—a share of the credit for writing some of the lyrics.)

On paper "Justify My Love" must have sounded rather simple—a funky drum pattern under a droning, aural synthesizer pad, with

Madonna speaking sexy verses over the music, Kravitz casually moaning a melody in the background. The result was one of the few songs in Madonna's career on which she didn't actually have her creative imprint. Except for adding a few words, she let Kravitz shape the track. The finished mix oozed pungent sex—it was just that passionate. The single would hit Number 1 on the *Billboard* chart, but not without the controversy that somehow always seemed to surround a new Madonna project.

Since *The Immaculate Collection* album was to be issued just before the release of her *Truth or Dare* documentary, Madonna was determined to keep the public's interest in her at a peak. She decided—no surprise here!—that the creation of a good controversy could only work to her sales advantage. The problem was that she had crossed the line of what most people would consider good taste so many times in recent years, it had now become more difficult for her to shock the public. She needed a new idea, and it came to her when, during an interview, a journalist asked if any of her videos had ever been banned from MTV.

The "Justify My Love" video—directed by Jean Baptiste Mondino—seems to have been made with the specific intention of having it be banned from television broadcast. In order to create the necessary outrage, Madonna incorporated into the video many of the themes that had generated headlines for her in the past. The concept is a simple one: Madonna, once again donning her Marilyn getup, stumbles into a hotel room where an orgy seems to be taking place. Intrigued, she watches as topless and butch-looking lesbians fondle one another, transvestites cuddle, a voyeuristic and drugged-looking Tony Ward leers. Later, Madonna deep-kisses an androgynous lesbian, and then runs out of the hotel, giggling mischievously.

Whether MTV was an unwitting participant or a co-conspirator in Madonna's scheme to create a sensation seems fairly clear. The convenient chain of events ran like this: after heavily advertising an "All Madonna Weekend," of which Madonna's "Justify My Love" video was to be the main attraction, the station suddenly announced with great fanfare that the video could not be broadcast because it was "religiously and sexually offensive." On November 29, 1990, MTV announcer Kurt Loder explained to the channel's international audience that, "When MTV programming executives got their first look at the video's steamy bed scenes, gay and lesbian snuggling, S&M and briefly bared female breasts, they decided they couldn't air it." (Certainly few people who watch MTV would be disinterested in such a video with that kind of description.)

Suddenly, Madonna had scored a coup that had previously eluded her: a banned video.

As soon as the video was banned, Madonna's publicity juggernaut once again began to roll. There was much protestation from Madonna, who talked a great deal about censorship and how "unfair" it all was to her. By this time, though, the media and public had long ago caught on to Madonna's game of "controversy before product." Still, Sire Records executive Seymour Stein seemed to buy into the game, or at least act as if he did: "When she went in to make the video for 'Justify My Love,' she didn't make a video for the purposes of having it banned, so it couldn't be shown . . . I think she just believes in what she is doing."

When ABC-TV's respected late-night program, *Nightline,* decided to air a special devoted to the controversy, and then show the video in its uncut entirety, Madonna agreed to be interviewed for the program on December 3, 1990. "There was this enormous hoopla over a music video," recalls Forrest Sawyer, her interviewer. "It was all kind of astonishing." During the interview, Sawyer pointed out the obvious: as a result of the controversy, the video—available in stores within a week of its ban, and just in time for Christmas at $9.95— would most certainly make even more money for all concerned. "Yeah," Madonna said, shrugging, "so, lucky me." The video single sold over 400,000 copies.

While "Justify My Love" was controversial, breaking all the rules, by comparison, the second single from *The Immaculate Collection,* the up-tempo "Rescue Me," written and produced by Madonna with Shep Pettibone, was standard, pulsating dance fare. It rocketed itself to Number 9 on the pop chart, inducting itself into the exclusive club formed by sixteen other Number 1 and Top 10 hits that made *The Immaculate Collection* a project both to behold and respect.

✝

On March 25, 1991, Madonna was scheduled to perform Stephen Sond-heim's Oscar-nominated "Sooner or Later" from *Dick Tracy* at the Academy Awards ceremony. However, she had a dilemma: who should accompany her to the awards? Who would make the biggest impact on the media, cause the biggest sensation? For Madonna, it was always about "sensation," when it came to public appearances with dates, as opposed to a selection based on with whom she might have the best time. She had no one in her life, anyway. She was between men and, after the quiet but powerful revelation that was Tony Ward, her standards had been raised. "Who is the last person on the planet people would expect me to be seen with?" she asked her manager, Freddy De-Mann.

"Prince?" he offered. No, she said, "I hate him, now."

"How about Warren?" No, she said, again. "I hate *him*, now."

"Tony Ward?" Again, no.

Then Madonna exclaimed, "How about Michael Jackson? Oh my God, what a great idea. Don't you love it?"

Freddy DeMann agreed that such a pairing would be "surprising," especially since Jackson had just signed the biggest recording deal in history with CBS Records, potentially worth $1 billion. "Maybe he can teach me how to make money," Madonna joked. "And maybe I can teach him how to spend it."

Since he had once managed Jackson, it was a matter of a few tele-phone calls before DeMann arranged a "date" between his present and former clients, two of America's greatest and most controversial pop-music icons. The date was set for dinner at the Ivy restaurant in Beverly Hills, a week before the awards show. But, on the appointed evening, Madonna almost forgot about it. She was having a bad day. Freddy had sent over to her home, as a gift, a three-foot wooden statue . . . of Madonna. "Now, why would he do that?" Madonna asked, scratching her head. "I mean, it's so spooky. Look at it," she told friends who hap-pened to be with her when it arrived. There, in the middle of the floor, stood the statue, carved in teak, a perfect likeness of Madonna, smirking. "I'm afraid that if I go to sleep, it'll come after me with a knife," she said, and she didn't seem to be joking. She sent the statue back to her manager.

An hour before she was to collect Michael (he told her he would drive but, according to Michael, she said, "Are you crazy? *I'll* drive!") Madonna was still wearing her hot-pink silk robe, eating a snack and watching a piece about herself on a tabloid television program. According to a friend who was with her at this time, as she watched the broadcast, she said, "Look at this report about me and Warren [Beatty] breaking up. Why, it's all true. Every fucking word of it is true!"

While spreading butter and marmalade on a croissant, she cocked her head and closely examined her friend. "Listen, if I ever find out you've been snitching on me to these shows, you are out of here. Do you hear me?" she said. When the friend assured her that she wasn't the source of the story, Madonna said, "Well, they got it all right, so *some-one* is a snitch around here, and it sure isn't me." Then, after a moment's thought, she concluded, "You know, I wouldn't be surprised if it was Warren. He loves publicity, no matter what he says, especially if it makes him look like a big shot." Meanwhile, as Madonna continued to watch the program, it hit her. "Oh my God, Michael Jackson," she exclaimed, jumping from the couch. "I completely forgot. How could I forget about Michael Jackson?"

There had probably been times when Michael Jackson wished he could forget about Madonna. As he once said, "She's always in your face, isn't she? I don't get it. What is it about her? She's not a great dancer or singer. She does know how to market herself," he said. "That must be it."

Two years earlier, in 1989, Warner Bros. Records had paid for an advertisement in one of the industry trade publications pronouncing Madonna "Artist of the Decade." Even though most people in the business understood that this ad was the kind of empty compliment record labels often paid artists in promotions they financed themselves, Michael Jackson was particularly annoyed by it. An irate Jackson, who had sold more records with his *Thriller* album than anyone in history, telephoned his attorney John Branca to complain that Madonna didn't deserve such acclamation. "See, it makes me look bad," he explained, as Branca later remembered. "I'm the artist of the decade, aren't I? Did she outsell *Thriller?*" Michael asked Branca. "No, she did not," he said, answering his own question.

In response to his client's agitation, Branca suggested that they approach MTV with the idea of a fictional award they could give to Michael. Off the top of his head, Branca came up with "The Video Vanguard Artist of the Decade" award. Michael liked it. "That'll sure teach that heifer," he said, referring to Madonna.

Now, two years later, Michael found himself sitting across from Madonna at a table at the Ivy, and staring at the object of his derision. Madonna was wearing a black jacket and short pants with lacy stockings and a cross around her neck. Her blonde hair lay shining, bright and brassy against her sleek, bare shoulders, dark roots proudly on display. Jackson was in black jeans, a red shirt and matching jacket emblazoned with a cartoon sailor's image. He had on his trademark fedora, his black, curly hair shoulder length. To the author he recalled of the date, "I had my sunglasses on. And I'm sitting there, you know, trying to be nice. And the next thing I know, she reaches over and takes my glasses off. Nobody has ever taken my glasses off . . . And, then, she throws them across the room and breaks them," Jackson continued. "I was shocked. 'I'm your date now,' she told me, 'and I hate it when I can't see a man's eyes.' I didn't much like that."

Later during dinner, Madonna caught Michael sneaking a look at her cleavage. With a lascivious grin, she grabbed his hand and put it on her chest. "How do you like them?" she asked, teasing him.

Jackson pulled his hand away, nervously.

Later, during dinner, she dropped a piece of bread down her cleavage, and then fished it out and ate it just to see Michael's reaction.

"Oh my God, you should see the muscles on that woman," Michael recalled. "I mean, she's got muscles in her arms way bigger than mine. They're, like, rippling, you know? I wanted to know how she got muscles that big, but didn't want to ask because I was afraid she'd make me show her *my* muscles."

A week later, the odd couple—described by *People* magazine as "Pop's Billion-Dollar Boy and the Queen of Steam"—showed up at the Academy Awards presentation at the Shrine Auditorium in Los Angeles.

Madonna looked perhaps more like Marilyn Monroe than ever before in a low-cut, strapless, white-sequined, body-gripping Bob Mackie gown and ermine wrap. Her lips were cherry red. Her blonde hair, which framed her face in soft waves, seemed to catch and hold all the light around her. On her neck she wore $20-million worth of jewels on loan from Harry Winston. Michael looked spectacular in a matching white-sequined suit with a large diamond brooch, gloves and gold-tipped cowboy boots. The two sat in the front row, on the aisle. During the broadcast, Madonna's performance of "Sooner or Later" was more than just a tribute to Marilyn; it seemed as if she had appropriated just about every one of Monroe's mannerisms and characteristics. The audience was appreciative. However, the crowd's acceptance didn't mean as much to Madonna as a telephone call she received the next day from her father telling her that he thought her performance was "great." Coming from the rarely complimentary Tony Ciccone, this was praise indeed. Much to her and Michael's clear delight, the song went on to win the Academy Award for Best Song.

During the annual Oscar party hosted by the late literary agent Swifty Lazar at Spago in Hollywood, Madonna and Jackson caused a media sensation with their much anticipated arrival. As flashbulbs popped all around them, Madonna was asked by Hollywood reporter Army Archerd how she was able to convince the usually reclusive Michael to accompany her to such a public event. "Oh, Michael's coming out more," she answered with a laugh.

Once inside Spago, however, Madonna drifted from the persistently shy Michael and wound up at Warren Beatty's side. Who can explain her actions? Perhaps because Michael is so insulated by power, money and his own obsessive need for privacy, she couldn't find anything to talk to him about regarding the real world. Beatty's date, model Stephanie Seymour, had neglected to show up, leaving him open to Madonna's attention; Madonna seemed not to hold a grudge against Warren. She was flirtatious, even.

Poor Michael Jackson stood awkwardly alone in the middle of a roomful of celebrities, many of whom couldn't help but gawk at him. Luckily, his mentor Diana Ross was present to take him under her protective wing.

"Well, I just don't understand it, Michael," she told him loudly enough for anyone standing near them to overhear. "I mean, she's supposed to be with you, isn't she? So, what is she doing with him [Beatty]?"

"I don't know," Michael said. "I guess she likes him better."

Across the room, Madonna cuddled with Warren, nibbling his ear and whispering to him as if they were still a couple. Diana Ross, sipping a glass of champagne, eyed Madonna with scepticism. "Well, I think she's an awful woman," Diana decided after a few moments. She drained her glass. "Tacky dress, too."

"Yeah," Michael agreed, glumly. "Tacky."

"Michael didn't much like her, but he knew a good thing when he saw one," one of his attorneys recalls, "and so Michael decided to ask Madonna to appear in the video for his song 'In the Closet.' They had a few meetings, which I personally arranged. She was interested, but she said something like, 'Look, if we're going to do this thing, it's not going to be just a silly little love song. I mean, we have to do something completely and utterly outrageous or I won't be into it. Agreed?' Michael said, 'Cool. Let's do it. Let's do something wild.' "

A few days later, Madonna telephoned Michael with her "outrageous" video concept: since the song was called "In the Closet," she would appear in drag as a man, while he would appear as a woman.

Perhaps because Jackson's sexuality had for years been a topic of discussion in the media, Michael was immediately concerned. He told Madonna that he would need time to think about her idea, and he then telephoned his closest ally, his sister Janet. Janet also never had much respect for Madonna. ("If I took off my clothes in the middle of a highway, people would look at me, too," she once said. "Does that make me an artist?") However, Janet felt Michael should agree to Madonna's terms. "They'll never expect that from you," Janet said of the public. "It'll be your way of making fun of them for the way they think of you. And with Madonna? Wow, what a statement." Still, Michael decided to pass on the idea.

Of Michael, Madonna said to the gay magazine the *Advocate*, "I keep telling Michael Jackson, 'I'd love to turn Jose and Luis [her dancers at the time] on you for a week. They'd pull you out of the shoebox you're in. Anybody who's in a shoebox in the closet cannot be in one after hanging around with Luis and Jose. Or me, for that matter.' "

Some years later (in October 1994) in speaking of Michael, and of Prince as well, she concluded to the *Los Angeles Times,* "I could never say that either of them were friends. I've spent a great deal of time with both of them. They're very different people, but I felt the same with both. I felt like a peasant next to them, like this big clumsy farm girl. Like, when I'm hungry, I eat. When I'm thirsty, I drink. When I feel like saying something, I say it. And they have these manners and they're just so careful about what they eat, and what they say. But it's never too late to start being a human being. If they could just try being something close to that. I can't imagine either of those guys putting on sweat pants and sneakers and going out for a run, playing outside with a dog or just being silly and hanging out with your friends without your makeup on. You know what I mean? I don't think they do that."

☦

Ingrid

After the Academy Awards of 1991, Madonna met a fascinating woman who was to become one of her closest friends, Ingrid Casares. Casares, an attractive and stylish Cuban-American, was introduced to Madonna by Sandra Bernhard. At the time, she was working as a model booker at Wihelmina Modeling Agency in Los Angeles when her lover, Sandra, took her to Madonna's birthday party. Casares, who proudly declared, "I don't classify myself sexually," has since become a staple in gossip columns for being involved with a string of female lovers, including Bernhard, k.d. lang, the model Maureen Gallagher and singer Billie Myers. "You get involved with certain groups, make social contacts," she explained years later, "that's how I met my friends, and Madonna especially, who's my best friend." Although she once quipped that she could "discover a cure for cancer and still only be known as Madonna's girlfriend," Casares has proved herself to be a capable businesswoman. She has owned three successful nightclubs in Miami—Liquid, Joia and Bar Room.

With her boyish, short, dark hair and contagious personality, Ingrid appealed to Madonna who, after meeting her, said that she wanted to get to know her better. The two became fast friends, much to the dismay of Sandra Bernhard.

Photographer Chita Mavros was a friend of Ingrid at the time. She recalls, "Ingrid and Sandra were having certain relationship problems. Sandra asked Madonna to talk to Ingrid, to intervene and help her work things out. However, in the course of doing that, Madonna and Ingrid became very close, very quickly. Suddenly, all Ingrid could talk about was 'Madonna, this' and 'Madonna, that.' Sandra was upset."

Since that time, Sandra has said she could have solved her problems with Ingrid if only Madonna had stayed out of them. "She felt that Madonna—with her show-business lifestyle and wild days and nights—was a complete distraction to Ingrid," said Chita Mavros. "Then, she accused Madonna of sleeping with Ingrid, though Madonna denied it.

"Madonna and Sandra had some horrible fights about Ingrid. One day, Sandra went to Ingrid's apartment, and who did she find coming out of the shower in nothing but a towel? Madonna. Sandra went berserk, screaming and hollering and accusing Ingrid of cheating on her with her best friend. There was no controlling her, she was that irate. After that, she and Ingrid broke up, and she and Madonna were no longer friends."

The irony, at least according to Chita Mavros, was that Ingrid and Madonna were probably not involved in a sexual relationship. Ingrid had said that Madonna wasn't her "type," and that she just appreciated her friendship. Certainly, both women deny the relationship went any deeper.

But the rift with Sandra Bernhard has continued. Today, she has nothing but contempt for Madonna. "Madonna is a woman who doesn't have the vaguest idea who she is," Bernhard says. "I gave her everything—friendship, love. How did she pay me back? By stabbing me in the back. I'm telling you as sure as I'm standing here, Madonna will steal everything from you, even your closest friends if she can get her grubby little hands on them."

Sandra—who was once Madonna's greatest ally and supporter—now says that she has always found Madonna's tributes to icons such as Marilyn Monroe and Marlene Dietrich reprehensible. "I could hear Dietrich screaming from her grave, 'Kill that trash, and kill her now,' " says Bernhard. "Did I tell you about my nightmare?" she asks. "I dreamed I was Madonna, shopping at Tiffany's, where I was trying to buy some class. Then, suddenly I turned into a toothless cleaning lady. I woke up with a big smile on my face and then it crossed my mind— didn't Carol Burnett already do this?"

Madonna seems wounded by Sandra's comments whenever she hears about them through friends, most of whom have managed to stay neutral. "I never did anything to her. Not a thing," she says. "The reason the relationship ended is the reason most friendships fall apart: envy and jealousy. She's a brilliant woman who has a lot of talent. I can't believe she would say those terrible things about me. Every year that goes by, I think she's going to just get over it, but she doesn't. So, on some level, I guess I must still be important in her life or she wouldn't keep trashing me in the press."

When the author once asked Madonna what happened between her and Sandra, she said, "I can only tell you this: there was a huge misunderstanding about something, and she went off the deep end and never returned. That's all I will say on the subject."

✝

Truth or Dare

In May 1991, *Truth or Dare* was finally released. In "pushing the envelope," as she would put it, this movie, along with several upcoming projects, would prove that even Madonna could push too much, and go too far . . . until finally crossing the line between good taste and bad.

Truth or Dare is fascinating to watch, not so much because its star is particularly witty or clever in it but rather because of what happens around her—the way her dancers fawn over her and vie for her attention, the way her manager Freddy DeMann is mistreated by her, and how she alternately rides roughshod over and also mothers everyone about her. It is truly a camp "performance."

It's also intriguing to watch a woman in action who is, apparently, narcissistic enough to believe that everything she says or does has great importance and relevance. Why otherwise would she want herself committed to film while having her makeup applied, or while talking on the telephone, or even visiting her mother's grave for the first time since she was a child—in a limousine, her eyes hidden by big and round Jackie O sunglasses? ("I wonder what she looks like now?" she mused of her deceased mother, her voice a monotone. "Probably just a bunch of dust.")

As the cameras rolled, Madonna bickered with Warren Beatty, whispered secrets to Sandra Bernhard, and recalled a sexual encounter with a high school girlfriend, who later turned up in the proceedings to say with a mixture of embarrassment and astonishment that she had no recollection of the incident. "But she *did* finger fuck me," Madonna insisted. "I remember looking at her bush!"

Shrewdly, she also showed her soft side by playing mother hen to her brood of vulnerable, pampered backup dancers and singers—some of whom were so young they were leaving home for the first time. Madonna led them in a prayer before every concert, she advised them on their love lives and refereed their arguments. In the film, she explains that she selected dancers and singers who were "emotionally crippled" so that she could "mother" them. She said, "This was the opportunity of their lives. I wanted to impress them. I wanted to love them." At one point, when twenty-two-year-old dancer Oliver Crumes—who kept insisting that he was the only heterosexual dancer in the troupe—was rumored to have become sexually involved with her, and the story made the front page of one of the tabloids, Madonna counseled the others as to how to deal with their jealousy of Crumes. During a scene when she learns that Canadian officials may shut down her show because of its alleged indecency, she prays to God because "all of my babies are feeling fragile." At the end of the movie, she cavorts in bed with all of them, in various stages of undress. "Get out of my bed and don't come back until your dick is bigger," she orders one giggling dancer. Her manner was one that suggested cruelty and humor at the same time.

"I see a huge paradox in me," she told the *Advocate,* in talking of her impression of the film, "the intense need to be loved and the search for approval juxtaposed with the need to nurture other people, to be the mother I never had. I didn't realize how matriarchal I am, how maternal I am, until I watched this movie."

Further, she told *Vanity Fair,* "People will say, 'She knows the camera is on, she's just acting.' But even if I am acting, there's a truth in my acting. You could watch it and say, 'I still don't know Madonna' . . . and good! Because you will never know the real me. Ever.

"I think the impression of me will be twofold," she said. "People will think, 'Oh, she isn't just a cold, dominating person.' I think that's the world's perception of me, that I'm power-hungry and manipulating. I think a great deal of the movie shows a gentler side of me."

When a journalist asked her if the movie was shocking, Madonna became defensive. "Is what shocking?" she asked. "Me giving head to a bottle? You see people doing it in movies all the time. It's a joke. What's shocking? Why don't *you* know if it's shocking or not? Don't you know your own feelings? It's a joke."

Her manager Freddy DeMann felt that the movie would damage Madonna's reputation. As she later recalled, he tried to convince her to cut several scenes.

"The one where you stick your finger in your mouth to indicate that Kevin Costner makes you want to vomit, that has to go, Madonna," he told her during one meeting.

"No. It stays," she said, shaking her head.

"Well, the one where you say that woman finger-fucked you, that has to go. It's disgusting."

"It stays," she said. "There's nothing disgusting about it."

"Okay, but the one where you are a bitch to everyone . . ."

Finally, Madonna cut him off. "Fuck you, Freddy," she said, according to his memory of the meeting. "Everyone knows I'm a bitch. Who cares? People think I'm Saddam Hussein. They compare me to Hitler. Leave my fucking movie alone! It's not telling people anything they don't already know."

Apparently, one aspect of her life that Madonna did not want revealed in the film was any that involved the running of her business affairs. While she is known to be open, revealing and forthcoming, on matters of business, she chose then (and still does today) to remain an enigma. So, cameras were forbidden in business meetings, even though director Alek Keshishian tried to force his way into them. "Get out!" she screamed at him.

Rather than have her public understand that a good deal of her immense celebrity had to do with her genius for public relations as well as her talent, it seemed that Madonna wanted the public to believe that it stemmed from only her talent. So, when magazine editors scheduled articles that were to focus on her extraordinary business savvy, she refused to discuss profits, revenues or business strategies. Likewise, Madonna instructed her staff and friends not to talk about those matters, either.

In 1991, Madonna's revenues from her assorted music, film and commercial projects would be about $60 million, including the $36 million generated by the "Blonde Ambition" tour. She put in long hours managing her holdings and investments, seldom delegating important responsibilities to others. She also set up a number of lucrative companies: Boy Toy, Inc., for music and record royalties; Siren Films, for film and video production (taking the place of Slutco, a video production company that she dissolved soon after starting); Webo Girl, for music publishing; and Music Tours, Inc., for live performance contracts.

Madonna was—and still is today—involved in all negotiations that relate to her career, always walking into meetings with a legal pad, a pencil and a great many questions. Says her former boyfriend John "Jellybean" Benitez, "She has a lot of people feeding her the information she needs, and she looks at it more creatively than other artists do. She absorbs everything, and she asks a lot of questions."

In 1991, Freddy DeMann received up to 10 percent of her annual earnings. Her accountant, Bert Padell, had his services capped at $1 million, annually. Her legal negotiations were handled by Paul Schindler of Grubman Indursky Schindler, a company that used a system called "instinctive billing," where fees are negotiated with clients *after* a deal has been struck, depending on how lucrative the outcome. Madonna felt that the attorney was worth the curious billing method. Still, says the manager of another rock star, "If she treated me the way she treats the other people who work for her, I would be gone in twenty-four hours. She is known for mistreating the people who work for her, and I think she feels that if she pays them enough she's allowed to treat them badly. Or, maybe the privilege of working for her at all is supposed to be some kind of reward."

Her fans, however, didn't really care what went on with Madonna behind the scenes, as long as she delivered to them onstage. Truly, the most wonderful part of *Truth or Dare* is the concert footage from the "Blonde Ambition" tour. The dancers, the sets, the music and, of course, Madonna . . . all are visually spellbinding. While watching her perform, one marvels at her level of commitment to her act and her audience. Certainly, few entertainers work as hard as Madonna to please a crowd. Few have even an inkling of Madonna's expansive imagination and vision. Also, in the video, when Madonna brought her father, Tony, onto the stage in Detroit so that her audience could sing "Happy Birthday" to him, it was a genuinely touching moment. Daughter paid homage to father by literally bowing down to him in front of her fans, and only those closest to her and her family saw the real significance of the gesture. "She was saying, 'I love you, Dad. I want you to accept me. Look at all of these people. Look at how they love me,' says Nikki Harris, who was onstage with Madonna at the time as one of her two singers. "It was a genuine moment."

Besides the jarring reality of how talented Madonna is as a performer, perhaps the one thing the viewer of *Truth or Dare* is left with is that—at least at that time—she was not someone most reasonable people would ever welcome into their lives. Certainly, she gave definition to the New Age phrase "high-maintenance friend."

No doubt, one of the sweetest memories Madonna must have relating to the documentary was her experience at the forty-fourth Cannes Film Festival that year when she went to France to promote it. She and her large entourage checked into the Riviera's most exclusive and glamorous Hôtel Du Cap at Eden Roc; Madonna stayed in the large and very pink Princess Suite, "which I loved, loved, loved," she said later. As usual, photographers risked their lives to take her picture, hanging from cliffs by ropes and trying to aim their telescopic lenses as she swam in a waterfall, or circling in chartered speedboats at dangerously high speeds as she caught some sun on a yacht. Rarely did she then—or does she now—ever have a moment of peace and quiet whenever she was out in public in Europe. Somehow, she has managed to become—or at least act as if she has—completely oblivious to the fact that strangers with cameras are crashing into each other all around her as they all try to capture "the perfect photograph." She first faced the press at Cannes draped in a stunning rose-colored satin gown. Her dark, curled hair was piled atop her head, like a crown. As flashbulbs popped all about her, and at just the right moment, her gown dropped, falling in a heap at her feet. Then, there she stood—posing this way and that way—in nothing but a white satin coned brassiere and matching panty-girdle hot pants. It was fascinating that even in this scanty, immodest outfit—which, worn by another woman, would just seem trashy—she looked polished, feminine and in control. "You could feel her presence—or the reflected glare of her celebrity—at a distance of twenty miles," wrote Robert Sandall of the London *Sunday Times*. "Everybody was talking about the real star in town—Madonna."

Shortly after *Truth or Dare* was released, some of the very dancers Madonna was seen "mothering" in it turned against her when they realized that they weren't getting paid any more money in the form of residuals (even though the movie would go on to gross millions). Sallim Gauwloos, also known as "Slam," pantomimed the Warren Beatty–Madonna duet "Now I'm Following You" (from *Dick Tracy*) in the concert. He says he felt "disillusioned" by the entire experience.

"After the tour and the movie, I never spoke to her again. The movie makes it look like we were this big happy family but it was not like that. We never went to her with our problems; we were never that close, even though that's how they made it look."

Of his former boss, he says, "She was a sensitive person in many ways. But she was very, very insecure, especially with other women. We would have parties, and there would never be beautiful women invited. Only guys. She would freak if there was someone in the room more beautiful than her. That was her rule. Only men would be invited to her parties, or women who were far, far less attractive."

He adds, "I thought we were really good friends. We always knew that she was making a documentary. And we had a meeting with her at one point to say, 'Well, look, we're getting paid to do the tour, true, but are we going to make money from this movie, too?' It was obvious to us that, hey, if you put a movie out there starring Madonna, a lot of money is going to be made.

"She got a little insulted that we even asked about money, and she said, 'If the movie is a success, then, yes, I will give you some more money.' So the movie came out, and it was huge. And we never got a dime. Nothing. I was very sad. She could have at least given me a phone call to tell me, 'Hey, the movie is a hit. Here's the money I promised you.' But, no. Nothing."

In January 1992, three of the professional dancers featured in the "Blonde Ambition" tour filed a lawsuit against Madonna relating to their portrayal in *Truth or Dare*. The dancers—Gabriel Trupin, Kevin Stea and Oliver Crumes—filed suit in Los Angeles Superior Court, alleging that Madonna had lied to them about her intended use of film footage she gathered during the tour. The dancers contended their privacy was invaded by personal offstage footage, and that they weren't paid for their appearance in the movie. Madonna was angry about the suit. "Those ingrates," she said to one colleague. "To think that I made them who they are, then they treat me like *this.*"

Shortly after the suit was filed, Madonna happened upon Oliver Crumes at a party. "If you want money," she told him, her tone arctic, "why don't you sell that Cartier watch I bought for you."

The suit would drag through the court system for years until the dancers simply couldn't afford to pay their attorneys. Finally, in September of 1994—the year *Forbes* magazine stated that she earned $37 million—Madonna offered an out-of-court settlement to the dancers. Terms of the settlement are still confidential, though one dancer has said, "For what her lawyers put us through, forget it. It wasn't worth it."

"We were nearly unable to pursue the claims in the case because of Madonna's superior financial resources," says attorney Debra Johnson, who represented the dancers. "All too often in Hollywood, a powerful figure like Madonna is able to act as if she is above the law," Johnson concluded.

☩

Sex

On October 21, 1992, Madonna's notorious book, *Sex,* was published by Time-Warner. When the book finally appeared—after months of speculation and hype—the public discovered that Madonna's foray into the publishing world would be in the form of an oversized and overpriced ($49.95), 128-page volume, spiral-bound between embossed stainless-steel covers, aptly titled, simply, *Sex.* As if to make certain that the public fully recognized the controversial nature of this publishing endeavor, the book arrived in book shops wrapped in silver Mylar (which also ensured that only paying customers were privy to what lay between its covers). Also included was a CD of Madonna's new song, "Erotica," in a silver Mylar Ziplock bag. "Warner Books is shitting in their pants about it," said Freddy DeMann in assessing the publishing company's nervousness about distributing such a work.

Some might say that the genesis of Madonna's *Sex* shows a typical side of her character and the way that she, as she has put it in the past, "takes a little of this and that and turns it into my own." Earlier, in the fall of 1990, Judith Regan, then an editor of Simon & Schuster Pocket Books, had an idea for a book of erotica and sexual fantasies which she felt would be ideal for Madonna. "I felt that it was right in line with what she was all about at that time," says Regan. "So I sent a box of material to her manager's office, which included erotic photos that I thought would interest her, as well as the kind of text I thought would be appropriate. It was colorful and imaginative, if I do say so myself. I was happy with it, anyway. As it turned out, she, too, was impressed and thought it would be a good idea. The next thing I knew I was in Los Angeles sitting with her and her manager Freddy DeMann. I was pregnant at the time, and the first thing Madonna said to me was, 'Well, you know, I don't have any children.' It seemed odd that she would think that I wouldn't know such a thing about her, one of the most famous women in the world."

"I just want you to know that I won't even think of doing this thing if you've offered it to even one other celebrity," Madonna cautioned Judith Regan during their meeting.

"Why is that?" Judith asked. Of course, she knew the answer, but still wanted to hear it from the woman herself.

"Because it has to be unique to me," Madonna said, predictably. "It has to be for me, and for me alone."

"Well, I started at the top. With you," Judith assured her. "If you're not interested, then I'll go elsewhere. But I hope that you will be interested. I think this could really work for you."

Madonna seemed satisfied. During the rest of the meeting, she made it clear that she would only do such a project if she could exert complete control over it. "She has amazing instincts, I learned that right away about her," says Regan. "She knew just what she wanted to do, and how to do it. She asked intelligent questions about publishing. Not surprisingly, I found her to be very eager, very smart. Shrewd."

Perhaps Madonna was even shrewder than Judith realized. By the end of the meeting, she had agreed "in principal" says Judith, "to do a book we would call *Madonna's Book of Erotica and Sexual Fantasies.*

She said that her manager would call me and we would work out the details. I never heard from her, and decided that she just didn't want to do it. Then, six months later, I learned that she was doing the project for Warner Books [an arm of Time-Warner, which owns Warner Bros. Records, and now distributes Madonna's record label, Maverick]. She had obviously taken my concept, my photos and ideas and used it as a proposal to secure a deal with another publisher. I never heard from her, not a word of gratitude, or an apology, or anything," concludes Judith Regan. "Frankly, I thought it was in poor taste."

The contents of *Sex*, when finally published, consisted of visual and verbal essays by Madonna (as herself but also in the role of a character named Dita, borrowed from screen goddess Dita Parlo of the thirties) regarding her personal, sexual fantasies—or, at least, what she wanted the public to believe were her sexual fantasies. "This book does not condone unsafe sex," she hastened to add in one of her missives to the reader. "These are fantasies I have dreamed up. Like most human beings, when I let my mind wander, I rarely think of condoms."

Photographed beautifully in black and white by Steven Meisel—who has photographed her throughout much of her career—Madonna was seen hitchhiking in the nude, posing lasciviously while clad in leather S&M outfits, brutally dominating a pair of butch lesbians, happily sucking somebody's toe, brazenly shaving someone else's pubic area, receiving oral sex from a biker, being viciously raped by skinheads (while dressed as a schoolgirl). She is at least partially nude in most of the photographs, and completely nude in many of them. In one, she is posed in a sexually suggestive position with a dog. "It turned out to be a lot more salacious, I think, than what I would have wanted to publish," says Judith Regan. "She went over the top with it. I wanted it to be imaginative, erotic . . . but not quite so prurient."

Indeed, much of the book reads like a letter to a pornographic magazine: "I love my pussy, it is the complete summation of my life," Madonna wrote. "My pussy is the temple of learning." A lot of attention is also paid to the joy of anal sex, "the most pleasurable way to [have sex], and it hurts the most, too." Many graphic paragraphs are devoted to the ways she enjoys making love, each position described in vivid detail, a great deal of it having to do with sadomasochism. She also waxes rhapsodic about the first time she masturbated.

Much of *Sex* is surprising, if not shocking. Rather than an "adult" book, it is really childish and impetuous. Though Madonna insisted that she was trying to demystify sexuality in all its many faces, knowing who she was and how she operated made it clear to any keen observer that what she was really just trying to get away with was as much naughty-girl text and as many pornographic photographs as she could get away with because . . . well, because she could get away with it. She was being a brat, not a revolutionary. That much is clear if one reads between the lines in an interview she gave to MTV in 1998. "I thought, 'You know what, I'm going to be sexually provocative, I'm going to be ironic, and I'm going to prove that I can get everybody's attention and that everyone's going to be interested in it . . . and still be freaked out about it.'" One might ask: Why? Hadn't she already proved her ability to be sexually provocative, ironic and attention-getting?

Those who knew Madonna well knew what was really going on with her at this time: the *Sex* book—and the outrageous antics that preceded it and would follow it—was really just something she used as a barrier between her and the rest of the world.

For years, it had seemed to Madonna that every moment of her life had been exposed to the world, her every word and mood flashed across the newspapers for comment, often biting and critical. She felt hunted, even though it was she who had started the hunt. By her own doing, she had become one of the most watched and most criticized women in the world. She had never let her public down, always at the ready with a provocative comment, a salacious anecdote, a shocking photograph. Now, because she was just who she had created, she was having trouble relating to "normal" people. She felt that they didn't understand her. And she certainly didn't understand *them*. She seemed to have lost herself somewhere in all the headlines. Terrible isolation was her ironic fate, isolation that came from being such a sensational public figure. Her relationships with men had been abysmal. Was some of that also due to her fame?

To prevent herself from having to be a part of the masses, either consciously or subconsciously—and only she would know which—Madonna created a persona that no one could begin to understand . . . one so outrageous as to defy explanation, one found objectionable by most people (at least those who were not pornographers). "She was losing touch," said one of her public relations handlers. "The barrier she put up between herself and the rest of the world was the notion of crazy, wild sex—pure and simple—and trashy and controversial sex."

Most mental health professionals are of the opinion that, in the human condition, there are two ways of being antisocial. In a man it can take the form of aggressive, hostile behavior. In a woman it can be presented as being sexually provocative and outrageous. In other words, when little boys are angry, they have fights. When little girls are angry, they show their panties. Some of us don't grow out of that behavior; it would seem that Madonna was "showing her panties" just because she was vexed by the intense scrutiny her personal life had generated over the years. In her view, she had no other way of fighting back.

Tony Ward, Naomi Campbell, Isabella Rosellini and rappers Big Daddy Kane and Vanilla Ice all made guest appearances in the *Sex* book in photographs which showed them in various stages of undress.

The photographs were taken during the eight-month period during which Madonna and Vanilla Ice (real name Rob Van Winkle) were romantically involved. Ice, whose song "Ice Ice Baby" was, in 1990, the first rap song to top the *Billboard* charts, says that the relationship with Madonna was difficult, "because she would change personalities a lot." He also says that he now regrets having posed with her for the book. "It kind of cheeses me out," he says. "It makes me look like I'm like all the other people in there, a bunch of freaks. I'm no freak."

Also prominently featured was Madonna's friend Ingrid Casares, who would later complain that her participation in the project would fuel years of far-fetched gossip about her own sex life. "I'm actually quite conservative," Casares states flatly. Casares and Madonna were photographed in male drag, kissing passionately.

Though initial fascination for the book pushed it to Number 1 on *The New York Times* best-seller list, the reviews were generally negative. Richard Harrington of the *Washington Post* called it "an oversized, overpriced coffee-table book of hard-core sexual fantasies sure to separate the wanna-bes from the wanna-be-far-aways. Is *Sex* shocking? Not really. Mostly because it's Madonna, and in a way we've come to expect this from her. Is *Sex* boring? Actually, yes."

With all the sexual posturing, it was ironic that in the summer of 1992 Madonna was seen in Penny Marshall's light comedy romp, *A*

An early publicity session. *Kees Tabak/Sunshine/Sipa Press*

Like a virgin? Madonna on stage in April 1985. *Roger Ressmeyer/Corbis*

Left: Wearing the famous Gaultier bustier-corset on a Los Angeles stage during the "Blonde Ambition" tour, May 1990. *Juan Venege/Sipa Press*

Right: "All of the gimmicks in the world mean nothing," Madonna has said, "if you can't deliver on stage." *Photofest*

No career retrospective would be complete without this popular photo . . . Madonna's well-known *Truth or Dare* publicity pose from 1991. *Everett Collection*

Wearing $20 million in diamonds and looking every bit like Marilyn Monroe, Madonna performs Stephen Sondheim's "Sooner or Later" from *Dick Tracy* in March 1991 at the Academy Awards. The song won an Oscar. *Philip Ramey/Corbis Sygma*

Even when androgynous—and sometimes, *especially* when androgynous—Madonna remains the sexy icon, here puffing away in the early nineties. *Richard Young/Rex Features*

The many glamorous faces of Madonna, evoking memories of the early days of the silver screen. *Photofest (top), Corbis Sygma (bottom, left and right)*

Left: In September 1993, carrying on with two of her dancers during her "Girlie Show" tour. *Archive Photos*

Right: Who has enjoyed being a star more than this woman? *Photofest*

In September 1993, dressed like the Hindu deity Shiva for her "Girlie Show" tour in Paris. *Thierry Orban/Corbis Sygma*

Never had she ever wanted anything more than to play Eva Peron in 1996's *Evita. United/Pictorial Press, Ltd.*

✝

She makes it all look so easy. On stage in 1995 at the Alexandria Palace in North London in a gown designed by Gianni Versace. *All Action/Retna Limited USA*

Another new look—sixties hip! Posing backstage at Radio City Music Hall with her MTV Video Music Award after the network's 1995 New York presentation. *AP/Wide World*

✝

Below, from left: With the two most important men in Madonna's life: Carlos Leon (father of her daughter, Lourdes), at the premiere of *Evita* in Los Angeles, December 1996; and Guy Ritchie (husband, and father of her son, Rocco), celebrating the release of her *Music* CD in Los Angeles, September 2000. *AP Photo /Chris Pizzello (left), Paul Smith/Retna Limited, USA (right)*

While looking "ghetto fabulous" for the video of her 2000 dance anthem "Music," Madonna stays contemporary and at the top of her game into the new millennium. *Globe Photos*

✝

Still sensational after all these years . . . on stage at Brixton Academy in London, November 2000. *JT/All Action/Retna Limited USA*

League of Their Own, about a women's baseball league in 1943. As part of an all-star cast including Geena Davis, Tom Hanks and Rosie O'Donnell, Madonna would again not have the burden of carrying an entire film on her shoulders. The movie was top-grossing in the summer of 1992, an added bonus for Madonna's acting résumé—though she was only fair in the role and most don't consider it memorable. However, any observer who thought that the movie would mark the emergence of a tamer Madonna knew he was wrong as soon as *Sex* was published. (Prior to this film, she was seen making a brief appearance in Woody Allen's black comedy, *Shadows and Fog*, a box-office failure that quickly disappeared from cinemas.)

☦

Erotica

To tie in with the publication of *Sex*, Madonna released a new album, aptly entitled *Erotica*.

It is unfortunate that *Erotica* has to be historically linked to other less memorable ventures in Madonna's career at this time because, unlike *Truth or Dare* and *Sex*, *Erotica* actually had much to recommend it. It was just that, coming on the heels of the two previous projects, *Erotica* seemed like more of the same to most observers. However, this record should be considered on its own merits, and not only as one linked to the other two adult-oriented projects, because it does have true value.

Madonna has often said that in her view—one shared by many cultural historians—one reason pop music is so powerful in society is because it often serves as a mirror of our culture. If one wants to know what's going on in the world, perusing the *Billboard* Top 40 might be a good place to start. While newspapers inform on a daily basis, pop music, at least on some levels, can render the big picture. For instance, one might not find any songs about peace, love or changing society in the Top 40; if so, their absence speaks volumes. It could mean that society is looking the other way at the moment, that it would rather trade its woes for a pretty pop ditty about good times and romance. Apathy and hopefulness, optimism and good cheer—wherever pop culture is at the moment, so, usually, is its music.

It is clear that few singers have their fingers on the pulse of society like Madonna, more so than Michael Jackson (who spends too much time in his own environment to be in touch), or Prince (who appears too self-obsessed to pay attention to anything else). Madonna's instincts have her plugged into life.

At the time of *Erotica*'s release in October 1992, much of society seemed to be reexamining its sexuality. Gay rights issues were at the forefront of social discussions globally, as was an ever-increasing awareness of AIDS. A generation seemed increasingly curious to explore, without guilt, shame or apology, a different slice of life, something more provocative, maybe darker . . . which involves the themes of *Erotica*. A concept album of sorts, its music boldly and openly focused on sexuality more so than any previous Madonna album. *Erotica* wasn't just about boy meets girl, birds and bees. Madonna had already effectively spoken about those innocent notions with such pop songs as the bubbly "Cherish" and the earnest "Open Your Heart." *Erotica* was deeper, franker and edgier. Somehow, Madonna knew that the timing was perfect for an album of such expression. (She also believed, apparently, that it was time for a book that would address these issues—thus her *Sex* book. However, while it's a good experience to *hear* Madonna's take on sexuality, it is a bad one to *see* it, page after page after page.)

Erotica wasn't a complete surprise to anyone who had been paying attention to Madonna's recent music. She had shown her hand earlier with *Breathless* when she sang "Hanky Panky," the song about spanking, with just a little too much authority. Then there was her single "Justify My Love," a beyond-naughty bit of sexy business. *Erotica*, though, was the full-blown musical exploration, an *exhibition*, of what we were to believe was Madonna's sexual reality.

For this album, Madonna again turned to producer/writer Shep Pettibone, with whom she had written and produced "Vogue." After having to work within the musical constraints of *Breathless*, Madonna wanted to do a clear and obvious dance record; Pettibone was proficient in this genre. Indeed, judging by the music they've created together, it would be safe to say that Pettibone is by far her best dance-music collaborator. After he laid down the musical tracks, Madonna would shape the vocal melodies and write the lyrics. Often (as on *Erotica*), she has ideas for the music tracks, as well; she's that versatile. They work well together, mostly because he understands her. "She's the opposite of calm," says Pettibone. "Her patience level is incredibly low, so you have to make things run smoothly. It's better to bring out the angel in her, because the beast ain't that much fun."

One didn't really need to hear the music to understand Madonna's intention with *Erotica*. If the title itself wasn't a tip-off, the CD's cover artwork certainly made the point clear. In pictures lifted from *Sex*, one photograph shows Madonna in S&M garb, toying with a riding crop and licking her arm; in another shot, she sits bound and gagged. The back cover features Madonna engaged in "foot worship"—blissfully sucking on someone's big toe. But for her *Sex* book, her public would have been surprised by the poses; on the heels of that published work, however, these photographs now seemed redundant.

The title track, also the first single to be released, consisted of an irresistible house-music beat, over which Madonna, in her "Mistress Dita" persona, spoke in a hypnotic, orgasmic style about the correlation between pain and pleasure and how it relates to sex. The spoken lyrics are separated by the hypnotic, teasing chorus, "Erotic, erotic, put your hands all over my body." The song could easily have been the theme to a Fellini film.

The "Erotica" video was quickly put into "heavy rotation" by MTV . . . after midnight, of course, to protect the kiddies. On the screen, Madonna appears as a masked dominatrix, complete with a gold tooth and slicked-down hair. She tongue-kisses a girl and does her S&M shtick, but it is too quickly edited to be really revealing. The video seems to be more about creating a montage of images designed to shock. Looking incongruous in leather and sunglasses, the usually clean-cut MTV announcer Kurt Loder tantalizingly explained that, "Some people have no objection to such role-playing games as long as they're consensual. Others find such practices repellent, which is why MTV is not airing this video in regular daytime or evening rotation."

Wrote columnist Molly Ivins, "You could tell you're out of touch with your fellow Americans when the reigning sex goddess is someone you wouldn't take home if she were the last woman left in the bar."

This time, a tamer Madonna did not act as if she objected to MTV's restriction of air time for her video. "MTV plays to a huge audience and a lot of them are children," she said in an interview on that cable network. "And a lot of the themes explored in my video aren't meant for children, so I understand why they can't show it."

True to course, Madonna's public was all the more fascinated by the song and video thanks to the controversy. It reached Number 3 on the *Billboard* singles chart.

"Deeper and Deeper," the second single from *Erotica,* was a change of pace from the title track. A straight-ahead house groove in the tradition of the funkiest New York clubs, the track had Madonna singing mainstream lyrics about falling hard for a lover. It worked its way up to Number 7 on the chart.

Erotica could have been ahead of its time. Madonna's song "Secret Garden," with its lyrics spoken over a jazz combo, is akin to the cool soul music acts such as the Roots and Erykah Badu would champion almost a decade later, under the banner of "neo-soul." Musically, *Erotica* was actually a melting pot of nineties urban music—burgeoning hip-hop and house, partnered with a more conventional synthesizer-based rhythm and blues. Madonna's most sexually promiscuous record was also her most R&B sounding.

However, it was the spectacle of the artist's sexuality on parade that seemed to have her fans and critics alike gasping for breath. *Erotica* was the first (and, so far, only) Madonna CD to carry a warning on its cover: "Parental Advisory: Explicit Lyrics." Obviously, Madonna didn't invent the images of S&M and bondage she so valiantly exploited, but it could be argued that *Erotica* was a soundtrack for the era's sexual liberation as people struggled to still find ways to enjoy their sexuality despite the threat of AIDS. Unlike her book, this music was an art form of which her public would not tire . . . and to which it could repeatedly return for entertainment. However, true to the nature of her self-inflicted career slide at this time, *Erotica* would become the least commercially successful of Madonna's releases, selling just over two million copies.

"Most people want to hear me say I regret putting out my *Sex* book. I don't," Madonna told *Time* magazine a couple of years later. "What was problematic was putting out my *Erotica* album at the same time. I love that record, and it was overlooked. Everything I did for the next three years was dwarfed by my book."

✞

By the end of 1992, many of her fans
Madonna had gone too far. The rele
Sex book and the *Erotica* album and
tion for some with a resounding "Ye
million in the United States. As its
vested $4 million into the movie,
However, after expenses, the film was not nearly as p
had hoped.)

Who was this woman, anyway? Was she a sexual renegade, or just a spoiled and internationally known brat who liked to take off her clothes and talk dirty? No one could answer the question with much accuracy, she had so clouded her true identity with scandal and sensationalism. Even when she tried to explain herself ("I love my pussy, and there's nothing wrong with loving my pussy") she sounded like a lusty porn star no one could take seriously.

"After the *Sex* book came out," she has recalled, "there was a time when I could not open up a newspaper or magazine and not read something incredibly scathing about myself."

Had she foreseen the negative publicity that would be generated by *Truth or Dare, Sex* and *Erotica,* Madonna might have chosen a different direction for her next film, perhaps continuing with light family-oriented movies like *A League of Their Own.* Instead, she chose a lurid thriller, *Body of Evidence,* as her next movie release—the final of the four unwitting steps in the dismantling of her career.

In the movie, which premiered on the heels of *Sex* in January 1993, Madonna plays Rebecca Carlson, a gallery owner accused of murdering a wealthy older man when he dies after having sex with her (raising the perplexing question of whether or not a sex partner's body can be considered a lethal weapon if the act results in a person's death). She ends up becoming sexually involved with her defense attorney, played by Willem Dafoe.

At the end of the movie, Madonna's character is murdered, causing some disgusted moviegoers to cheer at her demise. "She's a powerful lady," says the film's director, Uli Edel, of Madonna. "Sometimes you

n a she-lion in a cage. You have to force her to jump
hing hoop, and there are just two possibilities. Either
rough the ring of fire . . . or she'll kill you."

he movies of the forties, the bad girl has to die," Madonna
What I originally loved about the role [in the first script] was
he didn't die. And in the end, they killed me. So I felt that I was
otaged to a certain extent. For some reason, when that movie came
ut, I was held responsible for it entirely. It was my fault, which was absurd, because we all make bad movies. I mean *Diabolique* came out [in
1996] and Sharon Stone was not held responsible for the fact that it was
a crap movie."

Indeed, critics "murdered" Madonna in reviewing the film, declaring *Body of Evidence* a third-rate rehash of every murder mystery of
the past twenty years (and particularly of *Basic Instinct,* the box-office
blockbuster of the year before). Reviewers were quick to compare
Madonna unfavorably with that movie's leading lady: "It's not just that
Madonna does not make an effective Sharon Stone," a critic for *Rolling
Stone* complained. "She doesn't even make an effective Madonna. Instead of emoting, Madonna strikes poses and delivers stilted lines that
sound like captions from her book *Sex* read aloud in a voice of nerve-
jangling stridency."

Bad notices and the condemnation of religious groups had certainly never hurt Madonna's career before this time, but when it was reported that movie audiences had been laughing out loud at Madonna's
supposedly serious characterization in *Body of Evidence,* it became
clear that she had pushed the envelope as far as it was going to be accepted. It was becoming clear even to her that a new reinvention would
have to be in the offing, that is if she was going to be able to sustain a
career—especially when another film, *Dangerous Game,* was released
(in 1993) to terrible reviews and dreadful box office. In this one,
Madonna plays an actress with limited skills who has sex with practically everyone in her life. The sex is violent—Madonna gets to strip
several times, and does so with great zest. In one scene during *Dangerous Game,* actor James Russo says of Madonna's character, Sarah Jen-
nings, "We both know she's a fucking whore who can't act." Again, it
was all more than critics—or her public—could bear. What a disappointment this movie was, especially considering that it was directed

by the highly respected Abel Ferrara (known at the time for *The Bad Lieutenant*, starring Harvey Keitel, who also co-starred in *Dangerous Game*) and that Madonna had financed much of it with her own money.

Meanwhile, happily for her, Madonna's recording and performing career still had enough momentum to overcome the slump that had resulted from such exploits as *Body of Evidence* and *Dangerous Game*. Facing the barrage of publicity, Madonna chose not to hide. Instead, she decided to do what she had always done best: she took her act out on the road.

In the last quarter of 1993, Madonna forged ahead with a limited twenty-date, four-continent world tour—her first in four years—which she called "The Girlie Show." Wisely, she realized that a complete about-face in her career would be transparent, and at the same time would probably diminish much of what she had done prior to this time. She really had expanded the consciousness of much of her public, even if the way she'd gone about it was sometimes questionable. Now, if she was going to come up with a new image, the transformation would have to come about slowly. As a result "The Girlie Show," was a transitional tour. While still sexy, it was more of an innocent burlesque rather than a blatant attempt to shock. Gone were the hard core S&M images and the blasphemous religious iconology of the previous two years. Rather, this concert had the feel of a racy Barnum and Bailey circus, even revealing a softer, gentler Madonna.

Time described it as, "At once a movie retrospective, a Ziegfeld revue, a living video, an R-rated takeoff on Cirque du Soleil—opens with Smokey Robinson's 'Tears of a Clown' and closes with Cole Porter's 'Be a Clown.'" The critic concluded that Madonna, "once the Harlow harlot and now a perky harlequin, is the greatest show-off on earth." "The Girlie Show" enabled Madonna to end the difficult year 1993 on a successful note. Many observers and fans considered it to be her best show to date, reaffirming that, as a singer and stage performer—if not a movie star—Madonna could still please her audience. Still, she was now more sensitive than ever to criticism, probably because she'd had to endure so much of it in recent times. Even the slightest negative tone to a review would send her reeling. "No one understands me," she complained to one close friend. "I'm breaking the rules. Why don't people get that?"

"Maybe because people are sick to death of you and all of the sex nonsense," said the friend. "Even toned down, it's still too much." Madonna didn't speak to that person again for six months.

✝

Trash Talking on TV

While on "The Girlie Show" tour, Madonna engaged in a heated telephone conversation with her father, Tony, during which he told her that he wished she would "stop being so racy." According to what Madonna would later recall to intimates, he said he was embarrassed not so much by what she was doing, but by what people were saying about her. Rather than empathize with what her father was probably trying to say, which was that it hurt his feelings when strangers criticized his daughter, she took his comment as criticism. The two then became embroiled in the same battle they had been fighting for years, having to do with Madonna's belief that her father had never supported her aspirations or understood her art. Or, as Tony would later say, "When a father is concerned, does that mean he doesn't approve? Why is she such a hothead? Why does she take everything so personally?"

So many years had gone by, yet Madonna was still so hurt and angry by her mother's passing that there was really nothing Tony Ciccone could say or do that would be right, as far as she was concerned. It was the same story: she had to blame someone for her loss, so she blamed her father. Yet, she still wanted his approval.

No doubt, Tony had to have been concerned when he saw his daughter's appearance on *The Late Show with David Letterman* on March 31, 1994.

Madonna's recent understanding that her ability to generate interest in herself by shocking the public was no longer working must have been buttressed when she saw the public's reaction to her on the Letterman show. She made the appearance on the night of Holy Thursday, when Catholics commemorate the Last Supper during the Easter holidays.

In what was perhaps a last-ditch attempt to be shocking, sexy and controversial, Madonna embarrassed herself on Letterman's program almost from the moment she sat down. Dressed in a tight black velvet dress with matching scarred combat boots, her black hair pulled severely back, she walked onto the stage holding a pair of panties. Within seconds, she had launched into what many considered to be an offensive performance that included a string of obscenities she made while she smoked a cigar. She asked Letterman—whom she called "a sick fuck"—if he would smell her panties. Though Letterman attempted to avoid answering the question, Madonna would not let it go. "I gave him my underpants," she said to the audience, laughing, "and he won't smell them!" Then, after asking Letterman why he was so obsessed with her sex life (since it was often the subject of his comedy monologues), Madonna continuously tried to lead the conversation back to . . . her sex life.

In a verbal tug of war, a ruffled Letterman (showing an unsteady side of himself not often seen on television) tried to change the subject, but Madonna was unrelenting. "Would you like to touch my dress?" she asked him. Letterman promptly cut to a commercial. When they came back from the break, Madonna was smoking a cigar and explaining that it was "just the right size." Later, with the sex talk leading nowhere, and her attempts at double entendre falling flat, she seemed desperate to appear provocative. "Did you know that it's good to pee in the shower?" she asked, without provocation. The audience was silent. Undaunted, Madonna pressed on, "I'm serious. Peeing in the shower is really good. It fights athlete's foot. Urine is like an antiseptic."

"Don't you know a good pharmacist?" Letterman shot back. "Get yourself some Desenex."

By now it seemed to most observers that Letterman was hoping to cut her segment short, but Madonna, perhaps realizing that she was floundering, wanted to score some points before exiting.

"We have to say good-bye now," Letterman told her.

Madonna stalled. "She can't be stopped," David said. "Something's wrong with her!"

"Something *is* wrong with me," she shot back. "I'm sitting here!"

Inexplicably, Madonna picked up her peeing in the shower thread by declaring "everybody pees in the shower and picks their noses."

By now an audience member was shouting for her to get off the stage, and Letterman was nearly pleading with her to do the same, explaining that he had other guests waiting to appear. "Thank you for grossing us all out," he said to her before she finally took her leave.

Says Paul Shaffer, musical director for Letterman's program, "We know that Madonna is not going to appear on a show unless she can make an impact, and on this show she used language to make her impact. I remember saying to myself, 'The Material Girl has no material.' We were all amazed by it, shocked by it, really. And it was kind of shocking to hear the kinds of words she said on national television."

Though the show was one of the highest-rated of David Letterman's career, the press Madonna's appearance generated for her was some of the worst criticism she had yet received. Every report mentioned the fact that she uttered the word "fuck" thirteen times, causing the network to have to "bleep" it each time. The *New York Post*'s Ray Kerrison summed up the public's reaction: "Alas, it is what the world has now come to expect from Madonna. She has built a career, if you could call it that, around blasphemy, lewdness, profanity and smut. It is a pathetic reach for celebrity and notoriety by a woman short on talent and wit. She has nothing to sell but shock. Sadly, since she cannot soar with the eagles, she forages with the rodents."

"I called her the next day," says her friend chat-show host Rosie O'Donnell, "and asked her, 'What the heck was all of that about?' And she was upset. She said, 'They told me to do it. They set the whole thing up. It was mostly scripted, and now they [the Letterman producers] are acting like they had nothing to do with it.'

"She was pretty pissed off about it. She said that she didn't really want to do it. She said she knew better at this point in her career than to do it, but that she listened to them. 'People like it when you are shocking,' they told her. And she listened, against her better judgment. It was a mistake, she said. She didn't want to do it. They made her."

Maybe. Or maybe not.

Years later, Madonna would admit in an interview with Mary Murphy of *TV Guide*, "That was a time in my life when I was extremely angry. Angry with the way I was brought up. Angry about how sexist this society that we live in is. Angry with people who assumed that because I had a sexuality that I couldn't also be talented. Just everything. The press was constantly beating up on me, and I felt like a victim. So I lashed out at people and that night [on *Letterman*] was one of those times. And I am not particularly proud of it."

✝

Bedtime Stories

What was she to do now? She had practically trashed her image in recent years with one scalding controversy after another. The mostly negative reaction to *Truth or Dare, Sex, Erotica* and *Body of Evidence* caused Madonna to begin thinking—finally!—that maybe she had gone too far, that she had built a wall between herself and her public so high, it would be impossible for her to scale it and reconnect with the world in a way that had always mattered most to her—artistically. The dreadful appearance on David Letterman's show drove the point home. Even though she followed it with a more tame appearance on Jay Leno's show, and then another with Letterman at an awards program where the two acted as if they were now great friends, the public still seemed fed up with her.

According to one of her managers at this time, Madonna realized that she needed to make some dramatic changes in her career or, despite her huge record sales, she soon might not even have one. Always a smart woman, even though she had certainly slipped in recent years, she now realized that she needed to grow up, soften her image, and reconnect with her public. For the next few years, she would try to do just that . . . and her album *Bedtime Stories* would go a long way toward achieving that goal.

Bedtime Stories would also be the second of her albums to be released on Maverick, her own record label, funded by (its distributor) Warner Bros. Records with $60 million (the first was *Erotica*). For years, Madonna had wanted to release her own music on her own label and, expanding that vision, she wanted the label to be a full-service entertainment company specializing not only in music but also in television, film, book and song publishing.

Since Madonna was still very much a best-selling recording artist

235

by the early 1990s, the existence of her Maverick Records was an anomaly. One of the first female artists to have a *real* label, and one of the few women to run her own entertainment company, Maverick isn't just a company in logo only. It is a genuine venture for her with a staff and executives in place, all of whom were, at the time, governed by Freddy DeMann, who served as president of the company. The enterprise had its headquarters in a sleek, anonymous single-story office building in West Hollywood, close to one of Madonna's favorite shopping haunts, the chic Fred Segal department store on Melrose Avenue. Madonna had discussed such a venture with Warren Beatty on several occasions. He had encouraged her to do it, and was said to have been proud to hear that she'd finally launched the company.

"My goal, of course, is to have hits with the new company," she said when speaking of Maverick. "I'm not one of these dumb artists who is just given a label to shut her up. I asked for a record company. So, I'm not going to be invisible or simply phone in my partnership. There's no honor or satisfaction in palming the work off on someone else." (Certainly, the biggest artist Madonna has thus far signed to Maverick is Canadian singer/songwriter Alanis Morissette, whose album *Jagged Little Pill* had sold nearly thirty million copies as of the summer of 2000. The label also features Cleopatra, as well as the Deftones, Jude and Prodigy.)

That 1994's *Bedtime Stories* would follow the soft porn of *Erotica* might have seemed a bit odd to the untrained ear or to the casual Madonna fan. After all, though *Bedtime* was considerably tamer in tone than the ethereal-sounding, sexually charged *Erotica,* it demonstrated that, as always, Madonna had a keen instinct about where pop music was headed at the time of its release. By the early nineties, hip-hop music had completely permeated the national music sales charts. It was the "dance" music of the day, the "new" R&B of a generation of kids in fashionably sagging anti-designer designer jeans and backpacks. It was a trend, and, not surprisingly, Madonna wanted to be a part of it.

Bedtime Stories would prove to be Madonna's most unique recording to date. It marked the first time since Nile Rodgers and 1984's *Like a Virgin* album that she had worked with well-known producers. (For reasons that were as much about creativity as they were about control, she had chosen to work with relative unknowns on her recent recordings.) Certainly, at this point in her famously successful career, Madonna could have worked with any of the era's biggest record producers, from Quincy Jones (who'd navigated Michael Jackson's phenomenal success), to a high-priced journeyman such as David Foster (who had done wonderful work with Barbra Streisand) or Narada Michael Walden (longtime producer of the big-voiced Whitney Houston), or even New Jack Swing producer Teddy Riley.

For the tracks that would be included in *Bedtime Stories*, Madonna sought out the hottest young producers working in urban/hip-hop music. At the top of her list was Dallas Austin, the twenty-two-year-old songwriter/producer from Atlanta, Georgia, who'd found fame and fortune producing, among others, male vocal group Boyz II Men, teen R&B singer Monica and, especially, the young female hip-hop trio called TLC. Freddy DeMann was also instructed to place a call to another prominent name in pop/R&B, songwriter/producer Kenny "Babyface" Edmonds. Edmonds was black music's hitmeister of the moment, having penned chart recordings for Whitney Houston and Toni Braxton, among other R&B acts.

Austin's and Edmonds's names among the CD's production credits would have proved the seriousness of Madonna's intention to enter the world of R&B and hip-hop proper. However, she also rounded out her team of collaborators by pulling in Nellee Hooper, once the creative core of a British studio tribe called Soul II Soul who had enjoyed 1989 hits with the singles "Keep On Movin' " and "Back to Life (However Do You Want Me)." She also added Dave "Jam" Hall, then one of urban soul's most solid rising young songwriter/producers, who had scored hits with, among others, the R&B girl group Brownstone. "She knows how to man a project," says Freddy DeMann. "She knows how to surround herself with the biggest and the best, and I think that has been one of her greatest achievements. She's not like a lot of people who feel they have to do it all themselves. She wants assistance, but from only the most qualified people."

When "Secret," the first single from *Bedtime Stories,* was released, it surprised many Madonna fans, as well as her critics. It isn't a big-sounding dance track or a twinkling melodic ballad, both of which have been Madonna's style. Instead, it begins with just the sound of her voice singing over a rhythmic folksy guitar, before opening up to a sparse, retro rhythm section. Madonna's tangy voice remained at the center of the production. "My baby's got a secret," she sang, though she never shares with the listener just what that secret may be. She and Dallas Austin wrote the clever song which, no matter how many times one listens to it, never ceases to intrigue. It rode the *Billboard* singles chart up to the Number 3 position.

"Take a Bow" was the second single from the collection, a melancholy and beautifully executed ballad written by Madonna with Babyface. "Take a Bow" is a somber, sarcastic all-the-world's-a-stage song about unrequited love (a recurring theme in Madonna's lyrics) whose phoniness might have fooled everyone else, but not her. "Take a bow," she implored, for rendering a great, transparent performance in life and love. (The picturesque video was filmed over seven days in Ronda, Spain, with a bullfighting theme—using three bulls—and featuring popular bullfighter, Emilio Muñoz. It was partly because of the forties look of the video that Alan Parker thought Madonna might work in the part of Evita.)

Though he isn't listed in the credits as a performer, Babyface also sings on the track, vocally co-singing Madonna's lines in a way that makes their performance practically a duet. It proved to be a winner. "Take a Bow" put Madonna back in the place on the *Billboard* singles chart to which she'd become accustomed—Number 1.

✝

Stalked

In the spring of 1995, Madonna—now thirty-six—had concerns bigger than just the softening of her public image. Although she had become accustomed to being dogged by photographers and fans, she found herself being stalked not by a fan, but rather a fanatic in the form of crazed drifter, twenty-seven-year-old Robert Hoskins. Hoskins had actually deluded himself into thinking he was her husband. He had begun his campaign for Madonna's attention in February by sending her a disturbing series of bizarre letters which he signed "Your husband, Bob." He also began showing up at her home unexpectedly and ringing her security buzzer, perhaps hoping someone would allow him access to her grounds. One morning, Madonna was bewildered to see, from her bedroom window, Hoskins prowling around her estate. She alerted security, who handcuffed him to the garage for forty-five minutes as they waited for the police to arrive.

Frightened, Madonna promptly left town, fleeing to her new waterfront home in Miami. Undaunted, Hoskins turned up again on her property, scaled a twelve-foot fence, and crept to within twenty to thirty feet of the house, where he was confronted by security guard Basil Stephens. "I love her!" Hoskins screamed at the security guard. "I love her, don't you guys understand!"

Hoskins then lunged at the security guard, screaming for him to get out of the way, that he was coming home to see "his wife." When Hoskins allegedly tried to grab the security guard's gun, Stephens shot him.

Madonna was in her Florida home when she heard the news that her stalker was recovering at Cedars-Sinai Hospital from three bullet wounds in the arm and abdomen. The news promptly sent chills through many in the celebrity world. She had recently met Diana, Princess of Wales, at a party in London and had invited her to her home. That morning, she received word that Diana was interested in visiting her in the near future. "Tell her not to come," Madonna said to one of her associates. "My God, I don't want to be responsible if anything happens to her. Why should she have to be a part of my nightmare?"

"Madonna attracts a lot of crazy people," said Los Angeles private investigator Anthony Pellicano. "Madonna's about the worst. She goes out in public and likes to flaunt herself."

Madonna was truly frightened by the stalker's persistence, though she tried to remain unruffled and continue with her life and career.

"It really freaked her out," said one friend of hers. "It was difficult for her to come to terms with it. She was afraid to leave the house. She told me, 'When I was younger, I could deal a lot better with the crazies out there. But as I get older, it somehow gets harder. Maybe I'm losing my edge . . . or maybe I'm losing my mind.' She was hating her life and career, feeling strongly that her career was on the wrong track."

Once back in Los Angeles, Madonna showed up at her agent's office at CAA (Creative Artists Agency) upset. Her face was pale and seemed tiny. Her lips, so dazzlingly red, dominated her appearance. Looking startlingly thin, she wore a crisp white two-piece power trouser suit—all straight lines and starch—and matching hat. She also wore a single strand of pearls, matching earrings and a thin gold watch. No doubt, she was fully aware of the stares and whispers of those in the waiting room. "Can I help you?" the receptionist asked, her tone tremulous.

"You want to help me?" Madonna answered, abruptly. "Well, let's see. I need a new agent. This agency sucks. Recommend a new agency, and *then* you'll be helping me."

The receptionist did not know how to respond. Looking peeved, Madonna reached into a silver bowl on the secretary's desk and popped a chocolate mint into her mouth. She then made a beeline for her agent's office, and slammed the door behind her.

✝

Something to Remember

"So much controversy has swirled around my career this past decade that very little attention ever gets paid to my music. The songs are all but forgotten. While I have no regrets regarding the choices I've made artistically, I've learned to appreciate the idea of doing things in a simpler way. So without a lot of fanfare, without any distractions, I present to you this collection of ballads. Some are old, some are new. All of them are from my heart."

So wrote Madonna in the liner notes accompanying her eleventh album, *Something to Remember,* issued at the end of 1995. Perhaps no truer observation has ever been made of Madonna or of her musical career, and made by the lady herself. Like so many of the strong female entertainers from Hollywood's past who have inspired her, Madonna's personal life has often left her professional accomplishments sitting in the shade. Of course, she neglected to add that she has usually been the very source of the distracting madness. After all, she was the one who had practically ruined her image with her maddening, one-track-mind sexual outrageousness.

"She knew it was time to make a change," said one member of her management team who insisted on remaining anonymous. "She would have to be pretty stupid not to know it, and you could never say that Madonna was stupid. She was upset, a little frantic about what people were saying about her. That's why she put together the *Something to Remember* album, to remind people that there was more to her than just the controversy that had surrounded her almost from the beginning of her career."

Madonna was also correct when she wrote that some of her songs have many times been overlooked in favor of the current gossip and innuendo. Her savvy as a serious pop songwriter has attracted even less attention. For instance, the tabloids don't report that she has written most of her songs and publishes them through her own Webo Girl Publishing, Inc. "She hasn't shouted about her musical abilities," notes Mirwais Ahmadzai, a star of France's burgeoning electronica scene who would go on to produce her 2000 album, *Music*. "She is the consummate songwriter," he says. "She listens to classic musicals a lot. Not just the obvious ones, like *Singin' in the Rain*, but the lesser ones. She loves them. I remember one time we all had dinner in Germany, and somebody brought up old musicals, and she was the one who knew all the verses. Things our mum and dad watch, she's into it all. Really solid, melodic stuff like that. And she writes really solid, melodic stuff."

While such facts don't make exciting headlines, Madonna's interest in publishing is significant, especially in a business where, every day, famous singer/songwriters create valuable copyrights that they don't own. Nor is much made of the fact that Madonna is one of the few hands-on female record producers in the music business—and one of the most successful of either gender. She is certainly able to hold her own with such legends as George Martin, producer of the Beatles (whose chart performances Madonna's hits have challenged), and Quincy Jones.

So, whether Madonna issued *Something to Remember*, a collection of previously released love songs, because she had a point to prove or simply to keep a contractual obligation, the fourteen-track recording did make a statement. That statement began with the CD's packaging. On it, Madonna looks deliciously cosmopolitan in a form-fitting white cocktail number. On the front she's posed in meditation; on the back photograph she is coy, playful and just a bit sexy.

As she wrote in her notes, not all of the songs had been re-released; four of them were new. It's interesting that even though Madonna profits greatly each time she records a song she has written, she will gladly and eagerly perform a new tune by another writer, or, if she feels she can bring something new to it, even redo a classic. Such is the distinction of an artist more concerned with the whole of the project as opposed to how much money she can deposit in her current account as a result of its sales.

Long a fan of Marvin Gaye's 1976 classic, "I Want You," Madonna recut the song with the British dance-music unit Massive Attack. (It was also released on *Inner City Blues—The Music of Marvin Gaye* by Motown Records in November 1995.) The track was produced by Nellee Hooper. Whereas Marvin Gaye's version of the song, penned by veteran R&B writer Leon Ware and T-Boy Ross (younger brother of Diana Ross), is elaborately produced, Madonna's is pared to basically just her voice and Massive Attack's club beat. The result is a bit sexier than Gaye's version; one can almost imagine Madonna crawling seductively across the floor, after her prey.

"I'll Remember," another new cut, is just the opposite of Madonna's take on Gaye. Written by Madonna, Patrick Leonard and singer/songwriter Richard Page, the beautiful, gold-selling song was the theme from the 1994 motion picture *With Honors*. It sounds like a flick theme, too, equipped with smart chords and big emotion. It is reminiscent of another movie theme of Madonna's, "Live to Tell," also featured on the album, only better.

Also included were two new sentimental and expansive ballads, "You'll See" and "One More Chance," both written by Madonna with songwriter/producer David Foster. The working universe of a star as big as Madonna is small. At some point, she had to end up working (or consider working) with those who have had success with her peers, even competitors in the pop music world. Foster had produced Barbra Streisand and had written hits for Al Jarreau and Earth, Wind & Fire ("After the Love Is Gone"). It was interesting that, with all of his exciting musical ability from which to draw, he and Madonna would come up with two of the most somber songs she had ever recorded—but such is the excitement of collaboration: one never knows what will come from it.

The rest of *Something to Remember* consisted of some of Madonna's most important ballads, including "Crazy for You," "Oh Father," "Take a Bow," "Forbidden Love," a remix of "Love Don't Live Here Anymore," "This Used to Be My Playground" (a melancholy performance heard in *A League of Their Own*, and which went on to become her tenth Number 1 record in 1992, making its Madonna album debut here) and "Something to Remember," from the *I'm Breathless* collection. That she made the *Dick Tracy* ballad this CD's title track might indicate how she felt about the song she and Patrick Leonard had written—perhaps wanting it to have the attention it did not receive the first time around.

In any case, perhaps all that *Something to Remember* lacked was a bow around it. It was a valentine, a love letter from Madonna to her fans and music lovers alike. Like any Madonna project, it seemed to say just a little more than the obvious. In this case, the collection seemed to nudge teasingly at her contemporaries, ". . . And *these* are just my ballads."

✝

Perfect Casting?

She had wanted it for years, but never had she *needed* it as much as she did in 1995.

From the first moment in early 1995 that Madonna learned she had won the prized role of Eva Perón in Andrew Lloyd Webber's film interpretation of his musical *Evita*, she sensed a major shift about to occur in her life and career. "I really want to be recognized as an actress," she had once said. "I've learned that if you surround yourself with great writers and great actors and a great director and a great costumer or whatever, it's pretty hard to go wrong. In the past, I've been in a really big hurry to make movies and I haven't taken the time to make sure all of those elements were in line and good enough. It's a waste of time to do something mediocre. Unless you absolutely believe in every aspect of it, then you shouldn't waste your time."

For over a decade, much of the press and the public had speculated that Madonna was the perfect choice for the role of Evita. However, because her movie career had never really ignited, as a result of box-office disasters such as *Shanghai Surprise, Who's That Girl?* and *Body of Evidence,* a number of other actresses were considered for the part. It was a search that nearly rivaled the casting of Scarlett O'Hara in the classic *Gone With the Wind* back in the 1930s.

Patti LuPone, who had masterfully created the part on Broadway, was under consideration and was said to have wanted the movie role badly. Glenn Close, who had caused a sensation starring on the stage in another Andrew Lloyd Webber musical, *Sunset Boulevard,* was also vying for the part. Meanwhile, Meryl Streep diligently took lessons to better her voice for her own *Evita* audition. There were also sporadic announcements that genuine singing divas such as Bette Midler, Mariah Carey, Olivia Newton-John and Gloria Estefan were all interested in starring in what promised to be a big-budget, highly publicized movie musical. Not to be outdone, Liza Minnelli and Barbra Streisand—performers respected for their acting ability as well as their singing talent—were also associated with the project at different points along the way.

After years of announcements, denials, rumors and speculation, most Hollywood observers believed that Michelle Pfeiffer had finally been chosen by the film's director Alan Parker *(Bugsy Malone, Fame, Pink Floyd—The Wall* and *The Commitments)* to star in the movie. Pfeiffer had, indeed, expressed an interest in the project. However, it had taken so long for decisions to be made that, while waiting for the wheels to turn, Pfeiffer had a baby. When Parker met her just before he was to make his final casting decision, it was clear that her motherhood status now presented a problem. With two small children in tow (an adopted daughter as well as the new baby), the actress wasn't eager to tackle the long, difficult shooting schedule Parker had in mind. So, she was out. But who would be in?

It was upon hearing of Pfeiffer's rejection that Madonna, her uncanny instinct for perfect timing at work, just as always, sent Parker a handwritten, four-page letter. In it, she explained why she would be the perfect choice to play the role of Evita.

In her letter, Madonna promised that she would sing, dance and act her heart out if Parker would only give her the opportunity to do so. She would put everything else in her life and career on hold in order to devote her time and energy to *Evita*. She may have felt that she had no choice; Madonna was that desperate to do something worthwhile in films. In 1995, and then again in 1996, she would appear in supporting roles in movies of which most people didn't even know she was a part, just for the experience of doing them. The first had been 1995's *Four Rooms*, a series of vignettes, one of which featured Madonna as a witch named Elspeth. *Blue in the Face*, also released in 1995, was a sequel to the popular *Smoke*, in which Madonna is featured briefly, mooning Harvey Keitel after delivering a singing telegram. In 1996, she would appear in Spike Lee's *Girl 6*, in which she appears briefly as the owner of a telephone sex service.

"When I was chosen to make *Evita*, I know I wasn't Andrew Lloyd Webber's first choice," she would later say. "I don't think he was particularly thrilled with my singing abilities. I knew I was going in with odds against me. That's an awkward position to be in. You feel everyone's waiting for you to stumble."

Of course, there are clear similarities between Madonna and Eva Perón. Eva was a Latin-looking brunette who found fame as a dyed blonde, as did Madonna. Eva was strong willed, as is Madonna. Eva was emotional, dramatic and sometimes self-pitying, as is Madonna. The story of Madonna's rise to fame—a legend partly of her making and partly that of the media's—also parallels Eva Perón's in that both women exploited a series of relationships with men in order to survive early years of struggle and then, ultimately, clawed their way from obscurity.

Madonna as Eva Perón—Evita. Perfect casting, it would seem . . . and exactly what Madonna needed most to boost her career during a time she was trying to refashion her image. Throughout the eighties and early nineties, she had exhausted her aggressive sex symbol routine by using songs, films, books and outrageous quotes to sear a particularly scandalous image into the public's consciousness. However, by 1996, the notion of Madonna as a sexual pariah—the defiant and daring "naughty" girl of pop—had most certainly run its course. Finally, she of the many guises fully understood the need to reinvent herself completely. Thus, *Evita*. However, there would be a few challenges when it came to aligning Evita's story with Madonna's vision of it.

One major problem Madonna faced with her latest—and arguably most important—film venture was that the story of Eva Perón was not completely in alignment with the new, softer and uncontroversial image she wanted to project to her public at this time in her life. The story of a manipulative woman who really slept her way to the top—Eva's true story—may have worked better for Madonna in the eighties when all she could think about was how to shock the world, but not in 1995. Before she went into rehearsals, she spent hours going over the script, listening to the music, reading up on the history and suggesting to the producers changes to what was historically documented. Not to say that Andrew Lloyd Webber had been completely accurate in his own version of Eva Perón's life, but he was a lot closer to the truth, in tone and intention, than the version Madonna wanted for her break-out movie. Her desire was to rewrite history—even if just in a subtle way—in order to create a softer, more vulnerable Eva Perón. She wanted to craft an Evita more to her liking and, by extension, a Madonna more to her public's. In the end, her goal was to invent not only "Evita-Lite" but "Madonna-Lite," as well.

The real story was that the canny and intelligent Evita influenced an entire nation by aligning herself with a man who would become the country's next president, Juan Perón. Before her relationship with Perón, Eva Duarte was a minor actress in film and radio who had secured equally minor acting roles by virtue of other romantic relationships. However, as the protégée, and then wife, of the most powerful man in the country, the real-life Eva was able to turn her attention to politics, which was where her true talents lay. Ultimately, Eva became as important to Juan Perón's future as he was to hers. She instinctively knew she could endear herself to the country's working class, thus endearing her husband to them. She perfectly understood the masses. After all, Eva also came from an impoverished background.

While established Argentinian charities shunned her as the wife of the president, Evita had the power to establish her own charity foundations, which brought in enormous sums of money. Though she did a lot of good for the people of Argentina, she also spent lavishly on herself. She dazzled all by spending millions of dollars on jewels and haute couture. Born poor and illegitimate, she understood that the image of a woman who had attained great success against all odds was her most important weapon in reaching working-class people. The masses wanted her to succeed because her success meant the possibility of their own. "I'm one of you," she would say, throwing her arms forward and becoming a symbol of what an illegitimate child from an impoverished family could attain.

Fame, money and glamour were not enough for the ambitious Evita. She also craved power on a major scale and had ambitions to be the first woman elected to the office of vice-president. Sadly, her dreams would go unfulfilled. Cancer took her life in 1952 at the age of thirty-three, thereby assuring that she would forever remain, at least in her adoring public's eyes, a saint.

It was a terrific story just as it was . . . and certainly the story to which Madonna had originally been attracted. But now she felt it was in need of some tweaking.

"It's just not me," Madonna told director Alan Parker.

"Indeed, it's not," he shot back. "It's Evita Perón."

"But my public will think it's me. And it's not."

"But it's Evita Perón!"

And back and forth they went . . .

It seemed that Madonna was most offended by the implication of Evita having used so many men in her climb to the top, perhaps because the press and public had often implied just that about her. "It's a way envious people undermine your strength and your accomplishments," she observed in a *Vanity Fair* interview. "I didn't use any man who didn't want to be used," she said. "If anything, *I've* been used. I'm the one who has been used." Of course, Madonna was really not as blind to her past as that observation seemed to indicate. Anyone who knew her well would remember that she had admitted to having used people in the past—both men and women—and that her conscience had bothered her about such manipulations, going all the way back to feeling regretful for not having Camille Barbone at her side when she finally became successful with her first album in 1983. However, now was not the time for true confessions.

"I thought it [the original take of Evita Perón] was a male chauvinist point of view, that any woman who's powerful is a whore or slept her way to the top," she stated. "There's that implication right through the musical and it's ludicrous. You can't sleep your way to the top," she concluded. She then stopped abruptly, perhaps thinking about what she was saying, and quickly revised it: "Well, in Hollywood, maybe, but she [Evita Perón] influenced an entire nation."

"I hate that she looks like such a bitch," she complained, making clear her intention to tweak things. "I'd like it if she was . . . nicer, I guess. More dimensional."

"Well, a lot of people may have liked it if Madonna was nicer, more dimensional," said chagrined film critic Gene Siskel when the film was eventually released. "But, at least from what I hear, she's not that nice, and she's not that dimensional. What's true is true . . ."

As seen through Madonna's eyes, Eva Perón would no longer be a political animal. Instead, she would be "nicer, more dimensional." Gone would be the brilliant, scheming, conniving climber who used sex as a weapon to demolish anyone who got in her way—the truth of Evita's story, and maybe even of Madonna's, depending on how one chose to look at it. In her place would be a shy, reserved, ethereal Eva Perón who had been pushed around by men but who—by using her brains and willpower—would eventually rise to the top of the political ladder. Because she was so beautiful and persuasive, she would also go on to become a legend. After her death at the end of the movie, the viewer would weep, that's how much he would respect and love Eva Perón. "A couple of years ago, no one would have cried if I died, people were so sick of me," Madonna said, privately. "I only hope that will change with this movie."

Once Madonna was able to fashion the role in *Evita* to her liking, it was time to prepare herself to become Eva Perón. As had always been her style, the moment she was sure she had her goal in sight, she would make sure not to stumble. Throwing herself into the project, she began with a plan first to improve her singing range.

Being a filmed musical, all of *Evita*'s cast members would be expected to sing their parts themselves and not rely on other voices. Madonna's ability to do so—she was, after all, a singer—was at least one of the reasons the producers chose her for the starring role in the first place. However, the reason Madonna was thought to be ideal for the job could also have been the very reason she would have been terrible at it. Yes, she was a singer . . . but a *pop* singer. While Broadway and Hollywood's acting community pondered her ability to deliver her lines convincingly in front of the camera, Broadway's music sector smugly considered the idea of Madonna singing Tim Rice's lyrics over Andrew Lloyd Webber's musical creation with tongue firmly in cheek.

In some respects, Madonna felt she was up to the job. Over the years, she had unwittingly prepared for it through every little cheap demo she'd ever financed, through every music track she'd ever cracked her vocals over, through every recording studio couch she ever fell asleep on, toiling to make another hit record. The problem, however, was that nothing she'd ever done could totally prepare her for the recording of *Evita*—she'd never done anything quite like it. She'd participated in film soundtracks before, but in those situations she usually wielded considerable control over her musical contribution. She wrote and produced several of the songs for the *I'm Breathless* album, from *Dick Tracy,* but that was a "Music from and Inspired By" production, not a soundtrack album in the classic sense. The *Evita* soundtrack would be integral to the film. After all, this was a musical; the soundtrack *was* the film.

Madonna immediately went into vocal training with respected New York vocal coach Joan Layder. "She had to use her voice in a way she'd never used it before," observed Layder. "*Evita* is real musical theater—it's operatic, in a sense. Madonna developed an upper register that she didn't know she had."

Ironically, one of Layder's clients was Patti LuPone. Always competitive, Madonna feared falling short when being compared with the bombastic-voiced LuPone. Layder joked that Madonna felt that LuPone had her ear to the door during the lessons.

Vocal training for the film was difficult. Madonna was forced to stretch herself vocally in ways she had never before attempted. However, even she was amazed at her own vocal dexterity, once she became accustomed to using her "tool" (as Layder called it) in the proper way—singing from her diaphragm rather than her throat. Whereas she had often sounded tinny and thin on her recordings prior to this time, suddenly—after just a few weeks of training—her voice was full-bodied, rich and theatrical. Every time she opened her mouth to sing, she was amazed to find herself accessing elements of her voice she never knew were there. It was as if she had gone to bed and, magically, awakened a real *singer*. "Where did *that* come from?" she would ask Layder of her new sound. "God," she told her. "God!"

"I suddenly discovered that I had been using only half of my voice," Madonna later told *Los Angeles Times* pop music critic Robert Hilburn. "Until then, I had pretty much accepted that I had a very limited range, which is fine. Anita O'Day and Edith Piaf had very limited ranges, too, and I am a big fan. So I figured I'd make do with the best I had."

As it happened, she wouldn't have to "make do" with a limited vocal range. At the end of each lesson, she would excitedly telephone friends and say, "You won't believe this! Listen!" Then, she would sing into the telephone at full volume, completely amazed by her own proficiency.

When, in September 1995, Madonna arrived in London with Antonio Banderas and Jonathan Pryce to start rehearsals for the recording of the *Evita* soundtrack, she was ready. Every professional musical experience Madonna had up until this point—every song she sang, how she learned to breathe, how she learned to position her mouth in front of the microphone, how she learned to maintain vocal stamina, as well as her new vocal training—served to prepare her for the day she first stepped into the door of CTS Studios in London.

Parker was delighted to hear the "new" Madonna. Since all the filming would consist of the actors lip-synching to prerecorded vocals, the making of *Evita* was double the work for all involved. First, the actors were required to perform their roles in the recording studio, and then they would have to repeat the performance in front of the camera on a film set.

On the first day of actual recording, though, it became apparent that special consideration would have to be given to the film's female star. "I'm used to writing my own songs and I go into a studio, choose the musicians and say what sounds good or doesn't," Madonna later explained. "To work on forty-six songs with everyone involved and not have a say was a big adjustment. It was difficult to go in, spill my guts, then say, 'Do what you will with it.'" Moreover, Madonna was not comfortable laying down a "guide vocal" simultaneously with an eighty-four-piece orchestra in a huge studio. She was used to singing over a prerecorded track and not having musicians listen to her as she made mistakes natural to the recording process. "Three worlds were colliding," Parker observed, "musical theater, pop, and film."

Despite all of her hard work, the first day of recording was a disaster. She had to sing "Don't Cry for Me Argentina" on that day, and in front of Andrew Lloyd Webber. Believing that she had done a terrible job, she stormed from the studio, tears rolling down her face, pale as porcelain. ("How can I go on?" she lamented. "I can't work like this. I'm an *artist*. Not a puppet.") Later Parker would dub that first day "Black Monday."

"I was so nervous," she recalls, "because I knew that Andrew had had reservations about me, and here I am singing the hardest song in the piece. All of a sudden there, with everybody for the first time, it was really tense."

An emergency meeting was held among Alan Parker, Andrew Lloyd Webber and Madonna. The entire eighty-four-piece orchestra was fired, and Webber also brought in a new conductor. It was also decided that Madonna would record all of her vocals at a more contemporary studio in which she would be more at ease, while the large orchestrations would be conducted and recorded elsewhere. It was also decided that Madonna would sing only in the afternoons, and every other day. Days off were allocated for her to rest her voice. Still, regardless of the accommodations for her, the recording of the soundtrack was an arduous task. The cast and director worked for four months putting in over 400 recording hours—and that was before a single foot of film had been shot.

✞

The Stalking Trial

On Wednesday January 3, 1996, Madonna arrived at a Los Angeles courthouse under tight security in a large black luxury car with tinted windows. She could be seen inside wearing dark glasses as the automobile was driven into an underground garage that is also used to bring prisoners into the building. Reporters were brought into the courtroom before Madonna was led in by a contingent of armed bailiffs and bodyguards. The new, toned-down Madonna was dressed in a smart, double-breasted charcoal suit with a calf-length skirt, simple jewelry, black pumps and red lipstick, her auburn hair pulled back into a French twist. She looked lovely, but appeared to be nervous.

The time had finally come for Madonna to testify in the case against Robert Hoskins, charged with stalking and threatening her. Because she had previously ignored a subpoena to be a witness in the case, she was now ordered to appear in court under the threat of being jailed on $5 million bail. From the witness stand, she testified that she had not previously appeared because she was afraid of Hoskins and did not want to give him the opportunity to see her up close. She proceeded to describe how she had been disturbed by his unruly appearance and "the look in his eye," when she passed him one day as he stood in front of the gate at her entranceway. She said that she became terrified when Hoskins told Madonna's assistant (Caresse Norman) that he was Madonna's husband and would slit her throat "from ear to ear," and then kill Norman and everyone else in the house if he was not allowed to see his "wife." She said that she began to have "nightmares that he was in my house, that he was chasing after me."

As her stalker stared at her from just across the room, Madonna, at first visibly nervous but then becoming increasingly angry, made it clear that she was perplexed by the judge's decision that she be forced to testify in the trial. Her attorney, Nicholas DeWitt, had tried to convince Judge Jacqueline Connor to allow Madonna to videotape her testimony or at least to have Hoskins taken from the courtroom while she testified. The female judge ruled against both motions, saying that Hoskins had a constitutional right to face his accuser and that she did not want to provide him with grounds for an appeal. Madonna was amazed. "She's a woman," Madonna said privately. "Why would she be so spiteful?"

"I'm sick to my stomach," Madonna said from the witness stand. Looking grim, she elaborated, "I feel incredibly disturbed that the man who threatened my life is sitting across from me and he has somehow made his fantasies come true. I'm sitting in front of him. And that's what he wants." She avoided making eye contact with Hoskins during her seventy-five-minute testimony; she glanced briefly at him, twice.

The following day, on January 4, Madonna's bodyguard, Basil Stephens, testified that Hoskins had been at Madonna's Hollywood Hills property (called Castillo DeLago) on three occasions. On his first visit, Hoskins threatened to kill the bodyguard if he did not give Madonna a note he had scrawled on a religious pamphlet. On his third, Hoskins brought his bags with him and "looked like he was moving in." Although Hoskins's lawyer argued that he was just an unfortunate, homeless person, Stephens disagreed, saying that he considered the stalker to be "extremely dangerous." As further evidence, the jury was also shown footage from a security camera taken the day of the shooting. It showed Hoskins ignoring a "No Trespassing" sign, climbing the front gate, jumping from a wall onto Madonna's property, and peering into her front door.

On his last visit to Madonna's home in May 1995, Hoskins's behavior had gone from bizarre to violent. Stephens testified that he was forced to shoot him during an altercation. Thinking Hoskins was dead after having fired three shots at him, Stephens left the scene to call the police. However, ten minutes later, he returned only to find Hoskins sitting up, near Madonna's pool, with wounds to his arm and abdomen. Stephens told him that there was an ambulance on the way. In what sounded like a surreal scene from a bad movie, Stephens recalled having told the obsessed fan, "I'm sorry I shot you," to which Hoskins answered, "No problem."

When Madonna heard about what had happened at her home, she became so upset that she decided to sell the $7-million estate. She said, "How can I lie by the pool knowing this thing had occurred there? I felt it was an attraction to negative energy, and I had to get out."

After the eight-man, four-woman jury found Robert Hoskins guilty of stalking, the judge gave him a stiff ten-year sentence, noting that "his apparent mental illness appears to increase the danger."

After the trial, Madonna continued to have nightmares about Robert Hoskins who, if he intended to become her focus, was sickeningly successful. Madonna said that she couldn't help but feel that her dreams were premonitions to tragedy. Still, to this day, she has not gotten over the Hoskins ordeal. Say those closest to her, she now can't help but feel responsible for inciting this kind of potentially cataclysmic event in her life just by virtue of some of the overtly sexual publicity campaigns (such as the *Sex* book) she's done in her career, many of which could be perceived by some less emotionally stable people as an invitation to harass her. It would seem that growing up has not been easy for Madonna, especially the part having to do with facing the repercussions of, and claiming responsibility for, her past actions. Still, as an adult—and especially as a woman who was evolving into a person who understood that, as she put it, "each of our actions has a reaction"—she couldn't just dismiss the Robert Hoskinses of her life as merely a casualty of her celebrity. Perhaps he was just the inevitable result of some of the ways she went about achieving fame.

✝

Making *Evita*

In early February 1996, following the ordeal of the stalking trial, Madonna left Los Angeles for Buenos Aires. After recording the soundtrack to *Evita*, she may have thought the worst was behind her. However, Madonna was still in for a bumpy ride. When she arrived in Buenos Aires a few days before she was scheduled to begin filming, she realized that life wasn't going to be easy for her in "this godforsaken place" (as she referred to the city). Plastered all over the city was graffiti screaming, "Madonna go home." It was apparent that some Argentinians were unhappy with the notion that a brazen pop star would be portraying their beloved Evita.

To make matters worse, living conditions were, at first, a lot more challenging than those to which Madonna had become accustomed during the last twelve years of being a superstar. "No gyms! No decent food!" she groused. "I can't live like this," she shouted at one of the film's production assistants. "I need Evian. Do you hear me? *Ev-i-an!*"

Soon, though, Madonna was ensconced—at least on weekends— in a lavish $12-million mansion, renting it for $70,000 a week. Of course, as would be the nature of any diva, she made a couple of demands deemed outrageous by some observers—such as floating gardenias in the bathroom bowls, and white orchids in all of the other rooms—as well as some other less unreasonable requests: a blender, apple and mango juices, popcorn, Gummi Bears, Special K cereal, oatmeal, potato chips, assorted fresh vegetables, teriyaki chicken, and a CD player in every room. She also asked that one room be transformed into a gym equipped with a treadmill, Lifecycle, StairMaster, Versa

Climber and free weights. Of course, there was always shopping to keep her busy, as well. On one Sunday, she went on a shopping spree at the sprawling San Elmo flea market, where she stayed for three hours. Then, it was off to Antigona, a vintage clothing store where she bought fifty hats, ten pairs of gloves, a dozen dresses and ten lace mantillas. Bodyguards, chauffeurs and assistants waited to open doors for her, write out checks for her, or compliment her on her good taste.

Despite her comfortable lifestyle, there was still the nagging problem with which Madonna was so well acquainted: the burden of fame itself. Those fans who had migrated to this strange land "tormented" (her word) and "stalked" (again, her word) her when she wasn't at her weekend home but at her hotel, closer to the set, turning it into a virtual prison. A group of young, determined admirers kept a steady vigil outside the window of their idol's second floor suite, chanting and serenading the object of their obsession. "I slept like shit," Madonna complained. "The children outside my window came at two-hour intervals all through the night to beckon me to my balcony and profess undying love . . . Shakespeare this was not."

Leaving the hotel proved even more difficult. Each time Madonna exited, the crowds rushed her. "Unfortunately five hundred screaming fans made my departure almost impossible," she said later, describing the scene. Once, while attempting a quick getaway one afternoon, she and her entourage sped away in a car only to discover that a young girl was holding on for dear life to the roof of the vehicle. "So we stopped and pulled her off as she kicked and screamed and cried that she loved me," Madonna said. "I wanted to give her the business card of my shrink but my driver drove away too fast."

The stress, however, didn't dissuade Madonna from sticking to a strict agenda in order to continue to better herself during production. Since she would be called upon not only to sing, but to dance and, of course, act, she worked diligently to be at peak form in all three areas.

As for her acting, in order to become absorbed by the complicated character of Evita, Madonna traveled about Argentina meeting people who had known the real Eva Perón—diplomats, intellectuals, ministers and even a few of her childhood friends. "Of course, some refuse to meet me," Madonna said at the time. However, to those who would agree to talk to her, Madonna asked dozens of well-thought-out questions about the way Evita looked, the food she ate, the manner in which she behaved and what she enjoyed doing in her spare time. So grateful for the information she was receiving, she would kiss some of her interviewees on the nose, others gently on the lips. "It was fun to be the interviewer for a change," she laughed. As a result of this kind of research, Madonna began to understand subtle character traits she sensed would be necessary to guarantee her best performance of Eva Perón.

*

Filming of *Evita* began on February 13, 1996. In the first days of production Madonna became aware of the reality of how excruciating it was going to be to put all of her hard-earned, newfound acting, singing and dancing skills to the test on the *Evita* set. It was swelteringly hot in Buenos Aires in February and Madonna, as the fifteen-year-old Eva in her period costume and uncomfortable wig, on the first day of shooting was required to do take after take while saying good-bye to her family on the way to the big city. An ancient train billowed out a steady stream of noxious smoke and hot winds blew dust into her mouth as she lip-synched to her prerecorded song. It was a miserable experience, and only a foreshadowing of things to come.

In the days that followed, Madonna was required to spend long days in the intense sun alternating between waiting around for the proper light to film and performing in complicated song-and-dance numbers. "I was dying from heat exhaustion and being made a meal of by ants and flies and hornets," she said later.

Madonna was shooting six days a week and rehearsing on her day off. As filming dragged on in Buenos Aires she began feeling more and more lonely and alienated. "My family and friends are the people in the movie," she said at the time. "They have seen me bare my soul and yet they know nothing about me." She was also feeling dizzy and nauseous every day, conditions she blamed on the incredible heat.

Her moodiness aside, Madonna continued to prove herself the consummate professional while actually doing her job in front of the cameras. Cast and crew members, some grudgingly, couldn't help but admire her total commitment to the project. Even Jonathan Pryce—who played Evita's husband Juan Perón and who said after the first few days of working with her that he had never worked with anyone quite as rude—eventually found good things to say about her. "She's a strong, dynamic force and I can only admire that," he admitted. "I've grown to like her a lot. People have preconceptions about her due to the media but you soon learn she's a regular person. True, she doesn't discourage the media too much, but there's a lot of myth created around her."

Adding to Madonna's turmoil was the fact that Antonio Banderas's girlfriend, the actress Melanie Griffith, had become an annoyance. As soon as Banderas was cast as the movie's narrator, Ché, Madonna began hearing from certain associates of hers that Melanie Griffith was unhappy. Because Madonna is widely viewed as a "man killer," Melanie was concerned that her boyfriend would fall prey to her, especially since Madonna had made it clear in her *Truth or Dare* film that she fancied Banderas and thought he was "very sexy." (She also hastened to add, "He must have a really small penis because no one is that perfect.")

"What I don't need right now is a jealous girlfriend," Madonna told Alan Parker, according to one of Parker's associates. "I'm not even interested in Antonio. That crack in *Truth or Dare* was just a stupid joke. Antonio is too strait-laced for me." She was clearly upset. Alan Parker rested his forehead against Madonna's in an attempt to comfort her. Then, he kissed her on the nose and walked away. She stood in place, probably feeling that she had just been treated in a condescending manner.

Later, when Madonna was told that Melanie would be accompanying her boyfriend to Argentina, she couldn't believe it. "How could a woman be that insecure?" she asked. "If it were me, and he was my boyfriend, and I was worried about another woman—I'd say, 'Hey, go get her, tiger . . . and then get the fuck out.' And that would be the end of it."

Shortly before filming began, Madonna took matters into her own hands and decided to call Melanie Griffith.

"I understand that there have been some rumors," she reportedly told her, "and I just want you to know that they're completely ridiculous. I actually can't wait for you to get here, Melanie. We'll have fun!" Melanie's reaction to the call is unknown. After she hung up, though, Madonna turned to an associate and said, "Well, that should take care of *that*. And if it doesn't, I guess I'll just have to deal with her when she gets to Argentina with her henpecked boyfriend."

Despite having received the conciliatory telephone call from

Madonna, Melanie was still distant toward her when she finally did arrive on the set. "It seemed as if she didn't trust her," said Louise Keith, a Los Angeles–based friend of Griffith's. "Madonna was certainly flirty toward Antonio, but I think it was harmless and just the way Madonna is. However, Melanie didn't like it. She told me that Madonna did everything she could do to win her over, but Melanie wasn't giving in to her. 'I don't want to socialize with her, not really,' Melanie said when asked by one of Madonna's 'handlers' if she might like to join Madonna for lunch. Well, that really pissed off Madonna. Actually, I don't think they said two words to each other the whole time Melanie was there, a couple of weeks. Instead, they just shot each other frosty glares whenever they were in each other's company."

A crew member later recalled, "Madonna couldn't contain herself and she blurted out, 'Melanie hates me.' She told Parker, 'She won't accept an invitation if I'm in the same room. I don't know what Banderas sees in her but she's got him by the balls.' "

For publication, Madonna made light of the Melanie Griffith situation. In writing about the incident in *Vanity Fair*, Madonna refused even to mention Melanie's name: "The press is trying to make a big deal about my competing with his [Banderas's] girlfriend," she wrote, "which is ludicrous because everyone knows I would never date a man who wears cowboy boots."

For her part, Melanie remained diplomatic with the media. In fact, Griffith told the author that she was instrumental in smoothing the working relationship between her husband and Madonna. "They say she can be difficult, but I understand her," says Melanie Griffith. "In fact, I think I understand her better than Antonio, being a woman in this business. I know that she wants things perfect but that some men don't want to listen to her opinion precisely because she is a woman. Do you know how frustrating that is? I told Antonio to listen to her instincts. She has very good instincts. He did.

"Of course they never had an affair," Melanie said. "Would I tolerate such a thing? No, I would not."

Madonna's enthusiasm for the *Evita* project reemerged when the production moved to the location of her dreams—the balcony of the Casa Rosada, which was the shooting location for which she had pleaded with the president of Argentina, Carlos Menem, for permission to shoot. To make the scene as visually dynamic as possible, the company used every extra available, a total of 4,000. When Madonna walked onto the balcony, she couldn't help but gasp in awe of her surroundings. Looking down from the balcony, as far as the eye could see were . . . people. True, they were hired hands, but they must have seemed like fans just the same. When she began to mouth the words to the prerecorded "Don't Cry For Me Argentina" this audience erupted into unbridled cheers.

After the all-night shoot, Madonna was so exhilarated by her work she could barely speak. As the sun rose, the cast and crew quietly hugged each other. In spite of the difficulties they had been experiencing, on this morning they seemed to feel a keen sense of triumph. The filming of the many difficult Buenos Aires segments of the movie was finally coming to a close and now, after the emotional night of shooting at the Casa Rosada, everyone felt as if they were actually accomplishing what they had set out to do. Maybe things would work out after all. Maybe they really were working together to create something extremely special. After having sunk to such a desperate low only a few days earlier, everyone's morale was now suddenly elevated to a new high.

However, *Evita* was far from complete. After a few days of rest, the entire company would move to Hungary for many more weeks of grueling work. Once there, a new problem would arise, and it would be one that no one could have anticipated . . . and which, at least for the moment, only the leading lady suspected: Madonna was pregnant.

✟

Carlos Leon

In mid-March, with the filming of the Argentina scenes of *Evita* completed, Madonna flew back to America for a few days of rest before continuing on to Budapest. In Miami, she sailed, rode her bike and watched a Mike Tyson fight on television while lounging around in her nightgown, eating ice cream and reading Shakespeare sonnets. Then she headed to New York for a couple of days of shopping. All of this she dutifully reported in the March 19 entry for her "diary," published in *Vanity Fair.* What she did not report is that she also scheduled a visit to her doctor, who then informed her that she was pregnant. "I was stunned when I saw on the ultrasound a tiny living creature spinning around my womb," she later recalled. "Tap-dancing, I think. Waving its tiny arms around and trying to suck its thumb. I could have sworn I heard it laughing. The pure and joyful laughter of a child. As if to say, 'Ha-ha, I fooled you.' "

Actually, she had been talking about wanting a baby for years, but at the time of her marriage to Sean Penn, with her career progressing at a rapid pace, she kept postponing a pregnancy with her temperamental husband. She said that she regretted the abortions she'd had and that she considered the loss of those babies like missing fragments of herself she was not able to restore. She was concerned, now, that in her quest for success and fame, she had missed out on something she may have valued even more if she'd just given it a chance: motherhood. The harsh choice she felt she had—to be either a success or a mother—is uniquely a woman's, and one she was loath to make. "I want it all," Madonna said. "I don't know if I can have it all, but I do know that I want it all."

In newspaper articles throughout 1995, Madonna had spoken longingly of having a baby, but she was careful to add that she didn't want to focus on becoming pregnant until after she finished her dream role in *Evita.* The thirty-seven-year-old Madonna then began hinting that she was contemplating getting a sperm donor to help her have the child. She had joked to reporter Forrest Sawyer on the American television program *Prime Time Live* that her biological clock was ticking so loudly that she was going to put an ad out for a suitable man to sire her baby, to "take care of the fatherhood gig. I'm sure I'll meet the right guy," she said. "I'm sure of it." She also added, in a serious tone, that without a child she felt "a longing, a feeling of emptiness."

On Wednesday January 10, 1996, Madonna had a rendezvous with Sean Penn at the Carlyle Hotel in New York. The two stayed in the room together for twenty-one and a half hours, according to reporters waiting for her finally to emerge. Those closest to Madonna and Penn now say that she was trying to talk Penn into having a baby with her. "I've had a lot of men since our marriage ended, but you're the only one I want as a father to my children," she said, according to a friend of

Penn's. "You're the only man I've ever truly loved, Sean, and you know it."

"She really tried to talk him into it, saying that she still loves him but understands that the two of them have no future. Still, he was just the kind of man, she said, that she wanted to have father her baby. Sean really considered it. But, in the end, he didn't think it would be a good idea."

Penn, who already had two children by his second wife, Robin Wright, declined Madonna's offer.

However, she seemed more determined than ever to have a baby. "It's the one thing she wanted more than anything else," says her ex-friend, Sandra Bernhard. "I think she would do anything to have one." It's true that anyone who knew Madonna knew that once her mind was set on a goal, it was unlikely that she wouldn't find a way to achieve it.

It would be her darkly attractive, handsome new boyfriend, the six foot tall Carlos Leon, who would assist Madonna in achieving her goal of motherhood. Madonna met Carlos in September 1994, while jogging in Central Park. As he cycled through the park, she watched intently, impressed by his well-toned body and the way his sinewy arms and legs filled out tight black spandex. After asking her bodyguard to stay at a safe distance, Madonna approached the strapping stranger with finely chiseled Latin features. She asked him to join her for a cappuccino at a local coffeehouse. Over coffee, Madonna learned that the New York–born Cuban-American was raised in Manhattan and educated in parochial schools. He had aspired to one day become a professional cyclist, with aspirations of winning such races as the Tour de France. However, in order to earn a living, he was now a personal fitness trainer who received $100 an hour for his work, mostly at the gym Crunch. Still, he dreamed of one day making the Olympic cycling team.

Impressed by his seductive looks and contagious personality, Madonna asked Carlos to stay in touch. Of course, what is probably most amazing about the story of how the internationally known superstar performer met the anonymous fitness trainer is that, at this stage of her life and career, Madonna would actually pick up a stranger in Central Park. One can only imagine the practically unbelievable story Carlos Leon had for his buddies over drinks that evening. Shortly thereafter, they began dating.

Sometimes referred to in press reports as a "New York dancer," the amiable Carlos was soon seen holding the happy and animated Madonna's hand at functions in New York, Miami and Los Angeles. "We plan to start a family," Madonna suddenly announced at her thirty-seventh birthday party, "but we're waiting until I finish making *Evita.*" Of course, this proclamation of hopeful motherhood made little sense to interested observers, who couldn't figure out exactly who Carlos Leon was, or his purpose in Madonna's life. ("That's the difference between me and Madonna," her friend Rosie O'Donnell said. "She sleeps with her trainer . . . I ignore mine.") It also made little sense to her friends who knew that she had recently asked Sean Penn to be the father of her child. However, as one friend of hers put it, "trying to make perfect sense of Madonna's life is a lot like trying to make perfect sense of electricity."

It seemed that she felt she was unable to have a fulfilling relationship with a man at this time in her life, and simply didn't want to wait to find one before she had a child. Madonna is an impatient woman, as anyone who knows her will admit. After Tony Ward, she had raised the stakes when it came to the kind of man she would allow in her life. So far, no one had measured up. However, it was now time for her to have a child . . . the ideal relationship would have to wait.

During Carlos's visits to Buenos Aires, he and Madonna seldom slept in the same bedroom, causing speculation among the cast and crew about the state of their relationship. What was not known at the time, though, was that Madonna had been suffering from nightmares ever since she began the movie. "I was constantly being chased, caught and mauled in these awful nightmares," she later confided to a friend. "Every night, I would have these dreams. I would wake up exhausted." Madonna slept in the master bedroom of her suite, while Carlos slept in a guest room. (Often, the two would start the night in the same room, before Carlos then withdrew to the smaller one.)

After experiencing the joy of hearing her baby's heartbeat, Madonna became concerned about the future of the movie, only adding to her stress. What would happen to *Evita* now? Her doctor had informed her that she was approximately ten weeks pregnant. She estimated that she could hide her condition for, perhaps, another seven weeks. However, a number of major dance numbers had been scheduled for the end of the shooting. "Of course they could always get a body double for all my dance sequences [like Jennifer Beals in *Flashdance*]," Madonna mused, "but the idea of someone else doing my dancing is repulsive."

While trying to decide how to proceed, Madonna decided to reveal the news only to her immediate circle: her trainer, her assistant, and the child's father, Carlos. She chose not to tell her sisters, or any of her other friends. "Not because I was ashamed of anything," she later explained. Her biggest fear, she added, was that the story would somehow be leaked to the voracious press. She knew that the notion of Madonna-as-unwed-mother would become instant, worldwide news and cause a sensation that would, in her view, make her life a living hell. "They will send their camera crews to torture me," she said at the time, "and I am desperate to finish filming in peace."

Finally, when she realized that she had no choice but to inform Alan Parker, Madonna picked up the telephone.

"Are you sitting down, Alan," she asked by way of greeting. Then she blurted out, "I'm pregnant."

"How much?" the stunned Parker asked, dazed. "I mean, when is it due?"

†

A Race to the Finish

Alan Parker tried not to panic but, as he would later recall, he couldn't help but do some quick calculations after learning that his star actress was expecting a baby: how many shooting weeks were left on his $59-million film, against how many more weeks she would look slim and trim. What could he do but congratulate Madonna, and agree with her that they would both just have to "see what happens next." They also agreed to keep the pregnancy a secret, again for fear of the disruption the media's reaction might cause the film. Madonna would later say that she felt like a frightened adolescent trying to keep an unwanted pregnancy from her strict parents.

It wasn't long, though, before some of the crew began wondering about the unexplained and dramatic changes Parker began to make to the shooting schedule, especially where the dance sequences were concerned. "They started to wonder if I had finally lost my marbles," Madonna recalled. So, she and Parker had no choice but to fill the other producers in on the secret. Madonna, however, continued to keep her pregnancy from her friends and co-stars, realizing that the fewer people who knew about it, the greater her chances of keeping it out of the news. "I feel like we are all in a race against time," she said at the time. "How will I do all those glamorous photo shoots to promote the film when I can't even fit into my costumes?"

Alone in her hotel room at night, Madonna brooded. Being pregnant should have cheered her up, but it didn't. She had a nagging feeling that she was about to destroy what she and the crew had worked so hard to accomplish. But was success in this film really so important, she would recall wondering to herself. "All I want, really, is some peace in my life," she remembered saying aloud to no one in particular. "Is that so much to ask?"

The days were long, filming scenes outdoors in freezing temperatures, marching up and down the streets while leading torch-carrying masses, all of whom were singing for Perón's freedom. On some days, she was on her feet for hours at a time, mostly dancing. In one scene, as the increasingly ill Evita, she had to fall to the floor clutching her womb. Take after take, Madonna patiently repeated the fall until, when the scene was finally completed, she was covered in bruises. Although she bitched and moaned, she confided privately that she was very proud of her acting that day. ("I know it's going to be a very moving scene.") It was all hard work, perhaps even more so than she had anticipated when she lobbied for the role.

Back at the hotel, when gazing at herself in the mirror she did not see the happy glow of pregnancy. Instead, her reflection revealed an exhausted woman with an imperfect complexion. Clearly visible was a network of lines around her mouth, a web of wrinkles at the corners of her eyes. Sitting at her dressing table, she would begin the careful application of makeup. Her eyes would not leave her image until she was satisfied that her public mask was perfect. However, as she would later recall, it would take longer, with each passing day, for her to achieve that goal.

Constantly feeling chilled, Madonna just couldn't seem to warm herself. Nor could she put aside the memory of the day's work just completed so that she could relax and, hopefully (but not often), fall asleep. She felt panicked, on edge, "like Judy Garland in her final days," as she put it to one of her handlers. Later, she would have to admit that she couldn't shake the sick feeling that she was experiencing the unraveling of her carefully constructed life, that everything she had worked so hard to attain was about to be irrevocably lost.

It wasn't a good time.

✝

No Big Thing?

On April 13, 1996, Madonna's future manager Caresse Norman telephoned America's premier gossip columnist, Liz Smith—always a big supporter of Madonna's career—and confirmed the news of Madonna's pregnancy. Smith's article about it was published in newspapers around the world the next day. "Surprise, surprise, the stork couldn't wait," Liz Smith wrote. "The happy news from Budapest has just arrived—that Madonna is indeed pregnant."

"Madonna doesn't want this to be a big thing," Liz Rosenberg told Liz Smith in a follow-up call, "though I don't know how she thinks it won't be a big deal. But she is deliriously happy, and so is everybody close to her. I hate to resort to a cliché, especially about Madonna, but she is radiant!"

Just prior to the phone call that was made to Liz Smith, Madonna telephoned her father, Tony, with the surprising news. During the filming of *Evita,* she had developed a closer relationship with her family, ironically enough by long-distance telephone communication. Each time Madonna called her father from Argentina to let him know how she was faring, he was thrilled to hear from her. He was proud of her, he said. The frequent conversations he had with her about her life and career at this time were certainly more civil than talks they'd had in recent years. Inadvertently, Tony had always seemed to rub Madonna the wrong way.

For instance, a year and a half earlier, father called daughter to tell her he had seen the video for "I'll Remember" on television and thought she looked "pretty" in it. Rather than just accept the compliment, Madonna couldn't help but be annoyed.

"But, Dad, it's been out for six months and you just now saw it?" she remembered telling him.

"Well, we don't watch much television," he said.

"You would think you would keep up with what I'm doing," she told him. "My God. Do you even have cable?"

From there, the argument escalated. "My father just refuses to acknowledge who I am and what I've accomplished," she told a reporter shortly thereafter.

However, now so many miles from home and with so much on her mind, Madonna seemed able to distance herself from her vexation enough to feel nostalgic for her father and for the rest of her family. "She was homesick," says her brother Martin, whom she also called periodically. "She was calling all of us, her brothers and sisters and even some cousins." Or, as Tony told one relative, "We've been talking, and not fighting. I don't know, maybe things are changing." It was as if, in some ways, Madonna was actually transforming herself into a gentler, more reasonable person—the kind of woman she had been trying to convince her public she really was at this time. "Not that she was a saint," says Alan Parker, "but I did notice that as time went on with the film, she seemed to mellow."

When Madonna learned she was pregnant, she said that she didn't want her father to read about it in the press. She telephoned him with the news, and also confessed to him that he was the most important person in her life—and that she hoped her child would not let her down the way she had let him down so many times in the past. Of course, Tony was concerned that Madonna was unwed and didn't seem at all eager to marry Carlos Leon. However he was also elated and filled with genuine emotion by her call. "We cried on the phone," he recalls. "I knew my kid was growing up. And she was nice to me," he says, laughing. "No smart cracks."

Perhaps along with her pregnancy finally came a sense of acceptance and recognition for Madonna that she had only one surviving parent, and that she should at least try to be good to him. If she had directed her fury about her mother's death at Tony—and it certainly seemed to most people that she had done just that over the years— maybe she now realized how unfair she had been to her father. Or, maybe she had just grown to accept her mother's death as a terrible tragedy for which no one was responsible, and that her father's ability to move on with his own life was an act of strength and courage, not a betrayal of her mother's memory. Certainly, if a similar tragedy were to ever befall Madonna, she too would somehow carry on with life, as difficult as it would be to do so. The Ciccone spirit—as passed from father to daughter—is strong and unwavering. Or, as the saying goes, the apple doesn't fall far from the tree.

The expected media frenzy about Madonna's pregnancy was not a surprise to anyone in her camp; the news traveled across the globe as rapidly as a war bulletin. Her characteristic flair for the dramatic at work, Madonna complained about the attention: "Well, the world knows," she said at the time. "And I feel like my insides have been ripped open. The front page of the *Post*, CNN, even Hungarian Radio. What's the big deal?" she asked. "I wish everyone would just let me do my work."

Carlos's mother, forty-nine-year-old Maria Leon, who is a social worker, rose to Madonna's defense. "Everything people say about her is not true. When you get to know her, you know she's very affectionate, very warm. She's a real person, like you and me." His father, Armando, who owns several Manhattan check-cashing stores, added, "She loves Carlos very much. And we love her, too." (Armando has said that when his son first showed up at a family gathering with Madonna for what they would later learn was her favorite meal of black beans, "we couldn't believe it. We thought it was a lookalike or something. We played Cuban music and talked all night.")

At this important time in filming *Evita*, Madonna couldn't help but feel that the public and media's focus on her pregnancy was a nuisance. What she really wanted, she claimed, was privacy and peace of mind, so that she could finish her movie.

Making matters more interesting for the media to report, the jibes at Carlos Leon began instantaneously. He had been visiting Madonna in Buenos Aires because she wanted him at her side for moral support when she announced her pregnancy, but he quickly grew bored waiting around for her as she worked long hours on the set. Upon flying back to New York, he found aggressive media interest in him. "It's great to be back in New York," he snarled when a photographer snapped his picture as he sat on a bench in Central Park. Much to his dismay, the press now dubbed him, "Madonna's Top Seed," and her "Baby-Making Beau" (both headlines courtesy of the *New York Post*).

The press immediately learned that he was a native New Yorker who had grown up on West Ninety-first Street, in a very different neighborhood from Madonna's ritzy Central Park co-op (into which he had recently moved). Friends also recalled the slight street accent of Carlos's voice. Some sources hinted that Carlos hoped that meeting Madonna might provide the opportunity for a better life for him. "Carlos aspired to be more," recalls an old girlfriend of his who asked for anonymity. "He thought maybe he'd get into modeling or acting."

Loyal friend Michael Gacki quickly came to Carlos's defense. "He's not riding her coattails," he reported to the *New York Post*. "He's up at six A.M. every day working twelve or thirteen hours a day as a personal trainer to make it himself. He's been with her for a year and a half, and in my opinion it hasn't changed him one bit." Gacki went on to explain that he and his pal Carlos were both involved with women "more successful" than themselves but, he explained, "we both wanted to make sure that we paid our own way."

Patrice Gonzalez, who did not become a consort of Carlos's but who had a platonic relationship with him instead, now says of Leon, "He's really the kind of guy who can look at people and see them for who they really are, and that includes Madonna. He liked her from the time they first met. He was amazed that she was as timid as she turned out to be.

"But who's to say if he was ever really in love with her, head over heels. He never wanted to get caught up in her world. She was temperamental, difficult to be around. Also, he's a jealous kind of guy. If she complimented a model's looks in a magazine, he would get pissed off. They also had some arguments from time to time about the way she treated him. She's used to ordering people around."

Gonzalez was at the home of Carlos's parents when he and Madonna came to visit. As they were getting ready to leave, Madonna turned to Carlos and, in a rather abrupt tone, said, "Get my coat."

"Get it yourself," he snapped back at her, his eyes flickering with annoyance.

"What's the matter with you?" she asked. "You can't get my coat?"

"Carlos, go get her coat," his mother, Maria, said, trying to keep the peace. "Be a gentleman."

"Look, I'm not your personal assistant," Carlos told Madonna, ignoring his mother's request. It seemed clear to most observers that, for Carlos, a bigger issue was at stake than just the retrieval of his girlfriend's coat. Perhaps he and Madonna had engaged in previous discussions about similar matters. "If you want me to get your coat, say 'please'," he told her. "I don't work for you. I'm not on the payroll, you know?"

Madonna rolled her eyes and shot him a cool look. "My God," she muttered.

"Oh, now I understand," Carlos said. "You see, I had completely underestimated your capacity for being . . . *bitchy.*"

Though Madonna looked angry, she somehow held her temper in check. Perhaps trying to tone down the moment because Carlos's mother was watching, she acquiesced. "Carlos, can I ask you to get my coat?" she said, before adding, sweetly, "*Por favor.*"

As Carlos helped Madonna with her coat, his mother said, "Now, now. See how nice?"

When Madonna finally told Carlos she was expecting, he realized, according to Patrice Gonzalez, that this child would create a bond with her that he would live with forever. "This was a big adjustment for him," says Gonzalez, "and forced him to look at her another way, as a woman who would be in his life for the long run."

Many reporters went so far as to hint that Madonna was having the baby as some kind of extreme publicity stunt for her movie. Though outraged, she probably shouldn't have been surprised by the insinuation. After all, it seemed to many observers that she would do anything to promote a project. So, why not this? "People have suggested that I have done this [become pregnant] for shock value," she said. "These are comments only a man would make. It's much too difficult to be pregnant and bring a child into this world to do it for whimsical or provocative reasons. There are also speculations that I used the father as a stud service," she said. "Implying that I am not capable of having a real relationship. I realize these comments are all made by persons who cannot live with the idea that something good is happening to me. Something special and wonderful that they cannot spoil."

✝

Betrayal

Madonna understood the pitfalls of her worldwide fame. Certainly, it had cost her a sense of privacy, and she was used to dealing with that fact. She also understood that she had made some serious mistakes in her life when it came to romance. After Tony Ward, she had vowed to be more selective. However, she was a sexual creature with normal needs and desires. Though she wasn't about to commit to a serious relationship with the wrong man, she still wanted to share physical intimacy with someone. It was understandable to anyone who knew her that she would become intimately involved with libidinous basketball star Dennis Rodman. However, a bad choice is still a bad choice, even if it does result in mind-blowing sex . . . Dennis would end up betraying their relationship by writing about it in his memoir *Bad As I Wanna Be.*

Two years earlier, in 1994—before the filming of *Evita*—Madonna had begun dating Dennis Rodman, a basketball star two years her junior who had an eccentric reputation—on and off the court. With his outlandish appearance—bleached blond hair, tattoos and various piercings—as well as his flamboyant behavior, he relished the celebrity spotlight as much as Madonna did. In fact, borrowing a page from her career handbook, he often made controversial moves just for the sake of titillation—such as the time he announced his wedding and then showed up at the resulting press conference in full drag, complete with wedding dress and veil. He then declared that he was marrying himself.

The games between them began when Madonna first met Dennis and asked him for his telephone number. Instead of his phone number, he gave her his fax number. "You're trying to fuck with me," she faxed him the next day. "You gave me a number that's for your damned machine. What's your problem?"

It wasn't long, though, before playful and sometimes sexy love messages were flying back and forth between the two. "I want to have six kids," Rodman faxed Madonna, "what do you think?"

She faxed back to Rodman that six children would be fine with her, but they would have to get to work on it immediately. "You think I'm joking, but you'll see that I'm not," she wrote. She also mentioned that she would still be interested in Dennis even if he were broke and working at a car dealership. "Lay in your bed, close your eyes and fuck me at some point today," she concluded.

Perhaps because he was at the height of his own notoriety, Dennis Rodman seemed unimpressed by Madonna's fame or money, which only served to make him more interesting in her eyes. A friend of Dennis recalls being at a party with Rodman and Madonna. "He and I were flirting with some girls," he says. "Madonna kept trying to interrupt, but he just ignored her." Not one to be ignored, when Rodman finally did give Madonna his number (not his fax number, finally) she began a campaign to win him over. "She called ten to fifteen times a day," Rodman's friend reveals. "She kept asking him 'What's going on? What are you doing?' "

In early 1995, Dennis confided in friends that Madonna was "a lot of fun." Meanwhile, Madonna told her own confidantes that she loved Dennis, though it seems difficult to imagine that any of them would have believed as much—or that she believed it herself. It's more likely that she was just carried away by the sexual chemistry between them. When he was unavailable and she couldn't reach him on the telephone—perhaps he was screening his calls?—she flooded him with romantic faxes with salutations such as "Good morning, Daddy Long Legs."

These silly fun and games lasted for just a few months and didn't amount to much, other than a wild ride in the bedroom for both participants. Madonna ended the relationship when she heard that Dennis was gossiping about her to mutual friends. Later, when some of her faxes to him found their way into publication in the tabloid the *Globe*, she realized that, if anything, she had been unlucky in lust. Rodman's comments to *Playboy* that he had to end it with her when she started pressing him to impregnate her—certainly a running theme in her life at this time with the men she dated—made her even angrier at him. (Rodman recalled to *Playboy:* "She said, 'Be in a hotel room in Las Vegas on this specific day so you can get me pregnant.' " He declined.)

A little more than a year later, Rodman wrote his book. In it, he was explicit about his and Madonna's foreplay and pillow talk: "She wasn't an acrobat. But she wasn't a dead fish, either." When the memoir was published, Madonna ran to the store and purchased a copy herself. According to sources, she read the chapter about her and became so agitated that she threw the book into the fire.

"A certain disgusting basketball player I made the mistake of going out with decided to publish an autobiography and devoted a whole chapter to what it was like to have sex with me," Madonna later seethed. "Complete with made-up dialogue that even a bad porno writer would not take credit for. It's so silly I'm sure no one will take it seriously, but I don't feel like reading the headlines and of course I feel exploited once again by someone I trusted and let into my life."

She also explained, "When I first knew him, I sent him a few very silly faxes with really childish drawings on them, and months after I'd stopped seeing him, they appeared on [the tabloid TV program] *Hard Copy*, and I thought, "This is only the beginning . . .""

Her public may be surprised to learn that Madonna was too discreet to tell the truth about her relationship with Rodman which, as it happened, bore little resemblance to the way he portrayed it in his book. According to close friends of Madonna's and Rodman's, the couple only engaged in sexual activity twice—and not "fifty to a hundred times" as Rodman bragged in his book.

Says dancer Trina Graves, who dated Rodman in Chicago, "He told me very specifically that he and Madonna had slept together one time in Miami, and that it was a big disappointment. He blamed it on her, saying she was frigid. He said he couldn't get excited when he was with her, because she was too demanding in bed. He said that she emasculated him.

"But, after having been with Dennis myself, I can see the other side. He's much too selfish to make love to a woman in a way that would be considered memorable. Mine was a boring experience with him, bland. Nothing to speak of." Graves recalls that the basketball star didn't even take off his silk suit for their encounter. Rather, he just dropped his pants in a way that suggested a pornographic moment rather than a lovemaking session. "And, no," she allows, "he did not become aroused with me, either."

A friend of Madonna's who has known her for twenty years concurs, "Madonna made a vow a long time ago to only have sex one time with a man if he proved himself too selfish to care about her satisfaction—and that certainly defines Dennis's approach. Also, she wanted more from a man than what Dennis had to offer. Of that, she was certain."

To this particular friend, Madonna confided that after she and Dennis became drunk one evening, they tumbled into bed together. "The poor guy couldn't even get excited for her," said the friend. "She blamed it on alcohol that night. Then, the next night, she bent her rule and let him try again.

"This time, Dennis performed, but only to his satisfaction—not hers. The whole thing lasted about fifteen minutes. Then, that was it. They never had sex again."

Madonna's friend says that, after Dennis's book was published, the singer decided not to tell the truth about her affair with him because she didn't want to "be as mean to him as he'd been to her, lying about her in his book. None of it was true." Though she told the media that the book was "full of lies," Madonna decided to let Rodman maintain his macho image. She did not reveal that he was a dud in the bedroom. "Madonna could have put a dent in Rodman's machismo reputation if she had decided to tell the truth about his sexual prowess," says the source, "but, instead, I guess she opted to have mercy on him. She told me, 'I feel sorry for the creep.' "

During Madonna's interview with Oprah Winfrey, Oprah noted that she had read in the press that Rodman wished to apologize to Madonna for the book (which had spent eight weeks at Number 1 on the *New York Times* best-seller list and had clearly generated a lot of attention for him). Madonna said, "Well, he'd better crawl from here to China." In fact, Madonna and Dennis had already had a telephone conversation about the book. Somehow, Rodman managed to telephone Madonna in London to apologize "for any misunderstandings."

Reportedly, she said to him, "Dennis, you and I both know what happened when we made love . . . and it was nothing to write a book about."

✝

Because she is so well known for her public relations savvy, it wouldn't surprise anyone to learn that Madonna genuinely likes giving interviews to the media. Though she feels that she has said everything she wants to say to the press—and more than once—she fully understands the value of publicity and is always willing to play the game if it's at a necessary time in her life and career. She dislikes most reporters and writers—"parasites!"—but recognizes that dealing with them is a necessary evil. While filming *Evita,* she knew that she still had to engage with the press, even though she was exhausted by her schedule. After all, she was making an expensive picture with a lot riding on it, not only for her but also for its producers. Any publicity, she realized, would probably help the picture. Still, she couldn't help but be distrustful of the media, mostly because of the way her pregnancy was being handled in the press.

Madonna was hurt, livid at times, to read press editorials debating whether or not she was a decent role model for young girls. Angrily, Madonna told one reporter that society is "sick." When asked to explain she continued, "This bizarre interest and fascination with . . . well, you would think I was the first celebrity that wasn't married that got pregnant. It's just so absurd, the amount of attention and how it's skewed. Like it's so unusual, what I'm doing."

She was particularly angered to read that Camille Paglia, the controversial gay feminist, had implied that the reason Madonna was having a child out of wedlock was because she was unable to bond with a man. Paglia noted that the public had reason to be concerned for the well-being of the child. "Does anyone complain that neither Susan Sarandon nor Goldie Hawn is married to the father of her children?" Madonna retaliated, smacking a table with her palm. Who said a word when Woody Allen and Mia Farrow had a child and continued to live across the park from each other? Why are these people not expected to be role models?"

Madonna speculated—and perhaps accurately—that the public would be more comfortable if she simply married Carlos Leon, only then to have the marriage fail. But if she was to be honest about her future with Leon, she had to admit that there was no future with him. She certainly wasn't about to enter into marriage with him just to placate the public.

"I don't want to be a spokesperson for marriage, OK?" she railed to a reporter for *USA Weekend* news magazine. "I should be able to choose the things I want to be a spokesperson for. Why can't I be for freedom of expression and for practicing safe sex and those kind of things? *That* is freedom of expression—to say I don't feel like I have to get married to have a good relationship and raise children in a healthy way."

Perhaps the best course of action would simply have been to stop the madness . . . stop doing interviews, stop reading stories about herself, stop calling reporters to engage in debates with them about what they had written. However, she simply could not help herself. "If she knew that something was being published, oh my God! she just had to read it," said one of her former associates. "And, oh my God! she just had to debate it. One would have thought she had enough on her mind with the film, but no, not Madonna. She had to take on the media, as well. Why? I don't know . . ."

Perhaps the reason for Madonna's behavior with the press is that— as demonstrated by her past behavior—she seems to be a person who has to have as much drama in her life as possible. When it becomes too quiet, she seems compelled to find a reason for chaos. When she feels that she's finally focused on a project, she seems to have to find a reason for disarray. That's Madonna.

With two weeks left of shooting, the pregnant star was rightfully exhausted. For five months, she had been up each morning at six to endure three hours of fussing and styling, having her hair whipped into the elaborate braids and rolls of the forties. Her nails were manicured to expensive perfection, her eye color changed to brown with painful and irritating contact lenses, and false teeth were awkwardly put into place. For Madonna it felt as if she had put in a full day before she had even started work. Though she tried to focus her vision as she walked onto the set in full regalia, often her surroundings were just a blur. As set designers and costumers looked on approvingly, Madonna performed those last few weeks in a way that seemed somewhat disaffected.

At this same time, she also felt guilty about any concentration she was able to give to the movie. As she later said, she often found herself "apologizing to my unborn child for any uncomfortable bouncing around I was causing it." She longed to go shopping for baby clothes, she admitted, but knew that she would have to wait just two more weeks, until the movie was completed, before she could give in to the call of motherhood.

Ironically, some of the most grueling scenes in the movie were scheduled for the last two weeks. Feeling helpless and anxiety ridden, she was called to do Eva's draining death scenes, as well as close-up re-takes of the dramatic balcony scene, in the last weeks of production. She popped some aspirins in her mouth, and quickly downed them with some Evian water to prepare herself for the ordeal ahead. After throwing a terrified glance in Alan Parker's direction, she did what she knew she had to do. "The intensity of the scenes we've been shooting and the amount of emotional work and concentration needed to get through the day are so mentally and physically exhausting that I'm sure I will need to be institutionalized when it is over," she would later write in her *Vanity Fair* "diary."

Through it all, the one thing that kept Madonna going was that which had always kept her going: the hope of achieving greater success than she had known in the past. Her gut instinct told her that she was doing her best work in this movie. What she had always wanted for herself, more than to be a pop sensation or successful concert performer, was to be a movie star. Yet, it was the one goal that had always seemed the most elusive. If she could just hold on and continue doing the best work she could with the kind of quality performance she'd been giving since the beginning of work on *Evita*, Madonna felt certain that her future in movies would, finally, be assured. That kind of success would most certainly make all of the hell in her life worthwhile. Or, at least that's what she thought at the time.

✝

Anticlimax

After all of the hard work, anxiety and anticipation, the last day of shooting *Evita*, on May 27, 1996, proved to be anticlimactic for Madonna. She would later admit that she had fantasized an emotional ending to her long ordeal. Imagining herself breaking down in front of her co-workers once having uttered her final lines, she thought she would be completely overwhelmed by the experience. While she would feel grateful that the job was over, she would also feel sad that the time had come to say good-bye to all of those wonderful people she had so grown to love and admire, and who had shown her such love and admiration in return—or at least they had in this particular fantasy. Madonna had even gone to the trouble of rehearsing a dramatic, tearful farewell speech, one that each crew member and co-star would take home as part of his or her fond memory of her, one that they would be able to recount to family and friends . . . and maybe even to future Madonna biographers. Running a trembling hand over her brow, she was all but prepared to deliver her comments in regal, Evita style when, at the conclusion of the last shot, Alan Parker shouted out, "That's a wrap." However, before she had the chance to deliver her speech, everyone scattered and quickly went about the business of breaking down the sets. No one paid her a second thought.

Suddenly, it was all over. However, Madonna didn't feel the way she thought she would feel, as she later explained. There was no sense of sadness, elation or gratitude, as she would later tell it. Rather, she just felt . . . numb. She blinked as quick tears came to her eyes. Then, she looked about helplessly, as if she was trying to comprehend what had just happened. Perhaps noticing her confusion, someone came over to her—she doesn't remember who—hugged her warmly and then whispered something—she doesn't remember what—in her ear.

As the crew packed up its gear, there were no speeches, no sad good-byes. "I was just too damn tired," Madonna later recalled. "And so was everyone else."

All told, there had been 299 scenes. Four thousand extras appeared in period dress. Almost 6,000 costumes were needed from twenty different costume houses in London, Rome, Paris, New York, Los Angeles and San Francisco. Madonna's wardrobe consisted of 85 changes, 39 hats, 45 pairs of shoes, 56 pairs of earrings and as many different hair designs—while the art department created 320 different sets, including 24,000 props.

For Madonna, the filming ended just in time, for not only was her belly pressing against her tailored suits, she was on the brink of an emotional meltdown. "I couldn't have taken one more minute of it," she would recall.

Yet, even though she was finished with the movie, the pregnant star would not be permitted much of a rest. To sell *Evita* to the masses, Disney Studios' publicity machine went into top gear. The studio was determined to create an "event" around the opening of the film by announcing advance bookings, "exclusive-run" launches in major American cities. Within weeks of her return to the States, Madonna found herself an integral part of a massive campaign that included publicity in fashion magazines intent on promoting the "Evita look." In its November 1996 issue, for instance, *Vanity Fair* allowed her to publish what would, perhaps, turn out to be one of the world's longest press releases, something called "Madonna's Private Diaries."

"This is a diary of sorts," Madonna wrote in an introduction to the lengthy feature, "a sketchbook of feelings, ideas, and dreams, all relating to one subject—the making of *Evita* . . . the month before shooting began I made a promise to myself that I would write everything down that happened to me. I had butterflies in my stomach and I knew I was in for the ride of my life. I wanted to remember every detail." Madonna's public devoured this course, just as they did everything she served, not taking the time to figure out that people who keep "private diaries" to document important events in their lives usually don't publish them several months later in international magazines. But Madonna's "sketchbook" of feelings did provide some useful background information on the making of the film which, as it was designed to do, did make the reader curious to see it.

*

By September 1996, Madonna had been profoundly affected by her pregnancy. On September 9, she began keeping a journal about her pregnancy. In it, she wrote that there were days when she couldn't even function because she felt at the mercy of mood swings that made life impossible for her. She also wrote of hemorrhoids, back pains and said, "My life has been *hell.*"

Still, she managed to have some fun with friends. "Once she finished *Evita,* we got to spend a lot of time together," says her good friend Juliette Hohnen. "It was probably the first time in years she was forced to stay in one place for a while. We giggled when we went on our trial runs from her house to the hospital in preparation for the big moment. No matter how many times we practiced, we always made a wrong turn somewhere and then, like a couple of squabbling sisters, we would blame each other for bad driving or bad navigating."

As well as a written journal, Madonna also kept a video account of her pregnancy. Friends who have seen her video history say that it is so touching it should be released to the public. Says a source, "She talked about how hard the pregnancy was, how sick she became, how her face broke out in blemishes, how unattractive she felt and how she knew it would all be worth it for her child. I know that when her daughter sees these videos in years to come, she will feel a special closeness to her mom that Madonna never felt with hers—which was one of Madonna's goals with this project."

"M [many of her friends call her "M"] told me that feeling a baby growing within her made her want to make an effort to straighten out some of the things she'd done in the past that she wasn't happy about now," said her good friend. "For instance, I know that during her pregnancy she at least attempted to mend her years-long rift with Michael Jackson."

Michael hadn't spoken to Madonna since the time he put the kibosh on the video in which Madonna wanted Michael to dress as a woman. However, in the fall of 1996, Madonna sent Michael a note to wish him luck on the beginning of a tour on which he was embarking at the time, and sent a huge floral display to Prague where he debuted his show. She tried to refrain from making critical comments about him, which was difficult for her.

"She also began calling people she hadn't talked to or seen in years," says her friend. Said Diane Giordano: "She told me that she wanted to be a good mother, but was afraid that would not be possible because she had become so accustomed to being a self-centered person. She became spiritual, and started looking at herself in a new and more uncompromising way. So, M's pregnancy was an emotional and very human time for her—and also for all the people in her life who were getting surprising, middle-of-the-night phone calls from Madonna asking for forgiveness. Being pregnant and bringing the baby to term was the toughest thing she'd ever had to do, tougher than anything she'd done in her career. Just as it is for a lot of women, being pregnant marked a defining time in her life."

Though it was difficult, especially toward the end of her pregnancy, she still tried to enjoy her free time. Recalls Juliette Hohnen, "We decided to go to an art exhibition when she was nine months pregnant. In order to avoid the ever-present paparazzi, we had to lie down in the back of a dirty minivan. So much for glamorous transportation."

She also tried to attend as many parties as possible, just to stay busy. After a gathering for photographer Herb Ritts at Perino's restaurant in Beverly Hills in September 1996, a very pregnant Madonna (in a powder-blue cut-on-the-bias dress designed by Susan Becker, a simple matching sweater by Anna Molinari, and wearing the diamond-studded gold watch that Donatella Versace gave her for her birthday) confessed to close friends that she felt out of place, "fat and ugly and just awful." She was standing in the corner looking alone and miserable. Ritts walked right by her, not having noticed her, and when he did see her he apologized and said, "I'm sorry I missed you." She said, "I don't see how anyone could miss me. I'm as big as a fucking house."

She had been having cravings that were unusual for her: poached eggs and omelets of every kind, caramel and strawberry ice cream, pizza, cheeseburgers and other junk foods. One person had seen her in a small grocery store in a sleazy part of Hollywood, standing in a corner "eating one of those awful hot dogs with a soft drink."

☦

Lourdes

On October 14, 1996, thirty-eight-year-old Madonna gave birth to a 6-pound, 9-ounce baby girl she named Lourdes Maria Ciccone Leon at Good Samaritan Hospital in Los Angeles. Lourdes—her name inspired by the town in France associated with miracles—sported a full head of jet-black hair, just like her father's. It had been a difficult birth, sixteen hours of labor that ended in a cesarean section. Madonna had originally hoped for a natural childbirth, with the soundtrack of a romantic 1988 Alan Rudolph film called *The Moderns* playing softly in the background. Her dream of such a tranquil birth was dashed, though, when the reality of the pain involved changed her mind. "I just want this to be *over,*" she told the doctors. "Screw *The Moderns.* I can't bear this!" As they wheeled her into the delivery room, a groggy Madonna turned to Carlos Leon, her newly promoted manager Caresse Norman, publicist Liz Rosenberg and several other friends and security guards and said, "Good-bye everyone. I'm going in for my nose job now."

Despite the fact that she checked in under the alias Victoria Fernandez, the expected media frenzy ensued, complete with the inevitable "Madonna and Child" articles which were quickly disseminated around the world. Outside the hospital, eleven trucks were parked, each with pop-up satellite towers, plus dozens of camera crews and hordes of photographers and reporters, all patiently waiting for any news tidbits—such as the revelation that Madonna's pediatrician was Dr. Paul Fleiss, father of convicted Hollywood madam Heidi Fleiss. The birth was just two months before *Evita* was set to open. The coincidental timing of these two major events in her life "was incredibly poetic," Madonna said. "I waited so long for this movie and it finally happened. I wanted so badly to have a child and I got pregnant while making the movie. Suddenly, God gave me two gifts that were very important to me." She pointed out that "everything I do is scrutinized so I shouldn't be surprised that it continued when I was pregnant. I try to have a sense of humor about it, but it does irritate me. My child is not for public consumption. It's not a career move. It's not a performance to be judged and rated. Nor is my role as a mother."

Carlos Leon—who cut the umbilical cord with surgeon's scissors—would give Madonna sole custody of the baby. Of the notion of marriage Madonna stated emphatically, "I don't feel the need. I'm perfectly happy with the way things are." As for defining a father's role in raising children in general Madonna said, "I think it's just as important as the mother's. But I won't tell you specifically that I think it's a man's job to do this and a woman's job to do that. They both have nurturing roles to play." When pressed to answer if the ideal would be to have both a mother and father at home Madonna retorted, "I grew up without a mother and I did all right."

Madonna decided that she would not release an official picture of little Lourdes for mass consumption (that would come a year later in *Vanity Fair*), which only served to make a shot of the baby all the more exclusive. If a photographer managed to get a clear portrait, it was estimated it could bring in as much as $250,000. She was incensed that the price of a photograph of her baby was so exorbitant, yet she also must have understood that had she released a photograph, the price—and, maybe even the interest—would have decreased dramatically.

As Madonna recuperated from childbirth, media interest in her and her newborn did not ebb. With the *Evita* opening just a couple of months in the offing, subsequent magazine interviews that Madonna gave revolved as much around motherhood as the making of the movie. And, as the publicity machine rolled forward, the softer image that she had begun to orchestrate just prior to the filming of the movie also came into focus. Now, she was able finally to announce to the world that she was a kinder, gentler Madonna, one with new values, worthier agendas . . . and even a baby, no less.

"Madonna has repeatedly been depicted as cocky, shameless and curt," journalist Jonathan Alter wrote after his interview with her. "But I found none of this to be true. She was emotional about motherhood, impassioned about playing Eva Perón and surprisingly uncertain about what the future holds. In place of her legendary self-confidence, Madonna seemed unusually vulnerable."

In a cover story for *Redbook* magazine, Madonna said, "When I started seriously thinking about motherhood and taking care of a child, certain people that I found amusing and interesting didn't seem so terribly amusing and interesting. I did a lot of emotional housecleaning and I wound up with a much smaller handful of friends."

For the first four weeks after Lourdes was born, Madonna didn't do anything but take care of her, hold her and (breast) feed her. Then slowly she started getting back to work, sitting at her desk and talking on the phone, trying to run her record company. "It was a huge adjustment," Madonna said. "I used to make a list and know I'd get everything done. Now a lot of things don't get done, and that's OK."

Madonna sent for her father, Tony, and his wife, Joan, so that they could visit her in Los Angeles and meet Lourdes. It was a joyful time. If there was any acrimony between Madonna and her father and step-mother, it certainly wasn't evident during the time they visited her after the baby was born. Other members of the Ciccone family—and also the Leon family—also converged on Madonna's home to celebrate the new birth. Tony seemed to get along well with Carlos, and some ob-servers noticed that he tried to convince Carlos to marry his daughter. "Dad, stop it, please," Madonna said, good-naturedly. She was wear-ing combat trousers and a white tank top, with her bra showing (which may or may not have given Tony pause). "Carlos does what he wants to do. If he wants to marry me, he will." Of course, whether or not Madonna became a married woman really wasn't a decision that Carlos was likely to be the one to make.

One month after the baby's birth Madonna once again fixed her eyes on the future—and the premiere of *Evita* in December. The 5-foot, 4-inch superstar had tipped the scales at a hefty 140 pounds before the birth of Lourdes, and she was seen furiously pedaling around Los Angeles's Griffith Park trying to slim down to 115 pounds before the movie's opening. For the next few weeks Madonna stuck to a low-fat diet and extensive exercise, and by early December she was turning heads with her slimmed-down shape.

Just before she gave birth, Madonna put her 7,800-square-foot mansion—the former home of gangster Bugsy Siegel—on the market for $6.5 million. Madonna said that she felt the house, just below the legendary "Hollywood" sign, was haunted and didn't want to live there with her baby. Her Manhattan duplex also went up for sale for $7 million. In preparation for the baby, she had bought a cozy $2.7-million house in the Los Feliz district of Los Angeles. Built in the 1920s, the Mediterranean-style home has three bedrooms in about 5,000 square feet, plus a two-bedroom cottage. The home is on two acres, and Madonna would divide her time between that residence and her $4.9-million mansion in Miami.

✝

After all the publicity hoopla, *Evita* finally had its grand premiere in Los Angeles in December 1996 at the Shrine Auditorium in Los Angeles, which Madonna and Carlos Leon attended together. She wore a magenta Eva Perón–inspired dress designed by John Galliano, a feathered chapeau and veil, and sexy strapped shoes by Manolo Blahnik. Looking confident and smart, she was flanked by bodyguards as she made her captivating entrance in a bedlam of police, limousines, klieg lights and fans, almost 2,000 of them. Truly, she was in her element as the lights played on her while the entourage of reporters and photographers yammered for her attention. Madonna's smile stretched wide. Exultant, she laughed, waved and posed as the paparazzi flashed their lights and reporters jotted down notes.

"Yes, it was such fun," she said to one reporter.

"No, I have no plans for another movie," she explained to another, "but if you know a producer, tell him to call me," she added with a laugh.

"See the movie," she enthused to one on-camera commentator. "It's my proudest achievement, besides my daughter."

Once inside, she chatted with Antonio Banderas and Melanie Griffith, seeming genuinely happy even though she was facing emergency root canal surgery the following day. Then, there would be another star turn when she would fly to London with her baby for the *Evita* premiere there.

The $56-million extravaganza was a quick commercial success; generally, the movie's reviews were favorable. *Time* magazine's Richard Corliss wrote: "It's a relief to say that Alan Parker's film, which opens on Christmas Day, is pretty damn fine, well cast and handsomely visualized. Madonna once again confounds our expectations. She does a tough score proud. Lacking the vocal vigor of Elaine Paige's West End *Evita,* Madonna plays Evita with a poignant weariness. She has more than just a bit of star quality. Love or hate Madonna-Eva, she is a magnet for all eyes. You must watch her."

It's true; *Evita* is a spectacularly produced film. The direction and art direction are superb. The supporting cast is excellent, the sets breathtaking, the costumes captivating . . . all of which adds up to a visually beautiful movie. The film is always entertaining and, at times, moving. But what of Madonna's performance as its star?

There is no denying that she is a magnificent entertainer. In her pop videos and stage concerts she has a magic that, at its best, dazzles and electrifies. Perhaps, had she brought some of the flash and trash sexiness of her video persona to her role as Eva Perón (as she did in her first movie role, *Desperately Seeking Susan*), her interpretation might have been a smashing success. Her choice, though, was to downplay Eva Perón's ferocious hunger, her desire to succeed, her need to excel. Her determination to portray a more sympathetic image for the character—and for herself—ultimately strips Evita of her undercurrent of urgency. In the end, Evita's masterful manipulations become sweet suggestions; numbers that should burn with intensity instead take on a certain pallor. For example, Madonna's coy interpretation of the seduction called "I'd Be Surprisingly Good for You," dilutes what should have been a tour de force and makes it sound weak and whiny.

Madonna dances expertly and looks lovely in the period costumes (although she appears too old for early scenes when—filmed in deep shadow—she plays Eva as a teenager). But always we are aware of Madonna as a performer working extremely hard at a role. We never feel that she and the role become one. She is so calculating—just as she has always been in her work—that there doesn't appear to be one truly organic moment for her as an actress in the entire movie. The viewer can almost hear her mind working: *click*—look this way, *click*—feel this way, *click*—time to cry.

During the times she is weakest, there are pleasant distractions. For instance, her performance on the much-anticipated "Don't Cry for Me Argentina" scene on the balcony of the Casa Rosada seems wooden and disaffected, especially considering all she did to secure that location. Yet, it is somehow boosted and lent power by sweeping camera angles, dramatic lighting changes and especially by her supporting players. Antonio Banderas's sly looks of admiration and contempt, Jonathan Pryce's proud bolstering from the sidelines, and the strong emotions on the faces of the extras playing Evita's supporters all lend power to the scene that Madonna—for all her strained neck muscles—cannot seem to muster.

Whereas there may be ambivalence from some quarters about her work as an actress in the film, as a singer Madonna could not have been more wondrous. When the two-disc soundtrack album to *Evita* made its debut, the resulting performance made jaws drop. Madonna performed with a sense of technical and emotional discipline and depth seldom heard or seen in her acts, and a commanding familiarity with the work that allowed her to get inside the Webber/Rice songs in a way that seemed even deeper and more convincing than her on-screen transformation into Evita.

As Evita Perón, Madonna is responsible for singing on most of the songs in the musical, alone or with her co-stars. When she makes her first appearance on the soundtrack—as the wistful voice of Evita, reflecting from her grave during the sad passage of "Oh What a Circus"—she is supple and strong, and doesn't sound at all out of place. She then sounds even more self-assured during "Eva and Mafaldi/Eva Beware of the City," a movement with complex and conflicting tempos. Bigger voices than hers have certainly sung the festive, determined "Buenos Aires," one of the production's signature tunes, but Madonna also made it her own.

In the end, Madonna sang her way through a full musical's worth of what was unquestionably the most challenging material of her career. She didn't simply get through it, as some other singers-turned-actresses might have—but gave a performance that was, at times, captivating. Who can deny that her voice has remarkable and unmistakable presence when heard during "You Must Love Me"?

Two singles from the soundtrack, the aforementioned "You Must Love Me" and "Don't Cry for Me Argentina," reached Number 18 and Number 8 on the *Billboard* singles chart respectively, while the soundtrack itself in 1996 went to Number 2 on the trade magazine's album chart. The soundtrack sold five million copies stateside, and eleven million internationally. With this collection, she added just one more triumph to a world-class résumé already brimming with accomplishments . . . and she also silenced a good deal of snickering in the process.

If nothing else, the interest that surrounded *Evita*—the film and the soundtrack—should have given Madonna more opportunities to star in big-budget movies. The Golden Globe, given by the Foreign Press Association, acknowledged her by giving her the award for best performance by a female in a musical or comedy. Certainly, this award was a well-deserved honor symbolizing a year of extraordinarily hard work, dedication and commitment on the part of Madonna. Sadly, no other offers were forthcoming, at least none that she felt were worth her time and energy. Also, she was snubbed at the Oscars, though "You Must Love Me" did win one for Best Song (and the award went to song-writers Webber and Rice).

"I'm patient," she concluded in one interview. "Roles for women are not easy to come by, especially good ones. I'd like to say that the way I handle my career is by being smart about it, but then how would I explain *Body of Evidence?* When the right role comes along, maybe I'll know it. Maybe I won't. I'm not a genius. I just do the best I can do."

✝

No Future with Carlos

After the legendary film star Elizabeth Taylor had brain surgery to re-move a benign tumor in the spring of 1997, Madonna sent her a basket of fruit at the hospital. The accompanying note read, "You are my idol. There will never be another Elizabeth Taylor. Get well." When Eliza-beth was sent home, Madonna became a frequent visitor to her Bel Air mansion; a friendship between the two women began to blossom. Eliz-abeth urged Madonna to marry Carlos Leon and "give Lourdes a fa-ther. My dear, it's obvious you love the man." Taylor was also quoted as having said, "So why don't you marry him? God knows I've married many more who've given me a lot less than Carlos has given you. He's given you a beautiful baby and will give you more. Besides, he's gor-geous."

The two laughed about the fact that Madonna had wanted the pope to baptize Lourdes, but he turned her down. "Imagine, me being turned down by the Vatican," she said, according to one of her friends. "How dare he?" (Actually, Madonna didn't think the pope would con-sent to such a baptism. After all, she wasn't even married. But what did she have to lose by asking?) Instead, Madonna had the baby christened at St. Jude's in Miami. "It was nice, but it ain't the Vatican," she told Elizabeth Taylor. Madonna later indicated in an interview that she wanted Lourdes to be raised a Catholic because, "that foundation was important to me, and important to Carlos. Say what you will about Catholicism, the things you pick up along the way do help you by giving you something to turn to when you're in trouble. Then, when you have that foundation, you can start looking at other philosophies— which is what I've done."

The two cultural icons—Liz and Madonna—became good friends, and remain so today. In common with Elizabeth Taylor was Madonna's newfound spiritual pursuit; she had recently become interested in Kabbalah, a mystical, medieval branch of Judaism that emphasized the link between self and universe. Madonna began inviting friends to study it with her, describing it as "a mystical interpretation of the Old Testament."

With many reasons to be exhausted by her whirlwind life and career—countless Grammys, sold-out tours, worldwide adulation— perhaps it seemed that the only thing left for Madonna to do was finally and truly to embrace who she really was, and not just who she seemed to be when attached to her career, or to a man. She became such a devout follower of Kabbalah that she hosted a high-powered reception in Los Angeles on September 18 to discuss the philosophy with friends and business associates. "Kabbalah is the one place I don't feel like a celebrity," she said. Although she had spent most of her life discussing her Catholic upbringing both in positive and negative terms, Madonna now stated that nothing had ever spoken to her like Kabbalah and that only now did she feel fully equipped emotionally to take responsibility for her life. After returning to Los Angeles, Madonna surprised some of her associates by regularly attending Bible classes at the Kabbalah Learning Center in Los Angeles. This spiritual awakening would also plant the seeds for her next artistic breakthrough.

Although Elizabeth Taylor and other friends had urged her to marry the father of her daughter, by the early spring of 1997 Carlos Leon seemed to be rapidly disappearing from Madonna's life. Most observers believed that Madonna had ended the relationship with Carlos after she got what she wanted from him: a child. It wasn't that simple. In fact, it was Carlos who began to lose interest in continuing his relationship with Madonna and, conveniently, at just about the same time she began to distance herself from him. That they would not marry would actually be a mutual decision. After the birth of Lourdes, he told friends that he couldn't be married to a woman "who never goes to bed before two in the morning and who then wakes up at five to see what has been published about her in some goddamn foreign country." She has a taste for good living, he said, but no great capacity for enjoyment, "because something is always going on in her life, some big dramatic thing, that just ruins everything that day for her. It's not fair. She works too hard to have so many bad days."

Another problem, according to Patrice Gonzalez, had to do with the constant emphasis on Madonna's career, no matter where the couple were, or what they were doing. "It was all about her, all the time," says Gonzalez, "and this was very off-putting to Carlos. He understood it—she was who she was, after all—but he didn't always like it. He was a proud man. He felt overlooked."

Patrice and other friends of Carlos report one instance—of, no doubt, many—when they were at a cocktail party with Carlos and Madonna in Manhattan and able to observe as Carlos was pushed to the background.

"They arrived together," Patrice says, "but in a matter of moments, they were separated. The guests sort of backed off instinctively to let them pass as they walked into the room, and then they descended upon her like vultures, pushing him aside. For the next two hours, Carlos sat in the background while Madonna and her friends and associates talked endlessly about her and *Evita*."

Looking preoccupied, Carlos walked over to the bar, where he joined a friend. As he leaned on the bar, a heart-shaped tattoo (with the date he first met Madonna) was noticeable on his left bicep. He also wore an expensive, crown-shaped ring, a gift from her on their first anniversary. Perhaps noticing his absence, Madonna sauntered over to him. "What's wrong, Carlito?" she asked ("Carlito" is Carlos's nickname).

"To be honest, I'm sick to death of hearing about *Evita*," Carlos answered, quickly. "From the moment we arrived, every word has been about you and *Evita*," he continued, trying to hold his temper in check. "These people don't even know who I am, or what I do. And they don't care."

No doubt, Madonna had heard this complaint before from boyfriends. She knew it was difficult for any man to walk in her shadow, especially if he wasn't also a celebrity. "I wouldn't wish being

Mr. Madonna on anybody," she once said. Still, according to Carlos's friend who was present, she looked a bit hurt. "Everyone else here is proud of me," she said. "Why aren't you?"

Carlos shook his head. "You really don't get it, do you?" he asked, giving her a hard, knowing stare. "This isn't about you, Madonna."

Madonna didn't respond. Instead, with furrowed brow, she examined the inside of her nearly empty glass, as if hoping to find the answer there.

"It wasn't that he wasn't proud," said Patrice Gonzalez. "He was just tired of hearing about her and her recent achievement. He said he knew every line of every scene of that film, he had heard about it so much. Whenever they were together, the talk was always about *Evita*—how angry she was about something that had happened, how happy she was about something else, what a bad day she had, what a good day. Then, when the movie was over, the talk was still about it, how it had been, how she would never forget it. So, to go out in public and be surrounded by the constant chatter, it was too much for him."

"This is your life, not mine," Carlos said sadly, while he and Madonna stood next to each other at the bar.

"I know," Madonna said. For a moment, her expression conveyed deep despair. Then, she shook her head in annoyance and said, "Carlos, I think you're just being a big baby. Now, come on, have fun. I'll tell you what," she said with a grin. "We'll talk only about you for the rest of the night. How's that?"

He didn't respond, perhaps hurt that she was making light of his frustration.

"Come on, buy me a drink," she continued, trying to force a light moment. "My glass is empty. A lady's glass should never be empty."

After a silent moment which made it clear that Carlos was not in a joking—or even a drinking—mood, Madonna turned to his friend and said, "My baby is sick of me, huh?" On tiptoes, she reached up and kissed Carlos gently on the cheek. "Things will sort themselves out," she said. Carlos's friend recalls a tone of inevitability in Madonna's voice, an understanding, an acceptance. "Trust me," she said before taking her leave.

Carlos looked doubtful.

Rumors soon began to run rampant that Madonna's relationship with Carlos Leon was over and that she had had her handlers negotiate a financial arrangement that would ensure not only his financial security but also his silence. According to the agreement, as outlined in the press, Carlos would have certain visitation rights but would have to sign documents agreeing never to seek sole custody of their child.

If her intention was to make Carlos Leon a financial offer—and, realistically, it would seem somewhat naive to believe that no such offer was made and then accepted—Madonna's proposal would have to be a generous one. He had received numerous offers to write a book about his relationship with her, and one was for more than $3 million. Madonna was concerned when word got back to her of the possibility of a book by Carlos. However, she needn't have worried. Leon completely rejected the offer. Loyal to her without reservation, he promised that he would never write about her, or be interviewed about her, and that she didn't have to include such provisions in any agreement between them. "It just goes without saying," he told her, according to a friend of his.

Madonna suspected that she could trust Carlos to say little about her—and certainly nothing negative or revealing—and, as it happened, she could do just that. Though she hadn't always had the best judgment when it came to choosing her mates in the past, this time she realized the importance of not repeating the set of circumstances in her life that had led her to someone like Dennis Rodman. In Carlos, she chose well. According to their friends, she has become even more fully aware of his devotion to her, and genuine concern for her well-being, in the years that passed after they decided not to marry. After the tangle of so many unhappy and turbulent relationships—Penn, Kennedy, Beatty, Ward, even Rodman—Madonna had finally hit upon one of the good guys: Carlos Leon. But as often occurs in the domain of love and romance, it wasn't that simple. Though Carlos may have had the potential to be the ideal mate, the hard truth was that Madonna didn't feel the kind of abiding love for him that would make it work between them—and neither did he for her.

Carlos has never spoken of any financial arrangement with Madonna if, indeed, one exists. It is the opinion of one of his friends that "Madonna and Carlos did come to terms. I heard that he was paid a few million dollars, homes in Los Angeles and New York and $100,000 a year till Lourdes was eighteen. Let's face it. Even if that's not completely accurate, he must have gotten something, but that's not to say that she will be getting him jobs for the rest of his life. He doesn't want it, and she's not going to do it. He has a lot of pride. He considers Madonna to be one of his closest allies in the world, and even though they will probably drift apart as the years go by, they do have one thing in common, and always will: Lourdes."

Indeed, by the time of Lourdes's first birthday in October 1997, Carlos Leon was nowhere in sight. Instead, it was Ingrid Casares who accompanied Madonna and her daughter to watch the dolphins in an aquarium in Los Angeles. Meanwhile, Leon was snapped by photographers frolicking in the Malibu surf with a bikini-clad blonde. The photographs showed the pair running around in the sand, taking a dip and kissing in what appeared to be a passionate embrace. By this time, Leon even had his own "spokesman," Eric Weinstein, who, despite the existence of the revealing photographs, declared, "Carlos and Madonna are trying to patch things up right now." Madonna was unhappy when she saw the pictures published in one of the tabloids—all of which she reads religiously—not because Carlos was moving on with his life, but because she felt that his being able to do so made her appear to the public to be dispensable. "You don't go from Madonna to some little blonde chippy," she told one of her associates. "I think Carlos should be more discreet. But what can I do? I guess he has to live his life, too."

A year later, reporter Chris Wilson from the *New York Post* spotted Carlos at a party in New York passing out flyers for an upcoming independent movie, *Blasphemy*, in which he had a role. When Wilson asked Carlos if he still spoke to Madonna, he became incensed. "I don't talk about my personal life!" Carlos said, angrily. "This interview is over!" Carlos then demanded that Wilson return the glossy promotional flyer he had just handed him. When Wilson hesitated about handing over the card, Carlos grabbed his arm and growled, "I'll turn out your pockets," and beckoned over a thuggish-looking friend, who gruffly demanded the return of the card.

Madonna's instincts about him had been correct from the beginning. It would definitely seem that Madonna will not have to worry about Carlos Leon ever saying much to anyone about her. However, the author chanced upon Leon in a bar in the East Village, in New York in the spring of 1999, and had the opportunity to ask him a few questions. Leon said that he sees his daughter, Lourdes, "as often as I possibly can. She's the light of my life." He also stated that, "Madonna is the best mother in the world, and I know I can trust her with our child. But Lourdes is *our* child, not just hers. I hate it when writers act like I don't exist, like Madonna is a single mother. I do exist. We're not married, but I am involved." When asked if there was a contractual agreement between himself and Madonna, Leon succinctly replied, "We love each other. We trust each other. More people should try it."

✝

Andy Bird

In many ways, the nineties had been tough, challenging years for Madonna. Even though she continued to enjoy great commercial success, she felt that the fame she had once so craved was now nothing more than a hungry and insatiable leech sucking her dry, keeping her from being truly happy. Much of her public had the false impression that, because she was famous, she also felt an incredible sense of self-fulfillment and of truly being loved. But people who are famous can tell you that the opposite is true—that if you are not truly fulfilled in your personal life, many thousands of people adoring you can actually make you feel emptier. At its worst—as it had been for Madonna—fame had become a substitute for love, a disruptive influence in her life, often giving the feeling of happiness when, really, no happiness truly existed. "I used to be so unhappy," she said recently. "Maybe that's why I was so, I don't know, maybe mean to a lot of people . . . though I don't think I'm ready to cop to that," she added with a laugh. The birth of Lourdes helped an immeasurable amount in this regard, giving Madonna a sense of satisfaction she had never before known. "Ever since my daughter was born, I feel the fleetingness of time," she said. "And I don't want to waste it on getting the perfect lip color."

She proved to be an excellent mother, says her close friend and confidante Rosie O'Donnell. "She's a tough-love kind of mother," says Rosie. "For instance, she doesn't want her kid watching TV. Can you imagine that? Me, I use the television as a baby-sitter for my [four] kids. If it wasn't for the tube, I don't know what I would do to keep them occupied." (As a child, Madonna was also forbidden to watch TV by her father, Tony, who felt there were better ways for a child to stay occupied.)

It's true that Madonna insists that her daughter not watch television, saying that she doesn't want the girl to be influenced by sexual and, also, violent images. Even though she made a career out of being an outrageous sex goddess, she believes children should be protected from such imagery. (She also says that if she ever found out that Lourdes was dating a married man, "I would have to kill her.")

"And no junk food for Lourdes, either," says O'Donnell. "So when that girl comes to my house to visit for the weekend, forget it! She leaves here a totally different child, a candy-bar-eating, MTV-watching, spoiled little kid. To tell you the truth," says the comic, "I think Madonna knows how tough she is on the kid and lets her spend time at my house just to give her a break. But when she goes back to Mama, she toes the line. Then, when she visits me again, I have to start the process all over again of turning her into one of 'my' kids."

In her private life, Carlos Leon had served his purpose, whether it was as a partner in a temporarily committed romance, or as just a trusted friend who was able to give her the child she so desperately desired. Now, with him all but out of the picture, she was anxious to move forward with her personal life and career.

In September 1997, Madonna embarked on what would amount to an unsteady relationship with an aspiring British actor and screenplay writer, Andy Bird, after having met him in Los Angeles through mutual friend Alek Keshishian (who directed *Truth or Dare*). It would be with Bird that Madonna would pick up her romantic life after Carlos Leon. While her choice in men was flawless when it came to Carlos, it seemed somewhat weaker in the choice of Andy Bird. She may be the world-famous Madonna, but she is as fallible as anyone else when it comes to choosing a mate. True, she had learned certain lessons about love and relationships along the way, and perhaps she thought she was applying them to her life when she chose to be with Andy. However, as it happened, she was mistaken.

Madonna was immediately smitten with the six-foot, two-inch Englishman who wore his light brown hair at shoulder length and always dresed in black. "It was lust at first sight," a friend of hers revealed at the time. "Madonna calls Andy 'Geezer.' He isn't exactly rolling in cash. The guy didn't look like he had two bucks to his name, but

Madonna was totally smitten. When they were together, she couldn't keep her hands off of him."

On the surface, it was easy to see why Madonna enjoyed Andy Bird's company, for he is a man who genuinely appreciates women. On their first dates, he seemed intensely curious about her, seldom speaking of himself and, instead, asking thought-provoking questions about her. In doing so, he actually became more of an enigma in their early relationship than she was. Soon, Madonna found herself immensely intrigued by his sense of mystery. Based on what she had heard about him through mutual friends, he was also a man of wide sexual experience, though he rarely spoke of any of it. His discretion in that regard fascinated Madonna, who is old-fashioned in that she considers it chivalrous of a man when he doesn't kiss and tell. Also, that particular characteristic would bode well for any man in a relationship with a celebrity of her stature, she must have reasoned.

Soon after meeting Andy Bird, Madonna jetted to London for a two-month mission to search for a house there, saying that she felt that Britain was a safer place in which to raise her daughter. "I have really fallen in love with it," she said. "I've made some excellent friends in London and even thought about my daughter going to school here. I think the British are more intelligent than Americans." With her affair with Bird flourishing under the media's watchful eye, they moved into a rented house in Chelsea. Twice, Bird drove Madonna 140 miles to visit his parents in Stratford-upon-Avon, Shakespeare's birthplace. Bird's parents accompanied the couple to lunch at a local pub.

In what some of her friends called "record time," Bird and Madonna rented a 4,500 pounds a week house in Chelsea, while Madonna looked for a permanent home in London. Then, when she needed to return to Los Angeles on business, he moved into her Los Feliz home. He told one London-based reporter, "I'm living over there now and trying my luck as a film director."

Madonna's romance with chain-smoker but nondrinker Andy Bird was tumultuous from the start, generating reams of tabloid headlines over the course of about a year. At one point, she kicked him out of her California home and he ended up back in London, working as a doorman at the Met Bar. Another time, she left him stranded, penniless, in Florida for a week before begging him to come back in a string of heart-to-heart phone calls.

Who can say why Madonna was attracted to Andy Bird? They seemed to have little in common. She was driven and ambitious, he was more laid back about his career. She was a multimillionaire, he didn't have much money. However, he was a kind man, and also fun. A gentleman with a great sense of humor, Andy made Madonna laugh. He was polite, reassuring. He wasn't cruel and argumentative like Sean Penn. He wasn't emotionally crippled like Warren Beatty and John Kennedy, Jr. Actually, he was more like Tony Ward—loving and well-meaning while, perhaps, not terribly stable or financially secure.

To his credit, Andy treated Madonna not like a star, but like a friend, which she found irresistible. They had picnics, they talked about movies, they joked with one another. In July 1998, the two exchanged vows in a Kabbalah ceremony that supposedly united them for all time. Madonna wore a flowing white gown. Both she and Bird were barefoot. She told friends at the time that she hoped to have Bird's child, but that marriage might not be necessary since "we had this very lovely ceremony."

In a chapter that seemed right out of Julia Roberts's *Notting Hill*, Madonna didn't much care about Andy's bank account—at least not at first. However, as weeks turned into months, she could not reconcile the fact that Bird was unclear about his future ambitions while, at the same time, being such a spiritual person. To her way of thinking, the purpose of spirituality was to use it to move your life ahead to the next plateau, not to fall back on it as an excuse to stagnate. Bird, however, felt that career concerns were secondary to those relating to the metaphysical. On a trip to London in the fall of 1998, at his urging he and Madonna visited the Inergy Centre in Kensal Rise, West London, which specializes in teaching yoga. Afterward, she said, "Yoga is very physical and strengthens me from within, not just externally. It helps me be more flexible about how I see the world and other people."

"She was a lovely girl and seemed to be very fond of our son," said Bird's mother after she and her accountant husband, Horace, shared a cup of tea with Madonna. "I liked her. I must say, she surprised me because she was so polite. I don't know what I expected. I wondered if they would get married, but I knew that young people rarely get married these days. I know he cared about her a great deal. I have nothing but nice thoughts about her, but she had been around more than Andy, I think. She was more worldly."

At twenty-nine, ten years Madonna's junior, Andy did seem to have some growing up to do. He was also insecure. Perhaps a defining moment occurred in their relationship when he accused Madonna of having a fling with a young film director while she was in London making a video. Madonna was having no such affair. (At least not yet.) Also, when it came to discretion with the media—a requirement if one is to have a relationship with a major celebrity—Andy Bird was a novice. "She goes through boyfriends like there's no tomorrow," Andy told a reporter. No doubt that wasn't the kind of statement Madonna liked to hear her male companions make about her. She must have known that there were problems ahead.

Madonna didn't have many people she could turn to to discuss issues having to do with her boyfriend Andy. Those who had known her for years were not the best to give advice, she felt, because, as she put it, "they've all heard my stories a thousand times over, and they're sick of them . . . and of me." Perhaps this is the reason Madonna turned to a surprising new friend in trying to sort out some of her problems with Andy Bird.

✝

Gwyneth and Peter

Madonna has had many female friends over the years, but she seems to have trouble maintaining such relationships, perhaps because she is so competitive by nature. By the fall of 1998, however, she and actress Gwyneth Paltrow had become close. Says Paltrow's Los Angeles friend Jeannette Misterling, "It seems like a weird match, but they have so much in common, not the least of which is their desire to keep their friendship out of the public eye. They both have ambivalent feelings about the media, so they'd just as soon their friendship not be dissected. They both like to hang on to some things of a personal nature . . . and not just let the public have it all."

According to close associates of both celebrities, the two women first became acquainted in the winter of 1996 when nude photographs taken of Gwyneth and Brad Pitt on vacation appeared in the press.

297

Madonna was so outraged by the invasion, and felt so bad for Gwyneth (whom she did not know), she decided to telephone her. (One might wonder why celebrities always seem to know how to contact one another—even if they've never met—whenever they feel compelled to do so.)

While Madonna told Gwyneth that she'd had similar experiences with intrusive photographers, and that she sympathized with her, Gwyneth admitted that she was horrified by the invasive pictures, much more than she would ever let on to her fans or the press. "How will I ever show my face in public again?" she asked Madonna, according to a later conversation with friends.

"But what have you got to be ashamed of?" Madonna asked. "I've been seen nude many times and I actually think it's only *enhanced* my career. However, you might want to go to a gym," she advised Gwyneth. "You could use some toning. You're too skinny."

After that conversation, the two women continued to exchange letters and phone calls. Whenever Gwyneth found herself in Los Angeles, she would always be sure to visit Madonna. They would end long, confessional lunches with caramelized apple tarts and vanilla ice cream, a favorite dessert of Gwyneth's, along with great quantities of strong coffee.

"Gwyneth is experiencing the upsides and downsides of being incredibly famous for the first time," Madonna explained to her friend Juliette Hohnen. "I think people taking pictures of you and writing stories about you and putting their noses in your business for the first time is disorienting. I wish I could have had someone to turn to when I was at that point in my life. I don't think I would have taken a lot of things so personally. So I'm happy to help her. I do see her as a younger sister, although she is very sophisticated for her age."

Earlier, at the end of 1997, after Madonna expressed an interest in Viggo Mortensen [who portrayed Demi Moore's drill sergeant in the film *G.I. Jane*), Gwyneth helped arrange a date for her. (Gwyneth and Viggo were good friends and were scheduled to make a film together.) Though Gwyneth set the date for Madonna hoping that it would take her mind off Andy Bird, it did not go well; Madonna and Viggo had nothing in common. When Gwyneth asked Madonna if she and Viggo had slept together, Madonna laughed and denied it, adding, "By the time I got home all I wanted to do was go to bed . . . alone." Besides, one-night stands now held very little appeal for her.

Once in the States and away from Andy Bird—at least for the time being—Madonna began spending more time with divorced actor Peter Berg, who starred as Dr. Billy Kronk on the television show *Chicago Hope*. Peter advised her to let Andy go and move on with her life. He also promised to be there for her if she would do so.

By August 1998, Madonna and thirty-five-year-old Peter—often fashionably unshaven—were seen in New York together, huddling romantically in restaurants and walking through Central Park. When the two showed up at a Krispy Kreme doughnut shop at eight in the morning after having been up all night together, they caused a sensation in the store. "Oh my God, can I have your autograph?" asked the girl behind the counter. "Can I have my doughnuts?" Madonna answered, testily.

Two days later, the couple attended a concert by Savage Garden in New York at the Beacon Theater. Earlier in the day, Madonna had to discipline Lourdes for something she had done. She was upset about it, saying she felt terrible whenever she had to "raise my voice to my daughter." Berg suggested that Madonna go shopping while he took Lourdes out for ice cream. "Anytime a man is willing to give a mother a break from a toddler, that's a good man," Madonna said. When, with shopping bags in tow, she returned home from her day on Fifth Avenue, Berg had dinner waiting for her. A contented Lourdes sat in her high chair at the table, washed and dressed for the meal.

Peter Berg quickly became infatuated with Madonna, telling one friend, "She's strong-minded, intelligent and independent. Her looks are an asset equal to her wealth. What else can a man ask for?" However, Madonna seemed unsure as to how to proceed. After Carlos Leon and Andy Bird, she was wary. She knew what she was looking for—but how would she recognize it when she found it? She now found herself examining the nature of love and risk. "At my age," she said at the time, "love is a risky business—a risk I don't think I'm willing to take—especially since, really, do I even need a man?"

"I don't want much out of life," Madonna told Berg in front of mutual friends. She reached into her bag and took out her compact. After checking her reflection in the mirror, she went back into her bag to retrieve a stick of concealer makeup. She dabbed it under her left eye. "I just want a little peace and quiet as I approach old age," she observed while patting the offending area with her pinkie finger. Then, snapping her compact shut, she said, "Is that too much to ask?"

"You? Peaceful? Quiet?" Berg asked with an arched eyebrow. "Not in this lifetime. No. It'll never happen."

"I know," Madonna said with a smile. "Talk about wishful thinking."

At the Cafeteria, a New York restaurant, Peter Berg joined Madonna after she dined with Ingrid Casares, Sony president Tommy Mottola and fashion designer Victor Alfaro, one of the restaurant's owners. In front of the others, Peter told her he would wait for her, "for as long as it takes, until you and I can be together." With a sad smile, Madonna said, "Well, Peter, you'll be waiting a long time." For the rest of the evening, he seemed just to stare at her with admiration and love.

Peter and Madonna then went outside together, but—much to the disappointment of fascinated onlookers—simply kissed each other on the cheek and went their separate ways into the softly drizzling rain. After walking a block, Madonna stopped and took off her brown, strappy Manolo Blahnik sandals, ignoring the ever-present paparazzi who were, no doubt, disappointed by her conservative outfit—a knitted top, layered earth-tone skirt and a matching sweater tied around her waist. Barefoot, she walked across a slick Manhattan street—successful, intelligent, rich, beautiful . . . and alone.

✝

Ray of Light

By 1998, thirty-nine-year-old Madonna was all but finished with what was perhaps the most ambitious makeover in her entire fifteen-year career. For the last few years, always with great forethought, she had been going about the business of repairing the public relations damage of the downward slide that had been the result of sexually explicit projects in four different media: *Truth or Dare* in video, *Sex* in publishing, *Erotica* in music and *Body of Evidence* in film. Wisely, Madonna had decided to ease out of her role as a sexual revolutionary and slip into a more subdued persona as a mother and New Age thinker.

It was more than just public relations, though. She really had been affected by her experiences with *Evita* and her new baby, Lourdes. "It's just an evolution, really, since I made *Evita*," she told *Rolling Stone*'s Gerri Hirshey. "Because going down to South America and getting beaten up the way that I was in the newspapers every day—and sort of living vicariously through what happened to Eva Perón—then finding myself pregnant. Going from the depths of despair and then coming out the other side . . . you know, becoming a mother, I just have a whole new outlook on life. I see the world as a much more hopeful place. I just feel an infinite amount of compassion toward other people."

Her first album released after the birth of her daughter, *Ray of Light*, was released in March 1998. It would combine her recently adopted New Age beliefs—which she seemed to have fine-tuned with Andy Bird's help—with music that was both current and trendsetting. Indeed, if ever there was a recording that proved without a doubt that Madonna still understood how to stay ahead of the game in pop music, *Ray of Light* was it.

After the movies, the soundtracks and the haunting ballads, Madonna knew that at her very core, she was still a dance music artist. She also realized that trends in that genre begin in the places where people dance—which is where Madonna would find her new sound.

Techno and electronica had, for years, been the music played at so-called raves, hugely popular, illegal underground parties taking place in abandoned warehouses and deserted areas on the outskirts of town all around the world. This is where young music lovers, on alcohol and the popular rave drug Ecstasy, were zoning out on the beat of such ethereal, synthesized sounds. It was a hot sound, and one Madonna knew had not reached the masses. "It's definitely an area that's gone untapped," Madonna observed at the time. "And I need to be in on it."

Just as she had once sought out the hot dance/pop producer of the moment to assist her foray into mainstream success (Nile Rodgers with *Like a Virgin*) and employed hot, urban producers to accommodate her hip-hop move (Dallas Austin with *Bedtime Stories*), Madonna smartly realized that to make an authentic album of techno-pop she'd need to go to the source of such music. Originally, she intended to collaborate with Robert Miles, Trent Reznor, Nellee Hooper, Babyface and William Orbit. In the end, probably in an attempt to give the project a strong identity, only Orbit—a writer and producer renowned in the field of techno and electronica—was retained. (Madonna historian Bruce Baron notes that there may be early demos of the *Ray of Light* songs co-produced with one or more of the original lineup. None has turned up so far, he says.)

While William Orbit brought along his crew of collaborators, Madonna again called on the durable Patrick Leonard. Leonard would serve musically to anchor Orbit's technology and, as he put it, "keep the resulting album sounding like it was Madonna at its core. She didn't want to lose her identity," he explains. "She just wanted to expand her sound." Together, this team would create what could arguably be called Madonna's most ambitious project since she'd tackled the musically elaborate *Evita*.

With *Ray of Light*, Madonna by no means invented anything new. Madonna simply took the essence of the techno scene— its sound and personality—and then applied it to the commercial dance music sensibility she'd come to master so well. Just as pop culture heroes and icons before her, able to reshape themselves to the public's whim at a moment's notice (like the Beatles did in the sixties when they went from the goofy and melodic "She Loves You" to the psychedelia madness of "Lucy in the Sky with Diamonds" in the span of just a few years), Madonna simply did what she knew she had to do to stay current: she brilliantly "morphed" into the current trend. She just happens to change with the times better than most of her contemporaries, many of whose attempts at keeping pace with the musical times often appear unimaginably contrived.

The album's first single, "Frozen," is a simple yet majestic song about spiritual growth in a person who doesn't seem to want it, made irresistible by infectious vocal melodies and musical accents that can be best characterized as Moroccan. A big success, the track reached Number 2 on the *Billboard* singles chart.

The album's title track and second single, "Ray of Light," was the personification of what Madonna sought to achieve with the project. The track begins deceptively with a quiet, melodic guitar sound before giving way to a determined beat and whirlwinding synthesized sound.

Lyrically, it's a celebration of power and of self. Her sense of abandon is catching, and the track carries away the listener. The song was an instant hit, debuting at Number 5 in the *Billboard* charts—her highest entry to date. (Previously, in December 1995, "You'll See" debuted at Number 8 and, in March 1998, "Frozen" equalled that entry position.). "Ray of Light," which was Madonna's fortieth chart single and thirty-second Top 10 hit, captured the heady feeling of the era—the "new" energy of the coming millennium.

"The Power of Good-bye," a song about the strength that comes in letting go, has a catchy Europop feel to it. Indeed, lyrically throughout, *Ray of Light* offers a certain amount of reflection on the person Madonna feels she used to be, and who she's become. For instance, "Nothing Really Matters" has her owning up to selfish ways of the past.

"I don't really want to dissect my creative process too much," she has said when asked by reporter Jancee Dunn to explain the songs she writes. "What's the point, really? I want people to have a visceral and emotional reaction to things, rather than to have in their mind where all my stuff came from. You know, if I see a bug crawling across the floor and it inspires me to write the most incredible love poem, I don't want people to be thinking about their relationship, and then think of my bug crawling across the floor."

Without a trace of bondage or oral sex in a single lyric, this album's songs instead spoke of ecology, the universe, the earth, "the stars in the sky," angels and heaven and, surprising some observers, contained respectful references to God and "the Gospel." In one song she talks of "waiting for the time when earth shall be as one," while in another she does her best to make a pop dance tune out of a yoga chant. However, when the album was released, the music industry at large, though usually unflinchingly supportive of an artist as commercially successful as Madonna, didn't think it would be a success. The sound of the songs wasn't radio friendly, some observers argued. Other naysayers surmised that Madonna, at least by pop music standards, was too old to do this kind of album. They were all wrong. *Ray of Light* went on to sell four million copies in the U.S.—twelve million internationally. It also presented an older pop icon to younger audiences as an artist to whom they could relate and musically embrace.

Now nearly forty years old, Madonna had also unveiled a new physical image that included the wearing of togas and saris, and veils over long, flowing dark tresses. Gone were her come-hither looks and her underwear worn as outerwear. Now, she was photographed with reflective expressions on her face, heavenly winds whipping through her hair. Her face was retouched to give it the bronzed, flawless complexion one would perhaps expect to see only on an angel. Still, Madonna strongly objected to the perception that she was constantly reinventing herself. "I'd rather think that I'm slowly revealing myself, my true nature," she said. "It feels to me like I'm just getting closer to the core of who I really am."

With the critical raves for and commercial success of *Ray of Light*, Madonna's image transformation proved to be another triumph. Oddly, in her fifteen years of fame, she'd only received one Grammy, and that was for Best Video back in 1991. (It's not unusual for acclaimed artists never to receive a Grammy award. Madonna was in good company with the Beatles and Diana Ross, among other notables.) However, the stars were once again in her favor, and with a new career and image Madonna would earn four Grammys at the Los Angeles ceremony at the Shrine Auditorium in February 1999 (during which she performed "Nothing Really Matters" in a dazzling red kimono, oriental-style makeup and straight black hair)—Best Pop Album, Best Dance Recording, Best Short Form Music Video and Best Record Packaging. (The next year, at the 2000 Grammys, Madonna added another award to her collection when she won for Best Song Written for a Motion Picture: "Beautiful Stranger" from the film *Austin Powers: The Spy Who Shagged Me*.)

Although *Ray of Light* was well received—as was the newer, more mature Madonna—her plans for a tour were put on hold while she concentrated on her movie career. In 1998, she was close to signing a contract to star with Goldie Hawn in the high-budget film version of the Broadway musical *Chicago* (which never materialized) and had already signed to star in a romantic comedy, *The Next Best Thing*, starring Rupert Everett, fresh from his smash success in *My Best Friend's Wedding*, a commercially successful Julia Roberts vehicle. The new script— which Everett brought to Madonna's attention—took the secondary story of *My Best Friend's Wedding*—a straight woman/gay man friendship—and brought it to the forefront. In *The Next Best Thing*, the two friends enjoy one night of intoxicated intimacy and decide to go with the resulting pregnancy and raise the child together.

Once again, though, Madonna's film career would prove to be less than lustrous. When *The Next Best Thing* was finally released (on March 3, 2000), the movie would be attacked as viciously as anything she had ever done in the past. Under the headline "Her Best Is Bad," the *New York Post* stated, "There hasn't been a movie as smug or cheesy as *The Next Best Thing* in quite a while." It would go on to criticize, "For the first half of the movie, Madonna speaks with an unexplained English accent that draws attention to the singer's apparent inability to read a line." *USA Today* would be more succinct in its analysis: "Madonna still can't act." (She would have a hit record, however, with the song "American Pie," a version of the 1971 Don McLean pop classic which Madonna recorded for *The Next Best Thing*.)

"I think half of my movies have been good and half have been shit," she has said of her film career. "I've got two things working against me. One is that I'm really successful in another area and it's really hard for people to let you cross into anything else. Also, because I was in a series of really bad movies, it has given people a license to say, 'Oh, she can't act. She can't do this, she can't do that.' But, honestly, I can think of Academy Award–winning actors and actresses who have done more shit movies than I have."

✝

Exit: Andy Bird

A major schism in Madonna's relationship with Andy Bird occurred in October 1998 when he made a few choice but innocuous comments about her to the press. "[We have] a fiery relationship, but it's worth working on," Bird told the *Daily Mail*. "I've got a responsibility towards Lourdes . . . and towards Madonna." Madonna telephoned him when she read the comment and became quite emotional. She felt betrayed, she said. She was surprised, as well, because she still hoped he would be more discreet when it came to talking about their life together.

"If I can't trust the people I sleep with, who can I trust?" she asked. Bird denied that he had even talked to the reporter and apologized profusely for the fact that the news had rattled her. However, once Madonna feels that a person has betrayed her trust, it is difficult for her ever again to fully trust that person. "She can be open, until she feels that you let her down and said something about her publicly that you shouldn't have said," observed her now former manager Freddy De-Mann. "Once that happens, forget it. She never really trusts you again. Especially if you talked to the press. . . ." (In 1997, after fourteen years as her manager, DeMann became chief executive of Madonna's Maverick label. Then, in 1998, after much publicized and unfortunate legal wrangling, DeMann left Maverick; Madonna settled with him for $20 million.)

Contrite, Andy Bird hopped on a transatlantic flight to New York and—one might wonder why he would do this—told reporters at the airport that he wanted to patch up his relationship with Madonna. "It's worth working on and I'm certainly not going all the way to New York to have a fight with her," he said.

Despite the truce that they called, Madonna was ambivalent about Andy Bird. In many ways, the relationship must have reminded her of the ones she had had with musicians in her early New York days. She had cared about those men, too, but felt that their potential to achieve as much in their lives as she had in hers was limited. Though she often seemed to end up in relationships in which she made more money than her boyfriends—Carlos Leon being the most recent—that wasn't a problem for her anymore. "It is perfectly socially acceptable for a man to find a beautiful girl who hasn't accomplished the things that he's accomplished, and make a life with her," she told American *Vogue*. "Why does the man always have to be the one who makes more money? It's pathetic and sexist and disgusting, and if people don't change the way they view this thing—the man and woman's place in society—nothing's ever going to change." For Madonna, the issue wasn't a financial one as much as it was that she felt Andy Bird was not motivated to do with his career what she felt he should do with it. She has such great initiative and drive, she can't help but to be judgmental about those who she feels don't match her in that regard. Also, as she once told Tony Ward, she needed more from a relationship. Again, whatever it was that was going to make it permanent between Madonna and a man simply wasn't there with this one.

"I can't be what you want me to be," Andy said to her at a party in

Los Angeles in front of witnesses. As usual these days, she was dressed down, in a satin shift with a long hemline, a cardigan sweater and slip-on Fendi shoes. She looked so "normal," it was difficult for some on-lookers to believe she was really *the* Madonna.

"I'm not expecting you to be what I want you to be," Madonna shot back. "Just find some direction . . . please!"

"I am who I am," he said, shifting from foot to foot. His response seemed weak, even to the most casual observer.

"Well, maybe that's not good enough for me," Madonna countered. "I've been around the block too many times for this kind of bull-shit." As she walked away, she added, "I want another child, but I want to give birth to it. Not date it."

It was true that, by this time, Madonna had decided that she wanted another baby. She enjoyed motherhood. "I have memories of sitting on my mother's lap," she remembers, "or lying next to her in bed and having her arms around me. I know how much I cherish those memories. I do have moments with Lola [Lourdes] when I can almost feel transposed back to those times. I don't so much see my mother mothering me as I think, *I'm* going to be the mother *I* never had."

There had been a short time after the birth of "Lola" when Madonna wondered if she had made the right decision about having a child. For years, she had lived a selfish, egocentric life—she knew it, even sang about it on her *Ray of Light* CD. She had become so accustomed to the independence afforded by success and wealth, it had even been difficult for Madonna to compromise her wants and needs for the sake of a relationship with a man. For most of her life, she, and she alone, was her greatest and only concern. Every decision she had made—particularly as an adult, and about her career—had to do with what suited her needs best. Would she like to sleep late after an exhausting public appearance? Why not? A vacation with a new boyfriend to some far-off land for an exotic weekend? Certainly. Did she really want to clean out the hallway closet floor covered in Prada heels to make room for baby toys? Doubtful.

Then she gave birth to Lourdes. "Well, that changed everything," she explained in one interview. "It was a tough adjustment, and she really didn't know if she could do it," said a friend of hers. "She said, 'My God, I'm a terrible mother. I'm selfish. This baby is crying, and all I can think about is that I have to finance this video.' But when she relaxed into it, she realized that, 'No, this is what I *want* to do, not what I have to do.' "

Indeed, with the birth of Lourdes, Madonna experienced a rebirth of her own. She had always suspected that she would probably be a capable mother, but she was truly stunned by her capacity to love her daughter. As she would tell it, she was amazed by her devotion to Lourdes. It had impacted her, informed who she was as a person, as a woman. It gave her a sense of purpose much wider in scope than just show business, and also a sense of satisfaction she had never before experienced in her life. Whether she liked it or not, there were—and are—days when her superstar plans don't matter; Lola's needs come first. Of course, there was also something esteem-building about her ability to be a good parent. After all, it made her proud of herself, made her feel good about herself. "Like any woman—I'm no different—I had to come to terms with the fact that I am not the most important person in my world any longer," she concluded.

Now, Madonna wanted to give Lourdes a brother or sister. Again, she found herself in a familiar predicament. She wanted a baby. Should she wait to find a suitable partner? No. She was too impatient to do that. She asked Carlos Leon if he was interested in having another child. However, he said he wasn't so inclined, explaining that, emotionally, one child was all he could claim responsibility for at this time.

As usually happens in Madonna's life, as soon as she sets her mind on a goal, the media somehow seems to be in on the scheme. Stories that Madonna was interested in having another baby, though not looking for a husband, began materializing earlier in 1998 when the British press reported that she had wanted Bird to be the father.

"How do they always know exactly what I'm thinking and what I'm doing?" she asked one of her advisers of the British media. "If I miss a period, the first thing I feel I should do is read the *News of the World* to find out if I'm pregnant."

In fact, ironically, just days after she had officially ended it with Andy Bird, Madonna learned that she was pregnant. This was bad timing for her. Those who know her best say that as much as she wanted a child, she was now completely uncertain about the suitability of Andy as a father. After all, she had to plan on a long-term relationship with whoever it was who fathered her next baby. Whereas she was on good terms with Carlos Leon, her relationship with Andy Bird was strained and difficult. "She wasn't sure she wanted him in the picture any longer," says one of her closest friends. "Still, when she found that she was pregnant, she knew she would have to figure out how to get along with the baby's father, Andy Bird. An abortion was out of the question," reports that friend. "Not at this time in her life, at this stage of the game when she was wanting to have babies, not get rid of them. Someone suggested an abortion, and she said, 'Absolutely not. Those days are over. I would never have another abortion, not after giving birth. Forget it.' "

It appeared as if she would have to find a way to patch things up with Andy Bird, and even somehow make him a permanent part of her life. This would not be easy for Madonna. Once she is finished with someone, she's completely finished with that person. It's difficult for her to allow back into her life a person who has fallen out of her good graces. It's rarely—if ever—happened.

While attempting to sort out complex emotions having to do with Andy Bird as a constant in her life, the difficult decision was made for her—by Mother Nature. Madonna miscarried in her seventh week.

It isn't known if she told Bird of the pregnancy or not. Some of the couple's friends insist that she did—and that he was two days away from a trip to America to be at her side when she miscarried and told him to cancel his trip. Others say that her ever reliable instincts told her to wait awhile before informing Bird of her condition—and that she was glad she had done just that when the information was no longer relevant.

She was unhappy about the miscarriage, naturally. She was also somewhat relieved. She knew that she wanted another baby—and that she wanted to at least like the father, if not be madly in love with him.

✝

Enter: Guy Ritchie

Throughout her life, it has always seemed that elements of chance and circumstance have aligned themselves in such a way that Madonna usually gets exactly what she wants when she wants it. Or, maybe it's just that once she sets her mind on a goal, there's simply no stopping her until she achieves it.

At just about the time Madonna decided she wanted another child, she became serious about English filmmaker Guy Ritchie, ten years her junior and the director of the popular British film *Lock, Stock and Two Smoking Barrels*. Madonna had first met Ritchie at a weekend gathering in summer 1998, hosted by Sting's wife, Trudie Styler (a major investor in *Lock, Stock,* along with Peter Martin and Stephen Marks) at their fifty-two-acre country estate in Wiltshire. Ritchie later admitted that the prime reason he went to the party was to meet Madonna, "so he must have had something on his mind," Madonna observed, laughing. (Madonna would eventually agree to release the soundtrack to Ritchie's film on her Maverick Records, so maybe what he had in mind was just some old-fashioned show-business "networking.")

Madonna enjoyed a brief relationship with Guy at that time— found him to be "cocky and charming." However, she felt the same about Guy's producer, Matthew Vaughn, the wealthy son of *The Man from U.N.C.L.E.* star Robert Vaughn. "And he fancied her rotten [in the worst way] for years," Guy Ritchie has said.

While Madonna wondered about Matthew and Guy, she continued her relationship with Andy Bird. It wasn't long before word of Madonna's brief dalliance with Ritchie reached Bird. Predictably, he was upset about what was going on behind his back with Guy Ritchie. Madonna's brief affair with Guy had a certain irony to it, actually; Bird had earlier accused her of having an affair with another British film-maker, a man in whom she really was not interested. He was so certain that Madonna would one day be unfaithful to him, his prophecy became a reality.

At this time, Guy was in a long-term relationship with model and TV presenter Rebecca Green, the daughter of a British tycoon, Carlton TV chief Michael Green. Rebecca had helped Guy produce his first film, a short called *Hard Case*. She had also persuaded her mother and stepfather, wealthy banker Gilbert de Botton, to invest in *Lock, Stock and Two Smoking Barrels;* therefore Guy was, as one of his friends put it, "in deep with her." However, as Guy became famous, she became impatient with the succession of models he began dating on the side, until finally either she, or he (depending on whose story one believes), ended the relationship.

In the first weeks of 1999, Madonna and Guy began to be seen in public together—coinciding with the press reports that she was yearning for a new baby. At the time, Guy had just ended his relationship with Rebecca Green, who says that her relationship with Ritchie "came to a natural end," but adds, "Madonna was knocking about and that probably had something to do with it. We still speak," she says of Guy. "I'm not going to say when the last time was, because that's a bit of a sore one—not for me, but for her [Madonna]. I've got to be a bit kind."

Like Madonna, Guy Ritchie has been accused of rewriting his life story, perhaps for dramatic purposes. So, as with Madonna, one should always take what Ritchie says about his past with the proverbial grain of salt. He is savvy enough to know that coming from the streets projects a more interesting, and even sexier, image than being raised upper class. (Or, as he wrote in the dialogue for one of his characters in *Lock, Stock and Two Smoking Barrels,* men from the upper class have "mincey faggot balls" and are "poofs. Soft as shite   faggots.") "I've lived in the East End for thirty years," he was quoted as saying in 1999. "I've been in a load of mess-ups . . . I've been poor all of my life . . ."

*

Guy Ritchie is, in fact, the son of upper-middle-class parents. His father, John, had followed his own father from Sandhurst into the Seaforth Highlanders (a regiment of the British Army), after which he became an advertising executive, responsible for the Hamlet cigar advertisements. (Guy's grandfather, Major Stewart Ritchie, was a military hero, killed in action in 1940 after the 2nd Seaforth Highlanders were ordered to remain on French soil while most British forces were evacuated at Dunkirk.)

Ritchie's mother, Amber, is a former model.

Born in 1968 in Hatfield, Hertfordshire, Guy Ritchie lived with his parents and sister, Tabitha, in Fulham, West London. When he was five, his parents divorced and, shortly thereafter, Amber married Sir Michael Leighton, the eleventh holder of a 300-year-old baronetcy who once boasted of having had "104 affairs." Guy then went on to live a privileged life in the English countryside. He grew up at the seventeenth-century Loton Park near Shrewsbury, a manor house belonging to his stepfather.

"Guy loved it there and got on well with Sir Michael," says John

Ritchie. "He could roam around the estate and was really keen on shooting and trout fishing. He actually wanted to be a gamekeeper or go into the army to keep up the family tradition."

His mother, Amber, Lady Leighton, divorced Sir Michael Leighton in 1980. Today, she lives with her daughter, Tabitha, in Wandsworth, South London. Tabitha, two years Guy's senior, works in the health and fitness business.

Guy has lost touch with his stepfather, Sir Michael Leighton, who has remarried. He also has some distant connections to royalty. His paternal grandmother, Doris, is descended from the royal house of Stewart. Through her, Guy is a cousin (albeit three times removed) of Sarah, the Duchess of York, and the late Diana, Princess of Wales. Through Doris, Guy can also claim Sir Winston Churchill as a distant cousin.

Throughout his childhood, Guy battled dyslexia and, after attending ten different schools, gave up on his education at the age of fifteen. It was then, he claims, that he had been expelled from the 4,725-pounds-a-term Standbridge Earls School near Andover, in Hampshire, whose teachers specialize in teaching dyslexics, for "doing a line of sulfate."

"Education was lost on me," he told the London *Sunday Times*. "I may as well have been sent out in a field to milk cows for ten years. I had no interest whatsoever in what I was supposedly being taught."

Guy's father, John, now seventy-two, retired and living in a 1.3-million-pound house in Chelsea, has different memories of Guy's school days. "The headmaster rang saying he [Guy] had been a naughty boy and that if I brought him back next term he would have to expel him," he recalls. "But it wasn't drugs—he had been caught in a girl's room and wasn't going to his lessons."

What followed in his life, Guy Ritchie says, was a wild period of "hanging out with villains" and doing drugs. "I took everything and anything, and most of the drug dealers I met along the way were in public school."

"Guy has a certain wit, a certain humor that people don't always get," says his father. "He says things sometimes in joking, I think. Then the newspapers print it, and it sounds like he's pretending to be a scallywag. He hasn't really been one, though. Not that I know of, anyway."

When he was about eighteen, Ritchie took off to Africa, and then to Greece where he dug sewers for a time before returning to England. Some press reports have indicated that Guy worked as a bricklayer when he returned to England, but his father recalls his son as having worked as a "messenger" for Island Records, after which he worked as a bartender, and then as a furniture mover—a job that ended abruptly when Guy strapped an antique table to the roof of his van and inadvertently drove through a low tunnel.

He then became a messenger for his father's advertising agency and soon after, with practically no training in the field—but by using his father's contacts—began making music videos for "Eurotrash techno-rave bands." He soon applied his budding directorial talents—and entrepreneurial business sense—to making short films. Eventually, at the age of twenty-nine, he found critical and commercial success as the writer/director of *Lock, Stock and Two Smoking Barrels*. With Matthew Vaughn as its producer, the movie owed much to Quentin Tarantino's *Reservoir Dogs* and *Pulp Fiction*. Thanks to an audience for his films that was largely young and male, the film went on to generate 18 million pounds in Britain alone, though it cost only 1 million pounds to make. Moreover, after having been publicly embraced by Tom Cruise, *Lock, Stock and Two Smoking Barrels* also had a respectable—though not overwhelming—release in the United States.

It is both ironic and paradoxical that Guy Ritchie would find himself in a romantic relationship with Madonna—an entertainer widely considered to be a gay icon—since *Lock, Stock and Two Smoking Barrels* as well as the more recent *Snatch* both have obvious homoerotic undercurrents, as well as disturbing homophobic leanings.

For instance, in *Lock, Stock and Two Smoking Barrels* one of Ritchie's characters explains what he believes could be the perfect scam: place an advertisement for "Arse Ticklers Faggot Fan Club anal-intruding dildos" in gay magazines, and wait for the checks to roll in. Then, send out letters saying that you're out of stock and enclose a check stamped "Arse Ticklers Faggot Fan Club." "Not a single soul will cash it!"

"Do you have big brave balls," asks footballer-turned-actor Vinnie Jones in a confrontational moment in *Snatch*, "or mincey faggot balls?" (*Snatch* is a black comedy; a gangland story largely set in London's Hatton Garden, about diamond heists and bare-knuckle boxing. It stars Brad Pitt, who cut his normal fee by 90 percent to take the role of the gypsy boxer and who, incidentally, is almost entirely incoherent throughout.)

Mark Simpson of the *Independent* dubbed both of Ritchie's films "gay porn for straight males." In an article headed "Just What Sort of a Guy's Guy Is Guy Ritchie," he wrote of *Snatch*, "Its 'mockney geezer' dialogue is thick with references to 'aving me pants pulled down,' being 'bent over,' 'full penetration,' and being 'f—ked.' " This isn't very surprising since, as in Ritchie's *Lock, Stock* and the spin-off TV series he executive-produced, women are conspicuous by their absence—the only snatch in *Snatch* belongs to other men . . . "In an age of masculine confusion, [Ritchie] is the pre-eminent example of a rising phenomenon: the homo-hetero," Simpson wrote. "Exclusively and adamantly heterosexual in the bedroom, the homo-hetero is nevertheless entranced by masculine images, forever fantasizing about a world of homosociality that is just a dropped bar of soap away from homosexuality. Could it be that Guy Ritchie—who lives with the woman famously described as a gay man trapped in a woman's body—is a gay man trapped in a straight man's body?"

Perhaps analysis such as Simpson's is why Guy Ritchie seems prickly about his public image. When a reporter from male-oriented *FHM* magazine asked him about his taste in clothes, he became defensive, using words such as "fruity," "queeny," "fucking fruit-tree" and "mincey." He also said, oddly enough, that he would be happiest "in a gladiator outfit." Later, in another interview, he said that he "will not allow Madonna to dress me like a poof."

Guy Ritchie is tall and athletic-looking, with tousled dirty-blonde hair and dark brown eyes above sensitive, chiseled features. His charm is infectious; he draws people like a magnet (except when Madonna is around; her magnetic quality is obviously stronger).

When Guy was in Los Angeles in January 2001 for the United States opening of his film *Snatch*, the author had a chance meeting with him and was surprised by how young he seemed and acted. Though thirty-two, his demeanor is that of a friendly, outgoing college youth. There is nothing pretentious about him, as if he could be anyone's pal—all of which makes his relationship with Madonna more intriguing, even confounding.

No matter how one looks at it, upon meeting her, Madonna seems anything but "normal." It would stretch the imagination to think that she could quickly become anyone's "pal." Even when she wasn't a star, she wasn't the kind of girl one would feel was accessible, easy to know. Now, because she's been a celebrity for so many years, she carries herself with definite regality and a sense of glamour that springs not so much from her looks as from her character and personality. Her presence tends to create a distance between her and any admirer. One wonders, then, how she ended up with the much more grounded and affable Guy Ritchie—and how he ended up with her.

While it seems futile to analyze matters of the heart (especially when the romance is still in full bloom and can change in many ways), suffice it to say that these two probably balance each other's personalities. Maybe in this extraordinary mingling of contrasts, Guy adds a sense of normalcy to her life and she a sense of excitement to his. .

From the beginning, Madonna enjoyed being with Guy Ritchie, she said, because he treated her "like a normal person, not an icon." When he speaks to her, he has the priceless gift of making her feel that she is the most important person in the world to him. Also, she'd never met anyone so full of compliments; he raised flattery to an art form. "And he's not intimidated by fame," Madonna has said, "he calls me 'Madge' and even makes me wash his car with him," she says. Finally. This one—Guy Ritchie—seemed to have it all: he was handsome, sexy, gainfully employed, sensible and with a sure, clear-eyed maturity about him. More important, he loved Madonna and she returned his affection with equal emotion.

In any relationship, though, there are personality traits to which both partners must adapt. One issue the two faced early in their romance was that Guy sometimes contradicted Madonna in public. Rather than cause a scene, she would bite her lip. Later, she would let him have it. "Don't ever contradict me in front of people," she told him, according to two good friends. The four were sitting in a darkened pub, each drinking a pint of Guinness under a haze of cigarette smoke. Madonna was wearing what appeared to be a Versace turtleneck, a Gucci leather jacket and secondhand Levi's. ("Never in a million years could I have imagined myself sitting in a pub, drinking," she later said, amused by how relaxed her standards for healthy living had become.)

"But when you're wrong, you're wrong," he said, maintaining an almost clinical composure.

"Absolutely *not*," she insisted, dramatically. "When I'm wrong, I'm *still* right—in public." She took her hand mirror out of her bag and—with a rapid flourish—applied a fresh slash of what appeared to be black raspberry lip gloss. "If ever you have a problem with something I said," she concluded, looking at her reflection, not at him, "do take it up with me privately, won't you?"

It was as if she had to indoctrinate Guy to the way she had been living for almost two decades. If someone asked her to do something she didn't want to do—"which happens about thirty times an hour," as she has said—she usually just fibbed and said she had other plans rather than put the person off or make excuses. Once at a party when Madonna was being pestered by a photographer, she lied and said she couldn't allow him to take her picture that evening because she had dinner plans. Guy cut in and said, "No, Madonna, that's tomorrow night. You're free tonight." She shot him a glare, the intensity of which didn't escape anyone present to witness it. It's not likely that Guy Ritchie ever made that mistake again.

Guy, whose old-fashioned English charm is matched only by his impeccable, polished manners, also had to become accustomed to the way Madonna eats salad. The same two friends who were with them in the pub recall what happened at dinner later that night when the salad was served: Madonna began eating it with her hands.

"But that is so . . . *wrong*," Guy told her, his face registering disapproval.

"What do you mean?" Madonna asked. She scooped up a crouton using a salad leaf dripping with dressing, and popped it into her mouth.

"That . . . why, that whole thing . . . eating with your hands?"

"Oh," Madonna said, laughing. "That. Well, that is how I eat salad. Get used to it."

Possibly because of her increasingly serious romantic involvement with Guy Ritchie, and her professional involvement with Rupert Everett, one surprising change in the Madonna mystique by the end of the nineties was her startling habit of speaking in what seemed like an upper-crust English accent that also somehow embraced Italian. It's similar to the affectation Elizabeth Taylor picked up after she became involved with Richard Burton. "True, that," she is known to observe often. Madonna actually loved the British and was determined to make London her home base. "I hate to use the phrase, but it's true that you can start all over again in England," she said. "What I really think is that even the most stupid Englishman is about ten times smarter than the most stupid American." Soon, she traded in her $15,000-a-month rented home in Notting Hill to purchase a 200-year-old, four-story house in South Kensington for $5 million.

Madonna has grown up, and as a result she's a different person than she was when she was younger and more frivolous. For instance, she's no longer a shopaholic. She used to spend thousands on clothing a week. "I'm too puritanical for that now," she says. "I'm too reserved to spend my money that way. I'm careful, so careful that I actually forget I have a lot of money."

Madonna is so careful, in fact, that people who work for her say that she is thrifty beyond all reason. She keeps flowers in her home long after they have wilted, just so that she won't have to spend money on fresh ones. She insists that her housekeeper shop using coupons, so that she can save a few dollars on groceries. She runs throughout her home turning off lights so that her electricity bill will be low. She won't allow friends to make long-distance calls on her telephone. She seldom picks up the tab when dining with friends. She rarely has cash on her, and is always complaining that she's "cash poor," as she calls it—even though she is one of the richest women in show business. Her spokeswoman, Liz Rosenberg, admits that when she's performing on the road, she does her own laundry because she believes hotels charge too much. She goes over hotel bills herself to make certain that she hasn't been overcharged, and if she finds that she has been she then has her accountant take up the matter with hotel management.

One extravagance: shoes. She has hundreds of pairs, many of which she feels are too fragile and exquisite ever to wear in public for fear that they might be damaged in the mad crush that always seems to surround her. She keeps many of her favorites wrapped in tissue paper, stored in boxes. Now and then, she sneaks away by herself, takes the shoes out, admires them, strokes them, puts them on . . . then takes them off and puts them back in storage, again.

To writer Jancee Dunn in an interview (in the summer of 2000), Madonna said, "When I go to the Versaces' homes and see the way wealthy people live, I think, 'I know I can live that way,' but it wouldn't come natural to me. I do appreciate that people can sort of go full-bore and get into it and live a super, glamorous, decadent life. And have gold faucets and statues everywhere. I do appreciate beautiful things, and I have nice things in my house—nice art and I like Frette linens and all that stuff. But I just don't—I don't have to show it off. I like to show off when I'm onstage. I don't like to show off, like, 'Come in and check it out. Look how rich I am.' That's not my style."

Moreover, though Madonna is worth many millions of dollars, she still fears that her fate could revert back to that of the young girl she says used to eat out of trash cans in New York, back in those struggling days. "You never get over eating from a trash can," she says, "no matter how much money you make. I wish people could understand me. But I guess that unless you've had my experiences, you really can't relate to them, or to me. I think I am the most misunderstood person on the planet," she says.

"People think that my goal is to just have hit records and make movies," she concludes. "I don't sit here wondering if I'll still be making videos when I'm fifty. I hope that I'll have three children and that they'll be the center of my life . . . not being on MTV."

Guy Ritchie seemed to be the perfect mate. He loved her, he understood her need for children and he even encouraged her to take time away from her career to, as he put it, "really start thinking more about what will make you truly happy in life." Or, as Madonna had concluded of Guy, "This one is a keeper."

✝

Bird vs. Ritchie

It was on March 19, 1999, that Madonna's past crossed her future when Andy Bird and Guy Ritchie met for the first time in London's trendy Met Bar, which is attached to the Metropolitan Hotel in Park Lane. What happened said as much about Guy as it did Andy. The two, who just happened upon one another, began talking about Madonna—who was in Los Angeles at the time at pre-Oscar festivities, on the arm of Sugar Ray rocker Mark McGrath.

"We were comparing notes about her when he suddenly hit me," Andy Bird now says. "It came out of nowhere." Bird—two years younger than Ritchie—said the punch sent him reeling over two tables. "I just couldn't believe it," he observed.

Ed Baines, a London chef and a friend of Guy Ritchie, says, "Guy sat there listening for half an hour and got more and more wound up. He's very honorable. This guy [Bird] was going on and on. Guy got up to leave and this guy grabbed him by the arm and said, 'You're not going anywhere.' Guy then felt a punch on the nose wouldn't do any harm."

The breakup with Madonna had been difficult for Andy Bird as he went about the business of unraveling their intertwined lives—shared friendships, families, living quarters, possessions. Madonna had been the one to come to the conclusion of the necessity of their breakup, not Andy. It was a huge heartache for him, says a friend of his, "an actual physical pain because he really did have strong feelings for her."

In late 1999, Andy Bird became romantically involved with British television presenter and interior designer Anna Ryder Richardson. Unfortunately, the relationship ended after three months. "I think I'm a pretty confident person, but there's only so much you can take. I got pretty sick of the word 'Madonna' by the end of our time together," she has said. "It was a pressure I didn't need. Ultimately, she did ruin our relationship—if only because he couldn't let go of her."

Because he had lost something he wanted very badly, it was difficult for Andy Bird not to be bitter. Also, there was a public element involved in his breakup with Madonna, an element of humiliation since it was clear to most observers that she had been the one to make the decision, not him. Still, it probably wasn't wise for Bird to express any animosity about what had occurred to Madonna's current consort, Guy Ritchie.

Guy is a strapping man who doesn't say much in public but who, among his friends and business associates, is as much known for his tough-guy swagger as he is for *Lock, Stock and Two Smoking Barrels*. While he seems somewhat timid when on Madonna's arm, Guy's hobbies include karate and judo and, as he put it, "kicking a little arse." He calls himself "a smart, smug bastard." Whereas Carlos Leon was gentle and unassuming, Guy Ritchie is a bit of a brawler, much like Sean Penn—a personality Madonna finds irresistible. Like many Englishmen, he appears to be reserved when in public, but privately he is expressive, wild and a great deal of fun—until crossed. He has a small scar, which he wears like a badge, on his face. "All I can say is that it came as quite a surprise to me when my opponent produced a Stanley knife," he has said in explaining the scar. A pretty good line . . . whether or not it is true.

Though it is likely to have painted him in a chivalrous light, Guy Ritchie was discreet enough not to provide his side of the story. Unlike Bird—who discussed the fight with the media—Ritchie kept his mouth shut, which, no doubt, earned him Madonna's appreciation. About a year later, Guy commented to Steve Hobbs of *GQ*, "There's something honest about violence. Some things are just better settled there and then. Of course," he concluded, "it helps if you are a big bastard."

✝

Madonna's Moment

She had become a better person—not only as a mother, but also as a girlfriend. It seemed that by the end of 1999, Madonna's maternal accomplishments had also influenced the way she related to the man in her life. Now, as a result of dealing with the demands of her child, she was more patient or, at the very least, she tried to be understanding. Of course, it was difficult for her not to act in a self-possessed manner on occasion. After all, she was still a wealthy person who had spent the better part of the last fifteen years a pampered, self-involved star. However, she was now attempting to be a more well-rounded, giving person, not only because of Lourdes, but also because she had learned her lessons with all of those previous dreadful romances. "I finally figured out that if you want to have the right kind of man in your life, you have to be the right kind of woman," she told *Cosmopolitan*. Madonna's relationship with Guy Ritchie was working in ways that simply had not been possible with men like Sean, Warren, John Jr., or even Carlos and Andy.

Guy appreciated it when Madonna spent time talking about his projects rather than only about her own. It made him smile to see her with Lourdes, playing with her, disciplining her or just sharing a quiet moment. She wasn't as selfish as she had been in the past—though, really, he had never known that side of her. As difficult as it may have been for her detractors to accept—or maybe even believe—"the Material Girl" was now a mature woman, the kind a man might desire not only in his life, but in the life of his child. Certainly, a great deal of emotional baggage came with being Madonna's consort—there were days when she could be tough, demanding, impossible—but Guy seemed to feel it was worth it, especially when he was at home, alone with the woman he liked to call "the missus."

To the outside world, Guy and Madonna are an extraordinarily attractive couple, tanned and healthy, lithe and smiling, with the unassuming aura of two who have the best life has to offer. Try as they might to understand each other, their petty arguments and disagreements do mirror those of any normal couple . . . albeit in abnormal situations. For instance, at the end of December 1999, Guy found himself in the middle of a typical Madonna-related drama when the couple spent New Year's Eve at Donatella Versace's Miami Beach mansion.

Madonna asked for—and received—a police escort to the Versace bash, so she wouldn't have to fight traffic getting through the millennium masses crowding the twelve-bedroom, thirteen-bathroom Ocean Drive palazzo outside which Gianni Versace was slain in July 1997.

"Seemed a little extreme to me," Guy later observed in front of partygoers. He looked dashing, as always, in the kind of "couture" pinstriped suit that certain English gentlemen favor.

"Well, I absolutely detest traffic," Madonna explained in a petulant tone. She then took off her wrap and, wordlessly, handed it to Guy. Underneath, she wore a pinch-waisted blouse and a 1940s-inspired tailored skirt.

"But you weren't even driving," Guy noted as he took the garment. "We were in a limousine."

"And your point is?" Madonna asked, giving him a look.

"My point is—" Guy began to explain. Stubbornly, he did not seem to want to abandon the subject.

"Oh my God. Guy! Please," Madonna exclaimed, with a smile. She then grabbed Gwyneth Paltrow's hand and began walking with her into a crowd of people. (Gwyneth and her boyfriend Guy Oseary—a chief executive at Madonna's Maverick label—were staying with Madonna in the guest house of her home in Coconut Grove, Miami

Beach.) "He has a lot to learn about dating a woman of means," Madonna said of Guy, a conspiratorial grin taking the edge off her criticism. Smiling, the winsome Gwyneth, in skinny suede pants and a belted leather jacket, wagged an index finger at her friend as if to say, "Now, now. Don't be incorrigible."

"A double Scotch," Guy instructed a hovering waiter. He shook his head, good-naturedly. "No rocks."

At the dinner for seventy-five in the mansion's courtyard, Madonna and Guy Ritchie were accompanied by Gwyneth Paltrow, Guy Oseary, Ingrid Casares, Rupert Everett, Madonna's brother Christopher Ciccone, and Orlando Pita, her hairdresser. Giant plastic tarpaulins had been tied to palm trees on either side of the mansion to block the view of any fans or photographers as semi-clad men served hors d'oeuvres and champagne.

"It was a true night of decadence and debauchery," Madonna later recalled. "It was the best New Year's I've ever had. There were shirtless men with oiled bodies dancing on podiums and there was a mambo band playing and this really yummy food. People were pogoing, people were jumping up and down on the furniture. I don't know how many drinks I had. All I know is they kept sloshing out of the glass and pretty soon you have twenty half-drinks . . . I was with the perfect group of friends."

About half an hour before midnight—as Madonna and party devoured steak and salmon—actress/singer Jennifer Lopez sauntered in, uninvited. Jennifer was in Miami to avoid the media glare in New York following her recent arrest with her boyfriend Sean (Puffy) Combs. A dark mood seemed to envelop Madonna—who was a bit tipsy by this time—as soon as she noticed Jennifer. Standing up, she announced to her friends, "Dinner's over." She then walked to a far corner of the patio, dutifully followed by four of her five companions: the two Guys (Ritchie and Oseary), Ingrid and Rupert. However, Gwyneth remained at the table, gazing deeply into an empty wineglass and seeming lost in thought.

It had been a tense New Year's celebration for Gwyneth, who had recently decided to end her brief relationship with Guy Oseary, saying that he "just isn't right for me." However, she said she would keep a promise she had made to him to be his date for the all-important New Year's Eve.

Earlier in the day, Madonna and her friends had boarded her yacht and departed from the wharf on her property, their destination being Rosie O'Donnell's Miami home in South Beach, about fifteen minutes away by boat. The yacht was piloted by Madonna's bodyguard. Once at O'Donnell's, Gwyneth spent about an hour crying on Madonna's shoulder about how much she missed actor and former boyfriend Ben Affleck, whom she met in 1997 on the set of *Shakespeare in Love* (for which she won an Academy Award). Perhaps feeling caught in the middle of a delicate situation—since Guy Oseary was not only a business partner of hers at Maverick but also a good friend—Madonna did her best to be diplomatic and understanding. She cut the visit to her friend's short, and went back to her own home.

She had flown her yoga instructors to Miami so that she and her friends could relax and meditate. ("I have yoga wherever I go," she said.) Gwyneth, though, wasn't interested in yoga at this time and wasted the rest of the day at Madonna's just moping.

That night, much to Madonna's annoyance, Gwyneth spent the whole time on her cell phone talking to Ben Affleck, who was in Boston. Madonna was overheard telling Gwyneth, "You are absolutely smothering that poor man. Will you please get off the phone and just enjoy the evening."

"Oh, but I miss my sweet little Benny," Gwyneth said, mournfully.

According to a witness, Madonna rolled her eyes. "Your sweet little Benny is going to jump ship if you don't stop acting so needy," she said. As the willowy Gwyneth sat on the floor hugging her knees, Madonna studied her in a sad way, and then walked off.

There was a great deal of speculation as to why Madonna was so annoyed by the presence of Jennifer Lopez. The truth was that she was angry about comments the singer had made about her and Gwyneth in a recently published interview.

About Madonna, Lopez observed, "Do I think she's a great performer? Yeah. Do I think she's a great actress? No. Acting is what I do. I'm like, 'Hey, don't spit on my craft.' " About Gwyneth, she said: "I don't remember anything she was in. Some people get hot by association. I heard more about her and Brad Pitt than I ever heard about her work." Through mutual friends, Madonna also learned that Lopez had made other unkind comments about her, which the published interview did not include.

"Let's go dancing," Madonna said, finally. Then, she and her party moved on to Bar Room, one of the nightclubs owned by the entrepreneurial Ingrid (now also a talent manager representing Victor Calderone, a DJ who remixes many of Madonna's songs). Within fifteen minutes, Madonna found herself surrounded by a crowd of excited people, each of whom was vying for just a single, precious second of her attention. George Cukor once said of Marilyn Monroe that every time she entered a room "it was an occasion." Certainly, the same could be said of Madonna. Moving slowly and deliberately through the adoring throng, she smiled and greeted people as if the party were in her honor. Soon, she was enveloped by a group of revelers.

Meanwhile, Guy Ritchie sat at the bar, alone.

It had never ceased to astonish Guy, he would say, the way he became practically invisible whenever he was with Madonna in public. Most people just looked right past him to focus their attention on his internationally known girlfriend, and on whatever it was she was doing, and with whoever she was doing it.

"Guy, get over here," Madonna shouted out at him from the crowd. "I want you to meet someone."

The weary-looking Guy Ritchie turned to a man he didn't realize was a reporter for a Miami newspaper. He raised his glass to him before taking a sip. Then, he rose. "Hopefully, next New Year's Eve," he concluded, his voice drained and flat, "I will be home, in bed."

By four A.M., the New Year's party was in full, chaotic swing. As the hypnotizing strains of pumping techno music filled the room, Madonna jumped up on a table and began dancing wildly to the rhythm. "C'mon up here," she beckoned to Gwyneth Paltrow with a teasing smile.

After a moment's hesitation, Gwyneth leaped onto the table to join her friend. Once up there, to the delight of at least 200 partygoers, Madonna and Gwyneth locked eyes and began dancing, both seemingly in a seductive trance, their movements unabashedly voluptuous. With their hands arched over their heads, they teased and beckoned each other as they performed what looked like an impromptu version of a Greek ritualistic dance called the *tsamikos* (where each dancer clutches the corner of a white handkerchief held aloft—only there was no handkerchief between the two friends).

Though the music was already loud, it somehow seemed to grow louder.

As Madonna danced unrestrained, one can only guess at the kinds of images that may have crossed her mind. It was the end of the millennium. Ever since Lourdes's birth, she had been feeling contemplative. While blinded by streams of color from dazzling lights, perhaps faces from the past flashed before her—snapshots of Christopher Flynn and Camille Barbone and Dan Gilroy and Erica Bell and Jellybean Benitez and Sean Penn and Warren Beatty and John Kennedy, Jr., and Sandra Bernhard and Carlos Leon and Andy Bird and all the rest—names and faces of friends and foes from years gone by, all charging forward in a nostalgic rush of millennial reflectiveness, evoking feelings easily related to at that time of the year—only perhaps even more sentimental given that it was a unique period, the end of one millennium, the beginning of another.

While Gwyneth Paltrow moved about the table, Madonna circled her, a predator scrutinizing her mouth-watering prey. Just as she had always sized up her career, each challenge viewed as an adversary forced to submit to her will, Madonna looked at Gwyneth with hungry eyes. Then, as if she could no longer disguise her appetite for warm young flesh, Madonna pounced. She grabbed Gwyneth and pushed her backward so that her spine was arched. Forced to surrender to her friend's will, Gwyneth gave way. Then, as the crowd roared its approval with applause and whistles, Madonna did what she has always done best: she defied expectations. She kissed Gwyneth full on the mouth, letting herself go, giving herself to Gwyneth Paltrow, giving herself to the moment, breathing life into it and then living it for all it was worth.

Joyously lost in Madonna's Moment, Gwyneth continued moving her body to the music, her face magnificent in its concentration as she returned the kiss. When Madonna finally released her, Gwyneth remained in motion on the table, now with a satisfied smile and never looking more alive, more beautiful. Onlookers continued applauding and stomping in time as they watched Gwyneth become one with the pounding, reverberating music. Her romantic problems, her concerns about this fellow or that one, had apparently been erased, completely eradicated by Madonna's Moment.

Madonna jumped off the table to watch as the perfect, pristine prototype of the new generation of blonde, sexy icon, the sweet and innocent and naive Gwyneth Paltrow, danced on a tabletop—having just been kissed by another woman. Who knows what Gwyneth was thinking, or how her own life would be informed by the moment, if at all. However, for Madonna, it had been just another act of complete and typical disregard for anyone else. If anything, it had been a kiss that demonstrated a wonderful permanence about her personality. Yes, she's changed. Yes, she's mellowed. But Kabbalah or no Kabbalah, at the core, she's still who she always was—a woman at her best when creating outrageous moments and then giving herself to them completely, and forcing everyone else to participate as well, like it or not.

As Gwyneth Paltrow continued her one-woman show on the table-top, lost in her own pleasure, Madonna nodded in approval, her eyes flashing. Then, she hollered out, raising her voice above the strident din and employing her best Austin Powers impression. "Yeah, baby," Madonna shouted out at her friend. *"Yeah, baby!"*

☦

Music

By the year 2000, Madonna had been a certified, card-carrying icon for almost two decades. In the universe of pop stardom, she'd truly done it all. Out of nowhere she came—not on the back of a celebrity mentor or as any famous person's protégée, but on her spunky, anonymous own—to make a single record that soon morphed into a catalog of international, multimillion sellers.

She'd done concert tours around the world, becoming a captivating performer in the process. She'd developed into both a capable songwriter and record producer. She appeared on film, on Broadway. She formed companies, generating millions of dollars for herself and her entertainment conglomerates, as well as the individuals surrounding her. She made at least one comeback of sorts, the Grammy Award–winning *Ray of Light*. By the onset of the twenty-first century, it would seem that Madonna the pop star had done it all as one of the most controversial as well as most emulated female performers in show business history. After proving herself in nearly every category she tackled, there was really only one goal to which a self-respecting pop star could now aspire: make another hit record.

Equally as challenging as attaining pop stardom is maintaining it, a fact to which any million-selling artist will attest. By the latter part of the twentieth century, Michael Jackson—the only other pop star in show business as commercially and artistically successful as Madonna—had seen his career slip significantly. Of course, like Madonna, if Jackson never made another recording or never stepped onto another stage, his legend as one of the greatest entertainers of all time would still be assured. Still, his inability to keep pace with the ever-changing, trend-driven world of pop music became embarrassingly apparent in the late 1990s with the release of *HIStory: Past, Present, and Future, Book I,* a two-disc set of new and previously released material. The CD's disappointing sales could not be salvaged, even by a manic, supercharged duet between the King of Pop and his sister Janet called "Scream." In recent years, Madonna's peers Prince and Janet had also seen their record sales slip, the CD sales of both superstars certainly not what they were in their salad days.

By the late nineties, and into 2000, Madonna, the aforementioned artists, the music industry at large and in fact the entire contemporary pop music world had been taken over by what will probably be a fleeting trend for "boy bands" and sexy, teenage female bubble-gum artists, the craze's front line of offense being the million-selling Backstreet Boys, N'Sync, Britney Spears and Christina Aguilera. Still, it wasn't as if Madonna's career was in the doldrums at the beginning of the new year. *Ray of Light* had sold millions of copies worldwide, the project having been hailed as bold and refreshing. However, some of Madonna's critics viewed *Light* as another calculated ruse on the part of the artist to exploit rave-inspired electronica music, which was mostly off mainstream pop's radar until Madonna got hold of it.

Madonna's detractors didn't understand that *Ray of Light* was actually where Madonna's personal tastes were at the time—she wasn't just exploiting a new sound; it was a sound she had studied and enjoyed. Being a mature pop star with a wide range of professional experiences has not diminished her appetite for adventurous new music. While she still loves listening to songs like "Singin' in the Rain" from classic Hollywood musicals in the personal confines of home and office, Madonna relishes the works of alternative artists and eclectic musicians practically unknown by the masses, such as Anoushka Shankar, daughter of Indian music legend Ravi Shankar.

One day while listening to the various demo tapes and other music that pours into the Maverick Records offices on a daily basis from both aspiring and established songwriters and producers, Madonna happened upon the tape of an album from writer/producer Mirwais Ahmadzai, who had earlier praised her musical abilities. Except for lovers of rave music, Mirwais (he rarely uses his last name) is practically a stranger to America's pop music fans. "I heard it and was just like, 'This is the sound of the future. I must meet this person,' Madonna would tell *Rolling Stone*. "So I did, and we hit it off. And that's exactly how it happened with [*Ray of Light* producer] William Orbit, too."

In a meeting hastily assembled by Guy Oseary, Madonna and Mirwais had such a rapport that Madonna decided that the "sound of the future" would also be the sound of her next album. Three weeks after shaking hands, she and producer were in the studio together; most of the music was recorded in London, beginning in September 1999. By the end of January 2000, the record was almost finished.

Madonna has always considered competition between her producers to be the way to get the best out of them, but William Orbit said he didn't have a problem with Mirwais being on the scene. In any case, neither producer would hear the result of the other's toil until the album's arduous mastering process in London.

Since William Orbit was already well aware of Madonna's idiosyncrasies in the studio, it was Mirwais who had to familiarize himself with the artist's creative working style. As much technician as musician, the Frenchman would endlessly tinker with the music tracks, adding effects and taking away others, layering some sounds and remixing others. Like many artists with a clear vision of what they want in the studio, Madonna has a tendency to be impatient, and Mirwais's tedious manner would often drive her to distraction. She recalled, "I just put my foot down and said, 'It's good enough now. We're done. We're done working on it.' He [Mirwais] could just sit there in front of his computer screen, changing, honing, editing, cutting, pasting—whatever. And it would never end. But life is too short for that sort of nonsense. My persona in the studio is, 'I'm in a hurry.' I think he was more put off by the fact that I knew what I wanted so clearly, and I wasn't interested in lots of embellishments when it came to the production."

"She took a big risk with someone like me," Mirwais told a reporter after the album was completed. "When you arrive at that kind of level of celebrity, you can just work in the mainstream and just stay there. Everything she does, for her is like a challenge, and I like this kind of personality."

When the work was done—accomplished between London, Los Angeles and New York—what would emerge was *Music,* a slick, orderless landscape of pop melodies and swirling electronic pop funk where Madonna's coy, often indifferent emotion is often the only living thing on the terrain. *Music,* for all its masterful gadgetry, would be nothing if not passionate. The final selections for inclusion on the CD would include "Impressive Instant," rife with abstract sounds and driving grooves designed to do just what the synthesized refrain suggests, put the listener in a trance, and "Amazing," a stylized, guitar-powered, uptempo Orbit collaboration that could have been the musical cousin to "Beautiful Stranger" (the song Madonna and Orbit had contributed to the *Austin Powers. The Spy Who Shagged Me* soundtrack). Also included would be "I Deserve It," a moody, acoustic guitar ballad obviously dedicated to Guy Ritchie ("This Guy was made for me," Madonna sings).

Of course, the project's flagship track would also be its first single and title song, "Music." The song is a shot of electronic funk-pop, a dance anthem that reaches into the future but which also slyly conjures up images and feelings for the good ol' days of disco (with its affectionate call out to "Mr. DJ," a relic of disco days gone by). It's a sparse, determined arrangement that quickly gets under one's skin.

Like the song's lyrics, its playful video would have a very simple storyline that ventures no deeper than three girls out on the town, looking for fun. The concept was inspired by real days gone by of the late seventies and early eighties, when young Madonna Ciccone and her friends Debi Mazar and Nikki Harris used to prowl Manhattan's eclectic club and art scene in search of music and romance. Originally, actresses were cast in the roles of Madonna's video entourage. However, when the women proved to be too pretty and stiff, a frustrated Madonna, in the middle of the shoot, got on the phone and asked Mazar and Haris to join her on the set.

Just as she plugged into the electronica scene for the music, for the video Madonna would shamelessly imitate the notion of "Ghetto Fabulous"—an over-the-top look popularized by East Coast rap and urban music stars like Sean "Puffy" Combs, Lil' Kim and Mary J. Blige and characterized by designer clothes and floor-length furs, gaudily accessorized with gold and diamonds (including in the teeth). When Puffy steps out of his Bentley dressed in this fashion, he's serious. In the "Music" clip, however, Madonna would wear her flash and gold with a playful wink. To give the video humor, cast as the zany limousine driver was British comedian Ali G, whose brash, irreverent ways amuse Madonna whenever she's in England. (Ali G hosted a television talk show in character, insulting politicians and other upstanding members of British public service.)

At the end of January 2000, Madonna had great hopes for *Music*. "I have to stay current," she concluded over lunch with two of her friends in Los Angeles where some of the songs were being finished. She looked stupendous in a chocolate brown Balenciaga jacket and Donna Karan trousers. Though her hair was pulled back and she wore large sunglasses, she still drew stares. While being served a tomato and mozzarella salad, she said, "God help me, but I guess I have to share radio air time with Britney Spears and Christina Aguilera." She shrugged her shoulders. "What choice do I have?"

"Well, you could always retire," one of her friends offered jokingly.

Madonna dabbed at her lips with a napkin. "But what would the music business be without me?" she asked with a laugh.

✝

ROCCO

In February 2000, Madonna finally confirmed what the tabloids had been declaring for months, that she was determined to have another baby. "I think Lola should have a brother or sister," she had said in an interview. "I think she's incredibly spoiled. She needs a bit of competition. But I would want to be in a stable relationship." Though Madonna stopped short at saying who she thought the father should be, she probably had Guy Ritchie in mind since, by all accounts, her love affair with the British filmmaker seemed to be the real thing.

A month later, when Matt Lauer of the *Today* show asked Madonna if she was pregnant, her answer was a definitive "no." But, then, less than three weeks later she and Guy Ritchie released a joint statement to the media: "We're happy to confirm rumors that we're expecting a child at the end of this year." Actually, Madonna knew she was pregnant when asked about it by Lauer, but didn't want to announce it to the world before she told the baby's father—and she didn't want to inform Guy until he had finished his work on *Snatch*.

Having a second child seemed like a natural progression in Madonna's life. She's proud of the way Lola is being raised—of course she employs a nanny (not a team of them, just one), but she prides herself on doing most of the work herself—and she was excited about the opportunity to double her efforts as a mother.

"The last thing I'm going to do is raise my children the way I see a lot of celebrities raising their children," Madonna has stated. "I don't want to traipse around with nannies and tutors. I think it's really important for children to stay in one place and to socialize with other children. I had that [in her childhood]. I'm not saying I don't want to go on tour or make movies anymore, but I realize I'm going to have to make a lot of compromises, and I'm comfortable with that."

For his part, Carlos Leon offered his congratulations to Madonna via an odd medium, the television tabloid show *Inside Edition*. "I want to wish her all the luck in the world," he said to the mother of his own child. He stroked his goatee reflectively. "I am thrilled for her," he said. "I hope she has a very healthy and happy baby who will be a wonderful brother or sister for Lourdes."

Her second pregnancy was, for Madonna, about as boring—and as uncomfortable—as the first, particularly during the last couple of months. Guy noted to one friend his amazement that Madonna had become so shy in the bedroom around the seventh month, always turning out the lights before undressing. Perhaps, like many expectant women, she simply did not feel attractive.

On August 10, just a couple of days after Gwyneth Paltrow hosted a baby shower for her, Madonna began to feel unwell. That morning, she and Gwyneth had a telephone conversation (Madonna later remembered) during which they laughed about the fact that Madonna had worn the same maternity clothes during the second pregnancy that she had worn for the first—"and I don't care what anyone thinks about it," she said. She spoke about being photographed in a burgundy Abe

Hamilton–designed sheath with a black lace overlay for a recent charity event, and not giving a second thought to the fact that she had been photographed in the same outfit a couple of years earlier. "I guess it's safe to say that fashion is no longer my greatest concern," she said (not in the same conversation with Gwyneth, but rather to a reporter, later).

Upon hanging up on Gwyneth Paltrow, Madonna then gave a radio interview over the telephone to Los Angeles disc jockey Rick Dees. While sitting at the breakfast table, she announced that her second baby would be a boy. She joked that she would name the child "Baby Jesus." She then attacked British hospitals as "old and Victorian," when asked if she would have the child in the United Kingdom. Qualifying her criticism, she said she did not like the thought of the complications caused by giving birth in a foreign country, adding: "I like efficiency." (In truth, Madonna is known as an Anglophile, having sung the praises of stout, a love of the English countryside and a desire to send Lourdes to a private school in the United Kingdom. "I'm having a love affair with England," she said recently. Her "love affair" was a surprise to some friends because, as recently as 1995, she apparently despised the United Kingdom so much she wouldn't even attend her good friend Juliette Hohnen's wedding there.)

Having finished on the telephone, she paced restlessly before going to bed, complaining of feeling nauseous. That night, Guy Ritchie attended a private screening of his film *Snatch*. At nine P.M., Madonna called him on his mobile to tell him that she was having trouble and was going to the hospital. News reports had it that Ritchie rushed home to pick up his girlfriend and then rushed her to the hospital, carrying her into the emergency ward crying out, "Save our baby! Save our baby!" Actually, Madonna was already at the hospital when he got there, "though he likes to think he carried me inside," she has said. (She was driven to the hospital by an employee.) Months earlier, Madonna had been diagnosed with placenta previa, a condition in which the placenta covers the birth canal, causing the mother to hemorrhage and the baby's blood supply to be cut off. A cesarean was necessary, but not as the emergency procedure also reported in the press. She had made arrangements weeks earlier to have the baby by C-section, just not two weeks before her original due date.

Madonna was placed in a room just across the hall from where

Catherine Zeta-Jones had, a few days earlier, given birth to actor Michael Douglas's baby. Specialists then began monitoring her as carefully as the baby, hoping that perhaps she would be able to carry to full term. Unfortunately, like Lourdes's, the new baby's birth would not be an easy one. As she was wheeled into the delivery room, a sedated and most certainly scared Madonna was overheard telling Guy Ritchie, "Baby, I love you. We're all going to be okay." By this time, Madonna had lost a great deal of blood; she was actually hemorrhaging faster than the transfusions could replace the blood and was close to slipping into shock. The baby was born at one A.M. on August 11, about three hours after she entered the hospital, weighing in at a substantial five pounds, nine ounces. (By comparison, Lourdes, who was carried to term, checked in at exactly a pound heavier.)

Guy sat by the frightened Madonna's side, holding her hand and comforting her throughout the difficult surgery. They called the boy Rocco, a name which, it could be argued, has the requisite Italian ring but certainly also reflects Ritchie's strong cinematic interest in names associated with organized crime. Considering that there was speculation in the press that the writer-director might want to name his son Vinnie or Anthony ("Ant-ny," as he might pronounce it), Rocco perhaps represents a compromise.

Immediately after his birth, stories began to circulate that the baby might be brain damaged. Luckily, most of these reports were not heard by Madonna, who was sheltered from all such inaccurate speculation by the protective Guy Ritchie. In fact, because of his premature arrival, Rocco suffered a slight case of jaundice, which is normal in such births. Because his lungs were also not fully developed, he was placed in intensive care.

By August 15, despite statements from Liz Rosenberg to the contrary, little Rocco was still in the hospital and not scheduled to leave for another few days. Rosenberg had said the child was already home with Madonna, but she was fibbing, probably in order to protect mother and child from the media storm. Guy would visit Rocco in the mornings and early afternoons, while Madonna rested at home. Then, Madonna would quietly visit her son in Los Angeles's Cedars-Sinai Hospital each day, arriving at about five-thirty P.M. and staying for four hours of feeding and cuddling. At all times, the security around the child was intense, with at least four guards assigned to his suite of rooms, plus private nurses. When Madonna visited, she arrived with a couple more guards of her own.

When the baby was finally released from the hospital on August 16, 2000, five days after his birth and, also, on Madonna's forty-second birthday, his contented and relieved mother took him to her Los Feliz home. (The estate was up for sale at this time for $4.2 million; Madonna had just bought Diane Keaton's 1920s hilltop Spanish-style estate in Beverly Hills for $6.5 million and was in the process of a $1-million renovation program.) She went into her bedroom, sat down with a breast pump and her new infant—then she noticed a paper bag on the table. She looked inside and found a box. It held a diamond ring from Guy, who had been so wonderful to her throughout the pregnancy (he even gave up drinking during those months, just so that she wouldn't be tempted). In an accompanying note, Guy told her how much she meant to him, and how proud he was of her and their son. "This is nothing compared to the big present I will soon be giving you," he wrote. (Madonna would insist that this was her first diamond ring. Perhaps because she gave back Warren Beatty's, she doesn't count that one. When she married Sean, she had a simple gold ring.)

Later, the good friends Madonna usually entertains at her home ("an eclectic infrastructure of friends—writers, painters, poets, art dealers and jewelry designers")—naturally came by to meet the new addition to the family. Little Rocco—who resembles his father more than he does his mother—was curled up in his bassinet, sucking his thumb and nodding off, a teddy bear quilt tucked around his legs. "Why, he's just so perfect," gushed Gwyneth Paltrow, one of five visitors clustered in the nursery.

For her guests, Madonna had combed her shoulder-length honey blonde hair back from her face. She wore embroidered and patterned blue slacks and a simple white tank top underneath a short-sleeved T-shirt. Manolo Blahnik slingbacks with three-inch heels added a touch of cool, uncontrived elegance. ("Better than sex," she says of Blahnik's shoes—she missed high heels while pregnant—"and they last longer.") Cartier earrings were another nice, unusual touch. Her skin seemed translucent. There was one word to describe her: wholesome.

"He is perfect, isn't he?" she said, gazing down at her infant son with loving eyes. At that moment, Lourdes ran into the room with a baby bottle. "Here, Mommy," she said, holding it up to her mother. "For him," she added, motioning to her brother. Madonna swooped Lola into her arms and held her, tightly. "Not yet," she said, her voice a low and soothing whisper. "But soon."

"It was a feeling of such tranquility," said another of Madonna's guests. "Lola then started sucking furiously on the bottle. 'You're a big girl now,' M said as she gently took the bottle away. 'Let's go downstairs and get some juice.' Then she, Gwyneth, Lola and the rest of us tiptoed out of the room. We went into the kitchen and drank beer and ate Doritos. Doritos! I remember when she would never eat junk food, ever."

Later, when just a few guests remained, Madonna slipped out of her clothes and wrapped herself in a soft white robe. After joining her guests in the spacious, sun-drenched living room with the Diego Rivera oil painting over the fireplace, she sank into a couch, her infant curled in her lap. "I thought, 'My, my Here's a Madonna the public doesn't know, a relaxed, freer Madonna,'" said her guest. "A Madonna that maybe she, herself, didn't know until recently." (Or, as her brother Christopher said while watching Madonna as she breast-fed Lourdes, "I don't believe it. I'm looking at it, I'm watching it. And, still, I don't believe it.")

"Have you managed a routine with him yet?" one of Madonna's friends asked.

"We feed him at about ten thirty, before we go to bed," Madonna said, sounding more like a mother than anyone who ever knew her would have believed. "Then, he gets one feed in between two and three. Then, maybe again between six and seven. He's a good baby," Madonna said proudly. "He only cries when he wants something, and why shouldn't he? Guy and I agree that he should get exactly what he wants. Lord knows I always have . . ."

Says Debi Mazar, who later gave little Rocco his first hair trim ("and if you cut him, I'll fucking kill you," warned his mother), "She's in good shape, and she seems really in love—they [Madonna and Guy] seem to get along wonderfully. I don't want to say she's in a new place, because I hate it when people put her in a little box and say, 'Madonna does this new record, and everything is so different and light and new! She must be in a great head!' I mean, any day she could be in a good head or a bad head. But she is really happy and beautiful now, and seems very much in love."

"Madonna first fell in love with her daughter, and that taught her how to fall in love for real," says Rosie O'Donnell. "When you're ready, it comes to you. She's definitely ready. I've never seen her happier . . . more grounded, more able to leave the star part behind."

✝

Happy Endings

Perhaps no one is as proud of the way Madonna has turned out as her father, Tony Ciccone. While he didn't support her dream to be a dancer and had hoped she would go to college before beginning her career, he fully understood her wanting to, as he now puts it, "make something of herself, which she did—boy, did she ever!"

When Rocco was born sickly and prematurely, it was Tony who, by telephone from his northern Michigan vineyard, suggested that his daughter summon a priest to administer the last rites. Though Madonna is ambivalent about such sacraments, it's a testament to the respect she feels for her traditional Italian-American father that she even considered the notion of last rites for little Rocco. As it happened, such a sacrament would not be necessary. When it was determined that the baby would be fine, Tony and his wife, Joan, tearfully collapsed into each other's arms—and then toasted with a fine wine the new addition to the family, Tony's eighth grandchild. "Sometimes I think I'm better as a grandfather than I probably was as a father," he now says. "But, let's face it, Madonna was a special case," he adds. "I think anyone would sympathize with the father who had the job of raising Madonna."

The day after Rocco's birth, Tony Ciccone continued his hard labor on the structure of the Ciccone Vineyards and Winery, a vineyard which would open to the public a month later on a hilltop between the Grand Traverse Bay resort town of Sutton Bay and the hills of the Leelanau Peninsula. Tony founded his winery in 1994 after retiring from his job as a physicist and engineer at General Dynamics in Detroit. It is dedicated to his parents, Gaetano and Michelina, who immigrated from Pacentro, Italy, to the United States three years before he was born. The Ciccone Vineyards has been a joint project for Tony and his wife, Joan, the stepmother with whom Madonna never got along as a youngster but to whom she is now—thirty-three years later—quite close.

"It's our life together," he proudly says of the winery, one of twenty-five in the state of Michigan, "mine and my wife's. We have Pinot Grigio, Dolcetto, Cabernet Franc and Chardonnay planted here. I think it keeps me and Joan close, even at this old age we're in," he says of the winery. "We raised vegetables in Rochester [Michigan] before owning the winery," he adds. "My father was a vegetable farmer, too. Good, solid work. The Ciccones have always been solid workers."

It was about ten years ago, Tony explains, when he first began cultivating grapes. As a surprise gift, Joan purchased an antique grape press for him. "He always wanted a winery," she recalls. "It was his dream. We knew it would be hard work. But when the Sutton Bay property went up for sale, we also knew we had to buy it." (The Ciccones will not say if Madonna contributed to the purchasing of the fifteen-acre property.)

Most of his neighbors are not even aware that Madonna is Tony's daughter. "I don't advertise it," he says. "It's not necessary. If they find out, they find out. I don't tell them. Some know. But they don't make a big deal out of it."

Today, as an adult and a parent, Madonna seems to understand that Tony was doing his genuine best at the time he was raising her, and that his marrying Joan was not a betrayal of his first wife but his only alternative if he was to move on with his life—and give his children a mother.

Certainly, it can be argued that nothing matures a person more than becoming a parent. It seems that Madonna was now identifying with the parent role and not so much the child role, thereby putting her on the other side of the table for the first time. Perhaps she was finally able to see that she needed her father more than she needed her anger, and so she was finally able to give up some of that anger. Indeed, seeing things through a parent's eyes was, for Madonna, a hopeful sign—it would allow for significant changes in her relationship with her father.

"I love my father," she now says. "He is a say-what-you-mean-and-mean-what-you-say kind of guy. I'm the same way. Anyone who knows me knows that I *am* my father, at least in that way. He's strict, like me. Loving, too, I hope like me. His work ethic is ingrained in me. Now that I have a family, I have so much respect for him and the way he tried to hold ours together, back when I was a bratty little kid. He didn't have the privileges I have, either. It's hard to see all of that until you have children."

Some of Madonna's siblings have not fared as well as she has in life, perhaps in some ways underscoring the difference in her personality and in her determination to meet the challenges of her circumstances. She has blamed the instability of the Ciccone children on the death of her mother. "I have a very large family who are all emotional cripples in one way or another. Emotionally, we're all pretty needy because of my mother." Whereas some of her siblings may have allowed the trauma they felt over their mother's death to jeopardize their futures, Madonna somehow managed to put hers to work to enhance her life.

Madonna is closest to younger brother Christopher, who accompanied her on a number of concert tours before establishing his own restaurant. Out of her seven siblings, Christopher is the most loyal to her, despite some acrimony that resulted when, in 1991, she discussed his homosexuality with a gay magazine without his permission. Christopher has since traveled with his sister, working with her as artistic director on her concert tours. (People in her employ used to refer to him as "the pope" because of his powerful position in the organization.) He has also designed the interior of some of her homes. "She has her own vision," he explains. "I offer her a different way of looking at things. Other people do, too. But it's different with us. We fight a lot, and either she wins or I win, but we don't let up. Neither of us is afraid to be direct, and Madonna has always known what she wants."

An enterprising businessman, as well as owning the restaurant Orient in New York, he also has an interest in the popular restaurant Atlantic, in Los Angeles, which Madonna frequents. He says, "Our father spent most of his time preparing us for the rest of our lives. Things I learned from him were honesty, loyalty and the value of truth. He taught us discipline. We went to church every day. Our sense of art, drama—and decadence—all that came from him."

While Madonna is close to Christopher, she remains estranged from two other brothers. Martin is a recovering alcoholic who has suffered significant instability in his life and career. He's worked as a disc jockey in the Detroit area and has also been employed as a building contractor. In the early nineties, during Madonna's "Blonde Ambition" tour, Martin had a well-publicized setback in his recovery just a day after being released from a rehabilitation center (paid for by his famous sister). Perhaps somewhat unfairly, he is seen in his sister's *Truth or Dare* video apparently incoherent and irresponsible, and either too inebriated or too disoriented to attend her concert and visit her afterward. The way the scenes are framed, it is as if Madonna is let down by his behavior—making her the victim, as opposed to the more sympathetic notion that the troubled, heavily scrutinized Martin may be a victim of Madonna's celebrity. After his third arrest for drunk driving and a warning from the judge that he could be jailed, Madonna lost patience with Martin. In 1994, he told a U.S. newspaper: "Madonna won't lift a finger to help me." The two have not been particularly close since that time. "This is not the sister I grew up with, who mothered me, who was so full of compassion," he says. "I guess fame really changes people." (In December 2000, Martin was a patient at the Chabad Rehabilitation Center in Los Angeles, being treated for an addiction.)

Of Martin, Madonna has countered: "He's very tortured. I've had to get him out of the habit of calling me whenever he needed something from me. I have to feel that Martin loves me for just me and not my money."

Her half-brother, Mario, is a former cocaine addict who has also had a number of problems in life. At one point, he faced a ten-year prison sentence on a burglary charge. His salvation came only after Madonna hired a high-powered legal team to defend him on charges that he had broken into a florist's in Rochester, Michigan, and absconded with about $2,000. At the time, he was already on parole with a three-month suspended jail sentence for allegedly assaulting his then girlfriend. It had been his third conviction in six months, after he also allegedly battered a motorist and fractured a police officer's nose. "My big sister can't tame me," he has said. "I am what I am and she has no right to lecture me. I don't even like her music."

Of Madonna's other siblings, Anthony and Paula are both television producers, and Melanie is a musicians' manager in Los Angeles. Madonna has a cordial, yet distant relationship with her half-siblings Jennifer and Mario.

"We've had a hard time, but the family tries to stay strong," says Tony. "They grow up. They lead their own lives. I lead mine.

"Nonnie has said things about me in the past, probably all true," observes Tony, reverting to the affectionate diminutive of his daughter's childhood. "So maybe I wasn't the greatest father in the world, but life wasn't easy for any of us." He says that he has never felt a need to address anything Madonna or any of his other children have ever said about him, "Because we're Italian-Americans. In our hearts, we know that we love each other. That is all that matters. Sometimes you can't be close. But life is long and there is always another day.

"But, Madonna and I have been closer than people know," he concludes. "There's a peacefulness about her now that she has Lourdes and Rocco to look after. Why, look at how things have changed for her," he marvels. "If you were writing a book, this is how it would end. It would have a happy ending. Everyone loves a happy ending . . ."

✝

Taking Stock

"In the beginning of my career, I just did whatever I wanted to do and if it made me feel good, if it was fun, that was cool," Madonna observed in a recent interview. "Now, I feel like everything we do affects society in a potent way. I feel a sense of responsibility because my consciousness has been raised."

She wanted nothing more than to be famous . . . she worked hard at it by being creative, imaginative and, also, by keeping her public guessing. She was a veritable workhorse. The twenty-five-year-old woman who once told Dick Clark (in her January 1984 TV debut on *American Bandstand*) that her goal was to "rule the world" has, in the intervening years, acquired more money, fame and power than most people could imagine possible in a single lifetime. What she has is real, hard earned and clearly her own. In a business where success is entirely dependent on ever-shifting pop trends and the fickle taste of the public, Madonna is nothing if not still competitive. Her survival instincts are as finely tuned as a bat's sonar. As a result, she remains a chart-topping recording artist into her forties; she has sold more than 100 million records. An October 2000 *Rolling Stone* cover story estimated her worth at more than $600 million.

Madonna's "Music" single, to no one's surprise, made its way to

Number 1 in September 2000, after six weeks on *Billboard*'s singles chart. The hit record proved, once again, that unlike many of her peers, Madonna is able to bend to her will the concept of what is supposed to happen to familiar pop stars. She continues to make contemporary music that rocks the world, and does so despite the stronghold of alternative music, boy bands and successful Madonna-wannabes, many of whom have styled their careers after that of the original "Material Girl."

At the end of September 2000, Madonna celebrated the release of her new album *Music* with a party meticulously designed to connect the new, serene Madonna of the new millennium with the original, party Madonna of the 1980s. To do this, the star's camp took over Catch One, a funky, ramshackle, notorious black gay club near Los Angeles's ethnic south-central community.

On a regular night, Catch One hosts an urban cross section of drag queens, closet gays, trendy "Ghetto Fabulous" and a small battalion of uptown whites, who come to behold Los Angeles's black gay culture and dance all night to techno-funk music on the huge dance floor. On Tuesday, September 19, the club hosted perhaps its strangest crowd ever—six hundred people referred to by syndicated newspaper columnist Liz Smith as Madonna's "closest friends." Party co-hosts Warner Bros. and the celebrity magazine *US Weekly* paid a reported two million dollars to transform the normally gritty Catch One into a temporary haven for the Beautiful People, an A-list crowd spiced with an assortment of strippers and exotic dancers, all in the tradition of the Madonna experience of days gone by—those days almost fifteen years earlier when the young star generated all the energy at Catch One whenever she walked through its front doors, when she beckoned her allergy-prone, older boyfriend, Warren Beatty—her "Pussy Man"— to join her on Catch's dance floor: "Let's have fun!"

But these weren't the old days, and Madonna—who wore her honey-blonde hair straight and parted in the middle, and boasted a black T-shirt promoting Guy Ritchie's latest movie, *Snatch*—was no longer a gum-chewing, profanity-spewing party girl. While she did mingle with the famous guests, she spent most of her time off the dance floor with a small circle of friends and associates in a so-called VIP room. She left early, after only ninety minutes. It had been her first night away from Rocco since she'd brought him home from the hospital a month earlier, and she wanted to get back home to breast-feed him. Her career was on autopilot, anyway: *Music* would debut at Number 1—in fifteen countries, including the United States.

The morning after the party for *Music* was a morning like any other at Madonna's Mediterranean-style Los Feliz home.*

In order to keep tabs on the day-to-day operations of her companies, including Maverick Records, Madonna's residences are equipped with fax machines and multiple phone lines. Each morning, when she's not on the road, she makes a list of goals to accomplish that day, and also lists tasks for her two assistants and other associates. From eight to nine A.M., she answers and sends E-mail on her computer. From nine to eleven, she makes business calls to attorneys, agents and to her spokeswoman and dedicated and able publicist of eighteen years, Liz Rosenberg (whom Madonna's friends refer to as "The Validator"—the one who separates truth from rumor, or at least does her job well by protecting Madonna from negative publicity).

"My job is more casual than people might think," says Rosenberg. "Madonna does not wake up in the morning and plan her media campaign, nor do I. We don't think, 'Who are we going to fuck over today?' There's no master plan, no army of press agents and tanks."

If he's not similarly busy with his own career, Guy will often be found in the kitchen helping the cook prepare breakfast. (He's an excellent chef, whereas Madonna says she doesn't "have the cooking gene. I don't want to go into the kitchen and do things. I want to go into the kitchen and be served.") She keeps a maddeningly detailed daily planner. "If she wants me to look into ten things, and I'm only able to look into nine, she remembers the one thing I forgot," says Liz Rosenberg. "She isn't big on wasting time." The rest of the day is devoted to rehearsals, recording sessions and interviews. Intermittently, she somehow makes quality time for her two children—each of whom has their own nanny. (She also has an army of assistants helping her at home and in her Maverick office.)

* When this was written Madonna had four homes: the Spanish-style home she bought from Diane Keaton in the summer of 2000, into which she had just moved; a Central Park West apartment; a waterfront mansion in Miami; and a home in Chelsea in London. When in London, she and Guy Ritchie live in a rented house in Notting Hill Gate. However, Madonna's Los Feliz home was sold recently to television actress Jenna Elfman, and her homes in Miami and London are up for sale.

Maybe as a result of meditation and yoga—or is it that she's just grown up?—Madonna now projects the glow of someone who has come to terms not only with herself but also, possibly, with the death of her mother, and with her father's enduring place in her life. In recent appearances, her hazel eyes seem to flash with a new knowledge, a sense of triumph, maybe. "I came to the realization that I didn't really know that much at all," she said when analyzing the onset of her personal journey into metaphysics. "I started asking myself the most elementary questions: 'What's really important about life? Why am I here?' "

Perhaps what's most intriguing about the way Madonna has evolved is that, at least based on her now-conservative demeanor, she seems to believe that true sensuality—true female sexual power—derives not from exhibitionism but from its opposite, from peaceful elegance and calm detachment. Today, she handles her life and loves with greater dignity than before   though, of course, there will probably always be the occasional tabletop dance and public kiss with someone like Gwyneth Paltrow just to keep her life—and ours—entertaining. Now, her image is polished—not trashy. Her clothes tease without screaming and are by Versace, Dolce & Gabbana, Oscar de la Renta and Gianfranco Ferré (most of her clothes are given to her complimentarily because of the exposure she gives their designers). She's sexy and modern, truly her own person, more tolerant of others and—surprise!—even bashful at times. Most telling to some observers was the way she shrieked when, at the New York premiere party for *The Next Best Thing* at the Saci Club in Manhattan, she was asked if Guy Ritchie—on her arm—had ever seen her sexual and masochistic film *Body of Evidence*. Visibly blushing, she exclaimed, "He never did, and he never will, thank you very much."

"I've been incredibly petulant, incredibly self-indulgent, incredibly naive," she recently observed. "But I needed to do all of those things to get where I am now, and where I am now I'm happy with. I don't have any regrets, even though there are moments when I go, 'Oh, God, I can't believe I said or did that.' But you know what? I love that person too. She brought me here."

More growth on her part? Or just more media manipulation?

Only time will tell if Madonna is sincere in her spiritual pursuits and personal evolution. However, one can't help but hope that what she now projects is who Madonna Louise Veronica Ciccone really is, that the serene persona of this mother of two is the result of years of work on herself . . . and not just another interesting and transitional personality. If so, then maybe her real life—and not one just tied to some show-business fantasy, hers or ours—has only just begun.

By winter 2000, the media continued to speculate as to whether or not Madonna would marry Guy Ritchie, especially when she was seen wearing the diamond ring he had given her after Rocco's birth. In fact, the two had secretly decided to marry by the end of the year.

As much as he seems to love her, some of his friends felt there could be trouble if the proud Guy Ritchie was forced to tolerate the indignities that often go along with being in a relationship with Madonna, especially given his temperament. For instance, at the party at Catch One celebrating the release of *Music,* he became involved in a confrontation with a wide-bodied security guard who refused to grant him access to a VIP section of the club.

"But I'm Guy Ritchie," protested the writer-director. Wearing a tank-top shirt with the word "Music" emblazoned on it, Guy's impressive biceps were on display. His hair was cut short and dyed a light shade of blond. He wore a small diamond earring. In the background, the music was loud, pumping . . . and annoying. Ever-moving lights in every color of the rainbow bathed the scene. An irritating, thumping cacophony, which was actually "Impressive Instant" from Madonna's *Music* CD, could be heard in the background.

"I don't care if you're *Lionel* Richie," said the uniformed guard over the din. He wore a headset so that he could take orders. "Your name isn't on the list," he declared, chewing on an ice cube. "Not on the list, you don't get in. That's the way it goes."

"Step aside," warned Guy. As he tried to force his way past the guard, a camera's flash went off. He stopped, turned his head and scowled at the photographer.

Perhaps noticing that he was distracted, the guard put one hand on Guy's massive chest and pushed.

Guy whipped his neck around to face the guard, an incredulous expression on his face. He seemed amazed—and indignant—that the guard would dare touch him. "What, are you kidding me?" he asked in disbelief, his voice angry, his brown eyes threatening. "Are you mad?" It was as if he had taken a page out of the "Sean Penn Handbook of Social Behavior."

For a few tense moments, the two studied each other with severe expressions—their eyes inches apart—like playground adversaries about to rumble. The veins in Guy's neck were standing out. Luckily, one of Madonna's functionaries arrived on the scene. "I felt a spasm of alarm," she later recalled, "when I saw that Guy's jaw was clenched." Taking quick stock of the situation, she grabbed Guy by the arm and escorted him to the reserved area where Madonna was with friends. As Guy walked toward his girlfriend, she was laughing gaily, oblivious to what had just occurred. He whispered something in her ear and, apparently in reaction, she looked in the direction of the offending security guard and gave a disapproving frown. Just then, someone else said something to her. She tossed her blonde hair, flashed a gleaming smile and began laughing again, relaxed, chatty. Guy, standing at her side with his hands in his pockets, looked dour.

"We're better when it's just the two of us, and not all of the fans, groupies and press," Guy told a reporter after the confrontation at Catch One. Madonna, as usual, was surrounded by her coterie of enthusiasts as Guy spoke to the newsman. "When it's just me and the missus," he observed, motioning toward Madonna, "that's when it's good. This? This isn't good."

By Guy Ritchie's definition, it was "good" a month prior to the *Music* party when he took "the missus" to dinner at the Palm restaurant in Hollywood. The couple were there to celebrate Rocco's release from the hospital a day earlier. The best table had immediately been theirs, of course, as it was in every place they ever ate. As Madonna sat next to— not across from—Guy, she was constantly greeted by people who knew her, thought they knew her or wanted to know her. She took the intrusions good-naturedly, apparently happy to be out in public. Long hair with blonde streaks framed a face that seemed worry-free, content. Her skin held the translucence of youth. Her breasts were partly exposed by the cut of a daring, crimson-colored dress—she was still Madonna, after all.

An iced bowl of caviar, plates of smoked salmon and cold chicken, and a silver basket of fruit were displayed on the table.

Though talking to the waiter, who had inquired about the health of her child, she didn't seem to mind revealing herself in an emotional, honest manner. "My life is perfect now," Madonna said. "If I never do another thing again, at least I'll know I've done this."

"Hear, hear," Guy said, smiling broadly. He raised a glass of champagne in Madonna's direction. Giving her an admiring stare over the rim, he added, "Here's to a new life."

✝

Epilogue: The Wedding to Guy Ritchie

Publicity, or no publicity? For Madonna, if the choice had to be made, it had always been in favor of the former, and plenty of it—as long as it was on her terms. However, that was to change when it came time to plan her two-million-dollar wedding to Guy Ritchie.

As the consort of an internationally acclaimed superstar, Guy Ritchie has endured press coverage that he hasn't been particularly happy about, and treatment by reporters that has, in his view, sometimes bordered on the disrespectful. For her part, Madonna never stops complaining about the media's intrusion in her life. It's been her mantra for years: "I hate the press. I hate the press." With the passing of time, not much has changed in that regard: as much as she loves the attention, that's how much she says she hates it.

It was Guy's decision, then—and not Madonna's—that there would be no attendant publicity to their upcoming marriage ceremony. All of it—the nuptials, the reception, the parties—would be planned and conducted with an eye towards complete privacy, absolute secrecy. Madonna didn't seem to care one way or the other about the matter. If she had to deal with the press on her special day, she would do it. Certainly her staff was equipped with the means to keep it all under control. However, Guy felt strongly that their wedding shouldn't be made into a public spectacle, and so that was the way it was going to be. It's fortunate that Madonna so appreciates a man who can take charge, for that is certainly what she got in Guy Ritchie.

Two friends of the couple report witnessing a conversation between Madonna and Guy at Kensington Place restaurant in West London two-and-a-half months before the wedding, an exchange that, perhaps, betrayed some pre-ceremonial jitters on Madonna's part.

"I just don't think there should be any press at all about any of it,"

Guy told his fiancée. "I want it to be quiet, and private, don't you agree?"

"Well, look, if that's how you feel then we should just run off to Las Vegas and elope," Madonna declared, according to the witnesses. Even though she was indoors, she wore a knee-length, snake-skin coat (dyed red), because she felt chilled. "I guarantee you, though, it will be a circus . . . a zoo," she continued, "so don't kid yourself."

"Why do you say that?" Guy wondered.

"Because everything I do is a fucking circus," Madonna answered, snapping at him. "Or haven't you noticed? Christ! Haven't you seen the parade that passes by whenever I walk out of the house?"

"Just let me handle it," Guy said. He paid no attention to her tone, perhaps accustomed to it by this time. "As long as we agree: no media and no tricks. And you know what I mean, Madonna," he concluded, pointing a parental finger at her.

Madonna sighed heavily. "Look, I couldn't care less," she said, visibly irritated. Perhaps she was annoyed at the suggestion that she would purposely invite press attention to their wedding. Or, maybe she was just coming down with a cold; she didn't seem particularly well. She had complained earlier of having "the worst headache, ever since we started talking about this wedding." Finally, she said, "I just don't want the stress of trying to control it all. So, go for it," she concluded. "Knock yourself out, Guy."

In the end, though she didn't admit it at the time, Madonna was vastly relieved to know that Guy was handling matters concerning the media. To Madonna, controlling the press's interest in her every move had always been a chore. However, to the easygoing, sports-loving Guy Ritchie, it was nothing more than a matter of gamesmanship. The way he figured it, if a photographer managed to sneak into the wedding and shoot a role of film, Guy would lose the game. It wouldn't be the end of the world, though, because, after all, it *was* only a game. "However, I don't like to lose," he cautioned one confidante. "So, I can tell you right now, there'll be no press coverage of the wedding. We'll have to find a place that's so out of the way, no one will have access to it."

It was Guy's friend, Vinnie Jones, who suggested the "out-of-the way" Skibo Castle in Scotland for the ceremony. It's been said that Andrew Carnegie once described his Highland castle—now the home of the private Carnegie Club, a residential sporting club—as "heaven on earth." As the story goes, the Scottish-born iron-and-steel tycoon and philanthropist Carnegie left his native land at the age of thirteen to make his fortune in America. He returned one of the richest and most successful men of his generation. His search for a Highland home led him to the lush grounds and crumbling estate of Skibo, which he bought in 1898. After spending two million pounds—a phenomenal amount at that time—to rebuild the castle, he had made it into one of the world's great residences, home base for his social life and philanthropic endeavors. At Skibo, Andrew Carnegie entertained such luminaries as King Edward VII, the Rockefellers, Rudyard Kipling, Edward Elgar, Paderewski, Lloyd George and Helen Keller. In 1990, British entrepreneur Peter de Savary purchased the estate for six million pounds, and then opened it as a private club.

Today, the fully restored twenty rooms of Skibo Castle and the twelve private lodges on the grounds, provide a stately hideaway for the privileged and wealthy. The estate's beauty—perched on rolling hills overlooking Dornoch, Firth—is of such magnitude and stunning clarity that it generates an emotional experience when merely looking at photographs of it, let alone actually experiencing it firsthand. The club also has a reputation for extreme discretion, especially after hosting the near-secret marriage of publicity-shy movie star Robert Carlyle. Regular guests include Jack Nicholson, Michael Douglas and Sean Connery.

When he went to Scotland to scout out this playground for the rich and famous, Guy felt that it was the ideal site for his wedding to Madonna. He wanted a spectacular affair, partly because he wanted to impress his—and her—friends and family, partly because he felt that Madonna deserved it and also because he knew that they could well afford it. At first, when shown a brochure of Skibo Castle, Madonna thought that the location was too isolated and, as she put it, "it sounds scary, like something out of a Dracula movie."

"Oh, you'll change your mind about that," Guy said, knowingly. "Trust me."

"She did a lot of acquiescing to Guy," said a friend of Madonna's who would speak only if guaranteed anonymity. "She wanted a nice ceremony, obviously, but leaned towards having it in Beverly Hills. She didn't want her friends to have to fly all the way to Scotland. But she made a decision to let Guy do it his way. She told me, 'Look, I and my staff manipulate everything that happens in my world. I don't want Guy to feel that he's in for that kind of life. So, let him have it his way. I'm cool with it. Honest to God,' she said, 'I just want to get the whole goddamn thing over with.'

"With the two kids, the promotion of the new CD [*Music*], the planning of music videos and other career moves," says her friend, "she was always feeling completely exhausted, headachy and irritable . . . not in the mood to plan a wedding, and definitely sleep-deprived because of Rocco."

Madonna told her friend that she would "just as soon get married in my living room in Los Angeles wearing a nice tube top and some embroidered jeans. But," she she went on, "if I have to put on a big show, I guess I can do it. I haven't done a tour in a long time," she joked, "so I have enough energy for a good show."

She only had one concern: that Rocco's baptism—which she had promised her father would take place before the wedding—would be memorable. "That was her only real interest," said her friend. "Not the wedding, but the baptism," which she wanted to have at nearby thirteenth-century Dornoch Cathedral in north Scotland, about five miles north of Skibo.

When it came to the question of security, and how much of it there would be, Guy considered Madonna's first wedding in 1985 to Sean Penn in Malibu, California. Though it is widely believed that she had actually orchestrated much of the public drama and excitement that surrounded that ceremony, Madonna has never stopped complaining about it—to Guy, to friends, to the press and to anyone else who would listen. Because he hadn't been there, Guy really didn't know to what degree the madness had been manipulated by his "missus"—though, knowing her so well, he probably suspected some involvement on her part—and how much of it was truly an unwanted intrusion. So, to be safe—and maybe to ensure that he would not have to hear her grouse about her second wedding—Ritchie hired a security force of seventy professionals from Rock Steady, a well-respected private firm, in an effort to guarantee the security of this second ceremony.

With plans nearly finalized, Guy went on to book all fifty-one bedrooms on the 7,500-acre Skibo Castle grounds for five nights. However, there would be certain rules. Guests would not be permitted to come and go at will, and would only be allowed to leave the castle for Rocco's baptism at the nearby cathedral. They would be carefully monitored at all times, "for your safety and ours," Guy explained to one of his more sceptical invitees. There would be no televisions or radios in any of the rooms. Mobile phones had to be turned off. In effect, contact with the outside world would be all but denied the guests for the entire duration of their stay, five days. Of course, for some of Madonna's celebrity friends who always seem somewhat annoyed by having to live in the real world with real people, the thought of this sort of isolation was pure and perfect nirvana. For many of Guy's pals, however, it was a preposterous proposition. "I do think he's been hanging round the missus too much," said one, snickering.

Guy's guest list would be limited, anyway, since Madonna had stipulated that invitations be extended only to wives of male guests, or to girlfriends who were familiar to her. She didn't want her fiancé's single and unruly buddies bringing strippers or other women of questionable professions to the castle for a good time.

"Look, it's going to be brilliant," Guy promised one friend who balked at the amount of time he would have to spend at the castle accompanied by a woman with whom he was about to end a relationship, but who Madonna insisted he bring along anyway. "It's a special place. You have to experience it. It's the good life, and it'll be good for you. And, anyway," Guy concluded, "what the fuck? Why not join me and the missus for some fun, eh?"

*

On December 5, 2000, Madonna and Guy set off from their London home for Scotland to sign certain legal papers related to the forthcoming union, and to make the final arrangements. After the private jet (carrying the couple, two bodyguards and a personal assistant), touched down at Inverness airport at 11:30 A.M., it was met on the tarmac by two Range Rovers, provided by the Carnegie Club.

As flashbulbs popped all around her from the waiting and excited media, a glowing Madonna descended from the plane wearing dark glasses, a tartan coat and embroidered jeans. Guy followed, casual in a jacket and jeans. After quick smiles and a few waving gestures, the couple retreated into their Range Rover, and took off.

Before viewing the castle, Madonna had decided that she first wanted to see Dornoch Cathedral. So, fifteen minutes after landing, her small entourage began the drive to Dornoch.

The cathedral was founded in 1224 by St. Gilbert de Moravia, then bishop of the diocese. It boasts a magnificent stained-glass window, unveiled in his memory by Prince Charles in 1989. While small compared with most cathedrals, it dominates the surrounding buildings in the ancient royal borough. As soon as Madonna walked into the stately cathedral, she was awestruck by its beauty. Transfixed, she stood in the center of the church in the soft sunshine that poured in through colorful stained glass. All was peace and serenity in this place. Maybe too quiet, even.

She couldn't resist. What singer could? Without warning, Madonna opened her mouth to see how her voice would resonate when enhanced by the acoustics of a 776-year-old cathedral. Her personal assistant, a local resident who just happened to be praying in the cathedral, three male Spanish tourists and Guy, were the only people present to witness the impromptu performance. As Madonna sang "Ave Maria," her voice breaking the stillness of the hallowed place and soaring to the rafters, it probably never sounded better.

"Yes," she said with a satisfied grin. "I think this will do just fine." She then walked over to Guy and melted into his arms. "Think we can make out in here?" she asked, coyly.

"Better not," he warned her, a wide grin playing on his face.

"Oh, then, we simply *must*." She kissed his hair, his eyes and then his lips, passionately.

After the cathedral visit, it was off to Skibo Castle. Once there, Madonna had to agree with Guy's assessment of the sprawling, tranquil estate. It was truly breathtaking, the ideal romantic location for a wedding. It wasn't difficult, Madonna would later say, for her to actually visualize how it had once been so long ago when Andrew Carnegie entertained the affluent and beautiful on this great estate, at this great castle. As soon as she walked onto the grounds, she was quickly transported into the past. Later, Madonna admitted to one friend that she couldn't help but note Guy's almost tender understanding of history—and of nature and its beauty—in his selection of the austere and majestic Skibo Castle, the ambience of which was wholly masculine, yet vastly sensitive. "For him to pick this place," she marveled, "well, the idea of it—that it was his choice, not mine—it really speaks to me. And it leaves me breathless."

*

With Madonna and Guy back in London—the press heated up its scrutiny of their wedding plans although Madonna's press representative, Liz Rosenberg dutifully denied that any wedding was even being planned. However, once the banns had been officially posted at the register's office in Dornoch on December 6, the news was out: the couple would definitely marry in the Dornoch area of Sutherland. It could no longer be denied. However, the location of the event would remain a mystery to all but those within Madonna and Guy's inner circle.

On December 18, the couple again arrived in Scotland by private jet. Though a hundred journalists gathered to document their arrival, Madonna and Guy made no statement. Madonna smiled at the crowd, though her glow seemed to dim somewhat when she heard the sounds of a bagpipe artiste known as Spud the Piper (Calum Fraser) serenading her with his odd rendition of "Like a Virgin." Apparently bemused by the whole scene, Guy's eyebrows lifted quizzically when he finally recognized the melody. "I guess it proves that you can play *anything* on a bagpipe," he said.

The guests arrived shortly after Madonna and Guy. The Skibo Castle experience would, apparently, be a difficult five days for some of the invitees, a few of whom later complained of having felt trapped on the estate's grounds. Truth be told, though, how bad could it have been? Everyone present would spend the time in the relaxing Edwardian splendor of the castle's grounds, with free access to all the resort's amenities and activities such as fishing for salmon and trout, clay-pigeon shooting, archery, croquet, mountain biking, hiking, bird watching, falconry and pheasant shooting. There were also tennis courts and snooker and table tennis, as well as an indoor swimming pool, gymnasium, sauna and steam rooms. For the most part, Madonna found herself sequestered with the women, Guy with the men. Occasionally, the couple would rendezvous to sneak off for long, romantic walks, their arms around each other. During the evenings, the entire party indulged in elaborate dinners—haggis, ("I'm sorry, but I simply can't eat that," Gwyneth Paltrow was overheard saying to one guest. "Why, I don't even know what it is!"), lamb, oatmeal and spices.

On December 21, baby Rocco was christened in Dornoch Cathedral. A crowd of about a thousand spectators, which had gathered in front of the cathedral hours earlier, were kept back from the premises by a police cordon. "Rocco is our Ray of Light to Dornoch," read a placard proudly carried by one local resident, alluding to Madonna's Grammy-winning CD.

For his christening, little Rocco was dressed in a white, gold-embroidered $45,000 "romper" designed by Donatella Versace. During the private proceedings, the baby's godmother, Trudie Styler, read the lengthy "Lorica" hymn while her husband, Sting, sang "Ave Maria." (The child's godfather is Guy Oseary, Madonna's partner in Maverick Records.) Some of Madonna's family, in town for the wedding, also attended the thirty-minute christening, including her father, Tony, and his wife, Joan, Madonna's sister Melanie Henry and her husband, Joe. Guy's mother, Lady (Amber) Leighton, and his father, John—along with Guy's stepmother, Shireen Ritchie and her twenty-one-year-old son, Oliver (from a previous marriage), were all in attendance. As well as a Catholic priest, also present were about forty total strangers to the couple, the church's elders, described as parishoners with perfect attendance records. Without them, according to strict church rules, no ceremony is permitted to take place in the cathedral. "Well, who's to keep them from selling us out to the press?" Madonna wanted to know. "I don't trust a single one of them."

"The way I look at it, if you can't trust people who go to church every Sunday," Guy said, according to what he later recalled to this writer, "then who can you trust?"

So moved was Madonna by the baptism (performed not by the Catholic priest but by the Rev. Susan Brown, a minister), she is said to have three times burst into tears during the ceremony. Afterward, Madonna and Guy posed outside the cathedral with their baby for just a few moments. Guy delighted the crowd by holding Rocco aloft while Madonna—her hair swept under a veiled cap and wearing a long, double-breasted and fitted Chlóe coat—stood at his side, looking stunning, demure and . . . royal. Smiling broadly, she waved grandly to the score of cheering, teary-eyed fans. Meanwhile, photographers memorialized the moment on film . . . no doubt, never dreaming that this would be the only shot they'd get of anything that was to take place in the next twenty-four hours.

Later, Guy learned that authorities had arrested two men—James and Robert Jones, both former soldiers from South London—for sneaking into the church and attempting to videotape the christening. Robert, fifty-one, had actually hidden in the cathedral's organ for sixty hours—with two plastic garbage bags for body waste. He and James were discovered in the cathedral about an hour after the ceremony. "That's one for the other side," Guy said, gamely. "Almost."

"I was actually rather amused by it," Guy told me a few months later. "I mean, you have to have a sense of humor about it, now don't you?" he added. "Good show for them that they got that far, that's what I thought."

*

Finally, the Big Moment had arrived. The "main event," the wedding, on December 22, 2000, at 6:30 P.M.

As the plaintive sound of a lone bagpipe player filled the great hall of Skibo Castle, Madonna's four-year-old daughter, Lourdes, barefoot and in an ivory gown with short sleeves and a high neck, led the wedding procession. As flower girl, she delicately tossed red rose petals from a basket while descending fourteen red-carpeted stairs. Immediately, many of the women began to weep. Among the fifty-five guests seated at the foot of the stairs were Gwyneth Paltrow (who arrived alone); Donatella Versace (escorted by Rupert Everett); Sting and his wife, Trudie Styler; filmmaker, Alex Keshishian; designer Jean Paul Gaultier; and Madonna's good friends Debi Mazar and Ingrid Casares. As well as members of Guy's family, many of his buddies and some of the casts and crews of his films—including Jason Statham and Jason Flemyng of *Lock, Stock and Two Smoking Barrels*—were in attendance.

After Lourdes's moment, music of French pianist Katia Labeque served as the background score to Guy Ritchie's entrance as he walked down a middle aisle, past the guests, and up the stairs now strewn with rose petals. Though born and raised in England, Guy had been determined to marry in full Highland dress. The romantic notion of his family's Scottish lineage has always filled him with immense contentment and pride. He has come to believe the heritage of his ancestors is integral to who he is as a man, that their ancient blood flows through his veins, informs his identity. For his wedding—his first—he wore a Hunting Mackintosh plaid kilt of navy and green, custom-made by Britain's Scotch House and boasting his ancestral Mackintosh clan tartan. Underneath the kilt, Guy wore nothing, as is the custom. ("I'm not a wuss," he jokingly explained to a friend.) His teal blazer was tailor-made by London's Alfred Dunhill. He also boasted green and antique diamond cuff links, a wedding gift from his bride. (Four-month-old Rocco Ritchie, wearing a matching outfit—but with a diaper on underneath—sat in his nanny's lap in the first row of the congregation.) Guy mounted the stairs and stood at the top, handsome and proud in the warm glow of hundreds of candles.

Ritchie was trailed by his two best men: Matthew Vaughn (producer of *Lock, Stock and Two Smoking Barrels,* and *Snatch,*) and London nightclub owner Piers Adam who, like Guy, suffers from dyslexia (the two still attend classes together to overcome the disability). They were followed to the top of the stairs by Stella McCartney, Madonna's maid of honor.

It had been expected by many of Madonna's friends—as well as the press—that Gwyneth Paltrow would be maid of honor. However, according to one intimate, Gwyneth said that she couldn't "bear the pressure of such a performance" and begged Madonna to "let me off the hook, please." So, the honor was extended to Miss McCartney, designer daughter of Sir Paul McCartney. She wore a self-designed, understated, grey-and-beige silk pants outfit.

Then, at last, the bride . . .

As Madonna walked out from the wings, down the middle aisle and up to the top step of the grand staircase, she was a vision in a strapless ivory silk gown, a fitted corset bodice and a long train. An antique veil, embroidered with nineteenth-century lace and topped by an Edwardian diamond tiara, was draped over her face. It cascaded serenely to the ground. She looked slender, willowy, and dramatic. A 37-carat, 2.5-inch diamond cross hung delicately at her cleavage above a bosom that was no mystery to most of the free world. Pearl-and-diamond bracelets were the expensive and classic finishing touch. As she walked down the aisle, her father, Tony, in a black formal tuxedo, stood at her side, his arm entwined in hers, his step ringing with determination.

The two looked extraordinarily radiant as they walked to the top of the stairs, in perfect harmony with each other.

She had come so far that, most certainly, her middle-class youth in Bay City, Michigan, must have seemed light years in the past as forty-two-year-old Madonna Louise Ciccone gazed down at her guests, her manner composed, her demeanor regal. As she stood at the top of a majestic staircase, its balustrade laced with ivy and white orchids, she was resplendent in the supernatural light of the great old castle. She appeared as would a queen to her subjects . . . or maybe even as Eva Perón would have to her constituents, for this was a production that, at least to some observers, seemed on the same grand scale as her star turn in *Evita*.

Madonna's ensemble was the result of just weeks of planning: the gown was designed (free of charge) by Stella McCartney; the tiara—767 diamonds, 80 carats—loaned to her by Asprey & Garrard of London; bracelets courtesy of Adler of London; the diamond cross designed for her by Harry Winston in New York. It all had been co-ordinated as quickly as possible so as to get it out of the way. Madonna, her inimitable brand of efficiency well-known to those who have worked for her, has never been one for dawdling. If she has agreed to give a show, she'll give one—and a good one!—but it needs to be done quickly and efficiently. No fuss. Or, as she would put it, "Just do it!"

This isn't to say that Madonna hadn't been excited about planning her wedding. The invitations, guest lists, menus, travel plans, florists, musicians . . . she ploughed ahead with all of it, with the assistance of her capable staff. Once she became involved in the formal wedding attire, her designer's imagination and sense of style ran wild. She was soon in the swing of things, viewing the selection of each fabric with Stella McCartney and other close friends as one of her life's biggest adventures. "How often do you choose something, the memory of which you'll have all of your life?" she decided in conversation with a friend while reviewing sketches of gowns. "I don't want to look back on my wedding pictures in ten years and say, 'What was I *thinking?*' Plus, really, look how much fun all of this is. What girl wouldn't love *this!*" She wanted perfection, no matter the cost of time, money, or energy. Those who attended the wedding would say that, as usual, she got what she wanted.

When she reached the top of the stairs, Madonna kissed her father on the cheek and then left his side to stand by Guy's. From a distance, she seemed to be crying. Touched, Guy reached for her hand, regarding his bride with obvious warmth and affection.

The Ritchies' wedding ceremony—in front of Skibo's bay window of century-old stained glass—was just twenty-minutes long (as conducted by the Reverend Susan Brown, the first female minister ever to be in charge of a cathedral and, also, the minister who had earlier baptized Rocco.) In muted voices, the couple exchanged vows which they had written, sealing their promises to one another. They then exchanged wedding bands—Madonna's a simple platinum-and-diamond ring, Guy's a gold one. Even from a distance, Madonna's face seemed flushed the moment she and Guy were pronounced husband and wife. One spectator in the third row later recalled, "You could see, with sudden clarity, the intense love in her eyes for this man. Guy touched her cheek gently, maybe wiping away a tear, I'm not sure. It was a moment, though, like no other. There was a true bonding, on every level."

After the obligatory wedding kiss, the newlyweds finally descended the stairs as husband and wife, their guests cheering in appreciation. Flashing a beguiling smile, Madonna seemed to glow as she and Guy stood at the bottom of the staircase and accepted the good wishes of friends and family. Those who know her well say that she had never appeared happier than she did at that moment. She seemed filled with a contentment that she, perhaps, had never before known.

After the ceremony, everyone gathered in Skibo's drawing room for champagne toasts. Dinner was then served in the castle's oak-paneled dining room. As a traditional four-piece Scottish band played, guests drank champagne and red wine and ate lobster, salmon, mussels, Aberdeen Angus beef, roast potatoes and red cabbage. For dessert, a caramelized profiterole cake was served. At 11 P.M., the party moved on to a disco that had been set up in the basement of the castle. By this time, Madonna had changed into an ivory-white pantsuit. The new bride was also adorned by millions of dollars worth of jewels: diamonds that were on loan from Harry Winston. Guests then danced into the early morning hours to recorded music by Madonna and Sting, as well as artists who had contributed to the soundtrack of Guy's movie, *Snatch*.

Thanks to such careful planning by Guy Ritchie and certain members of Madonna's experienced staff, the event had been successfully shrouded in unprecedented secrecy, and had been a total media black-out. In sub-freezing temperatures, hundreds of journalists camped outside the locked gates of the castle, awaiting some word that the couple had married. It never came. Dozens of paparazzi, blacked up and dressed in camouflage gear, then crawled through the undergrowth of the castle grounds to get a closer look. They were hotly pursued by Guy's security officers who were armed with sophisticated, heat-seeking equipment, infrared cameras and other thermal-imaging devices. The photographers were picked off, one by one, like hunted deer. "If anyone manages to get past my guys, they deserve to get in," Guy had said, laughing.

"At the end of the day," as Guy Ritchie put it, he had certainly, "won the game." Not one salable photograph of the couple was taken by any paparazzi, though one photographer did somehow manage to shoot a blurry, long-distance shot of "the missus" standing in front of a window. Also, no firsthand observations were given to reporters. There was never even an official announcement that the wedding had taken place, only a statement from the minister who had officiated: "It did happen."

Slowly, over the course of three days after the ceremony, sketchy—and often contradictory—details of what had occurred behind the castle's gates began to emerge. Surprisingly, no wedding picture of the couple was issued to the press, though noted photographer Jean Baptiste Mondino had documented the entire experience. "If we're playing the game, we go all the way with it," Guy told one of Madonna's press representatives. "So, no photos."

Madonna could not have been more delighted by the notion of not releasing photographs to the media, perhaps never considering that the fans whose financial support had made such opulence affordable for her may have treasured at least one picture of the occasion. However, in her view, there was something appropriate, and even novel, about this turn of events. As she would later privately explain, it was often dismaying to her when she realized that the public was so fully aware of how she acted and appeared during practically every key moment of her entire life. It gave her a sense of satisfaction knowing that her second wedding remained a mystery. "I think it's fabulous," she told one friend. "I didn't get married for anyone's entertainment, anyway. Fuck 'em, all," she said, doubtless in reference to the media, not her fans. "I think I've given enough, don't you?"

In the end, the only real breach came from Guy's father, John, who had told a reporter—prior to his arrival at the castle—that Guy would be wearing a kilt of the family's Hunting Mackintosh tartan. Once he arrived in Scotland, the elder Ritchie was given a severe dressing down from one of Madonna's representatives. When he later heard about the rebuke, Guy became incensed—perhaps the only time he was angry during the five days at Skibo. "He's my father," Guy hissed at Madonna's handler upon confronting her. "How dare you speak to him in that way!" An argument ensued, a blowup that quickly ended when Guy walked away with a fierce expression, muttering something about "the fucking assholes that work for the missus." Though instantly forgiven by his son and his fiancée for the innocent transgression, the senior Ritchie was still shaken by the internal fracas. At the cathedral just prior to the baptism, a reporter from the Associated Press asked him what was going to transpire at the ceremony; John Ritchie responded, "I wouldn't dare ask."

After the wedding, Madonna's father, Tony, and his wife, Joan, left Scotland for the United States. Everyone who knew Madonna felt that her father's presence in Scotland had been a strong indicator that his relationship with Madonna—"Nonnie," as he sometimes still calls her— was now on firm ground. Whatever unpleasantness had occurred between them had been assigned to the past where, hopefully, it would remain.

One close friend reports overhearing a conversation between father and daughter on the grounds of Skibo Castle. Tony, awed by his surroundings, spent much of the time with Guy's father, John, soaking up the environment, feasting his eyes on the scenery. On the morning of the wedding, he and Madonna enjoyed one of many heartwarming moments on the grounds. Wearing what appeared to be a cashmere, pale pink turtleneck sweater with straight-leg jeans, Madonna sat under a sycamore tree, holding baby Rocco in her arms, close to her bosom. A cheerful nanny played tag with Lourdes, three feet or so away. Friends milled about, watching Madonna with the new baby and gazing out at the spectacular vista spread before them. This peaceful scene played out gently in the early morning hour's sunlight, abundant with beauty, harmony and a sense of timelessness that made it all seem so far removed from the outside world.

As Tony approached his daughter, she smiled at him. "Well, we've sure come a long way, Dad," Madonna said.

"I'll say," Tony agreed, "I never thought we'd be here in this place together," he added, waving a hand at their lush surroundings.

"No, Dad," Madonna responded. "I mean you and me. We've come a long way."

According to the witness, Tony's eyes began to fill with tears. He shook his head, a slow smile spreading across his face. "My God. Just look at you," he told his daughter. Madonna lifted Rocco in the air, and made a funny face at him. "A mother . . . soon a wife. Look how good you turned out, Nonnie," Tony concluded, his face filled with genuine pride.

"Da-ad!" Madonna exclaimed, drawing the word into two syllables. She seemed embarrassed, probably because she knew that people were listening.

"No, I mean it," he insisted.

"Well, stop it," Madonna said, her face softening. "You're gonna make me cry."

"And we couldn't have that, now, could we?" asked another voice. It was Guy, approaching from behind Madonna. He was wearing comfortable corduroys, a heavy, wool sweater and a big smile.

Madonna's head spun around. "Oh, I get it. You guys are gonna gang up on me, now," she concluded, good-naturedly. She handed the baby to Guy. "Take this kid," she told him as she stood up. "I'm getting out of here."

"Where to?" Guy asked.

"Somewhere I can have a good cry," she answered.

Guy carefully placed the infant into the arms of the nearby nanny, and then followed Madonna. Joining her, he put his arm around her waist. They walked off wordlessly, looking safe with each other, seeming to belong together, maybe lost in their own thoughts, no words necessary between them.

✝

Acknowledgments

☦

Madonna: An Intimate Biography would not have been possible without the assistance of many people and institutions.

First acknowledgment must go to my Simon & Schuster editor, Chuck Adams, who somehow managed to pull together the elements of this American edition under the tightest of deadlines. Also at Simon & Schuster: thanks to my publisher, David Rosenthal. And thanks also to my production editor, Dan Cuddy; designer, Jeanette Olender; attorney, Veronica Jordan; and publicists Aileen Boyle and Rachel Nagler. And thanks to Cheryl Weinstein for all of her assistance. This is the first time I have worked with Simon & Schuster and, I must say, it's been a class act all the way. I am relieved to find that, after a decade in development, this book has finally ended up where it seems to have always belonged: S&S.

Thanks also to Natalie Goldstein, photo researcher, for gathering such imaginative artwork for this edition.

I'd also like to thank Gordon Wise and Ingrid Connell, my editors at Macmillan Publishers Ltd. and Sidgwick & Jackson in the United Kingdom, for shepherding the original edition of this work. Thanks also to Lucy Henson and everyone else at Macmillan who worked with such diligence to make this book a national bestseller in the U.K.

My deepest appreciation goes to Dorie Simmonds of The Dorie Simmonds Agency. She is truly a positive force in my life, a trusted and valued friend. I appreciate her dedication, assistance and encouragement.

Thanks to Mitch Douglas at International Creative Management for so many years of friendship and of top-notch representation.

Thanks to Maureen Egen at Warner Books for making it possible for me to proceed with publication of this book in the United States. She's not only a gracious woman, but also a real pro. Thanks also to Jackie Joiner and Jimmy Franco at Warner.

I must acknowledge my friend, the late George Coleman, who first urged me to write this book back in 1990 while at G.P. Putnam's Sons. Though it took more than a decade to complete this project, my memory of George remained strong throughout that time.

My thanks to Jonathan Hahn, a fellow journalist and my personal publicist at Planned Television Arts. We had many discussions about how to present Madonna in a way that would be accurate and empathetic. While I am grateful to him for his vision, my close friendship with him is what matters most to me.

As an editor and a friend, Paula Agronick Reuben has been invaluable to me for many years. I thank her for her continuing encouragement.

Warmest thanks to Cathy Griffin for her professional assistance over the years, as well as her friendship. Cathy, a journalist and reporter in her own right, worked as an investigator and researcher on *Madonna: An Intimate Biography* at the beginning of its development in 1990, in 1991 and again in 1994, locating scores of sources and conducting in-depth interviews with them. To date, we have worked on five books together, each a pleasure, each a learning experience.

I owe a debt of gratitude to Wayne Brasler of the University of Chicago who has always supported my work. Al Kramer, a trusted friend and writing colleague for years, has also kept me on the right track.

I am appreciative to grief specialist, Dr. Marvin Eisentadt, the coauthor and American editor of Parental Loss and Achievement (along with Dr. Andre Haynal, Dr. Pierre Rentchnick and Pierre de Senarclens), for his observations.

In 1990, when I first began work on this book, Madonna historian Bruce Baron availed me of his great knowledge of this subject, even providing audio tapes of rare Madonna music, much of it unreleased at that time. Bruce was an invaluable asset to the research behind this work, and I do thank him for his great documentation and his dedication to accuracy.

Thanks also to Charles Casillo who helped fine-tune the ideas behind this manuscript, thinking about the characters involved and how to present them fairly and objectively. I am indebted to Charles for his time and attention to detail. He's a fine writer, and a good friend.

Without a loyal team of representatives, an author usually finds himself sitting at home writing books no one ever reads. So, I thank "Team JRT": James Jimenez, Esq.; Ken Deakins, Rae Goldreich, Harold Stock and Teryna Hanuscin of Duitch, Franklin and Company; and Michael Johnston of Capital Lending Resources. Also, my thanks, as always, goes to Ron Bernstein of International Creative Management in Beverly Hills.

Special thanks to Stephen Gregory for many years of friendship, loyalty and support, and all of that despite some rather challenging circumstances along the way.

Also, thanks to all of those who assisted me in tangible and intangible ways, including Richard Tyler Jordan, Jeff Hare, Iake and Alex Eissinmann, Paul Adler, Sven Paardekooper, Steve Ivory, James Pinkston, Billy Barnes, Roby Gayle, Hazel and Rob Kragulac, Sonja Kravchuck, Barbara Ormsby, Rick Starr, John Passantino, Linda DeStefano, Mr. and Mrs. Joseph Tumolo, Daniel Tumolo, James Spada, Tony and Marilyn Caruselle, David Spiro, Billy Masters, Mr. and Mrs. Adolph Steinlen, David and Frances Snyder, Abby and Maddy Snyder, Maribeth and Don Rothell, Mary Alvarez, Mark Bringelson, Hope Levy and Tom Lavagnino, Anthony Shane, Bart Andrews, Anne McVey, Bob Meyer, Daniel Coleridge, Lisa Reiner, George Solomon, Marcus Reymaga, Dan Sterchele and Yvette Jarecki. Also, R.T. and J.D., if you read this, know that I am thinking of you as well, and missing our times together.

Thanks also to Iake Eissinmann for his excellent photography, and for his friendship.

Thanks to Dale Manesis for all of his help with Madonna-related memorabilia to which I would never have had access without his assistance. And thanks to Camille Sartiano-Glowitz for all of the travel accommodations relation to *Madonna: An Intimate Biography*.

It's never easy being around a writer who can be annoyingly single-minded about his work. I recognize the patience it takes to understand such a process, and I thank Andy Steinlen for all of his many involvements in my life, and for his eternal friendship.

Thanks to my incredibly supportive Italian-American family: Roslyn and Bill Barnett and Jessica and Zachary, Rocco and Rosemarie Taraborrelli and Rocco and Vincent, and Arnold Taraborrelli. And, of course, Rydell and Dylan.

Special thanks to my father, Rocco, who has always been my inspiration, encouraging me in ways too numerous to mention. This book is dedicated to him because of the challenge it presented to his son. I most certainly would have abandoned it years ago if not for his influence on me.

I also send my love to my late mother, Rose Marie, who is always in my heart.

And finally, to those loyal readers of my work who have followed my career over the years, who have sent me letters of support and encouragement about my previous eight books (and who have also doled out harsh criticism when necessary), I humbly thank you for adding this work to your book collection. I hope you were as entertained reading about Madonna's life experiences as I was chronicling them, and I also hope you perhaps learned a little something about human nature in the process.

J. RANDY TARABORRELLI

June 2001

✝

I first began developing *Madonna: An Intimate Biography* in January 1990 as the intended follow-up to my first best-seller, *Call Her Miss Ross: The Unauthorized Biography of Diana Ross*. Though my career turned in other directions, I and my team of researchers never ceased developing a full-scale biography of Madonna.

After having written nine biographies, I know that it is impossible to write accurately about anyone's life without many reliable witnesses to provide a range of different viewpoints. A biography of this kind stands or falls on the cooperation and frankness of those involved in the story. Over the years, a great number of people went out of their way to assist me in this endeavor: hundreds of friends, relations, journalists, socialites, lawyers, celebrities, show-business executives and former executives, associates and friends as well as foes, classmates, teachers, neighbors, friends, newspersons and archivists were contacted in preparation for this book over a ten-year period. Obviously, considering the span of Madonna's life and career, I and my researchers had the opportunity to interview a wide range of sources. We purposely decided to focus on those who had not previously told their stories. These people were interviewed for this work over the last decade, either by myself or my trusted researchers, Cathy Griffin in the United States, Thomas DeWitt in the United Kingdom, and Teri Donato in Italy. Many of these sources are people I haven't seen or talked to for almost ten years, but my appreciation for their cooperation and assistance will not fade with time.

Whenever practical, I have provided sources within the body of the text. Some people were not quoted directly in the text but provided observations that helped me more fully understand Madonna and her life and career.

In writing about a person as powerful and as influential as Madonna is in the entertainment world, a biographer is bound to find that many sources with valuable information prefer to not be named in the text. This is understandable. Throughout my career, I have understood that for someone to jeopardize a long-standing, important relationship for the sake of a book is a purely personal choice. I so appreciate the assistance of many people close to Madonna over the years who gave of their time and energy for this project, and will respect their wishes for anonymity. Those who could be named are named in these notes.

I viewed every film Madonna ever made to determine which were important to my particular observations, and which were not. Also, I reviewed all of the press clippings, press kits and other studio-related material, biographies and releases for each of Madonna's films, which are on file at the Margaret Herrick Library. I thank the staff of that library in particular.

Also, obviously, I viewed hundreds of hours of Madonna's television appearances, special events and concerts, press conferences, documentaries and also listened to many hours of radio interviews and other broadcasts in which Madonna took part, or of which she was the principal subject. It would be impractical to list them all here. Thank you, Nick Scotti, for providing me with much of this material.

Numerous organizations and institutions provided me with articles, documents, audio interviews, video interviews, transcripts and other material that was either utilized directly in *Madonna: An Intimate Biography* or for purposes of background. Unfortunately, it is not possible to thank all of the individuals associated with each organization who were so helpful and gave of their time; however, I would at least like to express my gratitude to the following institutions:

Alvin Ailey American-Dance Theater; American Film Institute Library; Associated Press Office (New York); The Bancroft Library (University of California, Berkeley); The Bay City Public Library; *Bay City Times;* The Beverly Hills Library; *Boston Herald* Archives; Boston Public Library; The Brand Library Art and Music Center; British Broadcasting Corporation; California State Archives (Sacramento); *Detroit News;* The Detroit Public Library; The Glendale Central Public Library; Globe Photos; The Hartford Public Library; Hayden Library, Arizona State University; The Hollywood Library; The Houghton Library (Harvard University); The Los Angeles Public Library; *Los Angeles Times;* The Margaret Herrick Library (Academy of Motion Pictures Arts and Sciences); *Michigan Chronicle;* The Neal Peters Collection; New York City Municipal Archives; New York Public Library; New York University Library; Occidental College (Eagle Rock, California); Photofest; The Pontiac Public Library; The Princeton University Library; Rochester Adams High School; *Rochester Eccentric;* The Rochester Public Library; Starfiles; University of California, Los Angeles; West Middle School.

Of course, I have listened to nothing but Madonna in recent years—not that this has been a chore. I believe it is important for a biographer to have an appreciation and a sense of understanding of his subject's work. If anything, my crash course in Madonna's musical history has only served to deepen my respect for her artistry. Here, I must thank the esteemed music critic, reporter and my good friend of many years, Steven Ivory, for his assistance in dissecting and analyzing Madonna's music. This book would be very different if not for Steve's involvement, and I thank him for the hours he put into this project.

Madonna has many wonderful fan clubs. I decided not to impose upon the dedicated people who run these clubs for fear of jeopardizing their long-standing and cherished relationships with Madonna. However, through their newsletters and other forums of expression—including their Internet websites, chat forums, etc.—I was able to confirm details and add color to certain sections of my book. Madonna is fortunate to have so many fans devoted to preserving her legend and reputation. Look them up on the Internet . . . they're all there. (If you really want to know about Madonna, though, I suggest you point your browser to madonnacatalogue.com. This site, run by respected Madonna historian Stephen Michael Caraco, is stunning in its painstaking detail.)

As the former editor-in-chief of *Soul* magazine I had the opportunity to interview Madonna on several occasions during the early years of her career, in 1983, 1984, 1985 and 1987. I have also attended several press conferences given by Madonna over the years. In this work, I utilized many of Madonna's memories from those encounters.

Since chapter notes are usually not of interest to the general reader, I have chosen a more general—and practical for space limitations—mode of source identification, as opposed to specific page or line notations. The following notes are by no means comprehensive but are intended to give the reader a general overview of my research. In some instances, I included parenthetically the year(s) interviews were conducted.

Also, because of their voluminous nature, I have made the choice of not including complete listings of the scores of magazine and newspaper articles that were referenced. It would simply be impractical to do so. Those mentioned within these source notes are included because I felt they were important to recognize.

Interviews Conducted Relating to Madonna's Relationships (Some Dates in Parenthesis)

With John "Jellybean" Benitez: thanks to Jellybean Benitez (1984, 1985, 1990), Erica Bell (1991) and Melinda Cooper (1994). Also: *Teen Machine*, June 1991, "Spillin' the Beans with Jellybean" by Marie Morreale.

With Steve Newman: thanks to Steve Newman (1995) and April Dougherty (1999, 2000).

With Prince: thanks to T. L. "Boom-Boom" Ross (1998) and Jerome Quigley (2000).

With Tommy Quinn: thanks to Tommy Quinn for five interviews (1998–2000).

With Sean Penn: in 1988, I spent six months developing a proposal for a book entitled *Sean Penn: Lone Wolf*. The book remains unpublished. However, I used much of the material from it in this work about Madonna. I also referred to my own interview with Sean Penn in 1987. Thanks also to Meg Lowery (2000), Lori Mulrenin (2000), Isaac Benson (2000), Todd Barash (1999), David Wolinsky (1989) and Martin Ciccone (1992), Al Albergate (1999), Deputy District Attorney Lauren Weiss (1988), and Lieutenant Bill McSweeney (1989). I reviewed the police documents from the LAPD relating to Sean Penn's arrest in December 1988; I also referred to the September 1987 "Madonna Interviewed on Fame, Sex and Sean Penn" by Jane Pauley, NBC-TV. Also helpful: *Playboy*, November 1991, "Sean Penn" by David Rensin; *Fame*, November 1990, "Sean Penn: Is There Life After Madonna?" by Harry Crews; *USA Today*, July 5, 1988, "Sean Penn Comes Back Kicking"; *Time*, December 17, 1990, "Madonna Draws a Line" by Jay

Cocks; *New York Post*, January 6, 1989, "Madonna Sues Sean Penn for Divorce"; *People*, January 23, 1989, "Surprise! It's Splits, Fits and Quits Again for Sean Penn and Madonna" by James S. Kunen; *USA Today*, June 24, 1987, "Bad-Boy Penn Gets 2 Months in Jail" by Lorie Lynch; *People*, September 2, 1985, "Madonna Lands Her Lucky Star" by Roger Wolmuth; *People*, August 17, 1987, "Chris Finch, Madonna's High-Stepping Sidekick Who's Also a Penn Pal" by Kim Hubbard and Sandra Lyon; *Harper's Bazaar*, May 1988, "Madonna Broadway Bound"; *People*, July 8, 1985, "Desperately Seeking Matrimony" by Carol Wallace; *People*, December 14, 1987, "Diary of a Mad Marriage/The Divorce of Madonna & Sean" by Joanne Kaufman and Victoria Balfour; *Sun*, August 18, 1985, "Sean's Gunplay Upsets Madonna" by Rod Barrand; *Chicago Tribune*, August 2, 1987, "The Show Goes on Without Sean" by Gene Siskel; *Star*, June 16, 1987, "Sean Penn's Rampage Over 'Lost Love' Madonna" by Lorraine Tilden; *USA Today*, July 3, 1987, "Bad Boy or Bad Rap?/Sean Penn Is off to Jail" by Karen Peterson; *News of the World*, October 27, 1985, "Bride Madonna's Bizarre Bathtime" by Wendy Leigh; *Star*, February 4, 1986, "Sean's Tantrums" by Steve Edwards; *New York Post*, August 13, 1985, "Madonna and Sean Get Marriage License"; *Star*, November 11, 1988, "Sean Penn's X-Rated Animal House" by Barry Levine; *Rolling Stone*, March 1989, "Madonna—the *Rolling Stone* Interview" by Bill Zehme; *Vanity Fair*, March 1986, "Tough Act" by James Wolcott; *Los Angeles Times*, August 18, 1991, "New Directions for Sean Penn" by Kristina McKenna; *People*, December 14, 1987, "Everyone Said It Wouldn't Last . . . And It Didn't" by Joanne Kaufman; *US Weekly*, September 7, 1987, "How's That Girl?" by Fred Schruers; *People*, February 11, 1985, "Who Is Sean Penn—and Why Doesn't He Want Anyone to Find Out?" by Scott Haller; *National Enquirer*, January 24, 1989, "Madonna to Cops: Drunken Sean Beat Me and Tied Me Up" by Joe Mullins, Patricia Towle, Roger Capettini, Reginald Fitz and Michael Glynn; *Star*, January 24, 1989, "Sean Penn's 9-Hour Torture of Madonna" by Lorraine Tilden.

With Sandra Bernhard: thanks to Sandra Bernhard for the interview I conducted in 1996. I also referred to: *Penthouse*, November 1988, "Sandra Bernhard: The Queen of Comedy" by Richard Dominick. I also reviewed the tape of Madonna and Sandra on David Letterman's program, *The Late Show with David Letterman*, July

1988; *Star,* June 28, 1988, "It's All-Girls Night"; *Sun,* May 26, 1989, "Madonna and Sandra Shock Fans" by Allan Hall; *People,* June 12, 1989, "Gal Pals Sandra Bernhard and Madonna Monkey Around to Save the Jungle"; *USA Today,* October 24, 1989, "Bernhard Burning Over 'Sordid Press' " by Ann Trebbe; *Interview,* March 1990, "Sandra Bernhard" by Paul Taylor; *New York Post,* February 26, 1994, "Ex Gal-Pal Rips 'Grubby Madonna' " by Richard Johnson with Kimberly Ryan; *Laugh Factory,* April 28, 1994, "Tea Time from Hollywood—Sandra Bernhard Pours the Tea on Madonna" by Paul Mooney; *National Enquirer,* November 10, 1992, "Sandra Bernhard: "Madonna Stole My Lesbian Lover" by John South, Tony Brenna and Lydia Encinas.

With John Kennedy, Jr.: as the author of *Jackie, Ethel, Joan—Women of Camelot* (Warner Books, 2000), I have cultivated many contacts within the Kennedy circle. For this text, I utilized a number of them to learn about John's relationship with Madonna. Some asked for anonymity. However, two who did not are Steven Styles and Thomas Luft, both of whom I interviewed on ten different occasions regarding Madonna and John (1990–2000). I also interviewed two former members of the Secret Service, both personal friends of John who requested anonymity. My thanks also to Richard Wiese (1999), Senator George Smathers (1994) and Chris Meyer (1995, 2000) for their interviews. I also referred to: *New York Post,* October 4, 1991, "The Real Story Behind Madonna's Fling With JFK, Jr." by Marsha Kranes.

With Warren Beatty: thanks to Diane Giordano (1990, 1994) and Bill Hollerman (1990). Also thanks to Cathy Griffin for certain details and valuable information regarding Madonna and Warren. I also referred to: *National Enquirer,* June 20, 1989, "Madonna to Wed Warren Beatty" by Tony Brenna, Diane Albright and Jerome George; *Entertainment Weekly,* December 20, 1991, "Warren's World" by James Kaplan; *Interview,* September 1991, "Sean Penn" by Julian Schnabel.

With Tony Ward: thanks to Tony Ward for the interview I conducted in 1992; Jayme Harris (1993); and Sandra Bernhard (1996). Thanks also to Keith Saltar (2000) and Tina Stanton (2000). I also referred to: *National Enquirer,* February 26, 1991, "What Madonna Doesn't Know About Her Live-In Boyfriend" by John South, David Duffy and Alan Braham Smith.

With Michael Jackson: as the author of *Michael Jackson: The Magic and the Madness* (Carol Publishing, 1990), I have cultivated many contacts with the Jackson circle. I utilized some of them to flesh out the stories about Michael and Madonna found here. Thanks also to Michael Jackson (1996) and John Branca (1990) for the interviews I conducted with them from which I extrapolated information regarding his relationship with Madonna. Thanks also to Monica Pastelle (1995, 1998, 2000). Also, I referred to my own books: *Call Her Miss Ross: The Unauthorized Biography of Diana Ross* (Carol Publishing, 1989); *Motown: Hot Wax, City Cool and Solid Gold* (Doubleday, 1986); and *Janet Jackson: Out of the Madness* (which I co-wrote with Bart Andrews, Doubleday, 1994). I also referred to my research for: "The Secret Life of Michael Jackson" for the *Daily Mail*, August 24, 2000; *People*, April 15, 1991. I referenced "Madonna and Michael" by Steve Doherty, Todd Gold, David Marlow and Robin Micheli.

With Ingrid Casares: thanks to Chita Mavroo (1999, 2000). I also referred to: *New York Post*, February 7, 2000, "Casares Speaks" by Jared Paul Stern; *New York Post*, April 11, 2000, "Now It's Madonna [and Pal] with Child" by Linda Massarella.

With Carlos Leon: thanks to Carlos's parents, Maria Leon and Armando Leon (1996, 1999). Thanks also to Michael Gacki (1996), Patrice Gonzalez (1998, 1999, 2000). I referred to: *Daily News*, October 16, 1996; "My Lourdes, She's Daddy's Little Girl" by Corky Siemaszko; *New York Post*, April 17, 1996, "Man Who Stole Madonna's Heart" by Bill Hoffman; *Daily News*, April 17, 1996, "Beau's Mom Ecstatic" by Jere Hester and Wendell Jamieson; *Los Angeles Times*, April 16, 1996, "She's Now a Maternity Girl" by Liz Smith; *New York Post*, May 4, 1997, "Mr. Madonna Dematerializing" by Neal Travis; *New York Post*, April 24, 1996, "Madonna's Top Seed Jets Home" by Linda Massarella; *Newsweek*, April 29, 1996 "Get Married, Madonna" by Jonathan Alter; *New York Post*, June 30, 2000, "Don't-Ask Carlos Loses His Cool"; *People*, October 26, 1996, "Labor of Love" by Todd Gold; *People*, April 29, 1996, "And Baby Makes Three" by Karen S. Schneider.

With Dennis Rodman: thanks to Dennis Rodman (1996) and Trina Graves (2000). The faxed correspondence between Madonna and Dennis had been published in the *Globe* in 1995, and also broadcast on the television show *Hard Copy*. I also consulted: *Bad as I Wanna Be* by Dennis Rodman (Delacorte Press, 1996).

With Andy Bird: thanks to Andy's mother, Kathleen Bird (1998), Joseph Lafferty (2000), Elvin Bishop (2000); I also referenced: *People*, April 5, 1999, "Two Guys, a Girl and a Punch in the Nose" (no byline); Reuters, March 22, 1999, "Fighting over Madonna" (wire service); UPI, March 23, 1999, "Bird and Ritchie Clash over Madonna" (wire service); *Now*, December 4, 1997, "Madonna's English 'Geezer' " by Jon Clark.

With Gwyneth Paltrow: thanks to Jeannie Misterling (1999, 2000). I also referenced: Reuters, January 5, 2000, "Lopez Irks Madonna, Guests at Miami Y2K Party" (wire service); *New Idea*, January 3, 2000, "Madonna and Gwyneth Paltrow" (no byline); *Entertainment Weekly*, January 5, 2000, "How Madonna Became Gwyneth Paltrow's Role Model" by Liane Bonin. I also relied on research for these stories about Miss Paltrow which I authored: *Women's Day*, December 6, 1999, "Why Gwyneth Can Never Please . . ." by J. Randy Taraborrelli; *Women's Day*, December 13, 1999, "Gwyneth's Search for Love" by J. Randy Taraborrelli; *Daily Mail*, February 16, 2000, "Gwyneth Paltrow" by J. Randy Taraborrelli.

With Guy Ritchie: thanks to the many friends and family members of Guy Ritchie's who, because of his marriage to Madonna, asked for anonymity. Also useful: *Birmingham Post*, September 2, 2000, "At the Movies, Meet Guy's Gang . . ." by Alison Jones; *Independent*, September 2, 2000, "Guy Ritchie: Who's Afraid of This Guy?" by David Thomson; *Independent*, August 27, 2000, "Just What Sort of a Guy's Guy Is Guy Ritchie?" by Mark Simpson; *People*, October 19, 1996, "Mama Madonna / A Labor Of Love" by Todd Gold; *Vanity Fair*, October 1992, "Madonna in Los Angeles Times," March 1, 1998, "Madonna, Only More So" by Robert Hillburn; *New York Post*, March 2, 2000, "Madonna and Guy Do the Ex Best Thing" by Neal Travis; *Vanity Fair*, October 1992, "Madonna in Wonderland" by Maureen Orth; *Good Housekeeping*, April 2000, "Madonna Grows Up" by Liz Smith; *US Weekly*, October 2, 2000, "The Maternal Girl" by Todd Gold; *Los Angeles Times*, June 4, 2000, "In Search of the Next Best Thing" by Ruth Ryon; *Heat*, March 2000, "Has This Man Changed Madonna?" *Sun*, September 21, 2000, "Madonna, I'm Still Breast Feeding . . ." by Dominic Mohan; *Daily Mail*, March 21, 2000, "Madonna's Baby" by Randip Panesar and Oliver Harvey; *New York Post*, February 22, 2000, "Madonna's Boy No Toy" by Peter Fearon;

US Weekly, February 2000, "Madonna Announces She's Pregnant for Second Time," by Sarah Saffian; *US Weekly*, March 29, 2000, "Madonna and Ritchie Quash Rumors" by Jerry Rubinfield; *New York Post*, March 21, 2000, "Pregnancy Is 2nd Nature for Madonna" by Bill Hoffman; *People*, April 3, 2000, "Like a Family" by Steve Dougherty; *New York Post*, March 19, 2000, "Britain Beckons Madonna" by Neal Travis; *Globe and Mail*, August 19, 2000, "We Say a Little Prayer" by Gayle Macdonald and Alexandria Gill; *Toronto Sun*, August 16, 2000, "Madonna Despairs" by Sophie Vokesdudgeon; *New York Post*, May 14, 2000, "Madonna a Backyard Mama" by Neal Travis; *Daily Mail*, May 10, 2000, "All's Swell Between Madonna and Guy" by James Clothier; *Daily Mail*, May 1, 2000, "Side by Side, Madonna and the Apple of Her Eye" by Oliver Harvey; *Daily Mail*, June 4, 2000, "I Love My Guy ..." by Alison Boshoff; *GQ*, October 2000, "Guy Ritchie—Entrepreneur" by Steve Hobbo.

With her father, Tony ("Happy Endings'): thanks to Silvio Ciccone for the telephone conversation I had with him and his wife, Joan, in August 2000, which I used as a basis for this section. I also relied on: *Night&Day*, August 6, 2000, "Interview with Madonna's Father" by Caroline Graham and Melanie Bromley.

Evita

My thanks to all of those interviewed in Buenos Aires, including Simoné Sarella (1998), Isidrio Alvarez (2000) and Ceclia Nuñuz (2000) for pointing me and my researcher Jorgé Rodriguez-White in the right direction and giving us so many details—and so much color—relating to Madonna's meeting with President Carlos Menem. Thanks to the aides of Menem's who spoke off the record about that meeting. Also, the patrons of the La Cigale Bar (who asked not to be identified) in the Bajo area for leads and tips given to Mr. Rodriguez-White. As he explains it, the Costanera Norte and Las Cañitas in Palermo are where the city's young and wealthy go to drink and eat ... and when Madonna was in town for *Evita*, she was the subject of great fascination there. We thank all of the people who gave Jorgé so much information, and so many names and numbers. I also referred to "The Madonna Diaries" in *Vanity Fair* (November 1996) for background.

Thanks also to Martina Logan (2000), Joan Layder (2000) and Louis Keith (2000). I also referred to: *USA Today*, January 3, 1997, "Antonio Banderas: *Evita* Tests Press-Shy Star's Voice and Mettle" by Marco R. della Cava; *Time*, February 12, 1996, "People: All the Rage in Argentina" by Belinda Luscombe; *Time*, February 24, 1997, "Crying for Madonna, Experts Explain Why Oscar Snubbed the Studios" by Bruce Handy; American *Vogue*, October 1996, "Madonna's Moment As Evita, Mother and Fashion Force" by Julie Salamon; *Time*, December 16, 1996, "You Must Love Her" by Richard Corliss; *Billboard*, October 16, 1996, "Radio Embraces Evita" by Larry Flick; *New Perspectives Quarterly*, Winter 1997, "Evita or Madonna: Whom Will History Remember" (interview with Argentine writer Tomas Eloy Martinez); *US Weekly*, August 1, 1997, "Scaling Down" by Ty Burr; *USA Today*, December 23, 1996, "Madonna Stars, Banderas Shines in *Evita*" by Mike Clark; *Newsweek*, November 11, 1996, "Selling Evita to the Masses" by Susan Miller; *Los Angeles Times*, May 4, 1996, "She'll Surprise a Lot of People" by David Gritten; *Here!*, December 16, 1996, "What a Pri-Madonna!" by Caroline Peal; *Los Angeles Times*, September 29, 1996, "Madonna's Double Feature" by David Gritten; *Los Angeles Times*, December 24, 1996, "Q & A with Alan Parker and Andrew Lloyd Webber" by David Gritten; *Variety*, December 10, 1996, *Evita* [film review] by Todd McCarthy.

Among the volumes I consulted: *The Making of Evita* by Alan Parker (HarperCollins, 1996).

Madonna's Childhood and Early Years

Over the last ten years, I spent a great deal of time in Michigan where a number of people opened their homes—and their scrapbooks—to me as they remembered the young Madonna Louise Veronica Ciccone. I am indebted to so many people who lived in Michigan when the Ciccones did—many of whom live elsewhere today—and, also, to the sons and daughters of people who were friendly with the Ciccone family and whose memories of them and of Madonna remain intact. I was impressed by their affection for the Ciccones and appreciate their trust.

Thanks, also, to those who submitted to interviews, including: Christopher Ciccone (January 1993), Martin Ciccone (January 1993);

Carol Belager; Karen Craven; Clara Bonell; Beverly Gibson; Tanis Rozelle; Russell Long; the late Christopher Flynn (1987, 1989); Carol Lintz; Nancy Ryan Mitchell; Whitley Setrakian (1991, with this author, and also with literary agent Bart Andrews for the purpose of a possible memoir, which remains unpublished); Gay Delang; Tony Castro, Gina Magnetti; Pearl Lang (1989); Susan Seidelman (1991); Moira McPharlin Messana and Walter Pugni.

I culled quotes from many published interviews, as well as previously unpublished radio broadcasts and television interviews, with Madonna. Most helpful were: *Time*, May 27, 1985, "Madonna Rocks the Land" by John Skow, Cathy Booth and Denise Worrell; and "Now, Madonna on Madonna" by Denise Worrell; *Bay City* [Michigan] *Times*, August 1987, "Hey, Madonna, Come Visit Us" by Jeff Phillips; *Nightlife*, 1984, "Madonna: On the Borderline of Stardom" by Michael Kozuchowski; *News of the World*, August 16, 1987, "I Groped School girl Madonna on Very First Date" by Hugh Dehn; *People*, March 11, 1985, "Madonna" by Carl Arrington; *Globe*, March 30, 1993, "High School Heartthrob Spills Beans" (no byline); interview, April 1984, "Madonna: Borderline Angel" by Glenn Albin; interview, December 1985, "Madonna" by Harry Dean Stanton; *Chicago Tribune*, July 10, 1986, "Madonna Cleans Up Her Act, But Her Music Remains True Blue to Controversy" by Stephen Holden; *Time*, May 27, 1985, "Madonna Rocks the Land" by John Skow; 21st Century / *Soul*, September 1985, "Madonna: Exclusive Interview" by J. Randy Taraborrelli; *Spin*, February 1988, "Madonna: Goodbye, Norma Jean. The Material Girl Is Growing Up Just Fine" by Kristine McKenna; *Orange County* [CA] *Register*, July 20, 1987, "13-Year-Old Chris Finch Becomes a Lucky Star Dancing with Madonna" by Cynthia Hunter; *Washington Post*, June 28, 1987, "Tour Couture: Who's Madonna Wanna Be?" by Martha Sherrill Dailey; *USA Today*, July 23, 1985, "Madonna Keeps House-Hunting" by Jeannie Williams and Matt Roush; *USA Today*, July 9, 1985, "The Naked Truth Doesn't Faze Madonna" by Matt Roush; *People*, March 24, 1986, "Madonna's Beatle Boss" by Carol Wallace, Jonathan Cooper, Laura Anderson Healy and Jack Kelley; *Sunday Mirror*, October 5, 1986, "Madonna: Now I'm Just a Sweet Little Superstar"; *People*, March 11, 1985, "Madonna" by Carl Arrington.

Among the volumes I consulted: *Madonna: Blonde Ambition* by

375

Mark Bego (Harmony Books, 1992); *Madonna Unauthorized* by Christopher Anderson (Simon & Schuster, 1991); *Madonna: The Biography* by Robert Matthew Walker (Sidgwick & Jackson, 1991) *Madonna—Revealed* by Douglas Thomson (Carol Publishing, 1991).

I also studied the tapes of many television programs that aired for these years, including "Robin Leach's Madonna—Exposed" (March 1993), on which I appeared as a guest discussing Madonna, as well as "Madonna—The Real Story—An Unauthorized Video Documentary."

The Eighties and Nineties

I want first to thank Camille Barbone, who I believe is the unsung heroine of Madonna's life and early career. It is my hope that, with this volume, she is fully recognized for her contribution to the legend. She's a wonderful woman. I know that she has expressed interest in writing her own memoirs, *Making Madonna*. It's my hope that this project of hers is one day published.

I want to also thank Tommy Quinn, who has never before spoken of Madonna, and chose to trust me with his precious memories of her. His stories have so enriched this work.

Many notes, memos and correspondence relating to Madonna's early career can be found at the Lincoln Center Library of the Performing Arts. I utilized a great many of them throughout my research and I thank the staff of the Lincoln Center Library for all of its assistance throughout the years of research on this project.

Among those who submitted to interviews: Camille Barbone (1991, 1993); Erica Bell (1990); Martin Burgoyne (1988); Stephen Bray (1990); Gregory Camillucci; Anthony Panzera (1991); Martin Schreiber (1991); Norris Burroughs (1989); Dan Gilroy (1990); Stephen Jon Lewicki (1993); John "Jellybean" Benitez (1990); Bill Lomuscio; Mark Kamins (1988); Seymour Stein; Steven Sterning (1994); Rosanna Arquette (1996); Nile Rodgers (1995); Manny Parish (1991); Mark Kamins (1985, for 21st Century Publications); Bobby Shaw (1991); Carlos Leon (1989); Patrick Hernandez (1985); Michael Rosenblatt (1990); Reggie Lucas (1995); Ed Gutham (2000); Veronica Edwards-Long (2000) and Beatrice Furnell-Jarecki (2000).

Thank you to Barbara Manchester, David Morehouse and Stephen Witneki for allowing me to go through dozens of their photo scrapbooks about Madonna's life and career, and for making themselves available to answer my endless questions about Madonna's New York experiences.

Thanks to Betty Freeman and Thomas Styler, two generous people who were friends of Madonna's in New York. They spent hours with me, individually and together in the year 2000, and helped me re-create moments in Madonna's life, based on what she had told them. They also shared with me much correspondence from Madonna, which cleared up inaccuracies that had been published in other books. I am so grateful for their help and trust.

David Kelly allowed me access to his complete collection of Madonna memorabilia. This material was invaluable to me in that it provided many leads along the way. I am so grateful to him for his assistance. I am also grateful to Deidra Knight for her diligence in keeping such excellent notes relating to Madonna's early music.

Most important to my research was the *Advocate*'s two-part interview with Madonna, May 7, 1991, and May 21, 1991, "The Saint, the Slut, the Sensation . . . Madonna" and "The Gospel According to St. Madonna," both by Don Shewey.

I culled quotes from many published interviews, as well as previously unpublished radio broadcasts and television interviews, with Madonna. Most helpful were: Madonna's interview with Simon Bates, BBC, December 1987; *Glamour*, February 1985, "Meet Madonna, Multimedia Star" by Charla Krupp; *Rolling Stone*, September 10, 1987, "Madonna on Being a Star / The Madonna Mystique" by Mikal Gilmore; *Time*, May 16, 1988, "Madonna Comes to Broadway," by William A. Henry III and Elizabeth L. Brand; *Los Angeles Herald-Examiner*, April 30, 1985, "Madonna: Everywoman or Versatile Vamp?" by Mikal Gilmore; *Rolling Stone*, May 9, 1985, "Madonna and Rosanna: Lucky Stars" by Fred Schruers; *Rolling Stone*, June 5, 1986, "Can't Stop the Girl" by Fred Schruers; *The New York Times*, April 14, 1985, " 'Susan' Draws Spirit from the Sidewalks of New York" by Lindsey Grudson; *Vanity Fair*, April 1990, "White Heat" by Kevin Sessums; *Detroit Free Press*, August 7, 1987, "Madonna: She Breaks Rules, Sheds Images, Hides Her Real Self" by Gary Graff; *Time*, July 27, 1987, "How Artists Respond to AIDS" by Richard Corliss, Mary

Cronin and Dennis Wyss; *Time,* March 14, 1988, *People* page item; *The New York Times,* March 19, 1989, "Madonna Re-Creates Herself—Again" by Stephen Holden; *Desperately Seeking Susan* press kit, 1985, by Reid Rosefelt for Orion Pictures; *You,* April 21, 1985, "Madonna: I Was Born to Flirt" by Nancy Mills; *Star,* July 30, 1985, "Why Madonna Posed for All Those Nude Photographs" by Brian Haugh; *New York Post,* June 3, 1985, "Prima Madonna" by Pat Wadsley; *Record,* March 1985, "The Fifty Most Powerful Women in America" by Richard Price; *USA Today,* March 9, 1989, "Boycott and Pepsi/Madonna 'Ridicules Christianity' " by James Cox; *USA Today,* January 11, 1989, "The Empress's New Clothes" by Michael Gross; *The Warhol Diaries* by Andy Warhol, edited by Pat Hackett (Warner Books, 1989); *Boston Herald,* July 3, 1987, "Madonna on Madonna: I Do It My Way" by Simon Bates; *Penthouse,* September 1991, "Truth or Bare: Madonna—The Lost Nudes" by Nick Tosches; *Daily Variety,* April 21, 1992, "Madonna's Material Deal" by Bruce Haring; *Los Angeles Times,* May 3, 1992, "The Madonna Deal: Truth or Ego" by Chuck Philips; *USA Today,* October 21, 1992, "The Naked Truth" by Deirdre Donahue.

Among the volumes I consulted: *Madonna in Her Own Words* by Mick St. Michael (Omnibus Press, 1990); *Madonna: The Rolling Stone Files* (Rolling Stone Press, 1997) by the editors of *Rolling Stone; The Madonna Companion: Two Decades of Commentary* by Allan Metz and Carol Benson (Schirmer Books, 1999).

The Nineties and 2000

For this and other sections of this book, I referred to my research in: *Daily Mail,* March 27, 1999, "In Bed with Madonna" by J. Randy Taraborrelli; *Daily Mail,* March 30, 1999, "The Truth About Madonna" by J. Randy Taraborrelli; *Daily Mail,* March 29, 1999, "Madonna . . . Prince . . . Michael Jackson" by J. Randy Taraborrelli.

My thanks to Theresa Lomax for all of the hours of interviews (1999, 2000) relating to Madonna and Warner Bros. Records.

I referred to and am grateful for my interviews with Deidra Evans-Jackson, Doris Jenkins, Mark White, Joe Mantegna (1990); Ron Silver (1993); André Crouch (1995); Jean-Paul Gaultier, Diane Demitri, Sallim "Slam" Gauwloos (1990); Gabriel Trupin (1990); Kevin Stea

(1990) and Oliver Crumes (1990); Peter Cetara (1990); Raynoma Gordy Singleton (1991); Neal Hitchens (1998); Judith Regan (2000); Rob Van Winkle (1995); Rocky Santiago (1995); Paul Shaffer (1997); James Lucas (2000); Vinnie Zuffante (1991) and Camille Paglia (2000).

Other miscellaneous material consulted for this section:

Throughout this section, I relied on Larry King's television interview with Madonna on January 18, 1988 for certain quotes and other background information.

The Arts & Entertainment *Biography* series was invaluable to my research. My thanks to the staff of A&E who assisted me in my research, providing me with tapes, transcripts and other materials having to do with Madonna's life.

Thanks also to Eileen Faith, Nancy Wood-Furnell and Laura Cruz for their insight.

I am also indebted to the staff of the Department of Special Collections of the University of Southern California, which provided me with much material relating to Madonna's career.

Many published accounts and videos of television appearances were consulted. Most helpful were: *USA Today*, December 11, 1996, "Face to Face with Madonna" by Edna Gunderson; *USA Weekend*, June 8–10, 1990, "Totally Outrageous" by Richard Price; *Cosmopolitan*, May 1990, "Madonna—Magnificent Maverick" by David Ansen; *Los Angeles Times*, May 7, 1990, "Evolution of an Entertainer" by Robert Hilburn; *Ladies Home Journal*, November 1990, "Maybe She's Good: 10 Theories of How Madonna Got 'It' " by Laura Fissinger; *Los Angeles Times*, June 30, 1991, "$8-M Villa for 'Material Girl' " by Ruth Ryon; *Billboard*, February 21, 1998; *New York Post*, "Curse of the Material Girl—Talks Blue Streak on *Letterman*" by Michele Greppi; *The New York Times*, March 1, 1998, "New Tune for the Material Girl" by Ann Powers; *Entertainment Weekly*, May 10, 1991, "Justifying Madonna" by Owen Gleiberman; Madonna's appearance on *Nightline*, December 3, 1990; Madonna's appearance on *The Arsenio Hall Show*, May 1, 1990; *The New York Times*, May 5, 1991, "Madonna's Love Affair with the Lens" by Stephen Holden; *Spin*, April 1998, "Madonna Chooses to Dare" by Barry Walters and Victoria DeSilverio; *Vanity Fair*, March 1998, "Madonna and Child" by Ingrid Sischy; Madonna's appearances on *Live with Regis and Kathie Lee*, May 13 and 14, 1991; *MLC: The Madonna Fanzine*, Fall 1990, "Madonna Quote/Unquote" by Linda Perez; *MLC: The Madonna Fanzine*, Spring 1990, "Madonna Strikes a New Pose" by Ron Givens; *Los Angeles Times* October 23, 1994, "The Madonna Complex" by Sheryl Garratt; *New York Post*, April 16, 1998, "Keepin' Her Baby . . . Family Values" by Liz Smith; *Spin*, January 1996, "Live to Tell" by Bob Guccione Jr.; *People*, January 15, 1996, "Material Witness" by Steve Dougherty; *Entertainment Weekly*, December 14, 1990, "Some Like It Hot . . ." by Benjamin Svetkey; *New Musical Express*, March 1998, "Living in a Material World" by Sylvia Patterson; *New York Newsday*, October 23, 1994, "Madonna: A 'Secret' Chat" by Sheryl Garratt; *Redbook*, January 1997, "Madonna in Life Before and After Motherhood" by Peter Wilkinson; *Los Angeles Times*, May 5, 1991, "Madonna As She Likes It" by Patrick Goldstein; *Face*, February 1991, "Madonna and That Video: Breathless" by Sheryl Garratt; *Entertainment Weekly*, May 17, 1991, "Madonna: The Naked Truth" by James Kaplan; *Los Angeles Times*, January 4, 1996, "Madonna Tells of Fears About Alleged Stalker" by Andrea Ford; *USA Today*, March 7, 1991, "Madonna Justified" by David Landis; *Vanity Fair*, March 2000, "Madonna and Rupert Everett: Just Great Friends" by Ned Zeman; *Entertainment Weekly*, October 28, 1994, "Swinging a New Jack" by Jim Faber; *Working Woman*, December 1991, "Madonna and Oprah—The Companies They Keep" by Fred Goodman; *TV Guide*, November 23–29, 1991; "Madonna on TV" by Kurt Loder; American *Vogue*, October 1996, "Madonna's Moment As Evita, Mother and Fashion Force" by Julie Salamon; *US Weekly*, February 1993, "The Madonna Machine" by Jeffrey Ressner; *Los Angeles Times*, March 2, 1990, "Thoroughly Modern Madonna" by Barbara Foley; *Life*, December 1986, "An Affair to Remember" by Robert Hofler; *USA Today*, October 21, 1994, *Los Angeles Times*, October 16, 1996, "Madonna and Child" by Jeannine Stein and Bill Higgins; *USA Today*, February 1, 2000, "Madonna Serves Upper-Crust 'American Pie' " by Edna Gunderson; *TV Guide*, April 11, 1998, "Madonna—Confidential" by Mary Murphy; *USA Today*, March 1, 2000, "Madonna Role Isn't Much of a Stretch" by Elizabeth Sead; *Los Angeles Times*, November 25, 1997, "Another Make-Over?" by Steve Hochman; *Entertainment Weekly*, May 17, 1991, "Madonna—The Naked Truth" by James Kaplan; *Billboard*, July 11, 1998, "With 'Light' Madonna's Life Begins at 40" by Fred Bronson; *Billboard*, March 14, 1998, "Ray of Light" album review; *People*, January 18, 1999, "The

New Pop Divas" by Tom Gliatto; *Entertainment Weekly*, March 6, 1998, "Ethereal Girl" by David Browne; *Star*, September 15, 1998, "Madonna Flips for *Chicago Hope* Doc" September 15, 1998; *Globe*, September 15, 1998, "Madonna Getting TLC from *Chicago Hope* Doc" by Carole Glines; *Time*, March 16, 1998, "Heading for the Light" by Christopher John Farley; *Time Out*, August 16, 2000, "Warren Beatty" by Todd Gold; *US Weekly*, September 22, 2000, "Outta the Groove" by David Browne; *Daily Mail*, September 21, 2000, "Looking Swell, But Not Swollen . . ." by James Morrison; *New York Post*, January 11, 2000; *Jane*, March 2000, "My Friend Madonna" by Juliette Hohnen; *New York Post*, March 2, 2000, "The Best Thing" by Liz Smith; *US Weekly*, June 19, 2000, "Madonna's Candy Crackdown" by Marc S. Malkin and Marcus Baram; *Los Angeles Times*, January 29, 2000, "Madonna's Brand New Recipe" by Geoff Boucher; *Rolling Stone*, September 18, 2000, "Madonna Can't Stop the Music" by Janeec Dunn; *People*, March 13, 2000, "Lady Madonna" by Jim Jerome; *Vanity Fair*, November 2000, "Like an Artist" by Steven Daly.

Among the volumes I consulted: *Madonna* by Rikky Rooksby (Omnibus Press, 1998); *Madonna, Superstar* (Schirmer's Visual Library) (Schirmer/Mosel GmbH, 1988); *Madonna* by David James (Publications International Ltd., 1991).

Special thanks to Matthew Rettenmund for his comprehensive work, *The Madonna Encyclopedia* (St. Martin's Press, 1995). Wow.

Thank you to Debbie Monroe Thompson for her time, boundless energy and astute observations, and for ten hours' worth of interviews in the year 2000. Also to Betty Trundle, Debra Stradella, Marjorie Hyde, and others who provided me with audiotapes of rehearsals and concerts, and all of those outtakes from the *Sex* book. Thanks also to Steven Bishop, who had so much backstage footage of the "Blonde Ambition" tour; it took me weeks to view it all.

Thanks to David McClintock and Terrence Donahue for all of their notes, personal papers and other documents relating to Madonna's most recent recording career.

Thanks also to the following people for enlightening me on Madonna's current life: Buddy Adler, Diane Phipps, Mary Jenkins, Monica Hallstead, Beatrice King, Allan Melnick, Nelson Richards, Jessica Morgan, Paula DeLeon, Thomas Calabrino, Ethel Anniston, Bob Anthony, Patrice Mallard, Ida Banks, Josephine Barbone, Marjorie

Nassatier, Joseph Langford, John Parker, Steve Capiello, Carl Rick, James McClintock, Harold Chapman, Paul Clemens, Doris Corrado, Andrew Wyatt, Joseph Godfrey, William Godfrey, Shirley Jones, Thomas Lawford, Marilyn Lowry, Marion Bush, Elliot Schreiber, James Silvani, Steve Tamburro, Johnathan Treddy, Betty Wilkinson and Douglas Prestine.

Finally, thanks to Madonna Louise Veronica Ciccone for inspiring so many people with her life and career. Whatever one thinks of her, one fact remains: her success is the result not only of extraordinary talent but also many years of hard work, dedication and persistence.

"If I'm going to make it," she told me in 1983, "it's not going to be because anyone ever handed me anything, already I can see that. I'll probably have to fight my way to the top."

I asked her, "In the end, what do you want to achieve?"

She answered quickly. "Not much. Just the best of everything there is to have."

And so it is.